LITHUANIA

Stutthof

EAST
PRUSSIA

• Treblinka

U.S.S.R.

• Chelmno

POLAND

oss-
sen

Maidanek •

Belzec •

• Auschwitz

CHO-

SLOVAKIA

HUNGARY

Raoul
Ang

Raoul Wallenberg
Angel of Rescue
Heroism and Torment in the Gulag

Harvey Rosenfeld

Ƿ *Prometheus Books*

700 East Amherst Street
Buffalo. N.Y. 14215

Published in cooperation with
Russica Publications, Inc.

To Raoul Wallenberg—
  for his humanitarianism. . .
  for his future release. . .

Published 1982 by Prometheus Books
700 East Amherst Street, Buffalo, NY 14215
In cooperation with Russica Publications, Inc.

Copyright 1982 by Harvey Rosenfeld
Library of Congress Catalog Number: 81-86333
ISBN: 0-87975-177-0

Published in the United States of America

Contents

Acknowledgments

At a time when writing about the heroism of Raoul Wallenberg has become a popular practice, one should take note and cite those who have kept alive the story of his plight through decades when few paid attention to the Swedish Angel of Rescue. If there had been more journalists like Philip Slomowitz and Harry Weingast, perhaps the status of Raoul Wallenberg would be different today. As editor of the *Detroit Jewish News,* Philip Slomowitz has not only kept the story of Raoul Wallenberg on the front pages, but has also been of great assistance to his family and friends in their search for the lost hero of the Holocaust. In 1947 while editor of *The Jewish News* in New Jersey, Harry Weingast wrote the first full story to appear in an Anglo-Jewish newspaper that gave an eyewitness account of Raoul Wallenberg's heroism. Mr. Weingast has continually given prominence to the fate of Raoul Wallenberg.

Both Philip Slomowitz and Harry Weingast are outstanding journalists who have elevated the quality of the Anglo-Jewish press in America. We are especially grateful for their gracious assistance in helping prepare this book.

We also would like to thank Mrs. Margo Selby for her translation of Hungarian-language materials; Mrs. Margaret Hadad for her translation of Swedish-language materials; the late R. Lawrence Siegel, Professor Henry R. Huttenbach, and Charles R. Allen, Jr., the Rev. Robert A. Graham, Helena Afon, Joseph Salemi, Nathan N. Schorr, Reuben Blum, and Per Hollander for their meaningful suggestions, and Cynthia Haft and others at Yad Vashem who were of great assistance also in providing appropriate documentation.

We owe a special expression of gratitude to Barbara Bergstrom, whose concern for historical truth and knowledge of World War II have enhanced this book.

A final note of appreciation to Eli Zborowski, past president of the American Federation of Jewish Fighters, Camp Inmates, and Nazi victims, and member of the Executive Board of Yad Vashem. Mr. Zborowski and other survivors of the Holocaust have taught us the importance of remembering.

Introduction

We did not succeed in telling the whole truth. We can but continue to seek. It is not over. We believe every man in every generation must see himself as having been there in these times and places.

> — *The 81st Blow*
> Israeli documentary on the Holocaust, 1975

Much has been said, and much needs to be repeated about the atrocities of the Holocaust, for only by learning its lessons can we hope to prevent its repetition. Still, not enough has been said about those men and women whose nobility of spirit set them apart from so many who failed to act.

Raoul Wallenberg was one of these "soldiers of the soul." In every sense, the unassuming but relentless Swede was an Angel of Rescue. Through his dedication and courage he saved the lives of some ninety thousand Jews — an accomplishment unmatched even by the combined half-hearted efforts of the Allied governments. The late Arthur D. Morse said of Wallenberg in his book *While Six Million Died: A Chronicle of American Apathy*: "His gallantry bridges the chasm between the pretense and performance of the forces of international morality."

Raoul Wallenberg: Angel of Rescue is a compelling story. Harvey Rosenfeld has chronicled the far-reaching scope of the efforts made by Wallenberg and his colleagues. One of those associates is Tibor Baranski, one of my friends and constituents, and I am honored and privileged to know him. In his role of executive secretary to Angelo Rotta, papal nuncio in Budapest, Tibor worked closely with Raoul Wallenberg to save thousands of Jews from the clutches of the Nazis. They were the Davids against the Goliaths of Nazism. These deeds have been recognized by Yad Vashem in Jerusalem, which honored him as a "Righteous Gentile," its highest award for non-Jews who risked their lives for Jews during the Holocaust. Tibor has been appointed to the recently established U.S. Holocaust Memorial Council. Yet, the vast amount of literature on the Holocaust does not give sufficient recognition to Tibor Baranski's heroic deeds. *Raoul Wallenberg: Angel of Rescue* corrects this historical oversight.

It is ironic that after battling the Nazis, both Wallenberg and Baranski were victimized by the Nazi enemies, the Communists. As the Russian Army was taking Budapest on December 30, 1944, Tibor was captured under the assumption of being a Hungarian supporter of the Nazis. He was later released. After the war, Tibor became involved in underground anti-Communist activities, for which he spent fifty-seven months in Hungarian prisons. It was only after Stalin's death in 1953 that Tibor was finally released from prison.

Tibor Baranski is free. But the agonizing search for Raoul Wallenberg continues. *Raoul Wallenberg: Angel of Rescue* communicates the anguish of the Wallenberg family, the frustration and the confusion that has attended every step of the search. Thirty-seven years after his abduction from Budapest by the Russians on January 17, 1945, there are still prisoners coming out of the Mordvinia prison complex who claim to have seen Wallenberg alive in the special prison in Mordvinia that holds those inmates who have been officially proclaimed dead.

The Soviets have consistently turned deaf ears to pleas for more information about the fate of Raoul Wallenberg. After years of lies, contradictions and evasions, the Soviets return to the story that Wallenberg died in 1947. The question still remains—is he alive?

In September, 1981, Congress voted to take the extraordinary and nearly unprecedented action of giving Raoul Wallenberg honorary U.S. citizenship in recognition of his effectiveness in saving so many lives in a mission sponsored by the U.S. government. The bill was signed into law in early October by President Ronald Reagan, in a Rose Garden ceremony which I had the privilege of attending with Wallenberg's half sister Nina Lagergren, his half brother Dr. Guy von Dardel, the great Simon Wiesenthal, and others. It is poetic justice that among the leaders of this cause and attendees was my friend Tom Lantos, freshman Congressman from California, who along with his wife Annette, was instrumental in seeing this bill passed. Both Tom and Annette were among those who were saved from the Nazis by Wallenberg some thirty-five years ago who refuse to forget him, who refuse to believe that he is not alive.

Throughout the world there are many who feel the same way, who are still fighting to penetrate the web of deception the Soviets have woven around the destiny of Raoul Wallenberg. Their struggle to free him from the Soviets is in a very real sense a continuation of his own struggle to save the Jews from the Nazis.

For in its brutality, its suppression of basic human rights, and its eagerness to crush other nations and impose its will upon them, Soviet Russia has filled the totalitarian void created by the defeat of Nazi Germany. There was a predictable link between these two oppressive nations, for Hitler had "unqualified respect" for "Stalin the genius"; and Hitler, it was said, was the only person Stalin trusted.

No wonder the Soviets were aghast when Hitler violated his treaty with Russia. In 1956, Khrushchev revealed that the Russian military attaché in Berlin had warned his country of the precise time of the Nazi attack. Stalin had refused to believe that Hitler would break his word.

As early as 1945, there were signs that the policies of the Soviet Union would be a continuation of those of the Nazis, for in that year the Russian army had entered Hungary and carried out a wave of terror. One Hungarian citizen said to Lars Berg, a colleague of Raoul Wallenberg and now a Swedish consul in Brazil, "Lars, if you ever get out of this hell try to tell people, try to explain to them what savages, what barbarians the Russians are! Try to make them understand that all this might also happen to their countries, to their homes, to their wives! People won't believe you. They did not believe what was said of Hitler. People never want to believe disturbing warnings, but try anyhow. If they could only see what is going on here!"

The Soviets' present-day policy contains ugly echoes of the Third Reich. Their invasion of Afghanistan, their role in the military oppression in Poland, and their involvement in fomenting instability in Africa and the Caribbean—these are all signs that their thirst for world domination remains unslaked. In Laos, using biochemical weapons, the Soviets have waged a campaign of deliberate genocide against the Hmong villagers. And not since the preparations of Nazi Germany before World War II has a major nation "at peace" devoted such a large amount of its resources to military might as has the USSR.

After reading of the Soviet's incarceration of Raoul Wallenberg, a man so obviously innocent, one must be even more convinced that we must never cease to keep a constant and probing eye on the closed society that is Russia. Sadly, the Wallenberg affair is only part of a pattern of oppression and inhumane treatment of creative and individualistic lovers of freedom in that country.

Recent sessions of the Madrid Conference on Human Rights have helped to spotlight some of the Soviet violations of the terms of the Helsinki Final Act. Some of these violations include the reduction of Jewish emigration from the USSR by 50 percent, accompanied by increased harassment, and the persecution of such men and women as Yuri Orlov, Anatoly Shcharansky, Ida Nudel, Vladimir Preston, Andrei Sakharov and his wife Elena Bonner, Georgi Gutman, and many others whose only crime was to express opinions distasteful to the Soviet hierarchy. When Dr. Guy von Dardel, Wallenberg's half brother, traveled to Spain to bring up the Wallenberg case, the Soviets maintained a sphinxlike silence.

People did not speak out against the atrocities of the Third Reich. To avoid repeating this past mistake, we must now raise our voices to protest the Soviet violations of human rights. This commitment was articulated by Frans van Dongen, head of the Dutch delegation to the Madrid conference, who said, "When people are harassed or persecuted because of their attachment to the ideals of human rights and fundamental freedoms embodied in the Helsinki Final Act, we cannot and should not remain silent."

There is no more dramatic symbol of Soviet violation of human rights than the torment of Raoul Wallenberg, the Angel of Rescue. There remains disturbing evidence that he may be still languishing somewhere in the Gulag Archipelago, a tragically ironic "reward" for one who saved so many would-be victims of Nazism. To all of us, Raoul Wallenberg remains a shining example of decency, humanity, and courage in an otherwise dark and inglorious chapter of history. The world must not shrink from speaking out vigorously on his behalf.

Jack F. Kemp
Member, U.S. Congress
February, 1982

Raoul Wallenberg
Angel of Rescue

1

Hungary's Darkest Hour

I don't know whether I'm going as a prisoner or as a guest."

With these words Raoul Wallenberg, a handsome Swedish diplomat, bade farewell to his assistants in Budapest and to the outside world on January 17, 1945. From Budapest he was taken to Moscow, the first stop in a series of torturous destinations.

The bizarre story of Raoul Wallenberg still has no ending; only the questions remain: Why was Raoul Wallenberg abducted by the Russians? Where is Raoul Wallenberg? Where is the Christian diplomat who saved between fifty and one hundred thousand Hungarian Jews from the Nazi concentration camps and crematoria? Where is the heroic figure who in less than six months performed the amazing feats that earned him acclaim as "The Swedish Angel of Rescue" and "The Swedish Pimpernel"?

The dedication, determination, ingenuity, and skills of Raoul Wallenberg found an ideal setting in wartime Hungary.

For the precise, superefficient Nazi death machine built by Adolf Eichmann, the annihilation of Hungarian Jewry emerged as the most successful episode of the Final Solution, Hitler's plan for the total physical annihilation of European Jewry. The Hungarian operation broke all records for speed and efficiency, as well as cruelty and destruction. In less than one year of German occupation, over four hundred fifty thousand Jews — 70 percent of the Jews of greater Hungary — were deported, murdered, or died because of the inhuman conditions. Of this total, about two hundred eighty-five thousand were gassed at Auschwitz.

1

The liquidation of Hungarian Jewry was Eichmann's "finest hour" because Nazi brutality had been tried, tested, and perfected in Germany, in Poland, in Russia—throughout Europe. But the speed and barbarity in Hungary were without precedent. According to Winston Churchill in his letter of July, 1944, to the British foreign secretary, it was

> probably the greatest and most horrible crime ever committed in the whole history of the world, and it has been done by scientific machinery by nominally civilized man in the name of a great state and one of the leading races in Europe. . . . It is quite clear that all concerned in this crime who may fall into our hands, including the people who only obeyed orders by carrying out the brutalities, should be put to death after their association with the murderers have been proved.

Nazi ruthlessness should hardly have been a surprise for anyone aware of their past abominations. Political anti-Semitism first appeared in Germany at the end of the nineteenth century and became the official policy of the government and the ruling party of the Third Reich when Hitler came to power on January 30, 1933. The anti-Jewish policies were quick in coming: the legal and civil equality of the Jews was removed; they were excluded from the economy; social barriers were set up between Jews and the rest of the German population. These regulations and enactments reached a climax with the series of Nuremberg Laws, the first promulgated in September, 1935. The "Reich Citizens Law" specified that only persons of German blood were Reich citizens, while Jews or persons of "impure" blood were of inferior status, "subjects" and not "citizens." The "Law for the Defence of German Blood and German Honour" prohibited marriage and sexual intercourse between Jews and "bearers of German blood."

By November, 1938, about 170,000 Jews, out of a total Jewish population of 500,000 in the Third Reich, had left Germany. New measures, including mass arrests, looting of shops, registering of property for purposes of confiscation, the forced addition of Israel and Sarah to all Jewish names, were used in 1938. The central anti-Semitic incident of 1938, the infamous Kristallnacht, was triggered by the assassination of a German official by a young Jew whose family had been expelled from Germany and stranded in a camp of unwanted refugees near the Polish border. The incident gave the Nazis a convenient excuse to unleash a night of terror: hundreds of synagogues were burned down, 91 Jews were murdered, 7,000 Jewish shops were pillaged and destroyed, and 20,000 Jews were arrested and imprisoned in concentration camps. The 1938 pogrom marks the completion of phase one of the solution of the Jewish question: social segregation of the Jews, the exclusion of Jews from the economy, and the accelerated emigration of the Jews. All these policies had been enforced by legislative enactments; after 1938, legislation and violence went hand in hand, as manifested by the frequency and the amount of force used in acts of terror.

Phase two began on September 1, 1939—the outbreak of World War II. As the Nazis overran the countries of Europe, beginning with Poland, they put into effect measures designed to differentiate the Jews from the rest of the population: Jews were to wear special armbands, be herded into ghettos, and be excluded from every phase of the economy. This stage continued until June 22, 1941, the outbreak of the war with Russia. That date marked the start of mass murder by a variety of brutal methods, designed by Hitler as "the final solution of the Jewish question."

If one studies the atrocities committed by the Nazis in Germany, in Poland, in Russia—in every country they occupied—one should not be surprised at their ruthlessness in Hungary. Yet, the approval and cooperation given to Nazi policies in 1944 by nearly the entire population startled Hungarian Jewry because, ever since their emancipation in 1867, the Jews had participated in the economic, social, cultural, and political development of the country.

In 1930 the Hungarian Jewish population was nearly four hundred fifty thousand, about 5 percent of the total. Hungarian Jewry enjoyed the status of one of the most prosperous and thriving Jewish communities in central Europe. In a country with a distinctive landed aristocracy and a sizable peasantry the Jews were set off as middle class: more than a third of them were craftsmen or self-employed businessmen; nearly a third were wage earners in business and commerce predominantly, and the other third were primarily white-collar employees in industry, commerce, and banking.

The Jews of the small towns sharply differed from the Jews of the larger cities, especially those in Budapest. The small towns were inhabited by the *shtetl* Jew, an Orthodox Jew who rigorously followed Jewish tradition. Their synagogues, religious schools, rabbis and *rebbes* were as well known and respected as those anywhere in Europe. In contrast, the more than two hundred thousand Jews of Budapest, most of whom were highly acculturated and nationalistic, reflected their assimilative patterns in high intermarriage and baptismal statistics. In 1938 there were 35,000 baptized Jews in the country.

However, these outward appearances of acceptance and equality were somewhat deceiving. There was a long history of a distinct type of Magyar anti-Semitism. The German models of anti-Semitism in the 1870s fueled a counterpart in Hungary led by Gyözö Istóczy, a member of parliament. In the early 1800s, public opinion was aroused against the Jews by a notorious "blood libel," alleging that Jews use the blood of a ritually murdered non-Jew to prepare unleavened bread for Passover. It started in a small town in northeastern Hungary.

On April 1, 1882, a fourteen-year-old Christian girl from Tiszaeszlar mysteriously disappeared. Anti-Semites spread the rumor that some local Jews had murdered her in their synagogue for religious purposes in anticipation of the Passover festival. The town's Catholic priest even published an article implying that the Jews had committed ritual murder. Pushed into action by the provincial deputy, the authorities opened an investigation. Using brutal, unorthodox methods, they persuaded a fourteen-year-old Jewish boy to falsely testify that he had witnessed his own father and other Jews murder the girl in the synagogue, then collect her blood in a bowl. As might be expected, the investigation and subsequent 1883 trial in Nyíregy-háza attracted much publicity. There were angry debates in parliament, as Deputy Gyözö Istóczy fomented violent agitation that spread throughout the country.

A non-Jewish member of parliament, Károly Eötvös, acting as defense counsel, caused the tribunal to invalidate the false evidence and the Jews were acquitted. It was later determined that the girl had drowned herself in the Tisza River, but the damage had already been done, since many believed the false testimony. News of the acquittal caused the wave of anti-Semitism to gather momentum across Hungary. Angry mobs attacked Jews in Budapest and other localities. In some districts the authorities had to declare a state of emergency to protect the Jews.

Using the "blood libel" as a rallying point, Istóczy founded an anti-Semitic party which won seventeen seats in the 1884 elections to the Hungarian parliament. At the turn of the century, anti-Semitism was promoted by the Catholic People's Party and several national minorities, especially the Slovaks, who were angry that the Jews sided with the nationalist policies of the Magyars, the dominant and major Hungarian ethnic group.

Belief in the "blood libel of Tiszaeszlar" is an important factor in Hungarian anti-Semitism. Its effects were disastrously clear during the "White Terror" of 1919 to 1921, and even later during the anti-Semitic activity in Hungary during World War II.

The assassination of Archduke Francis Ferdinand on June 28, 1914, plunged the Austro-Hungarian Empire into World War I on the side of Germany. As the tide of war went against them, Hungarian nationalists sought independence from Austria, repudiation of the alliance with Germany, and peace with the Entente to safeguard the nation.

On October 31, 1918, Count Mihaly Károlyi became prime minister of an improvised administration based on a left-wing National Council. King Charles IV signed an armistice on November 3, then abdicated on November 13. The National Council dissolved parliament on November 16 and Károlyi became president of the independent republic of Hungary. Serb, Czech, and Rumanian troops quickly occupied two-thirds of the country. On March 21, 1919, a Communist revolution, supported by many Hungarian Jews, overthrew the Károlyi government. Expecting help from Russia against the Rumanians, Bela Kun, a Jew, replaced Károlyi as head of a "soviet republic."

The Russians had problems of their own and could not intervene in Hungary. Kun's doctrinaire Bolshevism, resting on a "Red Terror," managed to antagonize most of the country. He was overthrown on August 4, 1919, and Rumanian troops occupied Budapest on August 6. Following the overthrow of Bela Kun during a period known as the "White Terror," numerous riots and acts of violence were directed against the Jews.

The Allies managed to arrange a partial Rumanian withdrawal and handed power to a provisional government headed by Károly Huszár in November, 1919. Huszar's government repudiated all measures enacted by previous regimes. Admiral Miklós Horthy, who had organized counter-revolutionary armed forces in Szeged, was elected regent as provisional head of state on March 1, 1920. The Huszár government then resigned and a coalition led by Sándor Simonyi-Semadam took office. On June 4, 1920, the new government was forced to sign the Treaty of Trianon.

Hungary lost badly in World War I, not only on the battlefield, but also at the peace table. With the Treaty of Trianon, Hungary lost more than 70 percent of its territory containing about 60 percent of its former population, chiefly to Czechoslovakia, Rumania, and Yugoslavia, formerly Serbia.

Although the violent acts of the "White Terror" subsided in time, the policy of the Hungarian government remained anti-Semitic. In 1920 the parliament enacted a *numerus clausus* affecting the admission of Jewish students into institutions of higher learning. This legislation specified that no new students should be accepted into the universities unless they were "loyal from the national and moral standpoint." In a manner not unlike the "affirmative action" rules of today, it went on to state "the proportion of members of the various ethnic and national groups in the total number of students should amount to the proportion of such ethnic and national groups in the total population."

In his article on "Numerus Clausus" for the *Encyclopaedia Judaica,* Baruch Yaron states that the official reason for the legislation was "to prevent a surplus of people in the liberal profession, which the dismembered country was unable to integrate." However, Yaron says, "It was clear that the law was directed against the Jews only." Although an amendment was passed in 1928, the restrictions were not totally removed. Moreover, those who attended universities, Yaron points out, were often harassed and physically attacked by the non-Jewish students "whose 'ideal' was to achieve a 'numerus nullus.'"

The victory of the Nazi Party in Germany was accompanied by new anti-Semitic activities in Hungary. Several openly anti-Semitic terroristic organizations were formed, including Ébredö Magyarok Együlete (The Association of Awakening Hungarians). Subsidized by Germany, anti-Jewish Hungarian newspapers sprang up. A major figure in the dissemination of hatred was István Milotay, who later became a leading member of the most extreme of the Hungarian fascist movements that developed in the thirties. Known as Nyilaskeresztes Part-Hungarista Mozgaloms or Nyilas, this group endorsed the German Nazi doctrines, especially the "solution of the Jewish question."

The Hungarian fascists wore green shirts, with a set of crossed arrows as an emblem, a Hungarian variant of the swastika based on the weaponry of the medieval Magyar conquerors. The badge gave rise to the Nyilas also being known as the Arrow Cross.

But despite the restrictions and despite the Magyar anti-Semitism, Hungarian Jews felt that they were full, first-class Hungarian citizens. In fact, the Jews' major concern was not their own rights but the righting of injustices done to Hungary. In a 1930 memorandum from Hungarian Jewry to the worldwide Alliance Israelite, world Jewry was told that "the best service foreign Jewry can render the Jews of Hungary is to intervene in favour of a general improvement of the situation in Hungary and to remedy those grave injustices suffered by Hungary as a result of the Treaty of Trianon."

However, the situation changed drastically in the late 1930s. The year 1938 both determined and foreshadowed future actions. Spurred on by the growing strength of rightist circles and the increased Nazi influence, the Hungarian government passed the First Jewish Law in 1938. The number of Jews in the liberal professions, in public service, and in commercial and industrial enterprises was restricted to 20 percent. The term "Jew" was redefined to include not only members of the Jewish religion but also those who left the religion after 1919 or those born of Jewish parents after that date.

In part, these measures could be attributed to the Hungarian government's years of flirtation with Nazi Germany and Fascist Italy. Hungary hoped this romance would enable it to secure restoration of territory lost to the Western-influenced Czech, Rumanian, and Yugoslav states during 1919-20.

The territorial motives of Hungary became evident in November, 1938, when it joined with Germany in the disembowelment of Czechoslovakia. In the process Hungary seized some Slovakian districts and a portion of Subcarpathian Ruthenia.

A series of anti-Jewish laws enacted in 1939, known as the "Second Jewish Laws," was much more restrictive than the 1938 legislation. The definition "Jew" was now applied on a racial basis to some one hundred thousand Christians, i.e., to Jews who had left the faith and to their children. Jews were barred from further entry into any profession until their numbers fell to less than 6 percent of that profession. Jews were barred from leading positions in the media. The number of Jews in economic activity was fixed at 5 percent. As a consequence of these laws, some two hundred fifty thousand Jews found their livelihood taken away. As a further method of reducing Jewish influence, the government abrogated the voting rights of nonnative Jews, those whose ancestors were not permanent residents before 1868. The government was also given the authority to expropriate Jewish landed property.

An initial result of the Nazi blitzkrieg of 1939 was the influx of Jews into Hungary. Thousands of Jews fled to the comparative safety of Hungary when Poland was overrun by Germany and Russia. More than one hundred fifty thousand Jews were added to Hungary under the Vienna Award of 1940, which partitioned Transylvania from Rumania. Upon German insistence, Yugoslavia ceded former Hungarian territory in the Bačka basin with its twenty-five thousand Jews. All these additions increased the number of Jews in Hungary to about seven hundred thousand.

Restrictive measures continued in 1941. The "Third Jewish Law" defined the term "Jew" on racial principles so that the total number of persons subject to racial discrimination could be placed at a minimum of eight hundred fifty thousand. New measures also prohibited intermarriage. In every sphere of economic, social, cultural, and political life, Hungarian Jews were deprived of their basic rights. The government party, Magyar Elet Pártja, vigorously pursued a pro-Nazi, anti-Semitic policy.

The increase in the number of Hungarian Jews intensified the sadistic appetite of the Nazis. Almost at once, after the Yugoslavian annexation, thousands of these "additions" were placed in special labor battalions. Many of these Jews were later massacred, especially those serving with the Second Hungarian Army on the Soviet front and those who were slave laborers in the copper mines of Bor, Yugoslavia. The first large-scale slaughter of Hungarian Jewry occurred in the autumn of 1941. In July, 1941, the Hungarian Office for Aliens' Control forcibly "repatriated" about twenty thousand Jewish refugees to Galicia. In August the Hungarian government rounded up seventeen thousand Jews in the annexed Ruthenian territory and shoved them over the border to Kamenets-Podolsk in the German-held Ukraine. SS men murdered these deportees with the assistance of Hungarian troops. In January, 1942, some one thousand Jews were brutally murdered by Hungarian police and troops at Novi-Sad, formerly Yugoslavian territory.

Hungary's entrance into the war against Russia eventually brought labor battalions with fifty thousand Jews to the Eastern Front. After Soviet forces attacked near the Don River, the Hungarian Army disbanded and fled in panic. More than forty thousand Jews died during the retreat.

The plan to totally wipe out Hungarian Jewry was led by the Reich Security Office and the German Foreign Office. On December 8, 1941, the Foreign Office prepared a memorandum entitled "Desires and Ideas of the Foreign Office in Connection With the Intended Total Solution of the Jewish Question in Europe." The memorandum emphasized the "deportation of the Jews handed over . . . by the Hungarian Government . . . [and to] the readiness to deport to the East of Jews living in [Hungary]." On October 6, 1942, Martin Franz Julius Luther, head of Jewish affairs in the Foreign Office, issued a memorandum demanding the implementation of the "solution of the Jewish question in Hungary." Specifically, Luther demanded legislation for the total removal of Jews from cultural and economic life, the marking of Jews, their deportation to the east, and disposal of their property.

Hungary responded with token anti-Semitic measures that did not satisfy the Nazis. Prime Minister Miklós Kállay announced a law for the expropriation of Jewish property and spoke of removing Jews from the countryside. In April, 1942, he made a further commitment to "resettle" eight hundred thousand Jews as a "final solution of the Jewish question." However, Kállay said that the measures could only be carried out after the war. The prime minister told the Germans that deportation of the Jews would be disastrous for the economy of Hungary and also would be harmful to Germany since "80 percent of the Hungarian industry is in the service of the German economy." Moreover, Kállay told the Germans, the "solution of the Jewish question" could not be achieved because the Hungarian peasants were not anti-Semitic.

Kállay's resistance to German demands conformed to the agreement made between him and Regent Miklós Horthy when he succeeded the extremely anti-Semitic Prime Minister László Bárdossy on March 10, 1942. Contrary to German policy, Horthy, as a rule, recognized the validity of the conversion of Jews. With the goading of the Arrow Cross and other anti-Semitic elements, Jews were subject to further employment restrictions, forced-labor conscriptions, and greater expropriations of their properties, but that was all. In fact, more than fifteen thousand Jews from Slovakia, Austria, and Poland found refuge in 1942 and were not turned over to Germany by the Hungarians. At the end of 1942, the Horthy government said no to German demands for introducing yellow badges for Jews and for deporting them to Poland. In a public speech in early 1943, Kállay refused to go along with "resettlement" of the Jews as a "final solution" as long as the Nazis gave no satisfactory answer to the question of where the resettlement was to take place.

In short, while the Jews were being steadily liquidated throughout Nazi-occupied Europe, Hungarian Jewry continued to live in relative safety, despite certain discriminatory policies. Hungary even served as a haven for many Jewish refugees. This protection was afforded by an Axis satellite.

An incensed Germany continued to pressure the Horthy government. On April 17, 1943, Hitler and Foreign Minister Joachim von Ribbentrop met Horthy at Schloss Klessheim and told the regent to follow the lead of Poland, where "if the Jews did not want to work, they were simply shot." When Horthy said that he could not shoot the Jews just because they had been deprived of a livelihood, von Ribbentrop responded that the Jews should "either be killed or sent to the concentration camps." Meanwhile, Edmund Veesenmayer, who worked in the office of German State Secretary Wilhelm Keppler, was sent on a fact-finding mission to Hungary. In a secret report of April 30, 1943, Hungary was described as an "arrogant nation with very little national substance" and an "insignificant" ally. The Jews were blamed for promoting a defeatist attitude and for the "extensive sabotage of the common war aim." Veesenmayer said that Hungary was protecting the

Jews to escape serious air raids and to safeguard the country's interests after the war "by proving through the Jews that they waged the war on the side of the Axis Powers only because they were forced to." As for Horthy, he was seen as being surrounded by Jews and by "aristocrats with Jewish family relations."

In a second secret report of December 14, 1943, Veesenmayer stressed that "the Jews are enemy No. 1 and the 1.1 million Jews amount to as many saboteurs . . . and they will have to be looked on as Bolshevik vanguards."

In an attempt to hold off Nazi demands for deportation, by the end of 1943, the Horthy government had enacted a new series of anti-Semitic measures: Jews were removed from public and cultural life; a numerus clausus of about 6 percent was applied to economic life; Jewish land holdings were almost entirely expropriated; "race-protective" legislation segregated Jews from Hungarian society.

But while the government was putting these laws on the books to placate the Nazis, it was conducting secret negotiations with the Western Allies to withdraw from the war. As evidence of their good intentions, Hungary initiated military court procedures in December, 1943, against those involved in the 1942 anti-Serbian and anti-Jewish massacres in Bačka.

When evidence of these actions reached them, the already enraged Germans had had enough. Not only was the Horthy government protecting the Jews, it was also being an unfaithful ally. The Germans feared that Hungary would follow Italy's example of 1943: when Mussolini fell from power, the succeeding government of Marshal Badoglio promptly sued for armistice terms and pledged cooperation with the Allies. In fact, after the overthrow of Mussolini, Kállay took to the airwaves for a stirring peace speech.

The deteriorating German position on the Eastern Front helped to precipitate the darkest hour for Hungarian Jewry. Following their winter victory at Stalingrad, the Soviets prepared for the 1943 German summer offensive. In July when the panzers attacked Russian positions in the Kursk salient, they were soundly defeated by three Red Army groups that were dug into strong defensive positions. In the biggest tank battle of the war, the Germans lost most of the tanks and troops of their armored divisions, and with them, the initiative. The Russian counterattack drove them steadily back. By autumn the Red Army had recaptured Kiev and crossed the Dnieper. The 900-day siege of Leningrad was lifted that winter. The Soviets drove the Germans out of the Crimea during the spring of 1944. Everywhere the Germans were on the defensive.

The Germans decided to occupy Hungary, in part to protect their southern flank, but also to take care of the "unsolved" Jewish question in the country. An official pretext for the occupation was "the unrestricted presence of some one million Jews as a concrete menace to the safety of German arms in the Balkan Peninsula." The fateful day was March 19, 1944. Hitler gave the code name Operation Margarete 1 to the occupation of Hungary.

To avoid interference, Hitler summoned Horthy and his cabinet to Kless-heim. The Führer lectured Horthy on the treason of his government and told the regent that Germany would be forced to occupy Hungary. To stifle Horthy's opposition, Hitler had him held incommunicado for one day, under virtual house arrest. When Horthy returned home on March 19, the German occupation of Hungary had been completed.

The Nazi machinery was set in motion on March 22. The former Hungarian minister in Berlin, General Döme Sztójay, was installed as prime minister. This government of the right included Andor Jaross and László Endre, infamously identified as the "Hungarian Eichmann." But the real power rested with the SS and the German Plenipotentiary Edmund Veesen-mayer. The Gestapo was in full control. They had seized the railway centers, the government office buildings, and the broadcasting, postal, and telegraph centers in Budapest. The Hungarian Army, spread out along the frontier of Rumania awaiting invasion by the Russians, offered no resistance.

Terror came at once for Hungarian Jewry. On March 19 the master of genocide Adolf Eichmann arrived in Budapest, accompanied by experts at extermination, the most notorious representatives of the IV A Service of the Gestapo. They included Dieter Wisliceny and Anton Brunner, the extermi-nators of Slovakia and Greece; Theodore Dannecker, the director of the deportation in Bulgaria; Siegfried Seidl, who led the operations at There-sienstadt; Hermann Krumey, the executioner in Lodz, Poland; and mem-bers of Eichmann's inner circle: Franz Novak, a loyal friend; Rolf Günther, a trusted staff member; and Otto Munsche, his "legal expert." These emis-saries of death had already been responsible for the massacre of more than five million Jews. Eichmann assembled a hellish collection of individuals on Sunday, March 19, 1944, in Budapest.

Eichmann was ebullient at the prospect of directing this model operation of liquidation. Even before the series of meetings had ended, Eichmann joy-ously announced to his colleagues: "If everything goes as planned in less than six months we will announce to the Führer that the Jewish vermin of Hungary has been wiped out. It will be the fruition, the crowning of three years' effort, work, and thought. It will be another glorious page in the history of the Third Reich."

And how did Hungarian Jewry react to these developments? For them it was inconceivable, even absurd, that destruction awaited them. To their way of thinking, all signs militated against such a catastrophe. Final defeat of the Nazis was unquestionable. As the Red Army relentlessly advanced, it became obvious that the liberation of Hungary was imminent. Beaten and crushed on all fronts, was it not sensible to conclude that the Nazis would have more on their minds than the extermination of the remnants of Euro-pean Jewry? And even if the Nazis wanted to put the finishing touches on European Jewry, the arguments continued, time was an ally of the Hun-garian Jews. The Nazi death machine was efficient but not speedy. For example, as some of their more knowledgeable leaders had learned, didn't it take two years for the Nazis to deport 50,000 Jews from Slovakia?

How wrong the Hungarian Jews were. The Nazis were content to promote these illusions. The more deluded the victim, the less chance for resistance, had long been a Nazi premise. Hitler never considered sparing the last of the European Jews. As Paul Karl Schmidt, the Nazi theorist and Hungarian executioner, testified at the Nuremberg trials: "Maybe we were going to be defeated, but at least we would have accomplished that task." If the Hungarian Jews were caught off guard, how much more so was the world outside. Arthur Morse sums up the situation well in his book *While Six Million Died*: "The Germans' quickness to act in Hungary caught the world by surprise, for at that time the defeat of the Axis was certain and a softening of anti-Semitic persecutions was expected."

Jewish expectations were quickly eradicated. Without waiting for the Budapest meetings to end, preparations began for deportation and extermination. Eichmann ordered the leaders of the Jewish community to present themselves for a conference on March 22. At that time they were ordered by Sturmbannführer Otto von Clages to set up a Judenrat, or Jewish council, to carry out German orders. Within a few days Judenräte were organized for all centers of Hungarian Jews. Jews were deprived of their livelihood. They lost their jobs in government, theater, and the press. Their businesses were shut down. They were required to register all of their property, which was then instantly expropriated. All radios, telephones, bicycles, and cars were confiscated. They were only permitted to travel on streetcars. Jews were excluded from hotels, movies, and all other public facilities used by non-Jews. To further ensure disunity and confusion in the Jewish community, all other Jewish organizations were dissolved.

As the anti-Jewish legislation was being enacted, the Nazis resorted to the same pattern they had established in other countries: the arrest of hundreds of prominent Jews. By the end of March, 3,364 persons had been arrested in individual actions. The total reached 8,225 in mid-April when mass or "special actions" began. The wearing of the yellow star was introduced on March 31. On April 7 the Nazis started "regrouping" or "ghettoizing" the Jews into camps near the rail stations. The policy of the Germans was made clear: to free the country of Jews "within a short period of time." The Jews were herded into the ghettos with a small amount of supplies: the clothes on their backs, two sets of underwear and shirts, a fourteen-day supply of food, and baggage weighing up to fifty kilos. They were not allowed money, jewelry, or any valuables.

With a degree of superefficiency that even surpassed the precision of other Nazi death operations, the Nazis worked out a systematic arrangement for the deportations. Eichmann divided Hungary into six zones: Zone I, Carpatho-Ruthenia; II, Transylvania; III, northern Hungary; IV, southern Hungary east of the Danube; V, Transdanubia, including the suburbs of

Budapest; VI, Budapest proper. To facilitate the deportations, Eichmann made use of a special-duty commando (*Sondereinsatzkommando*) that he had brought from the Mauthausen concentration camp, and the Hungarian police. After a tour of the ghettos on April 24, Eichmann happily reported: "Everything is in perfect order. The provincial ghettos have the character of sanatoria. At last the Jews have taken up an open-air life and exchanged their former mode of living for a healthier one." But the conditions in the ghettos were absolutely wretched. They were located in brick yards or under the open sky in Dés Marosvásárhely and Nagybánya. The ghetto dwellers were brutally treated, deprived of their food supplies, and furiously beaten "in search of hidden valuables."

Typical of the horrid ghetto conditions was the situation at Nyíregy-háza, described in a memorandum of the Jewish Council of Budapest:

> 4,120 local inhabitants and 6,600 residents from the countryside—altogether 10,720 persons, were brought into the ghetto. These are lodged in 123 houses, whose area—including kitchens and halls—cover 9,165 square meters. Under these circumstances each person has less than one square meter of space to himself. Neither water supply nor drainage is available, which is clearly dangerous from the sanitary point of view. According to general regulations, the persons thus assembled were permitted to bring with them provisions sufficient for a fortnight, but the removal of the Jews from the villages took place so swiftly that they were unable to procure this amount of food. The Jews at Nyíregyháza have exhausted their provisions and the local Jewish Council has so far been unable to provide the ghetto with a supply of food.

Meanwhile, the death apparatus at Auschwitz was being enhanced for the wave of new arrivals. In anticipation of the daily twelve to fourteen thousand arrivals scheduled for the middle of May, a new railway line was laid and the debarkation point was moved so that it would be within 600 feet of the crematoria. The two special Jewish commando units assigned to the gas chambers were to be increased from 224 to 860. Also to be increased was the "Canada" commando, whose assignment was sorting the loot of those who were gassed. Eichmann selected Rolf Günther to "make all necessary preparations" at Auschwitz. As a means of consolidating last-minute details, a special "transportation conference" was convened in Vienna, May 4–6, attended by officials of the German railways.

Actually, two mass actions had taken place during April 28–29, with 1,800 Jews deported from Budapest the first day and 2,000 the following day. But the first organized, massive actions began on May 15 in Carpatho-Ruthenia and Transylvania. This was the first of four phases to eliminate the Jews from the Hungarian provinces, from all centers outside of Budapest proper. László Endre systematically and ruthlessly carried out the expulsion orders of phase one. The outside world was aware, but silent and ineffective. For example, it was reported in the British House of Commons that between May 15 and May 27, sixty-two rail cars left Hungary, filled with children between two and eight years of age; six cars filled with adults passed daily through a rail station near Cracow.

And the deportations, personally supervised by Eichmann, were carried out under the most dreadful and inhuman conditions. A day before the deportations, hospital patients, the blind and the deaf, the mentally disturbed, prison inmates, and newborn babies all were taken to the ghetto. When it was time for deportation, the ghetto inhabitants were driven to the railway station and loaded into freight cars. The eighty to one hundred people who were stuffed into one car were allowed one water bucket and one waste bucket. The Hungarian police escorted the trains to Kassa, where they were replaced by the SS. With all vents and windows boarded up, many deportees suffocated; many others committed suicide. At times the escorts turned murderers. On May 24 the SS robbed and killed many Jews at the Slovak station of Kysak.

Those who were not taken to Auschwitz were scattered to 385 other camps. Few survived the rigors and wretchedness of camp life.

Typical of these camps was the one at Mauthausen. The following report is from an extract published by the Hungarian Commission for the Welfare of Deported Persons, based on summaries of evidence submitted by survivors:

> On the average, the 240 cots of the "sick bay" in barrack-group 6 were occupied by 1,700 Hungarian Jews, five or six to each plank-bed, which was 87 centimetres wide. They were unclothed, covered with lice. Living sufferers lay among corpses and the dying. There were no medical stores or bandages . . . . Their food consisted of a soup with a calorific value of 50 calories . . . . Final balance of the sick bay: of 17,000 patients, 48 survived. The greatest part of the Jews and labour service workers taken to Mauthausen fell victim to the dysentery epidemic combined with general debility as a result of starvation.

Jacob König, a Hungarian engineer, gave the following testimony about his experiences in Auschwitz: "I was one of a group of 400 workers employed on draining the swamps. Our supervisors were German prisoners; they habitually beat the workers with shovels and cudgels until they collapsed."

The rules at the death camps were simple and sinister: they were detailed in a sworn affidavit by Rudolph Kasztner, former head of the Budapest Rescue Committee, on December 13, 1945.

> Children up to the age of 12 or 14, older persons above 50, the sick, people with criminal records—all were taken immediately upon arrival to the gas chambers. The other arrivals passed for inspection before an SS doctor, whose quick glance determined who was fit for work and who was not. Those who were unfit were speeded off to the gas chambers. The "fortunate" ones were sent off to the various labor camps.

Ernö Toch gave the following testimony before the Hungarian People's Court in 1945 on his experiences in Auschwitz-Birkenau:

It was about the middle of April when the first Hungarian transports arrived. The gas chambers and crematoria worked at full blast. The pyres burned day and night. Flames several meters high shot out of the chimneys. The smell of burnt flesh was noticeable for miles. It is beyond me to describe the scenes which occurred in the course of the executions. The prisoners employed on this gruesome work could only carry on after having been made drunk. Some of them went raving mad and threatened their superiors with their guns; they had to be shot on the spot.

To handle the seemingly endless piles of corpses, the crematoria at Auschwitz were kept in operation twenty-four hours daily. And for the overflow, six additional, large fire pits had to be dug. On the average the Germans killed ten to twelve thousand persons a day and burned their bodies. Of that total, eight to ten thousand were new arrivals. Those who were permitted to "survive" became the subjects of sadistic medical experimentation. Ten groups of barracks also had some four hundred female prisoners available for sterilization experimentation. To hasten child delivery, pregnant women were given special drugs. Skin diseases and yellow jaundice were produced artificially. Sterilization methods were also tried out on men. Other experiments, e.g., malaria and artificial insemination, were designed to eventually kill the inmates in as painful a manner as possible.

The first phase was completed—on schedule—on June 7. In three weeks, 289,357 Jews had been deported from Carpatho-Ruthenia and Transylvania. By June 30, there were an additional 92,304 deportees from northern Hungary and southern Hungary east of the Danube. With the deportation of 55,741 Jews from Transdanubia and the suburbs of Budapest by July 7, Eichmann had accomplished his goal of liquidating the Hungarian Jews in the provinces—and on schedule! In less than two months, more than four hundred thirty-seven thousand Jews had been sent to the death camps. Eichmann told Kasztner during the first week of June: "We accepted the obligation toward the Hungarians that not a single deported Jew will return alive."

But Eichmann was far from finished. He next turned his attention to Budapest, with its more than two hundred thousand Jews. Eichmann's plan was to set aside one day in mid-July for a massive operation.

The world could no longer be silent. The Swiss press, followed by the press in other neutral states and in Allied countries, published the gruesome details about the liquidation of Hungarian Jewry. Religious and political leaders throughout the world voiced appeals for Christian families to aid the Jews and for the Hungarian people to stand up against the Nazis. The Archbishop of Canterbury and Archbishop Francis Spellman (later cardinal) of the United States spoke out against the atrocities in Hungary.

The involvement of Archbishop Spellman received special praise in a report for the U.S. War Refugee Board prepared by Myron Taylor, personal representative of President Roosevelt to Pope Pius: "At a most critical point in the Hungarian situation, Archbishop Spellman wrote a truly impressive supplication to the Catholics of that country to protect and help the Jews. This moving statement was broadcast in Hungarian, and reprints of it were dropped over Hungary."

U.S. Secretary of State Cordell Hull called upon the people of Hungary to rise against the Nazis, with an implied promise that, after the war, such an action would be looked upon favorably by the victorious Allies.

Now was the time for action. But how was one to go about rescuing the remnants of Hungarian Jewry from their certain destination in the gas chambers? Even if the world was protesting — at this near midnight hour of the war — was there any possibility of overcoming the determination and monomania of Eichmann to complete his heinous mission? And if a rescue operation was undertaken, who would lead this herculean effort? Certainly this undertaking called for an accomplished individual with a worldwide reputation and following.

The choice: Raoul Wallenberg, a seemingly unknown young Swede.

2

Selection for
an Impossible Mission

If Raoul Wallenberg was known to few, the Wallenberg family tradition was known to many. Even though Raoul Wallenberg was untried and untested in the international arena, he had long displayed his unquestionable commitment to the ideals of justice and freedom. While Wallenberg had never acted as a diplomat, he had been an experienced observer of world conditions. And although Raoul Wallenberg had never been thrown into battle with the forces of evil, he brought to his mission an impressive history marked by ingenuity, resourcefulness, and achievement.

For generations the Wallenberg name had been synonymous with Swedish statesmen, diplomats, military leaders, bankers, shipping and industrial magnates, and bishops. André Wallenberg was a member of the Riksdag, the Swedish legislature, for the last twenty-one years of his life. One of his sons, Knut, served as foreign minister from 1914–17. Another son, Gustav Oscar, a figure in banking and shipping, became Sweden's first envoy to Tokyo and later acted as ambassador to China and Turkey.

The financial genius of the Wallenbergs began with André Wallenberg, son of the nineteenth-century bishop of the Lutheran Church at Linkoping. He founded the Stockholm Enskilda Bank in 1856 after a visit to America, where he had seen the consequences of the United States banking crisis in 1837. The fantastic growth of the Enskilda Bank brought inevitable comparisons between the Wallenberg and Rothschild families. André's son, Marcus, conducted special economic negotiations with the Allies in World War I. The sons of Marcus Wallenberg played a similar role during World War II: Marcus, Jr., in negotiations with the Allies; Jacob, with the Germans.

16

Jacob Wallenberg had become an intermediary for Karl Goerdeler, the leader of the German anti-Nazi underground. In this role he sought to be a liaison between Goerdeler, the mayor of Leipzig, and England. As the German's hopes of victory were sinking, Heinrich Himmler approached Jacob Wallenberg and asked him to sound out the Allies. The efforts were fruitless.

Raoul Wallenberg often spoke of his heritage with pride. This Wallenberg tradition extended to Raoul's father Raoul Oskar, an officer in the Swedish Navy, who was tragically stricken with cancer at twenty-three, and died four months before Raoul was born. In this atmosphere of sadness Raoul was born on August 4, 1912; yet, ironically his birth was under signs heralding good fortune. He was born on Sunday with the amniotic sack surrounding him: omens that in Swedish folklore foretell a life of great achievement.

A widow at age twenty-one, Raoul's mother, the former May Wising, daughter of a professor of psychiatry, went to live in her parents' home. But before long new tragedy struck with the death of Professor Wising. Under these circumstances Gustav Oskar Wallenberg, the paternal grandfather, emerged as the most respected and influential person in Raoul's life: he both shaped Raoul's thinking and guided his education. When he was six, Raoul's mother married Fredrik von Dardel, who became director of the Caroline Hospital, one of Stockholm's largest. To him, Raoul was not a stepson, but a son. Raoul's half sister, Nina, and half brother, Guy, were as close to him as blood relations. Today in 1982, they still actively search for an answer to the question: where is Raoul Wallenberg?

Despite his mother's remarriage, the molding of Raoul Wallenberg remained in the hands of his grandfather, Gustav Oscar. Raoul demonstrated brightness and sensitivity at an early age. One day his governess found little Raoul standing in front of a mirror, tears streaming down his cheeks. "Why is Raoul crying?" she asked. With much emotion he replied: "Raoul has no father, and I feel so sorry for him." While classmates and friends occupied themselves with childlike games and interests, Raoul studied the financial progress of Sweden's large companies: at the age of nine, he was already collecting and reading the annual reports of these companies. If only I were a company president, Raoul would often think to himself.

Before his undergraduate days at the University of Michigan College of Architecture, Raoul took much interest in constructions and buildings, in the houses of Stockholm, in its parks. He examined all the features of an edifice down to the most minute detail. If a building were going up in Stockholm, Raoul would be a regular observer at the construction site.

In his formative years, Raoul's compassion for those whose freedom was restrained took the form of concern for animals, especially hunting dogs. On one occasion he sneaked into the den of Swedish writer Axel Klinckowström and released the animals. Unfortunately, the liberated dogs devoured the neighborhood chickens—and even managed to leave a dirty remembrance in Raoul's own apartment.

Although an exceptional student at Östermalm public school and at the Swedish government experimental school, Raoul with his large dark eyes and wavy brown hair remained a mystery to his classmates. They could not understand how any boy could not enjoy football, other sports, or playing pranks, but they conceded his superior knowledge and his gifted manner of expression—he did not speak like a child. For example, when comparing lightning to fire, he said that one was the firework of God, while the other was the creation of man.

Raoul did not act like other children, largely because his Grandfather Wallenberg always treated him like an adult. Their talk was not of the trifles of childhood, but of weighty matters: governmental reform, international relations, import-export trade, and the like. Along with intensive study of music and the Bible, Raoul developed into a voracious reader, perusing from beginning to end the classic thirty-five-volume Swedish lexicon *A Nordique's Family Book.*

Travel enhanced Raoul's development. Under the tutelage of his grandfather, Raoul studied foreign languages and traveled widely throughout western Europe, spending the summers in England, France, and Germany. Before the age of fourteen he rode the Orient Express unescorted to visit his grandfather in Constantinople. (Unbeknownst to Raoul, his grandfather had instructed the railway personnel to watch over the ever-inquisitive youngster; however, Raoul, noticing a demonstration and seeking its source, evaded the conductor at Belgrade.)

After these trips Raoul fascinated his friends and classmates at the gymnasium with his reports. They listened in wonder at his accounts of culture, politics, economics, religion, and the like. In school Raoul strived to be the leader of his group, to outshine his classmates; rather than being jealous, they were proud of his achievements, especially his ability to influence people. Raoul endeared himself by his humor, often directed at himself. For example, the diligent Raoul joked about his laziness. He often made fun of his cowardice. Students looked forward to rap sessions convened by Raoul and dominated by his humor.

After graduation from high school in 1930, Raoul joined the Swedish army for some nine months of military training. And, with the same dedication he brought to all his endeavors, Raoul set out to perfect himself in the military. Although the rigidity of army regulations was never to his liking, Raoul finished army training with high commendations. Above all, he was well liked by his fellow soldiers, who called him the "Benjamin of the regiment" because of his youth. The most memorable episode of his army life occurred when some of his comrades, in an intoxicated state, smashed some furniture in the barracks. Raoul futilely appealed to his superiors for leniency toward his comrades. However, Raoul heartened the offenders with a party in their honor before their punishment was meted out; after they had endured their punishment, Raoul again treated them to a similar festive gathering.

Following military training, Raoul completed his "international studies" with a term at a French law school. A crucial moment had arrived in his development: the choice of a college. Once again, Grandfather Wallenberg took over and steered Raoul to an American university. The ambassador regarded the British upper classes, and hence Oxford and Cambridge, as too snobbish. This was not the sort of educational atmosphere he wanted for his grandson. He felt certain universities in the eastern region of the United States were too elitist and hardly less snooty than Oxford and Cambridge. Attention then shifted to a midwestern institution where Raoul could "imbibe the spirit of the pioneers." The University of Michigan, with its highly regarded College of Architecture, became an ideal choice.

Richard Robinson, a classmate of Raoul's at Ann Arbor, once asked the Swede why he chose the University of Michigan. Robinson, a retired architect from Ann Arbor, recalls the answer: "The eastern colleges were too exclusive, the colleges in the west were too progressive in their way of thinking, and the colleges in the south were too limited and restricted in their outlook. Midwestern colleges seemed just about right, and the University of Michigan had an excellent reputation in architectural studies."

The choice of the University of Michigan was a fortunate decision that neither Raoul nor his grandfather was ever to regret. Raoul adjusted quickly to the campus life at Ann Arbor. The undergraduate years gave Raoul an enthusiastic appreciation of the American way of life: its tempo, its informality, its unconventionality, its idealism, and, above all, its love of freedom. He mingled easily with the students and few imagined that he came from aristocracy. One who remembers Raoul well is his classmate Sol King, now retired in Palm Beach, Florida, formerly president of the Albert Kahn Associates architectural firm in Detroit. Sol King was the driving force behind the establishment of the University of Michigan Annual Raoul Wallenberg Architecture Lectureship.

Sol King recalls the simplicity yet brilliance of Raoul Wallenberg:

I still picture Raoul Wallenberg in gym shoes eating a hot dog—just a typical American college student. Neither his conduct nor his manner of dress gave any who knew him the slightest clue to his noble ancestry. In all that he did he managed to remain immensely unassuming. But one could not but realize the underlying brilliance. He was a modest person but a talented architectural student who showed great insight in finding simple solutions to complex problems. His deeds during World War II were totally in character with the warmly human yet maturely wise attitudes he exhibited while at the university.

In 1969, at the announcement of a campaign to establish the Raoul Wallenberg Lectureship, members of the University of Michigan family spoke in glowing terms of the former student. Mrs. Jean Hebrard, wife of a professor at the College of Architecture, called Raoul "a charming, serious young man who was unusually bright." Professor George E. Brigham remembered Raoul as an outstanding student who registered for more courses than anyone else and did very well in all his subjects with only minimal study. "I will never forget his personality," Professor Brigham recalled. "He visited in our home, and Mrs. Brigham still speaks of his warm, friendly, and outgoing nature." Indeed, Mrs. Ilma Brigham, a resident at the Westchester Care Center in Tempe, Arizona, talks excitedly about "that charming young gentleman who always won over those whom he met. His name will always be remembered at the University of Michigan. The life of Raoul Wallenberg should be a great inspiration to many people," she commented, upon hearing that a book on his life was being prepared.

Everyone agreed that Raoul was an unusually gifted student. In fact, he received the Silver Medal of the American Institute of Architects as the graduate with the highest scholastic standing. According to Richard Robinson, "Raoul studied little, but he performed quickly and very efficiently. It was not uncommon for him to do a project overnight." Robinson recalled that when Raoul broke his right arm, he attended classes with his arm in a sling. "He began drawing with his left arm," Robinson said, "and you know something, he drew better than all of us."

The most vivid recollections of Raoul's undergraduate days are those of his professor, Dr. Jean Paul Slusser. Now in his nineties, Dr. Slusser spoke lucidly and with exuberance about his outstanding student during an interview in his picturesque frame house in Ann Arbor:

> Raoul Wallenberg was one of the brightest and best students I had in my thirty-year experience as a professor of drawing and painting. If I were to make a list of my ten best students, Raoul would be among those at the top of my list. Raoul Wallenberg was so apt a student in drawing and painting that he got nothing but A's from all of us, I suppose. Finally, one day I asked him, "Raoul, why don't you become an artist?" He looked at me slowly and perhaps a little sadly. He then explained to me briefly and with enormous modesty, too, the history of his family and how the sons of the house of Wallenberg were educated. But what remained most clearly in my mind was the love he had for his grandfather and how his grandfather was not too proud to work in the steel mills of Sweden.
>
> I think most people on campus only vaguely knew about his family and its prestige. I found out that his family had greater wealth than that of the king of Sweden. But Raoul took his place in the student body just as another bright and eager young student of architecture. He lived modestly in a tiny frame house on Hill Street, now a garage, so small that he occupied the only rented room in it, on the ground floor at the front.
>
> So competent a draughtsman and painter was young Wallenberg that in his last class with me I encouraged him to create a large mural painting in pastel and crayon on the corridor wall across from my office on the fourth floor of the architecture building. He worked on it for days, maybe weeks, and it was so good that I allowed it to remain in place for perhaps a year or more. Probably

about 12' × 15' in size, it contained some excellent groupings of large figures in full color and had a true mural feeling, or so it seemed to me. The work was on heavy reddish-gray building paper bought by the roll.

It was not all study for Raoul. Two of the more memorable episodes during the Ann Arbor years were his working at the Chicago World's Fair during the summer of 1934 and his being robbed at gunpoint in his last year at school. Raoul loved to hitchhike, and one day in the summer of 1934 he hitchhiked his way to the World's Fair in Chicago. He immediately went to the Swedish Pavilion and asked for work. Nothing was beneath this descendant of aristocracy. He was a tour guide. He cleaned windows. He sold Swedish glass, furniture, and books. His most satisfying moment came when he convinced the director of the pavilion to properly illuminate the 200-foot skyscraper so that the "Swedish statue at the top would be swimming in spotlight."

In his senior year Raoul decided to make an adventurous hitchhiker's trip across America to the Pacific Coast and back. He left Ann Arbor in old clothes, with only a small piece of luggage. The trip proceeded smoothly until the last leg of his trek, between Chicago and Ann Arbor, when his two "hosts" robbed him of his spare cash. He pleaded with the driver and his associate that since they had robbed him, the least they could do was not throw him out into the dark. To prevent any resistance, the robbers ordered Raoul to keep his hands and luggage on his head. However, the robbers, worried about Raoul's nonchalant, calm attitude, precluded trouble by dumping him out on the roadside somewhere near Gary, Indiana. Raoul patiently waited in the bushes until sunrise when he stopped a train. The incident had little effect on his attitudes and outlook, but he vowed to never again keep money in his suitcase and to never volunteer information that he had money when hitchhiking. In fact, according to Professor Slusser, "Raoul loved every minute of the trip and enjoyed this down-to-earth adventure more than anything else."

The memories of Wallenberg's classmates at the University of Michigan point to an outstanding, resourceful individual with the potential for great accomplishments and with the personal qualities and character requisite for bravery. Fred Graham said,

After a lapse of forty-three years, one should not expect a complete recall of Raoul. It is certain to me, however, that his character made a lasting impression and that knowing him for that brief period had enriched my life. I remember visiting him in Stockholm in September, 1937. He was promoting his clever invention: an invisible zipper fastener for garments . . . . His demonstration that he could be brazen and brave is, to my understanding, an extension of his perception of things in a simple, direct manner.

Margaret Culver Ogden, of Wayne, Michigan, also remembers Raoul Wallenberg as a brilliant student. "I remember Raoul as an outstanding, gifted student. I first met him in my English class and was amazed at his tremendous vocabulary. He was a very adaptable individual. Despite being color-blind, Raoul lined up his paints in a precise way and his color combinations were always very pleasing."

Mrs. Ogden, who was an occasional dancing date of the young Swede, also recalls him as a sensitive and caring individual.

> To accomplish the humanitarian work in Budapest, Raoul obviously had to be a sensitive and caring individual. And that he was. I remember him sitting in the drafting room before leaving Ann Arbor. He once had told me that his grandfather had made him promise that he would have no serious personal involvements while in college. Raoul was close to one girl, whose name escapes me. Now that he was leaving he was saddened, not only because he would miss his friend, but even more that his friend would be emotionally hurt.

There has been much conjecture about Raoul's relationships with women. Although Raoul never married, he did have a fondness for beautiful women, but they seldom understood him. His wide and worldly interests fascinated the fair sex. He jokingly told relatives and acquaintances that he never met a woman who was both intelligent and beautiful. Moreover, he added, women only wanted him for his money. "Raoul had extremely normal instincts," Professor Slusser remarked. "He dated several girls and was always very accepted socially. He was a passionate dancer, always the life of the party. I recall the May Party Ball at the architectural school in 1935. Raoul came with a very attractive date and was most charming all evening." Richard Robinson spoke of his classmate as "a very nice person to be with. He had many friends, both men and women, but not one close friend." Another classmate, Fred Graham, called Raoul "a loner who got around a lot." Raoul was an "enjoyable classmate and companion but the friendships never seemed lasting."

Raoul also complemented his classroom studies and social activities with summer trips to Arizona, California, and Mexico. After graduation on June 9, 1935, he visited his Aunt Nita Söderlund in Mexico City, where Raoul first heard the story of the Söderlund family. After World War I the aunt and her parents were in China and a resourceful and courageous woman, Elsa Brändström, arranged for their escape through Siberia. The bravery of Elsa Brändström impressed Raoul, who often spoke of her noble deeds.

Upon returning to Sweden Raoul began working for an architectural firm whose major project was the construction of an open-air swimming pool in the center of town near the beach of Lake Mälar. The project has taken on much interest lately as part of an antipollution drive that has made the lake fit for swimming once more.

Since Raoul's aim was to modernize Stockholm while still preserving its historic flavor, he derived the most personal satisfaction, architecturally speaking, from enlarging the mausoleum on the Wallenberg estate—a plan that had been started by his father.

But, like other members of the Wallenberg family, Raoul directed his career to business. Leaving home for South Africa, which he had visited in 1929, Raoul went to work in Capetown for Ardener, Scott, Thesen, and Co., a firm that had close ties with Grandfather Wallenberg. There, the routine office work accounted for Raoul's departure from the firm after less than two months. Raoul's next employer, the Swedish African Company, gave him marketing assignments. A fellow Swede, Björn Burckhardt, who met Raoul en route to Capetown and later roomed with him, first in a hotel and later in a private house, remembers Raoul as an indefatigable worker who never kept nine-to-five hours. Although he personally disliked competitive sports, Raoul strongly believed in physical exercise and amazed athletes with his prowess and skills in bike riding and swimming. According to Björn, "Raoul did not do things in a normal manner. His way of thinking was so winding and involuted. But his intellect impressed everyone. And he could outtalk anyone. Perhaps his greatest asset was his charm, which influenced people to respect him. The result was that Raoul always seemed to achieve his goals sooner than anyone else. It is therefore easy to understand how he impressed those with whom he dealt in Hungary."

After six months in South Africa Raoul became restless and sailed for Haifa, then part of Palestine, in 1936. Grandfather Wallenberg placed him in a bank, where he worked under Ervin Freud. During his more than six-month stay in Haifa, Raoul met many German Jews who had fled Hitler's Third Reich. This was the first time that Raoul heard stories of the rampant anti-Semitism prevalent in Germany and accounts of the persecution of Jews.

Raoul did have Jewish roots. His great-great-grandfather Michael Benedicks, a German Jew, immigrated to Stockholm in 1780, seeking a haven from German anti-Semitism. When discovering that Sweden also barred Jews from the professions, he became a jeweler. Through hard work and an astute business sense, Benedicks succeeded as a financier, to the point of even lending money to the king of Sweden. Benedicks married a Lutheran and was himself converted. Although one of Raoul's maternal great-grandparents had been Jewish, this was never a factor in his life and did not influence or affect his later mission in Budapest. Raoul always considered himself a full Christian. But in 1936, as a compassionate, sensitive young man, the accounts of Jewish suffering in Germany had a profound impact upon him. These appalling stories grieved him greatly. Brute force and tyranny were alien to Raoul. He was not one to bend before force. He could only be convinced by truth.

Raoul left Palestine with a clear understanding of the extent and complexity of the "Jewish problem" in Hitler's Germany. He encountered recurring reminders of the gruesome nature of Nazism back in Sweden: one of Raoul's acquaintances, a Dr. Philipi, a Jew with a Swedish wife, was detained by the Gestapo in Berlin. Without formulating a plan of action or knowing whom to contact, Raoul stood ready to go to Berlin to intercede in the matter; however, the Swedish embassy intervened to get Dr. Philipi back to Stockholm.

Raoul spoke often — to those who were willing to listen — about the evil and dangers of Nazism. On one occasion in 1937, the actress Viveca Lindfors was introduced to Raoul through relatives, and they danced together. After the dance, in his grandfather's office, Raoul harangued on the subjects of Nazism and the Third Reich. "He spoke to me with much intensity about the developments in Germany. I was only sixteen then, and it was not the sort of thing that interested me. Moreover, I did not believe a word. In fact, I thought he was trying to seduce me. Looking back, I was a very silly dumb girl." Ms. Lindfors never saw Raoul again but is now a member of the Free Raoul Wallenberg Committee.

After returning to Stockholm, Raoul devoted most of his attention to business activities, including his own attempts to sell his patented sealing gadget for bottles and cans. In the summer of 1937 two college classmates, Richard Robinson and Fred Graham who now lives in Muncie, Indiana, visited Raoul. Robinson kept a diary of the visit in which he notes that "Raoul kept on talking without stop about his wonderful invention." His account also details Wallenberg's comfortable, unostentatious existence and happy family life: "The chauffeur took us to their home about six miles north of Stockholm. It was a very beautiful section, with lakes, very nice small homes, golf course, woods, and winding roads. His mother was much younger than I had pictured: very, very lovely. The father was quiet, very nice also. Raoul's brother, now in military training, was also very nice. The home was nothing fancy, rather plain, but very lovely."

Raoul's half brother Dr. Guy von Dardel quickly corrected a "mistaken impression" in Robinson's account. "We never had a private chauffeur. The chauffeur Mr. Robinson refers to," according to von Dardel, "must have been a mere taxi driver. There may be a misconception about our family. It is true that the Wallenberg family has very high standing, but it is not formally a noble or aristocratic family as specified in the Swedish Adelskalendern."

Raoul did not stay with his own business activities for long. As Nina Lagergren recalled, "Raoul detested working at the family bank. He was full of life, fun, and energy, and he could not be restricted to sitting at a desk all day, telling people 'no.' He believed in openness, in nature and in dealing with people. He loved traveling. As for taste, he was clearly anti-snobbish. His favorite movies were those with Charlie Chaplin and the Marx Brothers." In the early years of World War II Raoul met two individuals who were to play key roles not only in his business career, but also in his selection for the historic mission in Budapest. The two businessmen were Sven Salén, the Swedish magnate who headed numerous factories and corporations, and Dr. Kálaman Lauer, a Jew of Hungarian origin. In order to help place Raoul in a suitable business relationship, Jacob Wallenberg introduced his cousin to Salén. Raoul was advised to make an appointment with Lauer, who headed the Mellaneuropeiska Handels AB (Central European Trading Company), whose chief financier was Salén, perhaps best known as a shipowner. Lauer, who died in the spring of 1980, was quite impressed with Raoul's intellect—as many others had been. "I know you don't know the business," Lauer told Raoul, "but I have no doubt that you will learn." Late in 1941 Raoul was sent by Lauer on assignments abroad: to Germany, Switzerland, France, and Rumania. In fact, Raoul developed into Lauer's troubleshooter and international director.

The most memorable of these assignments were those to Budapest, the first taking place in February, 1942, the second in the fall of 1943. On the first trip Raoul had a long meeting at the Danube Palace with a Jewish merchant and his friend, a Hungarian general. Raoul listened with concern as they related the discriminatory practices being thrust upon Hungarian Jewry. Wallenberg realized that Lauer had many relatives in Hungary and shared his distress at this report. These business trips had familiarized Raoul with the social and economic conditions of Hungary and given him a grasp of its language and culture. Since the Central European Trading Company dealt in foodstuffs, Raoul became active in obtaining supplies for the Red Cross in several Central European countries.

The apprehension felt by Lauer, Wallenberg, and others was soon justified as conditions deteriorated for the Hungarian Jews in the spring of 1944, particularly after the Germans seized control of the country on March 19. Norbert Masur, a businessman and representative of the World Jewish Congress, closely monitored the situation of Hungarian Jewry. Frustrated by the worsening plight of the Jews, Masur wrote to Professor Marcus Ehrenpreis, the chief rabbi in Stockholm. "It would be useless to appeal to the Germans or to write to Hitler. In fact, such action would only embarrass Sweden." Perhaps, Masur suggested, the Vatican might be in a position to help. But it was Masur's letter of April 18, 1944, to Professor Ehrenpreis that became significant. In it, Masur proposed that a competent, reputable non-Jewish individual be named to direct a rescue campaign for Hungarian Jewry. The government of Sweden must have complete faith in that individual, Masur told Professor Ehrenpreis, give him proper diplomatic status, and ensure him both adequate funds and the full support of the Foreign Ministry. The proposal was meant to include a rescue mission for Jewish victims in Bucharest, Rumania; however, the Rumanian phase was abandoned as conditions changed in that country. In the spring of 1944, the Russians recaptured Bucovina, Bessarabia, and Odessa. In late August the Rumanians surrendered.

Masur's proposal initiated the first major humanitarian undertaking in Budapest for the rescue of Jews. After the German occupation of Hungary, the staff of the Swedish legation, headed by Minister Ivar Danielsson, together with other neutral diplomatic missions in Budapest, started offering aid to victims of the war. The seventy-two-year-old Valdemar Langlet, lector of Swedish language at the University of Budapest and delegate of the Swedish Red Cross during the war, proposed that less than seven hundred Jews receive so-called "emergency passports," to be issued because of familial or financial links with Sweden. Therefore, Masur's proposal had crucial importance for the survival of the Jewish community in Hungary.

In the middle of May, 1944, Professor Ehrenpreis first invited Lauer to see him about the proposed rescue mission. Without hesitation Lauer suggested Raoul Wallenberg, who had already offered to go to Budapest and help the relatives of Lauer's wife. The name of Raoul Wallenberg had previously been mentioned when Swedish businessman Hendrick Wohl sought someone to go to Budapest and save his relatives. Professor Ehrenpreis thanked Lauer for his suggestion and arranged to meet with Raoul. At this unfortunate meeting, Raoul kept stressing the huge sums of money needed for the rescue mission. Professor Ehrenpreis, displeased with this approach, attributed it to Raoul's immaturity. In the two weeks following this unproductive meeting Hungarian Jewry experienced the most intense period of deportations. While Professor Ehrenpreis dallied in choosing an individual for the rescue mission, thousands upon thousands of Hungarian Jews rode the death trains to Auschwitz. But Lauer refused to give up. His in-laws had sent a message to Stockholm about the desperate situation in Hungary. Lauer knew what had to be done—and Raoul Wallenberg was the man to do it. The Swedish Foreign Ministry complicated the situation by refusing to grant diplomatic status for the person selected to head the rescue mission. An additional obstacle arose when Raoul was called up for army duty. At this point American participation in the rescue effort was enlisted—that made the difference.

Sven Salén, the Swedish magnate, had his office near that of Iver Olsen, the representative of President Roosevelt's War Refugee Board. Olsen had first been assigned to Stockholm in 1943 as financial attaché of the American legation, but at the urging of Treasury Secretary Henry Morgenthau, when FDR established the War Refugee Board in 1944, he designated Olsen as its special attaché. At a meeting arranged by Salén, Lauer spoke with much emotion and conviction about the qualities of Raoul Wallenberg. "He is the only one with the courage to undertake the mission," Lauer told Olsen. The American attaché wanted to meet the young Swede himself, and a telegram to Raoul's regiment brought about a twenty-four-hour leave. Olsen first encountered Raoul at an auspicious meeting in early June, 1944. After the war, Olsen spoke of that meeting in an interview with the *Jewish News* of Newark, New Jersey: "Raoul Wallenberg impressed me as extraordinarily imaginative and vigorous. He was perfect for the job, not only because of his personal qualifications but because he had a nominal association with a Hungarian trading concern."

As a bachelor without family responsibilities, Wallenberg seemed ideally suited for the daily, around-the-clock assignment. For such an undertaking, marriage was not an advantage, but the ability to move with ease among various social circles, make many friends, and develop interpersonal relationships without forming one, permanent attachment proved very significant during Raoul's mission in Budapest.

Convinced of Raoul's fitness for the mission, Olsen invited Wallenberg, Dr. Lauer, and Herschel Johnson, the American minister in Stockholm, to a meeting on June 9, 1944, at Bellmansro, one of Stockholm's most exquisite restaurants. Johnson had looked forward to this meeting, not only out of humanitarian concern, but primarily out of his curiosity about Raoul Wallenberg, of whom Sven Salén had spoken so highly. "I would like to see with my own eyes," Johnson told Salén, "this gutsy young man who has volunteered to go to Budapest, to the lair of the hyenas." The American minister was very favorably impressed with Raoul. The intense meeting, which lasted from 7 P.M. to 5 A.M., produced a three-pronged plan: Raoul Wallenberg would be sent to Budapest as a Swedish attaché with a strictly humanitarian mission; the United States Department of State would be asked to support this undertaking; the duration of the mission would be fixed at two to three months. Johnson quickly contacted the Swedish Foreign Ministry. The ministry was obviously taken by surprise, without any prior knowledge or indication that an untested Raoul Wallenberg was being readied for this most delicate and important operation. "Such a decision does need much thought," was the measured response of the ministry. On June 13 Raoul Wallenberg received a telegram instructing him to appear at the Foreign Ministry.

It is true that Raoul Wallenberg knew nothing of "professional" diplomacy. But he did know what he did not like. He had a strong aversion to bureaucracy. He always said what he felt and what he thought. So, not surprisingly, the talks with the Foreign Ministry were prolonged, lasting several days. Wallenberg wanted a free hand. The sticking point was his insistence upon having the authority to buy off or pay off the enemy at any time, if it meant saving lives. The Foreign Ministry feared jeopardizing its ties with Germany. If Wallenberg were given free rein, a scandalous situation might be created. The timidity and hesitancy of the Swedish government in June, 1944, ironically foreshadowed the parallels of the postwar years when Stockholm tolerated extreme Russian provocation to avoid endangering its relations with Russia.

An agreement was finally reached between Raoul Wallenberg and the Foreign Ministry. The novice diplomat had proven himself a skillful bargainer. He was granted complete authority in saving lives — even if it involved payoffs. He was free to come home for discussions with appropriate officials at any time he saw fit. He would be given a list of trustworthy people on friendly terms with both the Hungarians and Germans. He had Stockholm's consent to ask for an audience with the Hungarian Regent Horthy. And perhaps most important, Raoul Wallenberg would leave for Budapest as secretary of the legation, the personal representative of King Gustav V.

Meanwhile, Johnson had succeeded in enlisting the support of the United States for Raoul Wallenberg's humanitarian mission. On June 21, 1944, Johnson reported to the State Department:

> Mr. Raoul Wallenberg will be appointed as Attaché to Swedish Legation at Budapest for the specific purpose of following and reporting on situation with respect to persecution of Jews and minorities . . . . Olsen and I are of opinion that War Refugee Bd. should be considering ways and means of implementing this action of the Swedish Govt. particularly with respect to financial support.

Raoul Wallenberg had hoped to stay in Sweden until the end of July, but he had to leave for Budapest in haste. As he told Dr. Lauer, "I can not stay until the end of July. Every day I stay costs human lives. I will prepare to leave as soon as possible." Olsen had warned Wallenberg of the dangers involved. If the Germans or the puppet Hungarian government learned of his rescue work, nothing could be done to save him. Without hesitation, Wallenberg replied: "If I can help, if I can save a single person, I will go."

In a most moving scene in the first week of July, Raoul Wallenberg said goodbye to Professor Ehrenpreis and other leaders of the Jewish community at the Great Synagogue of Stockholm. Sweden's chief rabbi had had his doubts about the suitability of Raoul Wallenberg for the rescue mission, but he was now highly impressed by the thirty-two-year-old cultivated, charming, and urbane gallant. With tears in his eyes, the rabbi embraced Raoul and reminded him of the Talmudic dictum: "Those who are on a mission for good deeds are protected from harm." The rabbi blessed Raoul Wallenberg with the Priestly Benediction: "May God bless thee and preserve thee. May the Lord make His face shine unto thee and be gracious unto thee. May the Lord lift up His face unto thee and give thee peace."

Raoul was visibly touched. In response he mentioned how important religion was in his own life and how it comforted him to read the Scriptures. "You have placed high expectations upon me," he remarked, continuing, "Of one thing you can be sure: the Wallenberg family name will always prove to be respectable. With that tradition guiding me, there is no limit to what can be accomplished."

Raoul Wallenberg left Stockholm on July 6, 1944, headed for his mission in Budapest by way of Berlin. He carried only a minimum of luggage: two backpacks, one sleeping bag, a raincoat, and a revolver. But the backpacks were stuffed with a list of names compiled by Swedes who sought information about relatives and friends in Hungary. Other, more significant lists of underground agents, anti-Nazis in Hungary, pro-Allied officials of the Hungarian government, and anti-Nazi Scandinavians in Budapest were provided by the former Hungarian minister in Stockholm, Vilmos Böhm; an unnamed Hungarian journalist; and the United States War Refugee Board. Detailed information accompanied many of these names. For example, the

War Refugee Board described one contact as "a lawyer who for a number of years very skillfully played the role of an ardent Nazi and anti-Semite with the objective of helping distressed or endangered Jews and liberals."

Raoul Wallenberg also left for Budapest with the comforting knowledge that his undertaking would have financial support. A secret account of 110,000 Swedish kronen (approximately $30,000) was deposited for his use at the Stockholm Enskilda Bank. The U.S. War Refugee Board and the American-Jewish Joint Distribution Committee supplied the funds.

Before leaving for Budapest, Raoul Wallenberg devised a coding system for communicating with Stockholm. He confided to Dr. Lauer that if unsuccessful, he would send a coded telegram for delivery to the Swedish Foreign Ministry, which then was to ask for his recall from Budapest.

As he boarded the plane on July 6, 1944, Raoul Wallenberg told his well-wishers, "The Foreign Ministry of Sweden is sending me to Budapest as a humanitarian attaché. What awaits me is very clear. I go to this mission with the commitment to serve with integrity and to fulfill my role to the best of my capabilities."

And so Raoul Wallenberg bade farewell to his homeland — perhaps never to return. His destination was Budapest — the lair of the hyenas.

If Raoul Wallenberg was known to few, in his thirty-two years he had developed the latent skills and qualities for what seemed a mission impossible.

3

The Mission Begins

Whatever skills, experiences, and determination Raoul Wallenberg brought to his mission, the assignment appeared to be an impossible one. When he arrived in Budapest on July 9, 1944, Wallenberg faced a seemingly overwhelming situation. Lars Berg, a member of the Swedish legation, now consul general of the Swedish embassy in Rio de Janeiro, describes the apparent desperation.

Raoul Wallenberg began from such a hopeless starting-point, with such small resources and with such a lack of actual force to back him up. When he arrived to organize help for the Hungarian Jews, he was nothing but a blank page. He was not a career diplomat. His knowledge of the Hungarian language was limited. He knew no one of importance in Budapest. However, he had a job to do: to stop the already initiated deportations of the Hungarian Jews, to give them food and shelter, and, above all, to save their lives.

The most remarkable thing about his work was that it was not based on any legal rights whatsoever. His task was not to protect any Swedish subjects, nor Allied prisoners of war, nor wounded, nor sick people. Neither he nor the Swedish Legation had any right at all to interfere with the manner in which the Hungarian authorities chose to handle their internal problems—in this instance the Jews. Nor was Wallenberg supported by physical force. Neither weapons nor soldiers gave weight to his words. He began his mission with only one source of power: an unfaltering faith in himself buttressed by the justness of his cause. His only protection was a diplomatic passport.

Following the Nazi installation of the Sztójay government in March, the Swedes had downgraded their Budapest embassy to a legation as a sign of nonrecognition. Minister Carl Ivar Danielsson remained as its head, and Per Anger, a career diplomat, served as second secretary. The B department, under the direction of Lars Berg, was entrusted with protecting foreign interests turned over to the neutral Swedish legation. Wallenberg was to head a special section known as Department C (Avdelning C). Although they each had their own responsibilities as diplomatic officers, Anger, Berg, and Danielsson were to play important roles in the rescue mission of Wallenberg.

In briefing Wallenberg about the conditions in Budapest vis-à-vis the Jews, Per Anger delivered an especially grisly report. Wallenberg determined to fully ascertain the situation for himself.

Using the lists of names he had brought with him to Budapest, Wallenberg filed his first report for the government on July 17. In an official, diplomatic tone, with objective statements and statistics, the concise two-page report chronicled the abominations heaped upon the dignity of humans. He wrote about the sealed boxcars, each with 75 or 80 persons—4 persons to a square meter. Inside the cars, there was little bread, one pail of water, and only one pail for the needs of nature. In the gas chambers 6,000 were exterminated daily. Some seven hundred thousand persons—70 percent of Hungary's former Jewish population—had already been deported.

But Wallenberg immediately concerned himself with the fate of the two hundred thousand Jews still living in Budapest. He noted that Horthy and the leaders of the Christian churches in Hungary favored an end to the deportations; yet, the fate of the Jews was complicated and threatened by pressure from Nazi Germany and the conflict of opposing political forces in Hungary. Wallenberg's first report is remarkable for its accuracy. In fact, today, more than thirty-five years later, scholars have not been able to surpass the report in its precision.

On July 18, Wallenberg based an even more detailed report on the accounts of one of the parents of a Wallenberg informant. The parents had managed to escape from Auschwitz and sent Wallenberg a letter confirming the atrocities occurring at the camp. Among other things, the letter discussed the medical experimentation at the death camp: castrations, sperm injections, and the like. The Wallenberg report also noted that twenty to fifty thousand Jews were being hidden by Christians. In the first week of July, many Jews were Christianized—a figure approaching seventy thousand. Although the local Hungarian population blamed the Germans entirely for the savagery, Wallenberg found that "anti-Semitism is very deep. Many people claim that they have lost the sympathy of the outside world because of the Jews, and this will be a consideration in the peace talks."

Wallenberg's suggestions for his rescue mission were offered in a July 19 letter to Dr. Lauer, who recalled,

I was very excited to hear from Raoul and was pleased that he was deeply involved in the rescue work. He suggested the establishment of a Red Cross camp to help the Jewish victims. He was also very interested in distributing money to the Christians who were hiding Jews. He needed additional money for producing false identification papers. Another idea which he brought up was the development of a transport system which would take the Jews to Sweden and Palestine. A final thought dealt with bribing Hungarian and German officials. However, Raoul was not too eager for this plan because it might introduce an endless system of blackmail.

While Wallenberg busily planned rescue methods, forlorn Jews awaited the final liquidation with great trepidation, but the arrival of Wallenberg did give them a spark of hope. "Their last chance," according to Lars Berg, "was to be protected by the Swedish Legation, and more specifically by Raoul Wallenberg, their savior and great hero." The hope Wallenberg inspired in Budapest is well described by the title of Joseph Wulf's monograph *Raoul Wallenberg: Il Fut Leur Espérance.* Wallenberg was quite distressed that hundreds of thousands of Jews had previously been massacred — almost all without resistance. This would change, Wallenberg vowed. No stone would be left unturned. In a memo of July 29, Wallenberg took issue with United States propaganda that condemned Nazi doctrines and severely warned the German leaders. In fact, he was much more complimentary toward Russian propaganda that stressed the imminent arrival of peace. "It is important to promise the people," Wallenberg wrote, "that help is on the way. . . . In one way or another, one has to awaken most of the Jews from their apathy in the face of their expected fate."

Wallenberg sought the advice of Rabbi Albert Belton (Béla Berend), now living in New York, who served as chief rabbi of the Budapest ghetto and as an executive member of the government-sponsored Federation of Jews in Hungary. They met at 12 Sip Street, the central office of the Jewish community, where, as Rabbi Belton relates,

> Wallenberg told me, that he wanted to hear "another opinion," or in other words the opinion of an Executive Member who advocated a total break with the Gestapo and preferred instead to work with Hungarians. When we discussed the entire situation I strongly urged him to work hard and concentrate all his efforts on the Hungarian quisling government. I advised him to deal with such officials as Döme Sztójay, Andor Jaross, and Lajos Reményi-Schneller. Of course, his most important dealings had to be with Regent Horthy. Although it was true that he "sold out his Jews" at Klessheim Castle, Germany, on March 18, 1944, one day before the Nazi invasion of Hungary, the situation had changed. Horthy had been softened up to listen to the voices of reason and international concern as a result of the protests of neutral countries and the threats from the lips of Churchill, Roosevelt, and Stalin that the Hungarian officials would be tried as war criminals.

Horthy had already ordered that deportations cease on July 7. In a statement addressed to the Swedish King Gustav on August 10, Horthy said that he would do everything "which in the present circumstances is in my power to make humanitarian and legal principles respected." The regent approved of the emigration of Jews to Palestine, Sweden, Switzerland, and other countries. Anti-Semitic decrees were suspended for those Jews who were married to Christians or who had received war decorations. Jews who were baptized before August 1, 1941, would not be sent outside the country. As for the other Jews, they would be transported to work outside the country only under "humanitarian laws."

Rabbi Belton, who had cultivated relationships with Hungarian officials in order to rescue Jews, told Wallenberg that his "underground information received through László Ferenczy, the lieutenant colonel of the Gendarmerie, had proven Gestapo looting, robberies, and racketeering with 'protection cards.'" Rabbi Belton feels that his encounter with Wallenberg honed the direction of the Swede's strategy with the regent. "Of course," Rabbi Belton said, "it would be immodest on my part to claim credit for Wallenberg's success. But Wallenberg was grateful for my advice and said that it would be useful. I should add that I was quite impressed by Mr. Wallenberg. He was sincere and committed in his desire to do anything and everything he could to rescue the Hungarian Jews from the hands of the Nazis and their associates."

Wallenberg's first major plan was the issuance of a new type of "protective passport." He knew about the Hungarian acceptance of protective documents from briefings on the situation. While such documents had been provided before by a few neutral legations in an attempt to rescue Jews, their scope was much more limited than Wallenberg now envisioned.

Switzerland had issued two types of protective documents. At the request of the American government, Switzerland took over the interests of El Salvador and, after prolonged negotiations with the Horthy government, was allowed to grant documents giving the bearer the status of "citizen of El Salvador."

After taking over British interests in Hungary, the Swiss had the responsibility for giving certificates to those Jews who had been granted entry into Palestine. Although German occupation of Hungary put an end to prospects of immigration to Palestine, it was important to put a seal of legitimacy to these certificates, whose numbers had increased to 8,000. Miklós (Moshe) Krausz, a Zionist leader in Budapest, contacted Swiss Consul Charles Lutz, who was entrusted with the protection of British and other foreign interests. As a result of their meeting, Lutz issued legitimations to the owners of the certificates. These documents stipulated that the bearer was under the protection of the Swiss legation until such time that the bearer could begin his journey to Palestine. True, these journeys never did begin, but these documents brought about the release of a great many persons from internment camps, from forced labor, and from the ghetto.

As mentioned previously, the Swedish legation had issued 650 safety passports to Jews with family or business links in Sweden, with the assumption that the individual only waited for the opportunity to return to Sweden.

Wallenberg intended to further extend the issuance of such passports to any Hungarian Jew who applied, despite the misgivings of the other Swedish diplomats who feared that greatly increasing the number of passports would negate their value. To counter this argument he proposed to redesign them. Although the existing passports were made out on legation stationery and contained the photo and relevant data about the owner, they did not look particularly impressive. Knowing that the Nazi mind had inestimable respect for the authority behind official looking documents, Wallenberg devised a much more formal passport, complete with a number, official seals, the Three Crowns of Sweden, and the minister's signature. This passport stated that the holder was to go to Sweden within the framework of repatriation authorized by the Swedish Foreign Office, and until departure, the carrier and his property were under the protection of the Swedish legation.

Wallenberg met with Horthy on August 12, accompanied by Dr. Charles Wilhelm, an officer of the Pest Jewish community who was appointed by the Germans to an "Advisory Committee." Dr. Wilhelm called the meeting "remarkable." Physically speaking, Horthy was an imposing figure, but Wallenberg, according to Wilhelm, "proved himself a giant, especially for an individual who was not large." Wallenberg himself was never awed by the stateliness of the regent. "The power of moral right was on my side," Wallenberg explained.

At Wallenberg's insistence Horthy agreed to recognize the new protective passports, allowing 5,000 of them to be issued. No precise precedent for this document existed in international law or practice; in fact, the document could even be considered a direct violation of the principles of international law. The League of Nations had issued Nansen passports for stateless persons who were refugees from their place of birth. However, those who held Swedish protective passports were citizens of the country in which they lived. In effect, the Hungarian government was being asked to ignore this fact.

By implication the Germans gave a silent consent to these passports. Why? Perhaps the Germans felt that without Horthy's collaboration, the total elimination of Hungarian Jewry was not immediately possible; so, they would be content to bide their time. The cooperation of the Horthy government might be attributed to self-interest, because if the Axis completely lost the war, the lives and property of the Hungarian officials might be saved because of their concurrence with Wallenberg's proposals. Moreover, since only a mere fraction of the two hundred thousand Jews of Budapest could receive these 5,000 protective passports, this rescue gesture might allow the Hungarian government to resume the large-scale deportations with only a minimal protest from the Allies, the neutral countries, and the church leaders of Budapest.

After negotiations with Wallenberg, Hungarian authorities agreed that the holders of the protective passports would be recognized as Swedish citizens after renouncing their Hungarian citizenship and would be freed from the obligation of wearing the yellow star. In the fall of 1944 Wallenberg informed the Hungarian government that the number of protective passports that had been given "to persons of Jewish descent, in which Sweden had interest" had been increased to 7,500.

Long lines became common in front of the Swedish legation. Although the agreed-upon plan stipulated one protective pass to a family, it was not unusual for all members of a family to obtain passports, often through falsification. Several underground groups obtained printing equipment and other requisite materials and began circulating as many forged copies as they could from many centers, including the Jewish community office at 12 Sip Street. One of the "distributors" of these false passports was Joseph Kovacs, now a New York travel agent. Before the Nazi takeover of Hungary, Mr. Kovacs was a prominent attorney and an active leader in the Jewish comunity; as soon as the Nazis arrived, they cut his phone lines. "I had a protective passport before Wallenberg came to Budapest," he related. "Because of a relative of ours in Sweden we were fortunate in obtaining one of those documents through the Swedish legation." As an added measure of protection, Mr. Kovacs also managed to get hold of baptismal papers.

For the other "distributors" through Budapest anonymity was important. If a distributor was arrested, it was important that the authorities not locate the other distributors. Kovacs was simply referred to as "the man in the black coat," and the back door at Sip Street was always open to him in case he had to make a quick escape. "I not only gave out the Swedish protective passports, but also forged Budapest certificates. Those who survived the deportations in other parts of Hungary made their way to Budapest in the hope that they would be relatively safe there. Once in Budapest, it was necessary for them to get a certificate that they were residents of the city."

While Kovacs sought specific individuals for whom he had protective passports, "it often became a matter of giving a document to anyone who looked Jewish." This often did not work out well for Kovacs—especially after the Nyilas or Arrow Cross came to power in the fall of 1944. "Once I passed a document to someone I was absolutely sure was Jewish," Kovacs recalled. "Much to my shock he turned out to be a Nyilas policeman. He pulled out his gun to shoot me when miraculously a woman screamed from out of a window. He turned around to look and I took to my heels like an Olympic runner." On another occasion when Kovacs had been arrested for his activities, he noticed a line in front of the police station "for those who had reason to be excused" from arrest. "I jumped into the line," Kovacs remembered. "When the policeman shouted, 'Hey, Jew, I didn't call your name!' from somewhere in the line came a heavenly response: 'You certainly did.'"

It is not surprising that there were so many forged documents in circulation. The need for Danielsson's signature—or a reasonable facsimile—limited even more widespread forgery. In Mr. Kovacs's words, "The Swedish minister turned his back at the practice of forgery. However, one should be fair to him. It was not unusual for him to keep silent and accept the forgeries as valid. He was well aware that a person without a protective passport might be snatched up for deportation and eventually the gas chambers."

However, a protective passport did not always guarantee protection, since the Nyilas thought nothing of ripping up these documents. But a protective passport—authentic or forged—was a means of gaining time, and this time was crucial with the total defeat of the Third Reich on the horizon. "A forged passport was better than no document at all," Kovacs said, "because it could become a mighty instrument in preventing deportation and death." In a paper given in 1961 before the Michigan Academy of Science, Arts, and Letters, Professor G. B. Freed, now at Denver University, remarked that "'protective passports' and other 'documents' were falsified by the thousands, and they often helped." Professor Freed, himself saved by Wallenberg, added that his "own father-in-law never saw a Swedish official but managed to survive those critical months in Budapest thanks to his false 'Swedish' papers."

While the Nazis might have been willing to overlook a protective passport scheme on a limited basis, they became uneasy and restless over the wholesale forgeries. In fact, Eberhard von Thadden, the watchful Nazi inspector and "Jewish expert," became so concerned that he wired a telegram to Berlin suggesting that the timetable for "action" in Budapest be advanced.

The Nazis did their utmost to try to invalidate forged documents. The Gestapo came to Wallenberg regularly and presented obvious forgeries for his examination. Nazi officials kept a constant watch over Wallenberg, trying to snare him with a technicality. Wallenberg knew that one mistake could destroy the entire protective passport scheme. He examined the documents with steely firmness and great care and never failed to contrive an explanation for the imperfections that the Nazis pointed out to him. With resoluteness, but also with courtesy, he insisted that the documents were genuine. However, Wallenberg had to be careful to avoid approving out-and-out false documents, which the Nazis hoped would ensnare him. On one occasion Hugo Grell, the Gestapo official in charge of Jewish affairs, gave Wallenberg a protective pass for a Dr. Arthur Kende. "Is it in proper order?" Grell asked. Wallenberg instantly concluded that the document had been doctored and quickly responded, "No such document has ever been issued." Kende had, in effect, been condemned to death, but Wallenberg had to act quickly and often ruthlessly in such matters, for only such action could guarantee the continuity of the protective pass scheme.

Although Wallenberg was successful in "legitimizing" the cleverly contrived forged passes, other Swedish officials, especially Per Anger and Lars Berg, still feared that the wholesale issuance of passes would negate their value. Berg said,

> We argued often with Raoul about these passes, that there was the frightening possibility that there would be an inflation of these documents to the point where they would have no value at all. Our arguments were pointless. Raoul was determined to have his way. When it came to saving lives, Raoul felt he knew best what would work. In general, you could say that Raoul was headstrong. When his mind was made up, nothing could reverse his plans.

And these passes — both real and forged — did work. Anger estimates that there were about fifteen to twenty thousand such documents in circulation, and some fifty thousand Jews were saved as a result.

The Wallenberg passes had an equally dramatic and gratifying effect on other neutral countries. While their previous efforts at rescuing Hungarian Jews had either been half-hearted or minimal, they now found the courage and determination to set up meaningful rescue programs. Inspired by Wallenberg's example, Carlos de Liz-Texeira Branquinho, Portuguese chargé d'affaires in Budapest, obtained the permission of his government to issue safe-conduct passes to all who could prove that they had had relatives in Portugal, Brazil, or the Portuguese colonies. Petitions for these passes were delivered to the office of the Portuguese consulate at Duna Street, where they were received by Consul General Gyula Gulden, who was also the managing director of the Herend porcelain factory.

In addition, Portugal and representatives of the Franco government joined in initiating a program for the protection of several hundred Sephardic Jews. Spain had previously maintained that it was unable to undertake any rescue operations. A heroic role in Budapest was played by Miguel Sanz-Briz, Spanish chargé d'affaires. The effort was also furthered in Madrid by American Ambassador Carlton J. H. Hayes.

The Swiss legation is thought to have responded most quickly and most dramatically to the noble pattern and pace set by Wallenberg.

With the assistance of Swiss Consul Lutz, Miklós Krausz, and Arthur Weiss, a leader of the Jewish community, an "Emigration Department of the Swiss Legation — Representation of Foreign Interests" had been opened in Mr. Weiss's business offices at 29 Vadász Street, a mirror company. To make this plan more diplomatically acceptable, the Swiss officially bought the so-called "Glass House" for use as an "annex" of their legation. According to Gabriel P. Katona, a New York attorney and the son of Mr. Weiss, "The Emigration Department was part of a large rescue operation totally apart from Raoul Wallenberg, who arrived on the Budapest scene relatively late. The Jewish leadership had been looking for a government that would be a sort of sponsor for the immigration department, which would be run entirely by Jews."

Once word spread of the Emigration Department, thousands lined up daily outside the Glass House to register for certificates to Palestine. At the end of July, 1944, more than two thousand collective passports to Palestine were issued. These documents included personal data and photos, the exit permit of the Hungarian Ministry of Foreign Affairs, and the transit visa of the Rumanian government. They lacked the endorsement of the Germans, whose objections nullified their value; however, the approval of the Hungarian government led the way for the issuance of a Swiss protective pass, printed in German and Hungarian and displaying the prominent white cross on a red field, that not only promised transit protection but also granted the bearer the rights of Swiss citizenship.

These passes, eight thousand of which were approved by Hungarian authorities, were certainly issued during the time that Wallenberg was distributing the Swedish protective pass. While it has been generally accepted that the Wallenberg plan set the pattern for other passes, there is no unanimity on the matter. In fact, Gabriel Katona maintains that his father "invented" the system of protective passes. "These passes," according to Katona, "were produced by a team of typists who worked around the clock. These passes were given out to applicants. In addition to filling the Glass House with countless Jewish refugees, my father rented an unused building next to his mirror company and filled that too."

The role of Lutz vis-à-vis the Budapest Zionists and Raoul Wallenberg has been viewed from different perspectives. Speaking of Lutz's role, Katona claimed that he was "paid off" for his endorsement of the plan, and "once the department was functioning, Lutz rarely made an appearance there." In the view of Per Anger, Lutz was a dedicated, scrupulous worker in the rescue of Jews. Not only did he issue protective passes to conform to the approved total of eight thousand, but he stayed in step with Wallenberg by exceeding the approved total: "At the Swiss legation, Consul Charles Lutz carried on a tireless labor in the Jews' behalf. While emigration to Palestine stopped altogether with the German occupation, this did not hinder Lutz from issuing papers or protective passports for a large number of fictional or actual holders of such certificates. The numbers approved by the Hungarian authorities rose to around 8,000, but in actuality the Swiss followed our example and took considerably more under their protection" (54).

In his book *Operation Hazalah* (Hebrew for rescue), the French correspondent for *Le Figaro* Gilles Lambert cites the joint efforts of Lutz and the Budapest Zionists: "Charles Lutz, working with Krausz, turns the House of Glass on Vadász into a refuge flying the white-cross flag. Every day lines of Jews form at its door in hope of receiving protection papers. Almost everyone gets one, because the Hazalah partisans have developed a certificate-duplicating system that—under Elisabeth Eppler's driving force—is working at full capacity" (125). But Katona sees it differently.

The Swiss activity was led by my father and was aided by various Zionist groups. False identification papers were supplied on a wholesale basis. Lutz played almost no role in these activities. When Wallenberg came to Budapest, our rescue operations were well under way. This is not meant to discredit Wallenberg or belittle his great achievements. Yet, the fact is that the Swedes modeled their rescue mission on the Zionist activities. In fact, my uncle, Istvan Gárdonyi, became a deputy coordinator for the new Swedish effort.

Another Zionist worker, Andrew Freeman, now a New York attorney, also spoke of the Swiss rescue effort and the role of Consul Lutz: "There were so many passports being produced, so many false documents being put into circulation that it became an embarrassing situation for Lutz. And the result was that he disavowed the false passes." Perhaps the severest disparagement of the Swiss consul came from a former Budapest Zionist who wishes to remain unidentified: "After the war one of the workers in the Emigration Department by the name of Alex sought to make profit out of our accomplishments. He devised a plan—with the concurrence of Lutz—that the consul's work would be magnified and presented in nomination for the Nobel Peace Prize. For his initiative Alex expected to share in the proceeds of the prize."

Lutz never did win the Nobel Prize, but his work in Hungary has been thoroughly documented and widely praised. According to Per Anger, Lutz was a central figure in the rescue operation and for that reason attended many strategy sessions with Wallenberg and other members of the Swedish legation. As a result of this involvement, there was close cooperation between the Swedish and Swiss legations and their respective Hungarian employees, especially in the late fall of 1944. As an example, Dr. Arié Breslauer, a lawyer, testified at the Eichmann trial that while in the hospital in the Jewish community he was visited by a member of Wallenberg's staff. Although he later worked for Lutz, Breslauer held a Swedish protective pass.

At the Eichmann trial prosecutor Gideon Hausner paid tribute to Wallenberg and Lutz, describing them as "two foreign diplomats who threw protocol to the wind to save human lives." Lambert cites the coordinated efforts of Wallenberg and Lutz and credits them with being the first diplomats to favorably receive representatives of the Budapest Zionists. The efforts of Lutz on behalf of Hungarian Jewry are also recorded in *Vádirat a Nácizmus Ellen,* the three-volume collection of documents relating to the Jewish community in wartime Hungary. (Yet, it seems to be an irony of "scholarship" that the authoritative, exhaustive *Encyclopaedia Judaica* has no entry for Lutz!) The Yad Vashem Remembrance Authority in Jerusalem honored Consul Lutz, who died in 1975 at the age of eighty, and his wife Gertrud with the title of "Righteous Gentile."

Mrs. Lutz, who resides in Gunten, Switzerland, has compiled an extensive bibliography of materials relating to the rescue work of her husband.

Notwithstanding the claims of his detractors, all the evidence points to the central role of Charles Lutz in the rescue of Hungarian Jewry. A fuller perspective on the contributions of the Swiss consul is presented in excerpts from two letters.

The first, dated May 28, 1946, is to Lutz from Bernard Joseph, the executive of the Jewish Agency in Jerusalem:

> Reports which have been reaching us steadily during the past year, and which are still coming to hand almost daily, all speak of the tremendous assistance which you gave to Hungarian Jewry during the time you were Swiss Consul in Budapest. All our friends agree that large numbers of Jews, probably running into thousands, owe their very lives to your courageous intervention with the authorities and your constant readiness to help in every way that was open to you.
>
> . . . The Jewish Agency, which speaks for the Jewish people all over the world, would like you to know that you will always be remembered in our annals as one of the relatively few men who had the honesty and courage to stand up to our persecutors.

A second letter to Lutz, dated Zurich, December 24, 1948, is from the former president of the Hungarian Zionist Organization Mikhail Solomon, himself a heroic figure in the rescue work. Solomon catalogs those saved through the "Swiss Action" and comes up with a total of sixty-two thousand persons. He is clear in his praise of Lutz: "I assert without exaggeration that nearly half of Hungarian Jewry who survived are indebted to your rescue work in this action . . . . With certainty I can assert that I convey the wish of all Hungarian Jewry in recalling with deepest thanks your noble activities."

Whatever the contributions of Lutz, it is necessary for historical correctness to distinguish between the Swedish protective pass and its counterpart issued by the Swiss legation. While Wallenberg's protective pass scheme was set in motion shortly after his arrival, the Swiss passes—not to be confused with the Palestinian collective passports issued earlier—were first distributed in late October, after the Szálasi Arrow Cross government had come to power. The Swedish pass also included a photo and the signature of the Swedish minister, while the Swiss safe-conduct or protective pass bore neither photo nor signature of the minister. These omissions often spelled disaster for the holders of those documents.

The crucial point is that the Swiss protective pass did work and did save thousands of otherwise doomed Jews. Two of the fortunate ones are David and Rella Gelberman of Oak Park, Michigan. As Mr. Gelberman celebrated his eightieth birthday on March 22, 1980, his thoughts were of the Swiss protective passports, the documents in German and Hungarian, which saved their lives and those of their children, then five and three. Mrs. Gelberman recalls the events of November 3, 1944: "Thousands of women had to march on that day with their children twenty miles from Budapest to a big football field. There the Germans sorted them out for work assignments, and separated the women from their children, who were sent away. But there were too many to process on that day, and I was ordered to return the following day." A miracle happened the next day. A neighbor's son appeared with a piece of paper and yelled, "Frau Gelberman, I bought you something today." It was a protective pass that the boy's father had acquired for the Gelbermans. "Fortunately," Mrs. Gelberman continued, "we had concealed some money before the Nazi takeover and were able to pay $5,000 for the paper." Mrs. Gelberman added that even those who had no money were able to receive the document. "All funds that were collected went for the expenses of Wallenberg's relief operation." Mr. Gelberman obtained his pass afterward, following escape from a slave labor camp.

Who deserves the thanks for these passes? "We owe our lives to God and to Wallenberg, that wonderful man who rode around Budapest in a big car and helped rescue Jews." Mr. Gelberman calls Wallenberg "a hero without equal."

The story of the Gelbermans also points out that the achievements of Raoul Wallenberg did not end with a protective pass. With pass in hand the Gelberman family entered the "international ghetto." The ghetto was comprised of a number of rented houses set apart for the Jews under the protection of the emblem overhead: Swedish, Red Cross, or the other neutral countries. The international ghetto was actually established by the Szálasi government but its creation was rooted in the operation of the "safe houses," which Wallenberg had effected during the Horthy regime. The protective passes for which Wallenberg had achieved recognition from the Hungarian government specified that the bearer and his property were under the protection of the Swedish legation until arrangements were completed for immigration into Sweden. In other words, Sweden had committed itself to accepting all Jews who had protective passes. The principle was fine, but there was no way that Germany would allow Jews to pass through it.

Wallenberg gained Horthy's agreement that the bearers of these passes would not be deported. As a result of arduous negotiations with Horthy, Wallenberg also secured permission for those with protective passes to live in designated buildings rented by the Swedish legation on the Pest side of Budapest, where Wallenberg also maintained his headquarters. The inhabitants of the "Swedish Houses" were given this right as they "awaited" departure for Sweden. As the number of protective passes increased, more and more people were conveyed into these buildings in the dark of the night, without the knowledge of the authorities. The number of houses enjoying "diplomatic immunity" eventually increased to thirty-two, sheltering from ten to fifteen thousand Jews. Not only did Raoul Wallenberg secure life-saving passes and shelter for the persecuted Jews, but he also made certain that they were fed daily. "Raoul accomplished feats that no other twenty diplomats in the world would even have attempted," one foreign diplomat told writer Ralph Wallace after the war.

Despite the resourcefulness of Wallenberg and despite his indefatigability in working twenty hours a day, even he could not do everything alone. Wallenberg began assembling a staff of primarily Jewish volunteers. Horthy agreed that the Jews on Wallenberg's staff be exempted from wearing the yellow star: this stipulation not only gave them greater protection, but also allowed them greater freedom of movement when carrying out their life-saving deeds. How did Wallenberg staff his office? According to Per Anger,

> Many people turned up at Raoul Wallenberg's office offering their services. They were businessmen and professionals. When the Nazis took over Hungary they had to close up their businesses. The professionals were now without professions. And there were those who were in Budapest as the heads of Swedish subsidiaries. Before Wallenberg came they had provisional passports because of family or business ties with Sweden and were waiting for an opportunity to travel to Sweden. To generalize you could say that the average member of Wallenberg's staff was middle class and well educated.

Among Wallenberg's army of workers was Agnes Mandl, now Mrs. Adachi of Forest Hills, N.Y. "I had been working for the Swedish legation before Raoul Wallenberg came to Budapest. When he was assembling his staff, it was a natural thing for me to present myself for service in his rescue mission," she recalls. Wallenberg issued a "Certificate of Employment" for her on August 11. "Many of those on our staff," she said, "were active in the Jewish community or had contacts there."

Hugo Wohl was one of Wallenberg's most trusted workers. His daughter, Mrs. Edith Wohl-Ernster, now lives in Stockholm and is first violinist of the Stockholm opera. As director of a radio parts firm, her father had visited Stockholm often since 1922. When the Nazis invaded Hungary, Wohl, as well as his daughter and her husband, László, received Swedish passports through Per Anger. Mrs. Ernster states that "Raoul Wallenberg recruited his staff from those who already had Swedish papers, perhaps because their safety was already guaranteed to some extent. This explains how my father became a staff member at the Swedish legation."

As Wallenberg's activities expanded from issuing and printing protective passes to overseeing the Swedish houses to supervising departments and offices throughout the city, his staff likewise grew. Eventually, Wallenberg headed an organization from his headquarters at 4 Üllöi Street, which was made up of more than three hundred fifty workers and some forty physicians. (A fuller discussion of the organization will be presented in a later chapter.)

With the rapid increase in the number of employees, it was not surprising that there were persons who did not do credit to the rescue mission. Berg recalls in describing his Budapest assignment:

> The number of employees in Wallenberg's section rapidly increased. It naturally could not be avoided that in such a big crowd some less desirable individuals

would sneak in. Some of them no doubt undertook to speculate in Swedish papers or to fabricate extra protection passports for their friends. Two hundred and fifty dollars for a Swedish protection passport was not considered an expensive black market price at that time. On the other hand, the insufficient time, the immediate dangers, and the overwhelming burden of work did not allow Wallenberg to keep complete control over every single employee. Wallenberg also tried – more than once – to cleanse his offices of unreliable persons, and if the Swedish passports had a big turnover on the black market, that was at least not his fault (10).

Those who worked for Wallenberg were expected to keep pace with him. As Mrs. Adachi relates, "Wallenberg stayed up nights to print identification papers for Jewish families so that they would not be deported by the Nazis. In short, we had to work around the clock because there was no other choice. Wallenberg set the tempo for those who worked with him. There were many times that we lay on the floor for an hour's nap. There was no such thing as a day off." Lars Berg also spoke of the untiring Wallenberg: "Innumerable were the times when I gave my daily reports to the Minister (Danielsson) after eight o'clock in the evening, and only after I had finished did Wallenberg appear with his thick bundles of papers to be signed."

Wallenberg's aides also knew that their lives were constantly on the line, and if they got into trouble, they should not expect or hope for help. Wallenberg expected his workers to perform at their best, according to Mrs. Adachi. His motto was: "If you have performed well, continue in this manner and do not wait for a 'thank you.'"

Even with all the dedicated workers at his side, there were limits to what Wallenberg could accomplish. There had to be certain guidelines. Wallenberg was aware that if his time, resources, power, and connections were to be most effective, they could not be devoted to individual cases. His mission was to save Jews – as many as he could – but the saving of a group or groups had prior claim over the rescue of an individual. Frantic persons who had learned that their father or mother had been seized for deportation desperately sought Wallenberg's personal assistance. But Wallenberg had to be firm and refuse such requests. Per Anger writes,

Wallenberg was always conscious of the fact that saving as *many* persons as possible was what mattered. "You know yourself," he remarked on one occasion, "how we're besieged every day by people who plead for a job at the legation, for asylum, or for a protective passport for themselves and their relations. When they can't come themselves, they send their Aryan friends to ask help for them. All of them want to meet me personally. I've got to be firm. Time doesn't allow me to devote myself to single cases when it's a question of life or death for Budapest's Jewish population" (86-87).

And no one could deny the effectiveness of Wallenberg's performance. His work quickly became known throughout the Jewish community. There was now an address to which it could turn for help. When Lajos Stöckler, head of Budapest's Jewish Advisory Committee, needed assistance, he knew he could count on Wallenberg. Here are excerpts taken from Stöckler's notes at an October 5 meeting with Wallenberg to obtain winter clothing, food, and medication:

> I went with Dezsö Sándor [a trustee of the Jewish community] to Wallenberg at the Legation. Wallenberg welcomed the discussion and listened with utmost interest. He made a statement that he is willing to help in any way possible. During the conversation with Wallenberg, he said that interventions for assistance had been sought through different channels. Because of this it was decided that there could be only one line of communication.
>
> At our suggestion, Wallenberg sent a telegram to Sweden in which he asked for a freight car of vests, food, and medication to be sent to Austria. At our request Wallenberg promised that he would ask the Hungarian Foreign Minister to determine the present state of discussions with German authorities.
>
> At our further request Wallenberg agreed to find out through diplomatic channels if any of those who were deported fell into Russian hands. During our conversation we dropped a word or two about our groups. Wallenberg said that he would be willing to go and meet with these groups accompanied by one of our trustees.
>
> At the end of the meeting we handed Wallenberg the original letter that was to go to the Swedish Red Cross. He was hopeful that the matter would be taken care of by him to our satisfaction.

While there was little rest for the weary Wallenberg, his efforts were personally gratifying and the situation in Budapest was under control. The rescue mission was proceeding vigorously. The work was adequately funded. On September 7 the Joint Distribution Committee authorized a check for $100,000 to be cabled to Iver Olsen. (However, the archives of the JDC indicate that $200,000 was appropriated for remittance to Stockholm.) Wallenberg's achievements were not unnoticed by American officials. The following letter of September 2 from Herschel Johnson to Sweden's Foreign Minister Christian Günther makes this clear: "I have the honor to inform Your Excellency that I have received instructions from my Government to express to the Government of Sweden the utmost appreciation of the Department of State and the War Refugee Board for the invaluable humanitarian services rendered by the Government of Sweden in connection with the Hungarian situation."

The conditions of Hungarian Jewry noticeably improved during August, 1944. Eichmann unwittingly had contributed with his support of a conspiracy to depose Horthy, led by Hungarian police head László Ferenczy and two pro-German officials, László Endre and László Baky. When the conspiracy failed, Horthy dismissed pro-German Prime Minister General Döme Sztójay, replaced him with the more moderate General Géza Lakatos, purged other pro-German officials, and declared Eichmann an unwelcome visitor on Hungarian soil. Seizing the initiative, Wallenberg further stirred up Horthy's animosity toward Eichmann and pressed for help in his own mission to save the Jews.

On August 23, 1944, with the advancing Soviet forces already inside the Rumanian border, King Michael decided to make peace with the Russians. Fearing that Rumania would become a battleground and that his sovereignty would be lost, the king met with Communist Party leaders and other groups opposed to the Nazis. With their support and assistance, he had General Antonescu, head of the pro-German government in Rumania, abducted and shifted his allegiance from the Axis forces to the Allies. With the change in political alliance, Soviet troops could rapidly advance toward the Danube, assisted by Rumanian units that turned their strength against the Germans.

Horthy, inspired by the Rumanian surrender to the Soviets, reopened peace negotiations with Moscow. He informed his ministers of his total opposition to further deportations of the Jews and, if need be, of his intention to offer armed resistance to prevent them. Ferenczy took this message to Eichmann, who was enraged and let loose with fury at the news that the deportations were being stopped. According to testimony of László Ferenczy at the postwar People's Court, Eichmann thundered: "In all my long experience, such a thing has never happened to me before . . . . That won't do . . . . This is contrary to our agreement , . . . It cannot be tolerated." Still, he refused to challenge the regent with armed force. Eichmann had been foiled. He had set August 27 as the beginning of the operation for deporting the Jews of Budapest; the last transport was scheduled for September 18. In preparation, Eichmann had ordered many German lorries to the capital and designated the brick factory in Bekasmegyer as the assembly center.

With their plans thwarted, Eichmann and his staff packed their suitcases for a return to Berlin in late August, following SS head Heinrich Himmler's advice that the obersturmbannführer "take a vacation."

Indeed, Wallenberg exuded optimism over the future. Aware of the steady advance of the Russian armies, he hoped to place the "safe houses" under their protection. He even entertained hopes that with the approach of the Red troops he could close up the C Section of the legation and return to Stockholm.

The spirit of optimism is reflected in Raoul Wallenberg's letter of September 29 to Káláman Lauer. One gets a glimpse of the great accomplishments of the Wallenberg mission:

> I have already made use of Olsen's money. Hardly anything remains. The money has served for the following purposes:
> The purchase of food, which is being warehoused for difficult times that will be here in two weeks. A shortage of food is already being felt. I have also

given 200,000 pengös. And today I have transferred to them an additional 300,000 pengös. And today I have given 35,000 pengös to the children's orphanage that was bombed. As part of the assistance operation of the Legation itself, I have spent a total of 30,000 pengös for needy persons. If possible, could you induce Olsen to grant us an additional 50-100,000 kronen . . . .

I am doing everything in my power to return home quickly. But you understand that one cannot disband a large operation such as this at a moment's notice. When the invasion will come, the disbandment will take place forcefully. As long as there is no invasion, our work is desirable and necessary. It is simply very difficult to cease this work. I will try to return home in a few days, before the Russians enter.

Yours,

Raoul

Wallenberg's first letters to his mother do not speak of a return home. Although the first letter paints somber scenes and refers to the uncertainties of the mission, there is an undercurrent of contentment with the job being done.

Dear Mother:

I have had perhaps the most interesting three to four weeks of my life here, although one sees tragedies of immeasurable extent. But the days and nights are so filled with work that one can react only now and then. I have acquired an office with forty people. We have rented two houses on both sides of the Legation and the organization grows day by day. It is of course utterly uncertain if a positive result can be achieved, as it essentially depends on the general situation.

Many Jews have disappeared, and in the countryside there are none left. Budapest, usually so gay, is completely changed. Most wives of the rich non-Jewish families have left the town. Their husbands are at the front. Business life is completely paralyzed. One hardly does anything but discuss politics.

My birthday was great fun. By chance my secretary, Countess Nákó, got to know about it, and two hours later on my desk there appeared a writing case, an almanac, an inkstand, flowers, and champagne.

I have rented a very beautiful house from the eighteenth century on the castle hill, with beautiful furniture and with a lovely small garden and beautiful view. Now and then I have official dinners there.

Best wishes to Nina, Father, and Guy

With best regards,

Raoul

A second letter also refers to Wallenberg's strenuous work schedule and the uncertainty of success but has a brief note of optimism. The most touching note speaks of the deaths of members of the family of Dr. Lauer, his friend and business partner.

Dear Mother:

We have had terribly much to do and have worked day and night. For the moment it looks as if we should be successful with our first effort within the framework of the humanitarian action. But we still meet great difficulties and I still find it hard to believe that this first thing is going to succeed.

Please inform Dr. Lauer and his wife that I have now established that his in-laws and probably also a small child in the family are dead. In other words, they have been deported from Kecskemet to abroad, where they cannot live for long.

Kindest regards,

Raoul

Everything crystallized on October 15. Wallenberg had information from the highest sources that the Hungarian government was secretly negotiating with the Russians for an armistice. The tip was not wrong. On October 15 Horthy announced on the radio that Hungary was prepared to put down its arms to save the country from becoming one large battlefield. The Jewish community was jubilant. The war seemed over. Hysterical joy gripped Budapest. Jews ripped off their yellow stars and burned them in stoves. Lars Berg describes the joy at the Swedish legation: "The Hungarians were not the only ones to be happy. At the Swedish Legation the deepest and most grateful satisfaction reigned. Wallenberg and Langlet had been successful in their difficult fight. The Hungarian Jews had been saved. This was the end of all deportations, the end of confiscation, ill-treatment, and gas chambers" (22).

The festivities were short-lived. By that evening, a German coup led by Otto Skorzeny forced Horthy to abdicate and turned power over to Ferenc Szálasi, chief of the Arrow Cross or Nyilas. Lars Berg spells out the disaster for all of Hungary, which would not be "occupied in peace and order by duly agreed-upon occupation troops, but by wild, merciless, plundering hordes that would leave neither women nor properties untouched." The prognosis was equally depressing for the rescue effort of the Swedish legation:

This development was also a serious blow to the Swedish Legation and its protégés. It was no longer Horthy and the equally influenced Hungarian authorities who were in power, but the worst scum of the country. The Nyilas were nothing but thieves and murderers who did not need any orders from the

Germans to intensify the mass killings of the Jews. Their cruel recklessness and their hatred against the Jews were more than enough. Wallenberg's and Langlet's task was not solved, hardly even started, and in a much more hopeless situation than ever before (25).

Another colleague of Wallenberg, Per Anger, also noted the troubled times that awaited them, but the secretary of the Swedish legation refused to admit defeat: "Eichmann and his henchmen returned, and for Wallenberg a hectic and dangerous period now began. But he never gave up, no matter how hopeless things looked" (62).

And so, the darkest days for Hungarian Jewry were ushered in, but Raoul Wallenberg, the Angel of Rescue, was there to accomplish the seemingly impossible, the truly miraculous.

4

"Death Was Now Armed with a New Terror"

The attitude of the new Arrow Cross government added a new dimension to the plight of the Budapest Jews. No longer could they count on the kind of protection provided by Regent Horthy's agreement with the neutral legations. Horthy's relative benevolence was replaced with a vindictive hatred. The Nyilas government began its regime with the resumption of deportations and the imposition of a "reign of terror" unparalleled in Hungarian history. The challenge for Wallenberg became clear when Szálasi issued his first official announcement: "This is a war of independence against Jewry. Whoever impedes the nation's war effort and disrupts the unity is a traitor."

A proclamation by Minister of the Interior Gábor Vajna contained the government's fully developed view on the Jewish question:

I will not acknowledge the validity of any safe-conducts or foreign passports issued by whomsoever to a Hungarian Jew. At present all Jews living in Hungary are subject to the control and direction of the Hungarian State. And we will tolerate interference from nobody, whether in Hungary or abroad.

For ten days the streets of Budapest were a study in terror. The government imposed a five-day curfew upon the Jews. On the sixth day, they were granted two hours a day in which to shop, but by that time most food stores were either closed or sold out. Throughout this period, government forces snatched Jews from their apartments and threw them out onto the rainy streets to join the long columns being marched to deportation sites. As Mrs. Hansi Brand testified at the Eichmann trial, "the major streets of Budapest looked as though they were full of ants."

49

Many Jews were led to a brick factory in Buda or to Saint Stephen's Square, both of which served as assembly points for deportees. When word reached the Swedish legation of the imminent departure of a trainload of Jews, the Angel of Rescue lost no time getting to the scene. Dr. Stephen I. Lazarovitz, now a physician in Toronto, will always remember October 28, 1944, and the intervention of the Angel of Rescue:

I was an intern, just before my final exams. When the Arrow Cross came to power I was not allowed to continue my studies and was drafted to a forced labor camp in Budapest. On October 28 we were yanked to the freight railway station of Józefváros, where we boarded the freight wagons. The doors of the wagons were locked from the outside. Suddenly two cars drove up between the railway tracks. Wallenberg jumped out from the first car, accompanied by his Hungarian aides. He went to the commanding police officer in charge, talked to him and presented official papers. Soon the officer made an announcement. He said that those who had authentic Swedish protective passports should step down from the wagon and stand in line to show their papers. Should anybody step down from the cattle cars who had no Swedish protective passport, he would be executed on the spot. The authenticity of the passports would be checked by him and by Wallenberg from the books of the Swedish embassy, which Mr. Wallenberg had brought with him.

In the meantime Mr. Wallenberg's aides pulled out a folding table from the car, opened it, placed it between the rail tracks, and put the big embassy books on top of it. The commanding Nazi police officer put his gun in front of the books. We, who were in the cattle cars, watched all this from the small barred windows of the cattle cars. The doors of the wagons were opened.

I did not know what to do because my protective passport was not authentic but forged. Suddenly I saw from the window that one of the aides was Leslie Geiger, a member of the Hungarian national hockey team, a patient of my father and a personal friend. I decided to step down from the cattle car. It was one of the most difficult decisions of my life.

I stood in line for an hour because I was at the end of the line. When I was close to the table, I stepped forward, went to Leslie Geiger, and whispered in his ear that my passport was forged. I asked him if he could help me. He said that he would try. When it was my turn, Leslie Geiger whispered a few words in Wallenberg's ear. Raoul Wallenberg looked at me, holding my forged passport in his hand, and said, "I remember this doctor. I gave him his passport personally. Let's not waste our time because it's late. We need him now at the Emergency Hospital of the Swedish embassy." The Nazi commanding officer then said, "Let's not waste our time! Next."

My feeling was then and still is that what happened was a miracle. Had the commanding officer insisted to check the books, I probably would not be alive. Raoul Wallenberg was certainly a courageous person who fought for the life of each person.

Mrs. Agnes Sereni, of Swampscott, Massachusetts, remembers that after spending months at a forced labor camp, she, then nineteen, fled to her mother when the camp was bombed. Back in Budapest they were stripped and herded into a clammy five-story warehouse. Nearby in the frost the railway cars were waiting to be loaded for the death camps. "It was such a crowd of people pushing, shoving, hoping to be among the few to be saved. It was chaos. All night long they came. The Nazis seized people from the first floor and the second, then squeezed them by the hundreds into the cattle cars. They stopped at the third. My mother and I were on the top floor."

Wallenberg suddenly appeared the next morning. "The messiah came," Mrs. Sereni recalled with much emotion. "He said that he was there to save lives. But he could only free thirty-eight, and those people had to have Swedish papers. We did not have these passes. However, a miracle happened. This messiah pushed my mother and me into a room along with the others to be saved. The others were taken to Auschwitz. He led us out of the building."

After one night at a safe house, the survivors were taken to the ghetto area of Budapest under the escort of the Angel of Rescue. "For me, for my mother," Mrs. Sereni said, "it was a genuine miracle."

As for Raoul Wallenberg, Mrs. Sereni will always remember him "not as an ordinary human being." Raoul Wallenberg, Mrs. Sereni said, "was a saint; to me a messiah." She added that the Swede "was a dedicated humanitarian. He rescued Jewish people because it happened to be the Jew who was persecuted at that time."

As October was drawing to a close, Veesenmayer, Hitler's ambassador to Budapest, summed up the state of the Hungarian operation in an October 28 telegram to Berlin: "Total number of Jews in Hungary on March 19 of this year, about 800,000. Already transported into the territory of the Reich, about 430,000. Jewish work force of the Hungarian Army about 150,000. In the region of Budapest about 200,000."

The first days of November were days of torment. Jews were dragged to the Buda brick factory and kept under guard beneath an open sky. Some three thousand men, women, and children were herded together awaiting deportation to the death camps. Ferenc Friedman, now in his eighties and a resident of Hamilton, Ontario, relives those moments when the Angel of Rescue arrived to perform another miracle:

"I was forced out from one of the Swedish safe houses and taken to a brick factory yard. It would be only minutes before we boarded the death trains. Suddenly two cars drove up. There was Wallenberg in the first one, with Hungarian officials and German officers in the second car. He jumped out, shouting that all those with Swedish papers were under his protection. I was one out of 150 saved that day. None of the others ever came back."

Mr. Friedman was not the only member of his family saved by Wallenberg. His wife, Giselle, also in her eighties, had another story to tell.

In September, 1944, I went with my nine-month-old baby and nine-year-old son to the Swedish embassy hoping to get a protection passport. The line in in front of me was hopelessly long, and we had only an hour of freedom in the ghetto. I was depressed and went around to the back garden, leaned on the wooden fence, and cried. Miraculously Wallenberg came out of the embassy with a pencil and paper in his hand. Fifteen minutes later I had the life-saving document in my hands.

Although the Szálasi government succeeded in making life miserable for the Budapest Jews, continued resistance by the Hungarian Army could not stop the inevitable Russian advance. Skorzeny's coup had only bought some time for Germany. As Horthy had feared, Hungary soon became a vast battleground. The Red Army fought its way across the country throughout October. By November 2 elements of Marshal Malinovsky's Second Ukrainian Front had broken through the German and Hungarian forces to the south of Budapest and pursued them to the outskirts of the capital, but could not capture the city. Jewish work companies that had been digging trenches under the watchful eyes of Nyilas guards were caught up in the rout. As retreating troops commandeered the roads, the tired Jews were pushed into the ditches alongside and forced to keep moving by the Nyilas. The guards shot any Jewish stragglers, leaving hundreds of their bodies strewn along the roadsides. On November 3, the Nyilas dragged sixty exhausted Jews to the edge of a large shell crater in Pestszentimre and shot them. Their bodies fell into this open grave and some earth was thrown over them.

As the Red Army drew near, the capital fell into unprecedented chaos. While the approaching Russians did not in themselves constitute a new danger for Hungarian Jews, their unsettling proximity created an unstable climate in which the SS and Arrow Cross became unmanageable.

One evening the Nyilas burst into the offices of the Swedish Red Cross, arrested the staff, and banned future activities. A sharp protest was made at the Hungarian Foreign Ministry, accompanied by the threat that if such acts were not stopped, the Swedish government would break off relations with the Szálasi government and its diplomats would be called home. Actually, the Swedish legation had no thought of leaving the Jews to the mercy of the Arrow Cross. In Per Anger's words, "We had received relatively dependable intelligence that the Arrow Crossmen intended to blow the protected houses sky-high the moment our mission left the country" (66).

During this period Wallenberg staunchly maintained his office in the Pest side of the Danube, near his protégés, while all other neutral delegations were in the hilly Buda part of the city, farther removed from the advancing Russians. The Swedish government exacerbated this hellish situation by some untimely decisions.

Wallenberg was aware of the disaster that would befall the Jews if a diplomatic vacuum were created in Budapest. Throughout the difficult negotiations with Szálasi and other Hungarian officials, Wallenberg and the other Swedish diplomats intimated that Stockholm would soon recognize the Arrow Cross regime and accept its representative in Sweden, but, of course, this was a ruse. The Swedish Foreign Office had already sent a message that it would not recognize the Nyilas regime. But, in a continuing effort to help the Jews, the Swedish legation did not disillusion Szálasi, who grew increasingly impatient.

Some leaders among the Nyilas had never accepted Wallenberg's interference in their handling of internal affairs, specifically his meddling in behalf of the Jews. These Nyilas did not hide their displeasure. According to Lars Berg,

> The aversion to the Swedes and the anger about their intervention in matters that actually were no concern of theirs at all grew worse and worse among certain Nyilas officials. Demands for countermeasures were raised. Who gave the Swedish Legation the right to interfere with the Jewish question! The Swedish diplomats were received with constantly diminishing courtesy. Even when we came on the most legitimate grounds, we were met by a "We don't help any Jew-attachés! . . ."

Sweden never chose to recognize the Nyilas regime despite Wallenberg's efforts. He often tried to influence Minister Danielsson to recommend that Stockholm grant it recognition. Wallenberg's diplomatic colleagues differ on Danielsson's stance. Lars Berg describes Danielsson's resistance to recognition, and his own pleasure that the Arrow Cross regime was never acknowledged: "But luckily enough the Minister stood firm in his resistance here, so the blasphemy never happened that Sweden acknowledged the Szálasi bandit government" (49).

Per Anger sharply disagrees with Berg. "It is not correct to speak of Danielsson's resistance to recognition of the Szálasi government. He tried his best to have the Swedish government offer some kind of recognition in order to help us save some more Jewish people." In his book, Anger writes: "In telegram after telegram during the fall of 1944, Danielsson pointed out the importance of extending some kind of recognition to the Szálasi government in order to make continued rescue work possible" (98). Anger adds that in recognizing the Szálasi regime, Sweden would be following the example of Spain, Switzerland, and Turkey.

While the haggling over recognition continued between the ministries, Hungarian interior policy was jeopardizing Wallenberg's mission: his Jewish staff had lost their hard-won privileges, and the validity of the protective passports, which they labored so hard to distribute, now had been revoked.

Joseph Kovacs, who feverishly worked to distribute protective passes during this hellish period, remembered the first days of November when the Nyilas seized hundreds of Jews wearing yellow stars and chased them into the Dohany Synagogue.

> In the afternoon of November 4, Wallenberg burst into the temple and stood himself in front of the altar and made this announcement: "All those who have

Swedish protective passes should stand up." That same night a few hundred Jews were freed, and they returned to their houses under the protection of Hungarian policemen.

People often ask me, "Why did Raoul Wallenberg succeed?" The way I saw it, Raoul Wallenberg was forceful, determined, and never hesitated in saying what he had to say and doing what he had to do.

Growing impatient with the diplomatic impasse, the daring and resourceful Wallenberg made use of a newfound ally, the young, attractive wife of Foreign Minister Baron Gábor Kemény. After learning that she had been born Elizabeth Fuchs, of Jewish descent, and had worked for a Jewish book company before the Nazi takeover of Hungary, Wallenberg combined his charm with intimidation to persuade her to influence her husband. Jenö Lévai, a historian chronicling the Holocaust's effect on the Hungarian Jewish community, writes of Wallenberg and the Keménys:

> The worried wife was deeply concerned about the life of her husband. In a conversation with the Foreign Minister, Wallenberg pointed out that he [Kemény] came from an illustrious family, and now his wife was expecting a child. How would it look if the father would be hanging from a rope. And that was precisely what would happen to him if he did not stop the persecution of the Jews. Wallenberg's prediction so shocked the Baroness that she strongly urged her husband to meet all Wallenberg's wishes (102).

In order to make local authorities and the public aware of the government's policy changes, Wallenberg made the foreign minister announce them over the radio on October 29. The baroness, not leaving anything to chance, forced her husband to go to the radio station himself and to remain until the announcer had read the new regulations. These restored the privileges of Wallenberg's Jewish staff members, including their exemption from wearing the yellow star, and, most important, certified the validity of passes issued by the neutral legations.

On November 7, Wallenberg filed a report stating that the protective passes would again be respected. All Jews with such documents would enjoy extraterritorial rights under the protection of the respective legations and would not be used for military or civilian work. Lévai calls Wallenberg's extraordinary diplomatic accomplishment an achievement without precedent: "There is no other instance in the history of diplomacy that a mere secretary from a neutral country could exert such influence and be so persuasive in dealing with a sovereign country" (103).

Wallenberg's diplomatic gains not only gave Budapest's Jews a new lease on life, but also calmed an anxious world Jewish community. Sweden's Chief Rabbi Ehrenpreis told the World Jewish Congress about the new agreements and they immediately sent the following message to the Swedish minister in Washington: "I need not reiterate to Your Excellency the assurance of our deep gratitude for the admirable action taken by the Swedish government on behalf of my unfortunate people."

During this period, the "international ghetto" was established on orders from the Szálasi government. This was an outgrowth of the safe-houses agreement that Wallenberg had worked out with the Horthy regime. The buildings in the international ghetto were marked with yellow stars and were protected by the neutral legations.

The actual creation of the ghetto was not a simple matter. On November 7, Ferenczy demanded that some fifteen thousand Jews relocate to the ghetto by November 10. Wallenberg protested strongly to the Nyilas authorities and, together with Lutz, negotiated for an extension of time to resolve the complications. Stalling for time, the Swiss legation told authorities that the non-Jewish families who had been living in the designated buildings for centuries were reluctant to leave, and it was difficult to dislodge them. Roving bands of Nyilas also caused severe problems. As many Jews moved into the ghetto, taking only those possessions that they could carry, Nyilas seized them, dragged them into cellars, and beat them. They then proceeded to strip the Jews of their winter coats and other clothing and stole their property. Other Nyilas robbed and beat up the Jews, then took them to the brick factory to inflict further atrocities.

The official count of ghetto residents showed the following numbers of protected people and their sponsors: Sweden, 4,500; Switzerland, 7,800; Papal Nunciature, 2,500; Portugal, 690; Spain, 100. Actually, there were more protected passes and bearers than appeared on official records; Wallenberg continually arranged for Jews to be sneaked into these houses. To accommodate this influx, mattresses were thrown on the floor and often twenty persons were crammed into one room.

To minister to the needs of those in the ghetto, Wallenberg and his highly dedicated and competent staff set up a complex organization, which is detailed in an elaborate report and organizational chart prepared in December, 1944. Ten houses on six streets were used for offices and living accommodations for workers. Two hospitals were maintained on Tatra and Wahrmann streets. The hospital that specialized in epidemic diseases treated ghetto inhabitants when dysentry broke out. All protected Jews and the staff were inoculated against typhoid, paratyphoid, and cholera; however, Wallenberg reported that the number of those with infectious diseases increased daily and "prompt intervention without conditions is desired." Wallenberg asked that the hospitals be allowed to increase their beds to accommodate 200 in-patients, instead of only 150.

Mrs. Paula Solomon Braun, now director of food services at the Hillel School in Stockholm, remembers Raoul Wallenberg's visits to the Swedish hospital. While working as a nurse, using false papers with the alias Anna Kovacs, she noted that the Swede brought much-needed supplies to the overcrowded facility. "But the most important thing was his talking with sick people, giving them hope, raising their spirits."

The hub of the vast relief network at 6 Tatra Street, the only office located in a safe house, was divided into four bureaus: social services, board, housing, and management. These bureaus met the medical and nutritional needs of thousands.

As part of the social services division, Wallenberg drew up programs and activities to meet the needs of the children, the elderly, and the sick. The "children's home," for those eight to eighteen in age, featured supervised activity by teachers and other specialists. Nurses were appointed to look after the elderly, whose nutritional needs were met through preparation of special diets. Whenever possible, the elderly occupied their own floors. Because of the shortage of hospital beds, "sickrooms" were set up in each safe house, with attending doctors, nurses, X-ray and other necessary equipment. Transport to the hospitals was organized by the Red Cross. In order to provide for the day-to-day needs of the ghetto inhabitants, as well as to train them for future employment, Wallenberg set up "industrial workshops" where basic skills were taught, such as shoe repair and sewing.

The board or provisions division bought food, valued at about two million pengös, for preparation in a common soup kitchen or in the individual cooking facilities that were maintained in the houses. The bureau accepted all ration cards, purchased provisions, and distributed them to thousands of people at breakfast, lunch, and supper. Wallenberg wrote of one major problem: "It is nearly impossible to procure the necessary quantity of bread; at most, 60–70 percent of the requirement is met."

The housing division, through its system of maintaining a house warden and deputy in each house, had the responsibility of keeping up-dated lists of the residents: who the inhabitants were, what type of protection pass, e.g., Swedish or Swiss, they possessed, and, of course, who among the inhabitants had no protection pass at all. In his December 8 report to the king of Sweden on the "Situation of Hungarian Jewry," Wallenberg catalogs the population of the international ghetto. "The ghetto is meant to shelter 17,000 but now accommodates 33,000, of which 7,000 are in Swedish houses, 23,000 in Swiss houses, and 2,000 under the Red Cross flag." Wallenberg adds that several thousand Jews under Vatican and Swiss protection had been taken out of their houses and either deported or moved to the central ghetto, while those in the Swedish houses had fared better.

The housing division also had the immediate responsibility for the safety and well-being of the protected persons. The warden and deputy in each house received the requests and grievances of the residents and conveyed them to the controllers, each of whom supervised four houses. The controllers visited the houses daily and reported their findings to central headquarters.

A management division with special financial responsibilities oversaw this vast network. Wallenberg's organizational chart indicates that some bureaus had offices at sites other than 6 Tatra Street. Among other matters, these bureaus dealt with information, housing maintenance, and legal questions.

While we have some detailed knowledge about Wallenberg's operation, much is missing due to Nyilas vandalism. As Wallenberg himself states: "A great part of the department's correspondence was destroyed."

In spite of the safe passes and safe houses agreed upon by Wallenberg and Szálasi, the situation worsened for Budapest's Jews. As the fighting approached the city, the reign of terror became more extreme. Fanatical SS units and Arrow Cross gangsters joined in abducting, torturing, and murdering Jews—even those with safe passes. At night the submachine guns roared as Jews were taken to the wharves and shot. Their naked bodies were hurled into the Danube.

The worst was yet to come. With the overthrow of Regent Horthy, Adolf Eichmann had returned to Budapest, determined to eliminate the last major pocket of Jews in Europe. But time and the tides of war were against him. The efficient killing machine he had organized the summer before was breaking down under the stress of the Russian advance. He could no longer rely on the railroads to move masses of Jews to the death camps in Poland. Most transport had been taken over by the military to move supplies for the upcoming battle for Budapest. The Russians were attacking from the south and east. The main roads to Poland were blocked. Only Austria was left as a destination for the Jews. Eichmann hit upon a new method of deportation that assured the remaining Jews a quick and brutal end—the death march.

According to one of the members of the Jewish Council, upon his triumphal return to Budapest on October 17, Eichmann gloated and offered this greeting of exultation: "You see, I have come back. The Hungarians thought that the events of Rumania and Bulgaria will be repeated here. They forgot that Hungary still lies in the shadow of . . . the Reich. The government will work according to our orders . . . . The Jews of Budapest shall be deported. This time on foot. We need our vehicles."

There were differing opinions on this action in the Reich foreign office. Himmler himself, sensing the inevitable loss of the war, opposed the death marches, preferring instead to negotiate with the Allies. Eichmann ignored Himmler's recommendation, preferring to carry the final solution to its conclusion. The death marches proceeded—with only temporary interruptions—for some five weeks, from mid-November through December 10. Forty thousand men and women, the elderly, and the very young, were sent on these marches and almost ten thousand died.

Thousands were seized wherever they happened to be—on the street or in their homes. Jews were grabbed and not even given a chance to put on proper clothes. They were forced to march from 15 to 20 miles a day in frigid weather, sometimes without any food, to Hegyeshálom at the Hungarian-Austrian border, 125 miles away. Lars Berg reported,

It was a march that only with the greatest difficulty could have been performed by well-trained infantrymen with all the necessary equipment. Thousands and thousands of old and young Jews were being asked to do this. It was horrible to have to be standing as a passive spectator when young girls were driven together, arranged in files and sent off, dressed in silk stockings, high-heeled shoes, and thin office clothes. Together with them were old people who would hardly be able to make the first mile without falling.

Many Holocaust survivors and their children recount Wallenberg's heroism during these marches. Yosef Lapid, director-general of the Israeli Broadcasting Authority, is grateful to Wallenberg for saving his mother's life. "The Germans came to the building where my mother was under the protection of the Swedish flag and ordered her and all the other Jews to join the march to an Austrian factory. My mother was marching in the bitter cold without food or medical supplies when suddenly she was taken out of line by Wallenberg, who had driven along the march route and flashed Swedish protection passes at the Nazis."

Susan Tabor, the librarian at Hebrew Union College in New York, encountered Wallenberg while she was on a death march. Neither a Swiss protective pass distributed by the Zionist leader Mikhail Solomon nor Christian papers could prevent her family from being forced to march.

My mother, my husband, and I had been two nights without food. Then we heard words, human words, the first we had heard in what seemed like an eternity. It was Raoul Wallenberg. He gave us that needed sense that we were still human beings. We had been among thousands taken to stay at a brick factory outside Budapest. We were without food, without water, without sanitation facilities. Wallenberg told us he would try and return with safety passes. He also said that he would try to get medical attention and sanitation facilities. And true to his word, soon afterward some doctors and nurses came from the Jewish hospital. But what stands out most about Raoul Wallenberg is that he came himself. He talked to us, and, most important, he showed that there was a human being who cared about us.

Nyilas sadism plunged to new depths. The Hungarian Nazis, many of them youngsters wearing their emblems of a red cross with four ends like arrowheads, pushed the doomed marchers on by brutally kicking them or by beating them with the butt ends of their rifles. Women who suffered miscarriages were mocked and taunted. To amuse themselves, the Nyilas staged simulated executions. The supposed victims were made to dig a common grave and then line up at the edge. After the guards were sufficiently amused, they dismissed the hapless Jews. Another "game" of the Nyilas was searching Jews for money. The victim was then undressed and beaten to death in front of the other Jews, or else put into a barrel and doused with cold water until he or she became a block of ice. Then, to increase their torment, the deportees had to file past the barrel or it was passed among them, so that they could witness the horrible sight.

These atrocities did not go unnoticed. A long, sharply worded memorandum (see Appendix) was sent on November 17 to Szálasi under the signatures of the minister of Sweden, the chargés d'affaires of Switzerland, Portugal, and Spain, and the papal nuncio. The neutral powers called on the Arrow Cross not to resume deportations and to cease all forms of cruelty. Unfortunately, according to the memorandum, the word is that

> deportation of Jews has again been decided on, and that this action is being carried out with such inhumane severity that the whole world is witness of the atrocities accompanying its execution (babies are separated from their mothers, the old and sick are exposed to the rigours of the weather, men and women are left without food for days, thousands of persons are herded into a single brick works, women are violated, and innumerable persons are shot for the slightest offence).

The officials also warned Szálasi that failure to honor past statements and promises protecting Jews would invite reprisals on Hungary after the war, "to say nothing of the possibility of an eventual Army of Occupation . . . applying the same measures against the Hungarian nation."

The memorandum produced no positive results. Wallenberg repeatedly sent notes to the Arrow Cross government, angrily telling officials that instead of being treated better because of past agreements, the Jews were now being treated much worse. Wallenberg's assignment was made more difficult by Eichmann's dominant role in the death marches and his monomania in carrying out the final solution. For the first time since he arrived in Budapest, the Angel of Rescue had the satanic Eichmann as his archenemy. Not only did Eichmann oversee the death marches from his office, but he was present at Hegyeshálom to see the new arrivals. Per Anger witnessed the doomed Jews being turned over to an SS unit under Eichmann. "He counted them like sheep," Anger said, "and had a receipt made out for the Hungarian officer stating that everything had been done properly." In a report of the "untenable" situation in Budapest, Wallenberg speaks of Eichmann: "We went all the way to the border. Eichmann, the SS Sonderkommando chief, was there to welcome the deportees with beatings and all kinds of mistreatment, before promising them forced labor on the military installations."

But Wallenberg did not despair. He offered a means of survival to the seemingly endless columns of people on the march, the old and shriveled, the feeble babes. In the words of Lars Berg:

> The persecuted Jews' only hope was Wallenberg. Like a rescuing angel he often appeared at the very last moment. Just when a deportation was about to start — some people were actually also sent by train — he used to arrive at the station with a written — false or genuine — permission to separate and set free all Jews with Swedish protection passports. If his protégés had already been

brought out of the city, he hurried after them and conducted back as many as he could on hastily procured trucks. His movable and always accompanying chancellery manufactured all kinds of identification and protection documents on an endless scale. Uncountable were those Jews who during the march toward Vienna had given up all hope, when suddenly they received from one of Wallenberg's "flying squadrons" a Swedish protection document, like their ancestors once upon a time during their long journey were rescued by manna from Heaven (38).

Often it took more than a protective pass to save the marchers. Wallenberg could outfox the Nyilas with quickness and craftiness. By suddenly appearing and announcing loudly in German that he had orders to take with him so many Jews, he would take that number from those standing nearest to him and disappear before the dumbfounded Nyilas realized what happened. He also duped the Nyilas with other stratagems, such as disguising Aryan-looking Jews in SS and Arrow Cross uniforms and raiding Hungarian camps and prisons. Sometimes such disguised Jewish youth would stop Arrow Cross members on the streets and demand to see their documents. By declaring their identifications false, the papers could be confiscated and then used as legitimations for future rescue actions. At times, Wallenberg succeeded in freeing large numbers of Jews on the grounds that they were being removed for deportation.

Not only did Wallenberg pull people out of death marches and pass out food and other supplies to the unfortunate deportees, he attempted to nip these deportations in the bud. Through his contacts in the governmental ministries, he received advance notice of intended actions and often convinced those in charge to revoke their plans. While the Baroness Kemény was still in Budapest, he effectively appealed to her. Lars Berg notes, "If the official channels did not produce the desired results, Wallenberg tried to buy time by bribing those who had to pass on or carry out the orders of the Nyilas."

The baroness, however, paid a price for her friendship with Wallenberg. On November 29 she was sent out of Budapest for relocation in Meran. "As is customary for a diplomat," writes Lévai, "Wallenberg appeared at the station to say goodbye" (103). The baroness was never heard from again, and Wallenberg lost his "friend of court."

If it became impossible to counteract the deportation orders, Wallenberg initiated another plan: at checkpoints on the roads out of Budapest and at the border station, Jews with protective passes were rescued from the ranks of deportees and returned to Budapest.

As atrocities against the Jews were stepped up, the increased responsibility rested ever heavier on Wallenberg's shoulders. A middle-of-November letter from Wallenberg to his mother points out the frenzied pace of of activity.

Dear Mother:

You today will receive these lines, which have been set down in a great hurry. I can calm you, for I am well. The Furies here are extremely agitating and exciting. But we work and struggle, and that is the main thing.

For the moment we are sitting at candlelight and trying to get the courier ready. The light is not working, and that is the only thing missing in this chaos. If you could only see me. There are a dozen people standing around me, everyone with urgent questions. I don't know to whom I shall give an answer or advice first.

I hope that you are well too. And I promise by all that is sacred that next time you will get a more detailed report. For today I conclude with regards and kisses to you all.

Yours,

Raoul

As can be seen from the letter, Wallenberg's staff also felt the hectic tempo. One of his key aides, Hugo Wohl, sought to have the staff members and their families live on Üllöi Street, both because it was closer to the heart of the Jewish ghetto and because it appeared that the Russians would soon liberate this center. In the meantime, the members of Wallenberg's staff contended with continual reports of thousands of families being dragged from their homes by the Nyilas; these developments frustrated and depressed the workers. "One day," Per Anger recalled, "Wallenberg hopped on his bicycle and made the rounds to his various offices to cheer up and encourage his Jewish colleagues. This was not a simple trip. It was at great personal risk because the Arrow Cross bandits would have liked nothing better than to snare him."

However, Wallenberg's aides were not always able to escape the bandits. Béla Elék, his assistant at the Austrian frontier, was caught, tortured, and murdered. Dr. Peter Sugár and Istvan Löwinger were among other victims from his staff.

Those fortunate survivors who were privileged to work with Wallenberg spoke of him in glowing terms after the war. Dr. Jonny Moser, a self-described "errand boy of Wallenberg," related his story to Swedish author Elsa Björkman Goldschmidt:

His [Wallenberg's] conduct, his power of organization, his rapidity in decision and action. What a strategist. It was like a celebration in the middle of Ragnarok when he turned up . . . .

I remember when we were told . . . that 800 Jewish soldiers were to be transported away. The deportations had started on foot to Mauthausen. Wallenberg caught up with them at the frontier. "Who of you has a Swedish protective passport? Raise your hand!" he cried. On his order I ran between the columns and told the people to raise their hand, whether they had a passport or not. He then took command of all who had raised their hand, and his attitude was such that nobody of the guards opposed it, so extraordinary was the convincing force of his attitude.

I think that Wallenberg was happy during the short time his epos took form. It is not given to many to live such a life, equipped with the spark of the initiative, an irresistible personal radiation, and a never tiring activity, and by these to be able to save thousands of one's fellow men (263-266).

Wallenberg's interventions earned no praise from Eichmann; instead, they greatly distressed him. Gideon Hausner spoke of the Swede's actions and the German's reactions: "Wallenberg followed the column of people with truckloads of food, clothing, and medicines. He removed from the marching columns anyone who could for any reason be declared Swedish and encouraged the local peasants to supply water and hot meals to the women and children. Eichmann was furious."

If Wallenberg himself could not be present at the death march, he sent his colleagues, most often Lars Berg or Per Anger, to the rescue. On one occasion, Anger rescued one hundred fifty persons, of whom only two actually held protective passes. Valdemar Langlet and Asta Nilsson, who worked with the International Red Cross, organized truck convoys for passing out food to the deported.

A November 26 report by Swiss Consul Lutz draws a shocking picture of those terror-filled days:

All the protected houses in the Szent István-Varós are overcrowded to such an extent that part of the people accommodated in them are obliged to live in the staircases, corridors, and cellars. In case of an airraid the lodgers of the house cannot, of course, use the shelters which are already overcrowded. It was reported on November 24, from the house at 54 Pozsonyi Street, that the number of people living there amounts to 1,800. Communication on the stairs is impossible as even they are crowded with sitting or sleeping people. For five days the inhabitants had no food at all, and very little afterwards. As Jews are forbidden to go out into the streets, it is impossible to provide for these houses. There have been instances when food brought there by Jews was confiscated by Arrow-cross men and the Jews were arrested. Endeavors have been made to provide the lodgers . . . with supplies, but the food transported there is hardly enough for the people living on the three lower floors; consequently, people living on the fourth, fifth, and sixth floors receive nothing at all. There are about 1,200 indigents in this house. Very many of them are ill, suffering especially of nervous diseases. The airraid shelter is jammed to such a degree that it is literally impossible to move about in it. Similar is the situation in the rooms, entrance halls, and bathrooms.

. . . On November 24 in 26 Tatra Street a policeman . . . appeared there. His number could not be taken. He declared that the protection passes were void and threatened their possessors that he would carry them off unless they paid him off 1,200 pengös immediately. The people gave him 950 pengös and the policeman said that he would return for the rest. In other houses it was Arrow-cross men who took the protection passes and sold them to others.

On November 28 the Nyilas attacked the protected house on 35 Pozsonyi Street, claiming that they had been fired upon from that building. Several hundred Jews were dragged from the house and either killed or placed in the central ghetto. On November 29 the Ministry of the Interior and Home Defense signed an agreement with the Gestapo to deliver an additional seventeen thousand Jewish laborers. While Wallenberg was able to save those with protected passes at Józefváros Station, several thousand Jews were herded into freight trucks, sixty to seventy in a truck. Instead of being taken for work assignments in Germany, as pretended by Szálasi, they were conveyed to villages in western Hungary, where they fell victim to typhus, starvation, and the sadism of Nyilas guards.

The last days of November are remembered well by Tibor Vayda, now living in Los Angeles, who was among Wallenberg's inner circle of Jewish assistants:

> I was selected to work for Wallenberg because I was blond and didn't look Jewish. This made it easier to carry out the rescue work. Every morning about six or seven of us met with Wallenberg and then left to aid those Jews who had trouble at the hands of the SS or Nyilas. One day at the end of November, I left at 5 A.M., accompanied by a fellow worker. We headed for a trouble spot on Jokai Street. Wallenberg told us he would be there before 8 A.M. We waited and waited, and there was still no Wallenberg. Some three hundred people were being lined up for deportation to Józefváros. We were ready to leave. Frankly, we were afraid that we might be in trouble too. Out of nowhere came a black car with Wallenberg, at one minute to eight.

Wallenberg's arrival did not mean immediate freedom for the would-be deportees, and his arguing with the SS officer was to no avail. Vayda continues, "But Wallenberg was a person who never gave up. The next day he went to the highest SS commander, and he got every one of those three hundred people back, even if the entire process took up to two weeks."

The Jews of Budapest and the worldwide Jewish community obviously appreciated Wallenberg's prodigious feats. The American government was also aware of the developments in the Wallenberg mission. A letter to Wallenberg in early December from J. W. Pehle, executive director of the War Refugee Board, indicates that the Roosevelt administration was closely following the developments in Hungary:

> My dear Mr. Wallenberg:
>
> Through the American Minister in Stockholm and Mr. Iver Olsen the War Refugee Board has kept closely informed of the difficult and important work

you have been doing to alleviate the situation of the Jewish people in Hungary. We have followed with keen interest the reports of the steps which you have taken to accomplish your mission and the personal devotion which you have given to saving and protecting the innocent victims of Nazi persecution.

I think that no one who has participated in this great task can escape some feeling of frustration in that, because of circumstances beyond our control, our efforts have not met with complete success. On the other hand, there have been measurable achievements in the face of obstacles which had to be encountered, and it is our conviction that you have made a very great personal contribution to the success which has been realized in these endeavors.

On behalf of the War Refugee Board I wish to express to you our very deep appreciation for your splendid cooperation and for the vigor and ingenuity which you brought to our common humanitarian undertaking.

Despite the encouragement of the War Refugee Board, Wallenberg faced a continuing struggle against the terrorism rampant on the streets of Budapest.

At 2 A.M. on December 4, the corpses of hundreds of Jews from Jewish labor companies were thrown from the backs of trucks. The entire length of Népsinhaz Street, from the corner of Aföldi and Fiumei Streets to the corner of Jozsef Boulevard, was strewn with bodies, all shot through the back of the neck.

On December 8, the Russian army laid siege to the city. Interestingly, on that day, Wallenberg had written a "Report on the Situation of the Hungarian Jews" and a letter to his mother. In both of these he spoke of the steady decline in the status of the Jews and presaged the ensuing pandemonium. A courier, who amazingly was able to leave the besieged capital, forwarded the report to the king of Sweden. Its first lines tell the story: "Since my last report, the situation of the Hungarian Jews has noticeably deteriorated." He provides a brief, gruesome description of the death marches and conditions in the central ghetto, where "the Jews have been crammed" into an area "supposed to accommodate 69,000 persons — but in actual fact containing many more." Wallenberg cites the structure of his multifaceted organization, but adds a concise, grim prognosis: "the food situation will shortly be catastrophic." He also relays talk of a new, intense reaction against the Jews; however, he feels it will not be widespread: "Rumors are circulating, according to which the Brigade of Death, closely associated with Minister Kovarcs, is preparing to incite a pogrom. I do not believe that this pogrom will spread very far, as for instance the SS organs have received no order to arrange a systematic mass-murder of the Jews."

The December 8 letter to his mother is the only extant letter from Raoul still in his family's possession. Although the text is in German, a brief postscript in Swedish clearly indicates that he will not be returning to Stockholm for some time.

Dear Mother:

I really do not know when I can atone for my guilt. Today there is another courier leaving. Anyhow you receive all the accounts from me. The situation is very disturbing but very exciting. My work is overwhelming, nearly inhuman. The bandits roam around the city beating up people, torturing people, shooting people. There are 40 cases of brutality against persons under my care. On the whole, however, our mood is good and we look forward to the struggle . . . .

We hear the artillery thunder day and night from the approaching Russians. The diplomatic frenzy began after the arrival of Szálasi. I alone do all the legation work relating to the government. So far I have met 10 times with the Foreign Minister, twice with the Deputy Minister, twice with the Interior Minister, once with the Security Minister, and once with the Finance Minister. I had become quite friendly with the wife of the Foreign Minister. Unfortunately, she now has left for Meran.

The food supply is not large in Budapest. But we have taken care to maintain a good supply. I have a feeling that it will be difficult to come home until the occupation. I think I will not be in Stockholm until Easter. But this is all speculation. No one knows how the occupation will turn out. In any event, my thoughts are continually about returning home as soon as possible.

Today one cannot make plans. I had thought to be home certainly for Christmas. But I must bring you my Christmas greetings in this manner and also send my best wishes for the New Year. I hope that the long-awaited peace is not far away.

Dear mother. I am sending you two recently taken photographs. I am in a circle with my aides and workers, at my desk. Because of all the work, time passes very quickly. And it often happens that I am invited to dinner, where there are steaks and Hungarian specialties.

I must apologize to you now because the courier's sack is now ready. I greet and kiss you and the entire family with much fervor.

Yours,

Raoul

Many kisses for Nina and the little ones.
P.S. I will remain for a long time.

The strained relations between the Arrow Cross and the Swedish legation came to a head near Christmas time, when the Szálasi government announced its intentions to relocate to Szombathely. The move was motivated by a desire to escape encirclement by the Soviet armies. It was made quite explicit that failure to follow Szálasi to Szombathely would jeopardize the extraterritoriality of the Swedish legation and the lives of the diplomats and staff. The Swedes tried to stall, never saying no, but never giving their agreement to the move. Among the officials who left with Szálasi was Baron Kemény, who was replaced as head of what remained of the Foreign

Ministry by Ladislas Vöczköndy—a most unfortunate development for the Swedish legation.

Vöczköndy had good cause to detest Swedish officials. When the officials who served under Horthy resigned after Szálasi seized power, Vöczköndy, the assistant military attaché at the Hungarian legation in Stockholm, named himself the Hungarian chargé d'affaires in Sweden. His self-appointed leadership did not last forty-eight hours before the Swedish Foreign Ministry ordered him out of the country. Now, as head of the Hungarian Foreign Ministry, he could display his vindictive spirit. In a note to the Swedish legation on December 23, he demanded that the Swedes leave for Szombathely at once and that the Swedish Red Cross stop its work immediately. From that point on Wallenberg and his rescue mission struggled to endure amid the Nyilas's brazen lawlessness. Anger squarely blames Stockholm. If the Russians had not stormed Budapest so quickly, the Arrow Cross bandits would have been fully aware of Stockholm's attitude and would have undone all of Wallenberg's accomplishments.

> There is not a shred of doubt that it was the Foreign Office's action in expelling Vöczköndy and the Swedish government's stiff-necked unwillingness to recognize the Szálasi regime that set off the operations against our legation. If the Russians had not arrived at just that time, the consequences for the Jews in the Swedish houses would have been terrible. In all probability, the Arrow Crossmen, having discovered that no recognition by the Swedish government was to be had, would have carried out their threats and blown the Swedish houses with their tenants to kingdom come, or liquidated them in some other way. All the Swedish efforts would have been in vain (98).

The Swedish writer Rudolph Philipp makes a more scathing indictment of Stockholm in the January 14, 1955, issue of *Vi*:

> To oust the Chargé d'Affaires of another country is an unequivocal message that one does not want "diplomatic relations" with that country. Even so, our Foreign Office made no move to call home Raoul Wallenberg or our mission in general, despite having by this brusque move pulled the juridical rug out from under both Raoul's rescue assignment as a neutral diplomat and the mission's activities as the sheltering power for Allied and Russian citizens. The Foreign Office's action and its passivity thereafter completely abandoned our Swedish diplomats as private citizens to the tender mercies of the Arrow Cross regime!

Philipp's comments touch on another interesting facet of the pre-Christmas period: the refusal of the Swedish government to recall Wallenberg and other members of the legation. Actually, Danielsson had convened a "war council" and put forward the suggestion that members of the legation return to Stockholm, but, according to Berg, "Wallenberg and Langlet immediately declared their intention not to abandon their posts, and all the others agreed that we were duty-bound to remain in Budapest."

On Christmas Day, 1944, the traditional day for peace on earth, good will toward men, the Nyilas intensified their enmity and ill will toward Sweden. A season commemorating the time-honored, hallowed values of decency and kindness was perverted into a period of unprecedented acts of vulgarity and barbarism. The Nyilas violated the diplomatic sanctity of the legation, arrested its members, paraded them through the Jewish ghetto, and heaped a volley of verbal abuse on them.

While the Neanderthal Arrow Cross were foraging, Raoul Wallenberg escaped the clutches of the beasts of prey and immersed himself in the saving of lives. For Stephen I. Lazarovitz, Raoul Wallenberg became a deus ex machina — for the second time. After Wallenberg had intervened to rescue him on October 28, Dr. Lazarovitz joined the staff of the hospital at Tatra Street. He recalled,

We worked and lived at the hospital. We attended surgical and emergency cases. There was a group of well-known physicians, among them my parents, Dr. G. Varga, a laryngologist, and Dr. F. Foldvari, both professors at the University of Budapest. On Christmas Eve, 1944, a group of Nazi Arrow Cross people in uniforms came to the hospital. They planned to take us to the Danube, where thousands of people had been executed. One of us was able to get in touch with Wallenberg, who arrived within ten minutes with his aides and the books of the embassy. He argued with the Arrow Cross people with calm and determination, showing them official papers. Finally, the Nazis left. Wallenberg had saved the life of my parents, and had saved my life — for the second time!

The new boldness of the Nyilas forced members of the Swedish legation underground. Wallenberg never considered forsaking his protégés in Pest. Berg remembered, "Not even armed Nyilas with a warrant on his person could keep Raoul away from his duties. No power on earth could have made Wallenberg give up his visits to his many houses and protégés."

Many of the sadistic activities of that period are recorded in the logbook of the Budapest ambulance service. The Nyilas book shop on 4 Kossuth Street had been blown up by unknown persons on December 14. On the following day among the debris, the ambulance crew found bodies of members of the Jewish forced labor companies — all shot in back of the neck. On their necks were tags reading, "Revenge for the outrage on the Nyilas book shop." That same day similar tags were found on the necks of Jews hanging from the trees of Szabadsag Square.

More than violating the sanctity of the legation, the Nyilas demonstrated that their barbarism had no limits. They raided the children's homes of the International Red Cross and the Jewish orphanage in Vilma Királyné and Munkácsy Streets. While bombs rained down, the children were driven across the Danube to Buda and into the Radetzky Barracks. Many children were shot during this march.

Wallenberg was not prepared to stop: the Nyilas were determined to annihilate the Jews of Budapest. An account of the Institute of Forensic Medicine in Budapest describes the ghastly period:

> In the most brutal manner, the Nyilas made short work of their victims. A few were simply shot, but the majority were mercilessly tortured. From the distorted faces of the corpses the conclusion could be drawn that their sufferings had been ghastly. Very few blown-out brains or heart shots were to be found; on the other hand, there was overwhelming evidence of the most brutal ill-treatment. Shooting out of eyes, scalping, deliberate breaking of bones, and abdominal knife wounds were Nyilas specialties.

According to the same institute, the number of suicides in December exceeded the total number of Jewish suicides committed during the entire year of 1943. Conditions were so bad, the institute reported, that "old men, young girls, expectant mothers committed suicide. A mother would stun her daughter, who protested against the thought of suicide, with a rolling-pin, and would then lay down beside her in front of the open gas pipe. Thousands of individual tragedies took place in those days."

During the last days of 1944, unmatched barbarism raged in the streets of Budapest. On December 29, 20 men and women were forced out of 39 Légrady Karoly Street, a house under Swedish protection, to Nyilas party headquarters at 35 Pozsonyi Street. They were stripped naked, lined up against a wall, and shot. At 21 Katona Street, another Swedish protected house, 279 Jews were marched to Szabadsag Square and stripped of their clothes. Eighty of the younger men were shot, while the others, including the naked women, were led into the international ghetto.

Nothing was sacred to the Nyilas. On December 30 the Arrow Cross invaded the Glass House, where more than two thousand five hundred Jews had been hiding in a building kept up by the Swiss legation. The Jews were driven out onto the street, as the Arrow Cross began beating them and looting their apartments. On the following day the Arrow Cross returned and killed Arthur Weiss, the respected Zionist leader and commander of the house.

On New Year's Eve, the Arrow Cross invaded the Hotel Ritz, a building that had always enjoyed international protection. Among those who were dragged away and killed were Ottó Komoly, chairman of a Zionist group and of Group A of the International Red Cross, as well as a member of the Jewish Council, and Janos Gábor, another member of the Jewish Council.

At the beginning of the new year 1945, Wallenberg learned of a new crisis: the Ministry of Foreign Affairs and the Ministry of the Interior had decided to transfer the inhabitants of the international ghetto into the sealed or central ghetto. On January 3, Wallenberg addressed the highest responsible authority in Budapest, the German town commander. The transfer,

Wallenberg pointed out, would mean the crowding of some seventy thousand Jews into an area meant for fifteen thousand. Moreover, the food supply in the ghetto was disastrously low; by January 5, the ghetto would be starving. "For humane reasons," wrote Wallenberg, "this plan must be described as utterly crazy and inhuman. The Royal Swedish Legation is not aware of any similar plan ever having been carried out by any other civilized government."

Wallenberg's efforts failed. On January 4, the inhabitants of the protected houses were told that they would have to leave and move into the central ghetto. Since food was very scant, they were advised to take with them what they could; but removing money, valuables, and tobacco from the international ghetto was forbidden. Wallenberg prepared detailed instructions for the move for his staff in a "Proclamation" that realistically appraised the situation: "The Legation considers that the protection hitherto afforded will no longer be effective."

The Nyilas explained that the international ghetto was to be dissolved because the neutral countries did not recognize the Arrow Cross regime; therefore, the Nyilas government was not bound to honor past agreements. On January 4, four of the protected houses were evacuated. The inhabitants were transferred to the closed ghetto, and their possessions were plundered. On the following day those living under Swedish protection on Pozsonyi Street, and inhabitants of the Portuguese and Vatican-protected houses were also transferred to the central ghetto. As those who lived on the right side of Pozsonyi Street were being readied for transfer, Wallenberg negotiated with Arrow Cross leader Imre Nidosi to obtain a twenty-four-hour delay. Wallenberg later negotiated with Dr. Ernö Vajna, brother of the minister of the interior and a special delegate of the Ministry of Foreign Affairs. Dr. Vajna, a difficult man with whom to deal, had previously told Wallenberg, "Take your Jews away. If not, they will be swimming in the Danube." Upon announcing his decision to transfer the protected Jews to the sealed ghetto, he calmly said that the inhabitants "will be exterminated with machine guns in due time." Wallenberg prevailed in this instance, and no further transports were to be made into the central ghetto. But, in return, Vajna extorted a high price. Wallenberg had to turn food stocks over to the Arrow Cross police, food that had been bought in the Hungarian countryside in the fall of 1944 and delivered, under the escort of Wallenberg's workers, to the Swedish houses for storage. The agreement, as confirmed in a January 6 letter to Dr. Vajna, also called for the hospital to remain in the international ghetto and for "liberty of movement of Jewish officials" in the international ghetto. Although an agreement was reached, Wallenberg was well aware that the Nyilas were difficult to control. To prevent them from plundering food supplies and mistreating his protégés, Wallenberg asked Dr. Vajna "to do everything" in his power "to restrain hotheads among the party members and to prevent these inofficial side actions of the party."

To further legitimate the agreement, Wallenberg wrote a note on January 9 to Dr. Vajna, then identified as commissioner of defense for Budapest and delegate of the Nyilas "Hungarista" action. Wallenberg enclosed a list of persons with Swedish protective passports, being careful that the list did not exceed 3,700, the agreed-upon number of Swedish protégés in the international ghetto. However, there were legal and extralegal means to sidestep the agreement. The Nyilas could not exercise control over the list of persons whose protective passes remained at the legation until "formalities" were settled. Wallenberg also stipulated that the lists "do not include the names of those holders of passports who have disappeared or have been enrolled in the forced labor companies and who, in the meantime, have returned unbeknown to the Legation." Minors were included on their parents' passports. Moreover, duplicate passports were circulated by claiming that the original passport had been lost — as a result, people could use the same number and name by attaching different photographs.

Wallenberg marshaled his staff and resources to work with the cooperating agencies in Budapest to save the Jewish children. In describing Wallenberg's efforts for the children, Lévai writes: "On behalf of the children he [Wallenberg] was like lightning as he moved from the Nyilas to the police. In this work he penetrated the hideout of the hyenas in the Sváb Mountains" (160–161).

Wallenberg, Hans Weyermann, chargé of the International Red Cross, Valdemar Langlet of the Swedish Red Cross, and Asta Nilsson played a central part in the "Save the Children" operation and provided shelter for some seven thousand children.

In addition to the six homes for children under the protection of the International Red Cross, countless children were hidden in Catholic institutions. Many Catholic nuns and monks dedicated themselves to rescuing children and were often tortured by the Arrow Cross for their efforts. When the Arrow Cross daily searched the Jesuits' house, Father Jacob Raile, the prior of the Jesuit College, dressed his protégés in police uniforms and transformed the house into a "police station."

During the first half of January, Wallenberg intensified his efforts for the central ghetto. He busied himself providing food to starving residents and at times succeeded in holding off the terroristic forays of the Arrow Cross. As one of his most important and most enduring acts, Wallenberg foiled a plot by the SS and the Arrow Cross to destroy the central ghetto and its seventy thousand inhabitants. At the very last minute, before the Russians had liberated Pest, five hundred Nazi soldiers and twenty-two Nyilas were prepared to annihilate the ghetto. The German General of Police Hitschler and his deputy, Major Gottstein, also head of the political division, instigated the Arrow Cross leaders to "see that not one Jew escaped alive from encircled Budapest, this being the particular wish of Hitler and Himmler." The report was forwarded to Pál Szalay, a top police officer of the Arrow Cross but an ally of Wallenberg. Szalay went to Dr. Vajna, who not only knew of the plan, but had an administrative role in the scheme: he certainly would not stop it. When Wallenberg learned this, he demanded that General August Schmidthuber, German commander of the SS panzer division, stop the planned massacre. Otherwise, Wallenberg threatened, Schmidthuber would be executed for his villainy when the Russians liberated Budapest. The Angel of Rescue had performed a miracle once more: Schmidthuber was startled by the threat. He called in Dr. Vajna and other leaders of the planned massacre and ordered them to cancel the action. If necessary, he warned, he would crush the plot with the forces under his command. Wallenberg's action in frustrating this massacre was fully detailed on October 24, 1945, when Professor Béla Zsedenyi headed a Hungarian delegation to convey the thanks of the Hungarian people to the king of Sweden, the Swedish people, and Wallenberg. Professor Zsedenyi cited Wallenberg's actions in saving and protecting persecuted Jews and praised his decisiveness in stopping the annihilation of the ghetto, which avoided the further defilement of the name and humaneness of the Hungarian people.

Wallenberg's strivings for the Jews in the central ghetto earned appropriate praise from the writer Jenö Lévai, himself saved by the Swede:

> It is of the utmost importance that the Nazis and the Arrow Crossmen were not able to ravage unhindered — they were compelled to see that every step they took was being watched and followed by the young Swedish diplomat. From Wallenberg they could keep no secrets. The Arrow Crossmen could not trick him. They could not operate freely. They were held responsible for the lives of the persecuted and the condemned. Wallenberg was the "world's observing eye," the one who continually called the criminals to account (174–175).

Indeed, the Angel of Rescue had accomplished much, and as the Russians marched closer to Pest, Raoul Wallenberg's thoughts were filled with optimism: the peace at hand, a Budapest and Hungary rising from the abyss of war and Nazism, a society rising from the nadir of wretchedness. The Angel of Rescue now dedicated himself to becoming a master rebuilder of Hungary.

With the liberation of Budapest only moments away, Wallenberg saw one mission completed and another beginning.

5

How Many Divisions Has the Pope?

According to Winston Churchill, Joseph Stalin posed this question to mock the importance of the Vatican's moral opposition to Hitler. This comment and many later ones criticize the pope for his allegedly "weak" response to Nazi atrocities during World War II. The story of Raoul Wallenberg would not be complete without examining the conduct of one of his most important allies—the Roman Catholic Church.

Discerning the "official" role of the church in opposing the Holocaust has been extremely difficult: until recently, many papal documents relating to this period were locked away in the Vatican archives. Lacking this material, some authors have been sharply critical of Pope Pius XII for tolerating the Nazis' genocidal policies. While a thorough examination of the Vatican's role throughout World War II is beyond the scope of this book, documents, testimonies, and known incidents of church involvement on behalf of the Budapest Jews after March, 1944, can offer some illumination of those days of despair. In Hungary, a predominantly Catholic country, many Catholic individuals, both laity and clergy, actively involved themselves in rescuing Jews—perhaps their acts best indicate the real importance of the church's moral opposition to the Holocaust.

Monsignor Angelo Rotta had been a faithful representative of the Vatican from the time of his appointment to Budapest as papal nuncio in 1930. The mass deportations of Hungarian Jewry after March, 1944, disturbed him greatly. According to the Reverend Robert A. Graham, a coeditor of the Vatican documentation on World War II, the information Rotta provided to the pope "on the gravity of the situation" in Budapest led to the famous open telegram from the Vatican to Regent Horthy on June 25, 1944, asking him "to save many unfortunate people from pain and sorrow." On July 6, Rotta vented his anger in a confrontation with Sztójay. He held back no words, calling the Hungarian government's treatment of Jews "abominable" and "dishonorable." It would be simplistic to say that the efforts of the pope and the nuncio were responsible for the halt of the deportations. (For example, at a 1974 conference in Israel, Holocaust scholar Dr. Yehuda Bauer said that Horthy had been influenced by an American air attack on Budapest July 2 and by information that fell into the hands of the Hungarian secret service that proposed the bombing of railway lines from Hungary through Slovakia.) However, the pope's attitude was an important factor. In fact, in a July 13 telegram to the Foreign Office, Veesenmayer said that Horthy's attitude had "changed" because of the protests of such leaders as the pope and the king of Sweden.

On July 13, reacting to Allied urgings, the nuncio asked the Ministry of Foreign Affairs to permit all interned for racial, religious, or political reasons to receive food parcels from the International Red Cross. The Hungarian government consented.

On July 28, the nuncio wrote a sharp letter to Prime Minister Döme Sztójay in which he questioned the "good faith" of the government for allowing the "viciousness" towards the Jews to continue and for doing nothing to alleviate the situation for Jews and converts.

Towards the end of August, the nuncio received word that the Germans were making new preparations for deportations. The nuncio convened an August 21 meeting of the neutral envoys of Sweden, Spain, Portugal, and Switzerland. The nuncio formulated and presented a note to Lajos Reményi-Schneller, the deputy prime minister: "It is the human duty of the representatives of the neutral countries to protest against these actions, which are opposed to all Christian and humane feelings. The representatives of the neutral powers herewith request the Hungarian Government to forbid these cruelties, which ought never to have started."

On August 22, Horthy told Reményi-Schneller of his decision: tell Eichmann that there will be no more deportations; if the decision is opposed, the Hungarian government would offer armed resistance.

Within a week after the Arrow Cross came to power, Rotta met separately with Kemény and Szálasi. On October 21, the nuncio met with Szálasi for more than two hours, with most of the agenda dealing with the rights of Jews. Rotta extracted a promise from Szálasi that the Jews would neither be deported nor exterminated. He also demanded that forced labor should be carried out only under humane conditions, and that protective passes and documents honored in the past continue to be respected. The nuncio won on these points also.

Bishop Rotta's involvement on behalf of the Jews went far beyond meetings with the Hungarian government. After Wallenberg's arrival, the church dropped the requirement that Jews had to be baptized before receiving help.

With the implicit consent of the Vatican, the nuncio received permission from the government to issue protective passes and provide safe houses for the Jews under papal protection. In order to receive information about Nazi and Nyilas activities, he also maintained extensive contacts with the underground.

Following the imposition of the Arrow Cross government, the day-to-day operation of these rescue programs came to be administered by a twenty-two-year-old theology student, Tibor Baranski, who had impressed the nuncio with his wit and bravado.

In the middle of October, 1944, young Baranski returned to Budapest from the university at Kassa in order to escape the advancing Russians. Upon returning home he discovered that his maternal aunt, active in an underground movement that helped the Jews to find hiding places and acquire false documents, had adopted a Jewish baby while his family was in hiding. She asked Tibor to obtain papers for the boy's family, who faced deportation. With a baptized Catholic in the family, they were eligible for a protection pass from the nunciature—if they could get one. Baranski explained that the Germans and Hungarians accepted the principle that a "family could not be divided. So, if there was one Catholic spouse, for example, only one baptismal certificate was necessary. However, to cover the entire family, individual protection passes were needed, stipulating that the family was under papal protection." As Baranski related, "When I went to the nuncio's residence in Buda, I was amazed at the long line of people waiting to get their passes. I was not discouraged. Nonchalantly I pushed my way through the line and said that I was on official business. A few days later I repeated this act, and thereby saved nine members of the Szekeres family. With these protection letters in hand, I afterwards led the family to one of the houses under Vatican protection." (See photograph section for the safe-conduct pass. The father of Gábor Lászlo Spitzer, the baby for whom the safe conduct was issued, changed his name from Spitzer to Szekeres, the family name of Dr. Hedvig Spitzer nee Szekeres. The original safe-conduct pass remains in the possession of Dr. Hedvig Szekeres, now living in the United States.)

Baranski had done more than save nine lives; he had impressed Angelo Rotta. The monsignor summoned Baranski several days later. "No one can get to see me as easily as you did," the nuncio said. "Can you fool the Nazis like you fooled me?" From his underground contacts, who used boys playing soccer by the brick factory to retrieve notes tossed over the fence by the captive Jews, Rotta had learned that nearly fifty baptized Jews were being held for deportation. He needed someone to rescue them.

Baranski remembers, "The papal nuncio asked me if I would go to the factory the next morning and get them out. I said 'No.' His excellency's face dropped like this," Baranski said, holding his hand on the floor.

He said, "What do you mean? You won't go?" I told him, "I will go now. I do not want to wait."

The nuncio then offered me the keys to a small Opel. I told his excellency, "The Nazis are primitive people. A little shoehorn car would not show any representation of power. The Nazis would be impressed by a Rolls Royce." The nuncio smiled like a friendly old cat—he saw that I understood the Nazi psychology.

Armed with protection papers, Baranski and a few aides drove the Rolls to the brick factory. When the Nazis refused to open the gate, Baranski threatened to crash through it. They opened the gate. The guards offered to escort him around, but Baranski told them to get lost, he knew his way around. "How?" they asked. He replied, "None of your business. I know where the Jews are being kept."

He witnessed an appalling scene. Over two thousand Jews were crowded inside a mammoth brick-making kiln, and some were already dead on the floor. Baranski called out the names of the people he sought. After finding forty-seven of them, he took them to another small building on the grounds. There they were watched by "two guards who had the swastika on their lapels but not in their hearts." The next day these Jews were released. Before leaving, he berated the Nazis for leaving the dead among the living inside the kiln. "Do you think that if there is an epidemic here the germs will care that you wear a uniform?" The Nazis began removing the dead bodies soon after.

Those who had no baptismal papers were not forgotten: while Baranski occupied the attention of the Nazi guards, his assistants instructed the remaining Jews on how to escape by contacting the underground. The nuncio was quite pleased at Baranski's success at the brick factory and eagerly recruited him for "a few more tasks."

A few days later, Baranski was named executive director of the Jewish Protection Movement. Through this position, Baranski came into contact with Wallenberg.

I first met Wallenberg at a meeting of the neutral legations. The meeting took place at the Grasham Palace near the Chain Bridge. I seated myself in the back. When the representatives found out that I was from the office of the nuncio, I was brought to the head of the table. Because I was considered the representative of the highest ranking legation, I was asked to chair the meeting. I was stunned. Not only was this new to me, but I also had no instructions from the nuncio. The agenda, as was true at all meetings, dealt with the present political situation, new regulations and orders concerning the Jews, the protection of safe houses, protective passes, and the meeting of food, medical, and other needs.

Baranski also worked in Budapest with the underground, a covert organization that diligently labored to rescue and hide as many Jews as possible, both within the Vatican safe houses and outside of them. Many were hidden in private houses; others were concealed inside of factories, in secret rooms constructed by the workers. "When I needed food for three or four times more Jews than I was supposed to be holding in my apartments, then I knew my underground system was that large."

Through his aunt who worked in a pharmaceutical company and was also active in the underground, Baranski was able to obtain medicine and other needed supplies for his own protégés as well as those of Wallenberg. In return, Wallenberg was often able to procure extra food for the safe houses under papal protection. But most of Baranski's time and energies were occupied in supervising the 3,000 Jews in the Vatican houses. "Actually, the Nazis had agreed to house 12,000 Jews in 42 houses, but those dogs didn't keep their word. With no warning, they changed to 3,000 Jews in 12 houses."

Some confusion seems to exist about the exact number of Jews protected. In a November 27 letter to the Vatican, the nuncio speaks of more than 13,000 letters of protection. Perhaps he referred to the number of documents filled in throughout the death marches.

The Nazis violated the safe-house agreement about eight times, according to Baranski, and seized Jews from the protected buildings. "Each time, I went to the Nazi district headquarters where they were held and obtained their release from the disgruntled Nazis."

On one occasion when Baranski was required to go into the safe houses and inform the holders of protection passes that their validity had been revoked, he devised a ruse to sidestep the rules of both the Nazis and the church. He reported later to the nuncio: "Your excellency, I went to each Jew and declared their documents invalid—but I did not collect it from them." The Jews kept their protection papers—it was up to the Nazis to try to enforce their invalidity.

The nuncio also sent Baranski to the Austro-Hungarian border, to retrieve Jews who had been dragged off on death marches despite their protection papers.

During the death marches, the nuncio gave permission to Sandor Ujváry, a volunteer worker of the International Red Cross, to carry hundreds of blank documents, forged protective pass legitimations, and faked baptismal certificates with him. Ujváry and nuns took convoys of motor lorries with medicine and food for the woeful Jews. After telling the nuncio how he tried to rescue the nearly dead Jews from the hands of the Arrow Cross, Angelo Rotta replied: "My son, your action pleases God and Jesus, as you are rescuing innocent people. I grant you absolution in advance. Continue your work to the glory of God!"

Having given his implicit assent to the counterfeiting, the nuncio set the tone for the young Budapest Zionists who disguised themselves as "envoys from the Vatican." They hurried along the route of the death march and, joined by girls in nuns' habits, gave food and medicine to the woebegone marchers.

An overlooked hero in the rescue at Hegyeshálom was the Lazarist priest, Father Köhler. At the townhall of Hegyeshálom, Ujváry and his aides selected those marchers who appeared to be in the worst condition and filled in papal protection passes in their names. Father Köhler demanded that the Nyilas free these people, and he often succeeded. On one occasion, he helped free 4,700 marchers, who were returned to Budapest.

The following is a report of Ujváry: "The Nyilas men once again attacked Father Köhler, rating and abusing him for saving Jewish lives and threatening violence. The Father bravely faced the armed Nyilas men and shouted: 'I am not afraid of you. Shoot if you dare!' The Nyilas men were so impressed by the daring behavior of the priest that they sneaked away."

Baranski disputes historical accounts citing the counterfeiting and forgery of the papal protection passes, particularly Ujváry's account of receiving the nuncio's blessing for such activities. "Because of my position as executive secretary, and because of the warm personal relations between us, the nuncio discussed almost everything with me; he never mentioned anything about false safe conducts to me. The nuncio would never have agreed to anything illegal, even though the Nazis themselves operated illegally." The main reason that the Nazis respected the papal safe conducts, Baranski notes, is that there was an insignificant amount of forged papal documents, and those in circulation did not have Angelo Rotta's approval. When the Nazis seized the protected Jews to drive them out of Hungary, they would also destroy their original safe-conduct passes. Because the papal embassy at Budapest never seemed to have enough printed safe-conduct passes, most were mimeographed or simply typewritten. Armed with these "official blanks," Baranski would arrived at the Austro-Hungarian border to redeem those Jews whom he could find among the death marchers.

Possessing such blank protection passes was dangerous in itself, since the church's position in regard to the Nazis was always very tenuous. Baranski remembers an incident when Nyilas learned of the existence of blank protection letters and reported it to the Gestapo, who promptly appeared at a rectory where Baranski was staying. The Gestapo put a gun to the head of the chaplain and questioned him in German about the blank protection letters. The chaplain kept insisting, over and over again, that there were no blank protection letters, that such things simply could not exist. Finally the Gestapo left, convinced that he had told them the truth. After they left, Baranski tossed some papers into the fire. The chaplain asked him about what he had so abruptly destroyed. "Blank protection papers," Baranski replied, and the chaplain nearly fainted.

"Not a single Jew under my protection died at the hands of the Nazis." It was a statement of fact for Baranski, not an expression of arrogance. "I never slept more than five hours, many nights a half hour or hour. Some days I didn't have a second to eat."

Baranski's rescue work ended on December 30, when the Russians captured him, assuming he was a Hungarian supporter of the Nazis. He was forced to march 160 miles during the next sixteen days, with Russia the destination. A sympathetic intercession of a Russian solder saved his life. After the war, he was involved in anti-Communist activities, spent fifty-seven months in Hungarian prisons, and gained his release after Stalin's death in 1953. He left Hungary in 1956 during the Hungarian Revolution to request help from the West. By the time he got to Andau, Austria, it was too late to stop the Russian takeover in Hungary.

Baranski emigrated to the United States, his exploits forgotten by a changing world. However, Baranski, now 59 and living in Snyder, New York, is beginning to get his due recognition. In 1979 he was honored by Yad Vashem as a Righteous Gentile for his rescue of Hungarian Jewry, and in 1980 he was appointed by President Carter to the U.S. Holocaust Memorial Council.

The active involvement of Baranski, Ujváry, Father Köhler, and the underground in the rescue of Hungarian Jewry offers an opportunity for studying the roles of Nuncio Rotta and Pope Pius XII during the genocide in Hungary. Angelo Rotta has been universally praised.

In his *Memoirs* the Hungarian Cardinal József Mindszenty provides an interesting report on Angelo Rotta's service. The nuncio was expelled by the occupation force that, according to the cardinal, "obviously wanted no witness to its work of annihilation." However, on November 16, 1945, Premier Zoltán Tildy visited the cardinal and asked for a resumption of diplomatic relations and the return of Angelo Rotta because he "was generally esteemed throughout the country." Mindszenty was amazed because the Russians had expelled Rotta. The cardinal suspected that Tildy was "trying to make a good impression on the Vatican and thus undercut whatever information I might be expected to give the Pope on the regime's hostility to religion."

Although Pope Pius XII was willing to send Rotta back to Budapest, Mindszenty advised against it because of the antireligious position of the Communists. Rotta never returned and died in retirement in Rome in 1965, at the age of ninety-two.

"The nuncio performed with extraordinary dedication to the saving of Jews," according to Baranski. "He was not a young man [Rotta was past seventy] and he was not a healthy individual; yet, he never stopped working until late in the night. I have never understood why Yad Vashem in Israel has never given him the deserved honor of Righteous Gentile." A Yad Vashem spokesman told us that there are two criteria for designation of the Righteous. First, there is the question of whether the person has placed his life in danger to save Jews. Secondly, the request must come from those whom he saved. In the case of the nuncio, "no request was received from those he saved." When such a request is made, "it will be considered in due course."

In his book *Med Raoul Wallenberg in Budapest,* Per Anger cites the nuncio's achievements and contrasts those efforts with those of the Vatican:

"Ever since the German occupation began, the Nuncio, Angelo Rotta, had been making energetic representations to the Hungarian government to help the Jews. Rotta's actions were in stark contrast to the passivity shown by his chief Pope Pius XII . . . . As regards Hungary, Rotta had to work alone, without any particular support from the Vatican" (54).

Documents released by the Vatican in 1980, as well as statements by the nuncio's aide in Budapest, sharply challenge Anger's appraisal of the relationship between Pope Pius XII and Angelo Rotta. The Rev. Robert A. Graham, one of the coeditors of the Vatican's documentation on World War II, has written us of this problem: "For the final dramatic months in Budapest . . . the documentation is sparse. Communication by courier was almost out of the question. Telegraphic connection was with Switzerland and thence by radio to the Vatican, and back the same way."

As secretary to the nuncio, Baranski had access to correspondence from the Vatican. "I myself had seen correspondence to the nuncio from the pope himself, as well as from other offices of the Vatican. I saw handwritten letters from the pope to the nuncio instructing him to do everything in his power to help the persecuted Jews. This included food, shelter, and protection. There were other letters from the pope that gave no detailed instructions but just general hints about aiding the persecuted Jews. And I must emphasize that there never was and never could be any suggestion of doing anything that was not on legal, humanitarian grounds."

Baranski's comments on relations between the nuncio and the Vatican find support from the Reverend Graham:

> The documentation leading up to the November-December nightmare illustrates quite clearly that Rotta did everything on the approval of the Pope, although some of the material details were never communicated to Rome. For instance, the issuance of the "Protective Passports" (15,000) was never notified to the Vatican — it was impossible and not even necessary . . . . I think you will find on close examination that Rotta had the full confidence and support of the Pope in his attitudes and actions in regard to the Jews. Rotta was in this, as in other cases, the representative of the Pope.

The documents Graham refers to were released in 1980 and contain the correspondence between Angelo Rotta and the Vatican. Some of them appear in translation in the Appendix.

On October 21, Monsignor Domenico Tardini, head of the Vatican Section for Extraordinary Ecclesiastical Affairs, telegrammed the nuncio telling him that the pope relied on Rotta to protect the persecuted Jews:

"According to news that has arrived, the Jews in Hungary may be once again threatened with deportation and persecution. I urgently implore Your Most Reverent Excellency to send me any information regarding this.

"The Holy See relies upon your constant action, Your Excellency and Episcopate, for every possible protection for the persecuted."

On October 23, the nuncio telegrammed the Vatican Secretary of State Luigi Maglione to inform the Vatican of his approaches to the Arrow Cross government on behalf of the Jews. "I insisted to the President of the Council of Ministers, in the name of the Holy See," Rotta writes, "that the conditions of the Jews be ameliorated."

However, it is the telegram from Monsignor Tardini to Nuncio Rotta, also on October 23, which clearly states the Vatican's concern for aiding the persecuted. The Vatican reacts to reports of the atrocities in Hungary and asks that the nuncio carry on his "beneficent" activities:

> The Holy Father has received the news [of the atrocities] with sorrow. He is happy with the diligence with which you keep the Holy See informed. He sends special Apostolic Blessing. Weighty appeals continue to reach here imploring the intervention of the Holy See in favor of so many persons who are exposed to persecution and violence because of their religious faith, their race, and political beliefs. May Your Excellency continue with the well-known zeal your beneficent activity, enjoying at the same time the collaboration of your episcopacy—supporting as much as possible the paternal preoccupations of the August Pontiff and showing to all that the Catholic Church leaves nothing untried in order to accomplish its universal mission of charity, even in the difficult conditions of the present.

The nuncio, in a November 27 letter to Monsignor Tardini, details what has been done for the Jews in the midst of the "incredible brutality":

> Not that any practical result can be expected, given the demonstrated mentality of religious ignorance and fanatical hatred against the Jews by the majority of the Arrow Cross, who in execution of given directives proceed with a truly incredible brutality. But it [actions of the Nunciature] which is required by a civilized and Christian conscience.
>
> The Nunciature for its part has made it possible to alleviate much suffering, by insisting to various concerned ministries and by releasing more than 13,000 letters of protection. These, to some extent, have helped at least to impede—for a certain time—the deportation of many Jews.

Upon reading of the nunciature's assistance to the Jews, Monsignor Tardini exclaims, as recorded in a Vatican notation of January 3, 1945: "Bravo Mgr. Rotta!"

In a footnote to a November 17 letter from Angelo Rotta to the Hungarian foreign minister, Kurt R. Grossman, an official in the Rescue Department of the World Jewish Congress, tells Archbishop Cicognani how the protective passes have helped the Jews:

"At least in appearance the documents by the neutral governments have helped and is still helping the Hungarian Jews. I share this news with Your Excellency with the hope that the Holy See will continue its laudable actions in favor of the Jews."

Throughout the Arrow Cross reign of terror in Budapest, Angelo Rotta and his aides labored diligently on behalf of the Jews. Other Hungarian Catholics risked their lives in the underground: hiding Jews from deportation, giving them food and drink during the death marches, distributing forged documents, or reporting Arrow Cross and Nazi plans to leaders like Wallenberg or Rotta. Their efforts saved thousands of Jews from death. This perplexed the Nazis. An SS officer once asked Tibor Baranski, "Why do you, a Christian, save Jews?" Baranski replied, "You are either silly or an idiot. I save Jews because I *am* a Christian."

Baranski makes it clear that he was acting on behalf of the nuncio and the pope in saving Jews with baptismal certificates (the majority of whom, he feels, remained Jewish). He maintains, "It is a disservice and distortion of history to say that the pope did nothing. Plays like *The Deputy* are untruthful. The agreement of the protected houses was between the pope and the Nazis. What Angelo Rotta did and what I followed through to save Jews is to the credit of the pope. If the pope had spoken out, would the godless Nazis have listened?"

6

The Angel of Rescue

"There are no great men, only ordinary men facing a great challenge." Winston Churchill's words certainly describe Raoul Wallenberg and his rescue mission in Budapest. With only the meager personal protection offered by a diplomatic passport, he confronted SS and Nyilas gunmen: racists, psychopaths, torturers, murderers, the dregs of a civilized society. Wallenberg literally snatched thousands of Jewish victims from the jaws of death using the only weapons at hand: some money, his wits, his courage, and an overwhelming moral commitment to save lives. His sense of responsibility to humanity allowed him to transcend his personal fears and shortcomings in order to overcome seemingly insurmountable obstacles with the perseverance of a true hero.

On the surface Raoul Wallenberg did not look like a hero, an Angel of Rescue. He certainly lacked the traits of the Scandinavian prototype of courage and strength, the dauntless Beowulf. With Wallenberg's medium height, dark eyes, and dark, thinning hair, he did not even resemble the Swedish stereotype. However, unlike exploits of Beowulf, the superhuman heroics of Raoul Wallenberg are not legend; they are fact. Colleagues, classmates, and family have all reflected on Raoul's phenomenal achievements.

Tibor Baranski had much in common with Wallenberg: they were both young, nonprofessional representatives of neutral legations, highly motivated for idealistic reasons, who succeeded through resourcefulness and indefatigable dedication.

Baranski's first impressions of Wallenberg were of "a thin man, rather shy and virtually fearless. He dressed elegantly and was always clean-shaven. He had a good nose to sniff out danger and immediately respond with the appropriate action. Although we did get to know one another, there was little time for friendship in those hectic times."

The representatives of the neutral legations met regularly, always at a different place so as to escape detection by the SS and the Arrow Cross. After one of these meetings, Baranski approached Wallenberg and asked if he would like to meet the nuncio. Wallenberg, very enthusiastic about the idea, asked Baranski to find out if the hour was not too late for the nuncio. "I called the nuncio, and he was excited." Baranski recalled the nuncio's words. "'Would he really like to come? Are you sure?'"

Wallenberg visited with the nuncio for about an hour and a half. "They spoke about many things," Baranski said, "mostly about their countries. I tried to ensure their privacy, so most of the time I was at a distance from them." The next morning, Baranski was anxious to get the nuncio's opinion of Wallenberg. The nuncio was "very much impressed by him," Baranski said. "In fact, he said, 'I never met such a nice Protestant.'" Wallenberg's impressions of the papal representative were reciprocal. "It was amazing," Baranski said. "Wallenberg told me, 'I never met such a nice Catholic.' You could say that Wallenberg and the nuncio both saw each other as human beings, both on missions motivated by divine love towards man."

After one meeting of the neutral legations, Baranski and Wallenberg sat together for two hours in a Budapest restaurant.

> We were fantastically near to each other. We were both nondiplomats who acted for the sake of humanity. At one point, he asked me whether I was Jewish. "Why, just because I look Jewish?" I quipped. "No," Wallenberg answered, "I just imagined that you must be Jewish because you were so zealous in trying to save them." I then asked him about his zealousness. He told me that he had a Jewish ancestor, but that had little influence on his motivation. He did say that he spent some time in Palestine and met refugees who fled from German persecution. At that time he made a commitment to help such victims if he ever got the opportunity.

According to Baranski, Wallenberg had much to say about his family, especially about his mother. "Wallenberg was a very loving son, who wanted me to meet his mother. His mother had always told him that he was too shy. 'You should come to Sweden,' Wallenberg told me. 'You have the big mouth that mother would want me to have.'"

No one is better acquainted with Raoul Wallenberg than his family. Mrs. Nina Lagergren, his half sister, expresses no surprise at Raoul's feats. "I always felt my brother would do something very special with his life. My family was not surprised at his acts. We knew what he did was the greatest challenge of his life. It took hold of him."

Mrs. Lagergren recalled that Raoul had said that he was going to Budapest with "all sorts of lists with people to contact." The family never actually thought that his life would be constantly on the line. "Raoul knew that it would be a very difficult undertaking, but no one expected that he would risk his life. One did not think of such things because diplomatic immunity has been accepted worldwide."

Mrs. Lagergren said that Raoul approached the mission with "much energy and eagerness. Because of his business trips, Raoul had developed many pleasant relationships. So in that sense, the mission became something very personal for him. His many business trips abroad had proven that Raoul was a skillful negotiator and that he could deal effectively with people. Undoubtedly, this is one factor which helps explain why my brother was able to accomplish so much in Budapest."

Mrs. Lagergren added that her brother was very skillful at intimidation. "He was a great actor. He could imitate brilliantly. If he wanted to, he could be more German than a Prussian general. Shouting louder, sounding more authoritative than the higher-ups, he could wrest concessions from the Nazis."

On one occasion before a train departed for Auschwitz, Wallenberg appeared on the scene with several lists of his protégés. Per Anger observed, "He demanded in an authoritative tone whether any such persons had by mistake been taken aboard. The Germans were taken by surprise and, right under their noses, Wallenberg pulled out a large number of Jews. Many of them had no passport at all, only any kind of paper whatever in the Hungarian language – driver's licenses, vaccination records or tax receipts – that the Germans did not understand. The bluff succeeded" (84–85).

Anger also tells about Wallenberg's arrival in Budapest with a revolver in his pocket. "He said he was never going to use the revolver because he was too afraid, too much of a coward. But of course he was very courageous."

Lars Berg describes Wallenberg:

Wallenberg's daring appearance at the scene of rescue was all the more admirable, as Raoul was not at all a brave man by nature. During the air raids he was always the first to seek shelter, and he was sometimes affected when the bombs fell too close. But when it was a question of saving the lives of his protégés, he never hesitated a second. He acted with a challenging boldness and bravery, though his life then mostly hanged by much thinner than a thread during the air raids.

Thomas Veres experienced Wallenberg's bravery firsthand. Mr. Veres, a commercial photographer in New York, rode in Wallenberg's big black Studebaker almost daily, taking pictures of the rescue mission. Thomas Veres's father, Paul Veres, a well-known Hungarian photographer, stopped practicing his trade when the Germans took over Hungary, and Thomas found himself with an abundant supply of film and other photographic supplies. Per Anger introduced the younger Veres, then twenty, to Wallenberg, and the right person and a vital assignment coincided.

Veres recalled the dangers involved, both for him and for Wallenberg. But, he said, Wallenberg never backed away from a dangerous situation:

I came to the Swedish embassy in October, 1944. Raoul Wallenberg said that he would like to take advantage of my profession and take pictures of the life-saving activities. He said that the pictures would serve as historic documentation. At that time, it was dangerous, in a sense forbidden, to take pictures on the streets. When I mentioned this point to Wallenberg, he said that he had already signed a pass for me, and thereby it would be legal for me to take pictures. In spite of this, Wallenberg constantly put his life in danger. Wallenberg dealt constantly with the Nyilas, and he knew their underhanded behavior. Legal or no, Wallenberg certainly knew that it was dangerous to take pictures, and at the beginning I couldn't bring myself to take pictures. However, the bravery of Raoul Wallenberg got to me. It may seem that I am exaggerating or just being trite, but the truth is that Raoul Wallenberg didn't know the meaning of danger.

Wherever Wallenberg's rescue operation went, Thomas Veres followed. He witnessed the death marches to Hegyeshálom and includes in his "collection" a "before and after" picture of a mother and daughter who survived the march, but whose excruciating experience is apparent in their faces. He recorded the freeing of Jews at the rail station and their return to the Swedish safe houses. He photographed hundreds of Wallenberg's protégés for identification on the protected passes.

Because of his many experiences with Raoul Wallenberg, Veres saw not only the bravery of the Swede but also his delightful sense of humor.

One day our car was in heavy artillery fire and there was our car with one license plate in the front, a different license plate in the back. In fact, we had many plates and signs, depending on who asked: the SS or the Arrow Cross. For example, we had a sign that said "rushing mail," to avoid being stopped. On that particular day, in the midst of gunfire, Wallenberg jokingly remarked, "We should get an automatic gadget so that when one license plate appears the others will disappear."

Despite Wallenberg's bravery and determination, Veres remembers times when even Wallenberg couldn't succeed. At the end of December, 1944, the Arrow Cross attacked a protected house and dragged out some of the protégés. Veres reconstructed the following dialogue between Wallenberg and a member of the Nyilas:

Wallenberg: "Where are the protected ones?"
Nyilas: "In the Danube."
Wallenberg: "Why?"
Nyilas: "They were dirty Jews."
"At that point," Veres said, "even Wallenberg was stunned and couldn't help."

Another Wallenberg aide presently heads a pharmaceutical company in Los Altos, California. He was one of the Swede's personal drivers on the rescue missions. Although he did not want to be identified, he said that "after years of silence, it is important to tell the story of Raoul Wallenberg. Perhaps all the talk, all the print will help locate this heroic person."

The driver presented himself at the Swedish legation when the Nazi invasion forced the closing of the universities. "Wallenberg was a modest, retiring individual with steellike determination," the driver said. "He wasn't the Patton type. He was adept in administrative detail and understood the German mentality. He knew that Germans reacted to formal documents and authority. When it came to rescue work, he was workmanlike, precise, and cold."

Taking Wallenberg to many deportation points, the driver got a first-hand view of the Wallenberg modus operandi: "He always overwhelmed the German SS with double talk. Wallenberg would threaten to call their superiors if they didn't cooperate. He used every possible deception and trick, including bribing them and telling the SS he would write a favorable report about them after Germany lost the war."

Wallenberg's daring spread among his workers.

Raoul usually had with him a book with names of passport holders. Sometimes the book had all blank pages. When he arrived at the train, he then made up Jewish names and began calling out. Three or four usually had passports. For those who didn't, I stood behind Raoul with another fifty or more unfilled passports. It only took me ten seconds to write in their names. We handed them out calmly and said, "Oh, I'm terribly sorry you couldn't get to the legation to pick it up. Here it is. We brought it to you." The passport holder showed it to the SS and was free.

I myself carried forged identity papers for various occasions. One set identified me as a doctor for the German SS; another proved I worked for the Swedish legation. If anybody had ever searched and found those phony papers, I would have been shot there and then. All those who worked with Raoul Wallenberg took unbelievable risks. But we were his disciples and followed his courageous example.

The driver never really got to know Wallenberg personally—few did. Raoul Wallenberg had a mission—that was all that mattered. "We never got very close," the driver said. "He never shared chitchat or confidences. It was strictly business. Wallenberg went to fulfill a mission. He never once thought of personal glory."

Another of Wallenberg's workers was his driver, Sandor Ardai. (Actually, Wallenberg had another chauffeur, Wilmos Langfelder, who was abducted along with him by the Russians.) Ardai was summoned to Wallenberg's office in November after Langfelder had been arrested by the Arrow Cross. Wallenberg asked Ardai to become his driver, but pointed out the dangers of the assignment. Ardai reflected on this meeting and on Wallenberg in the weekly journal *Aret Runt* (July 4–11, 1957):

"It is dangerous and difficult," underlined Wallenberg. "You do not need to if you do not want it."

I did not hesitate a second but accepted. And many times afterwards I have remembered my meeting with this remarkable Swede. He did not at all look like a hero, not as you imagine a courageous, strongwilled and freeborn hero type. He rather seemed dreaming and weak. My first mission was to drive him to the headquarters of the Arrow Cross and wait outside until he got Langfelder back. I thought silently "that this will never go well," when he disappeared with long strides. How could the Hungarian Arrow Cross release a prisoner, just because one man requested it?

But when I saw him again on the stairs he brought Langfelder along. They jumped into the car and I drove them to the legation. Nobody commented on what had happened and I started to understand the extraordinary force which was in Raoul Wallenberg.

I never heard Wallenberg speak an unnecessary word during the month and a half I and Langfelder took turns as a driver—not a single comment, never a complaint, even if he could not sleep more than a few hours for several days.

On one occasion we had come to a station where a train full of Jews was on the point of leaving for Germany and the concentration camps. The officer of the guard did not want to let us enter. Raoul Wallenberg then climbed up on the roof of the train and handed in many protective passports through the windows. The Arrow Cross men fired their guns and cried to him to go away, but he only continued calmly to hand out passports to the hands which reached for them. But I believe that the men with the guns were impressed by his courage and on purpose aimed above him. Afterwards he managed to get all Jews with passports out from the train. His only aim was to save as many as possible. And by his personal courage he managed to save thousands.

Wallenberg's insistence on helping groups rather than individuals became even firmer during his hectic round-the-clock rescue mission after the Arrow Cross took over. However, a dramatic, storybook episode, that of the Vandor family, proved an exception. On November 3, a frantic Tibor Vandor sought out Wallenberg. Vandor's wife was in labor with their first child, but all hospitals refused to help. In the middle of the night Wallenberg took the Vandors to his room, while he slept in the corridor, covered with his coat. At 7 A.M. the Vandors invited Wallenberg into the room to see the new arrival and to name the dark-haired girl. He chose the names Nina Maria Ava. "She looks like my grandmother," Wallenberg laughed. "I am honored to be her godfather." With Wallenberg's permission the name was changed to Yvonne Maria Ava.

After the war the Vandors went to Switzerland, Holland, and then Montreal, where Yvonne was raised as a Christian. "My parents always wanted to forget the past," Yvonne, now Mrs. Ron Singer of Toronto, recalled.

"All I knew was that I was born in Hungary during the war. I always felt that I had roots, that I didn't belong. When I married Ron fourteen years ago I converted to Judaism because I wanted to identify with Ron and with a group that had roots."

Years later, when the Singers were living in England, a relative told Yvonne that she was Jewish by birth. "I became driven with a desire to know more about my past, but my parents refused to say more." Then like a bolt from the blue, on October 20, 1979, a story dealing with the heroics and search for Raoul Wallenberg appeared in the *Toronto Star*. This article referred to the Vandors and the birth of Yvonne. In Mrs. Singer's words:

> I was reading the story aloud to Ron, when I came to those lines where I read my own name. I burst out crying. Ron and I clung to each other and we were both crying. It became very difficult to go on reading. I finally found myself. The reaction in the community has been incredible since that day. There is a sizable Hungarian Jewish community in Toronto. Many others have also found their roots. They have discovered that they are Jewish. They have come to the realization that they are only alive because of Raoul Wallenberg.

If Raoul Wallenberg could be said to be the Angel of Rescue, one could also say that the forces of Satan were arrayed against him. Chief among these infamous Nazi devils was Adolf Eichmann, Hitler's Bloodhound, the man who made mass murder into an efficient, mechanized process. The conflict between these two men provides a study in contrasts: the Angel of Rescue versus the Bloodhound. Whereas the arrival of the Swede in Budapest was an event of joy, the Nazi's appearance in Hungary prompted gloom and despair. While Wallenberg was a man of culture and learning, Eichmann was an individual of little knowledge but much pretense. Lévai describes Eichmann's entrance into Hungary in the *Black Book on the Martyrdom of Hungarian Jewry*:

> There is reason to believe that "Eichmann" used a new name in every country he went in order to prevent creating a panic, so terrible was the record of the atrocities for which he was responsible. Eichmann was fond of pretending that he was born in Palestine and spoke Hebrew fluently; in point of fact, no one ever heard him say anything in that ancient tongue beyond a Biblical quotation regarding the creation of the universe, and that can hardly be taken as conclusive proof of his knowledge of the language . . . . When Eichmann made his first appearance at the headquarters of the Jewish Congregation in Budapest, he opened the conversation with the following pleasantry: "Sie wissen nicht wer ich bin? Ich bein ein Bluthund!" (So you don't know who I am? I am a bloodhound!) (108).

In his relentless efforts to save Jews, Wallenberg worked around the clock, at times without eating and sleeping. He was forced to change apartments to escape the assassination plots of the Nazis and the Nyilas. Eichmann, however, was immersed in a hedonic existence. He was a permanent guest at the estate of László Endre, where they were united, according to Lévai, by three things: "their passion for horses, their love of alcohol, and their insane hatred of everything Jewish" (109). The wild orgies at the Endre estate were common knowledge.

The Angel of Rescue and the Bloodhound both resorted to deception: the Swede used subterfuge to save the targets of the Holocaust; the Nazi employed chicanery to facilitate his plans for genocide. After learning of the atrocities taking place in the provincial ghettos, the Jewish Council of Budapest compiled a memorandum and turned to Eichmann requesting an improvement of the situation. The Bloodhound responded with typical Eichmann dishonesty: "Not a single word of the report is true, for I have just inspected the provincial ghettos. I really ought to know. The accommodation of the Jews is no worse than that of German soldiers during manoeuvres and the fresh air will only do their health the world of good!" When the Jewish leadership continued to press, the Bloodhound replied with another attempt at deception. The treatment of the Jews was no fault of the Nazis, but of Endre, who "will die Juden mit Paprika fressen!" (who wants to devour the Jews with sweetpepper). When the Jewish leadership later received reports of the deportations in Sub-Carpathia and in the northern and trans-Danubian districts, Eichmann lied brazenly once more, telling the leaders: "If the Hungarian Jews behave themselves and do not join the Ruthenian partisans, there will be no deportations."

Wallenberg's family, friends, colleagues in Hungary, and the protégés whom he saved have attested to his graciousness, gentility, and courage. Before his execution in Bratislava after the war, Dieter von Wisliceny, the Bloodhound's collaborator in Budapest, enlarged upon Eichmann's boorishness, crudity, and cowardice:

In 1944 Eichmann met a woman in Budapest, whose name was Ingrid Schama (?). She was living separated from her husband and I think she had private means. She had absolute power over Eichmann. When the Russians were advancing in Hungary, Eichmann prepared poison for the woman in case she was captured by the Russians.

In Hungary Eichmann had another love affair, too, with a young Viennese woman, called Margrit Konschir. In the last years preceding the debacle, Eichmann, who would get drunk by night, was anyway an easy prey to women.

In spite of his high rank, Eichmann could never get rid of his lower middle-class habits and mentality. He most carefully avoided any encounter with personalities of the elite. He sent his deputy, Günther, to official receptions. Not as though he had been reluctant to receive any honours; it was rather because he did not trust himself; he was afraid of making a fool of himself in a milieu alien to him. He always wished to remain "the mystery man." He was living in constant fear that they were after his life. He only travelled by his own personal motorcar and never dared to fly because he was afraid the plane might crash.

There were always weapons in his car: two revolvers and hand grenades. In one of his pockets he always had a hand grenade and in the other a percussion cap . . . . Actually Eichmann was afraid.

In September, 1944, in Hungary, he feared lest the house he was staying at would be blown up. He had bunkers built in his garden. So cautious was he that he did not let himself be photographed. When he needed a photograph for an identity card, he had his likeness taken at the photographic studio of the Gestapo and ordered only a few prints.

The adversaries first caught sight of each other at the bar of the Arizona nightclub in Budapest. Eichmann appraised Wallenberg as yet another effete diplomat, a playboy as dissolute as himself. His misperception of the Swede's character was quickly corrected as their opposing missions came into conflict.

Wallenberg was probably the first person who had ever dared to frustrate and countermand Eichmann's orders. As he thrust his type of devastation on Europe, Eichmann had met only token resistance to his wishes. Wallenberg's presence, therefore, became a new and unwelcome experience for Eichmann. As a means of becoming "acquainted" with the opposition, Wallenberg invited Eichmann and a top aide to his home for dinner. "Wallenberg was well aware," Berg said, "how much easier it is to bring a difficult transaction to a successful conclusion after an indulgence of good food and fine wines." Unfortunately, the overburdened Wallenberg completely forgot about his "distinguished" dinner guests. When Wallenberg arrived home at his usual late hour, the exasperation of the hungry, thirsty Nazis had peaked: not only had Wallenberg forgotten about the invitation, but it was the cook's day off. Wallenberg, never easily rattled, kept the Nazis at bay with a few drinks and called Lars Berg, who agreed to have all the guests for dinner. With typical poise Wallenberg told the placated guests that there had been a misunderstanding and that the dinner had been set in the home of attaché Berg.

Berg and coworker Göte Carlsson had a most charming residence at Hunfalvi Street and a cook of the highest quality. The house had previously belonged to nobility, and the owner left the new tenants his exquisite tableware. "The count's best porcelain and silver were laid out for the guests," Berg said, "and thanks to our excellent cook, the dinner was a great success. I am sure that Eichmann never even suspected that Wallenberg had forgotten him."

Berg recalls that the dinner was held late in the fall of 1944, and as they dined the Russian guns could be seen on the distant horizon. "Raoul was very relaxed that evening," Berg recalls, "since there were no emergencies or interventions which required his attention at that moment. Our little salon became a battlefield for one of Eichmann's many defeats against Raoul Wallenberg." The latter's opening salvo was a cool discussion of Nazi doctrines and the military outlook for Germany. Berg observed, "With clarity and logical precision, Wallenberg fearlessly tore Nazi doctrines into shreds and predicted that Nazism and its leaders would meet a speedy and complete destruction. I must say that these were rather unusual, caustic words from a Swede who was far away from his country and totally at the mercy of the powerful German antagonist Eichmann and his henchmen."

But Wallenberg's attack on Eichmann had a definite purpose: he actually sought to influence Eichmann. "In his prediction of the imminent doom of Nazism," Berg said, "there was also a sincere exhortation to Eichmann to bring to an end the senseless deportations and the unnecessary killing of Hungarian Jews."

Wallenberg pointedly put the question to Eichmann: "Look, you have to face up to the facts. You have lost the war. Why do you not give up now?"

As the discussion went on, Eichmann could not conceal his surprise that anyone would have the gall to attack not only him, but also Hitler so openly! "He soon discovered," said Berg, "that he was losing the battle to Wallenberg. Eichmann's well-learned propaganda phrases sounded empty and had little strength against Raoul's forceful, intelligent presentation." Stunned, Eichmann replied in a very open, revealing manner:

I admit that you are right, Mr. Wallenberg. I actually never believed in Nazism as such, but it has given me power and wealth. I know that this pleasant life will soon be over. My planes will no longer bring me women and wines from Paris nor any other delicacies from the Orient. My horses, my dogs, my palace here in Budapest will soon be taken over by the Russians, and I myself, an SS officer, will be shot on the spot. But for me there is no rescue any more. If I obey my orders from Berlin and exercise my power ruthlessly enough here in Budapest, I shall be able to prolong my days of grace.

After making this admission and stating his resolve to continue, Eichmann served notice on Wallenberg: "I warn you, Herr Legationsekretär. I shall do my very utmost to defeat you. And your Swedish diplomatic passport will not help you, if I consider it necessary to do away with you. Even a neutral diplomat might meet with accidents."

According to Berg, the Germans are very "correct" in diplomatic dealings. And, not surprisingly, Eichmann left without anger or bitterness. "With the unfailing politeness of a well-brought-up German officer, Eichmann bid us goodbye and thanked us for a charming evening."

Berg speculated on the purpose behind Wallenberg's lecture and rebuke of Eichmann: "Perhaps Raoul did not achieve much by his frank argumentation, but sometimes it could be quite a relief for a Swede to be able to tell his straightforward opinion to a German SS officer. Without doubt Eichmann left the house very much impressed by Raoul's fearlessness and strong personality."

Wallenberg certainly left an imprint on Eichmann. A few days after their charming evening together, Wallenberg's private car was out on official business, but Wallenberg was not inside. A big, heavy German truck rammed straight into Wallenberg's car, wrecking it completely. Wallenberg lodged a firm protest directly to Eichmann regarding the attempt on his life. Eichmann was "sorry" about the "accident," but quickly told his adversary, "I will try again."

However, Eichmann had more important things to attend to, such as the planning and implementation of the death marches and other schemes to complete the final solution, so neither Wallenberg nor his cars were ever attacked again. In fact, Wallenberg is reported to have dealt directly with Eichmann in bargaining for the release of Jews. But Eichmann continually voiced his hatred of the Swede. One of his outbursts sparked an international incident. During a conversation with a staff member of the Swedish Red Cross, Eichmann made known his desire to shoot "Jew-dog" Wallenberg. "It is possible that Eichmann's statement was an empty threat," Anger said, "but we were not prepared to leave it unchallenged." After receiving a telegram from the Swedish legation, the Foreign Office in Stockholm instructed the embassy in Berlin to lodge a protest to the Germans, complaining about the threat against Wallenberg and demanding that the SS command in Budapest respect the legation members and their staffs. Edmund Veesenmayer, Hitler's ambassador in Budapest, "apologized" to Stockholm, assuring Sweden that Eichmann's words were not to be taken literally. However, Veesenmayer explained, Eichmann's reaction had to be understood in light of Wallenberg's illegal activities on behalf of the Jews. Wallenberg acted in a "far too unconventional and unacceptable way." In that sense, Veesenmayer maintained, Eichmann's words should be viewed as a future warning, meant to restrain Wallenberg from persisting in his rescue efforts.

Unwilling to be on hand for the arrival of the Russians, Eichmann hurried out of Budapest on December 23, 1944, but before leaving, he conceded that Wallenberg had been "a brilliant chess player." Their conflicting goals—Wallenberg's, to save as many Jews as possible; Eichmann's, to kill as many Jews as possible—had made them bitter, determined foes, but Wallenberg had outfoxed and outmaneuvered the Bloodhound. With his chief adversary Eichmann gone, the Angel of Rescue next directed his efforts towards outsmarting the Nyilas and contending with a more deadly group of villains.

Wallenberg's rescue activities brought him many potent enemies—aside from Eichmann. Although Wallenberg was able to influence Foreign Minister Kemény through the baroness, he had no success in dealing with Deputy Foreign Minister Zoltan Bagossy, Wallenberg's "particular antagonist," according to Berg.

Bagossy was a real sadistic Nazi and hated Jews with all his heart, if he had any heart at all. He was absolutely unsusceptible to persuasion whether in form of bribes or reasoning. He remained the master spirit of the deportation of the Jews. Not even the menace of blacklisting him with the Russians seemed to have any effect on him. In distinction to almost all other German and Hungarian Nazi big-shots he was not even interested in Wallenberg's very last means of influence—a Swedish protection passport either for the person in question himself or for his mistress or somebody else near of kin. Bagossy could just not be swayed (29).

Despite Bagossy's animosity towards Wallenberg, the deputy foreign minister never considered having his foe assassinated. The same could not be said for two other satanic forces: Kurt Rettmann and SS Hauptsturm-führer Theodore Dannecker. An instigator of the Nyilas's atrocities, Rettmann was quite incensed over Wallenberg's continual thwarting of his plans to "kill all Jews." Rettmann sent a warning to Wallenberg that he would have him murdered if he did not cease his rescue work. Dannecker also wanted to do away with Wallenberg. He planned the near catastrophe of a German truck ramming into Wallenberg's car and publicized it, by bragging that it was his scheme. Wallenberg's worker Charles Wilhelm was also aware of Dannecker's intentions and warned Wallenberg.

Despite these warnings, Wallenberg's response always remained the same: the Angel of Rescue would never give up his mission. In answer to Rettmann's death threats, Wallenberg said, "It is not my intention to worry about myself or about my safety. The more help I can dispense, the more safe passes I can give out, the happier I am."

Mrs. Paula Auer, of Newark, New Jersey, recalled Wallenberg's heroism during the final days of 1944. On February 14, 1947, the Newark *Jewish News* presented her experiences in perhaps the first account of a Wallenberg rescue. Mrs. Auer and her family had found refuge in a Swedish protected house. She said, "When the Russians reached the gates of Budapest, the Nazis broke into this and other Swedish homes and like crazed beasts shot all the Jews they saw. They then threw the bodies into the Danube. Somehow I escaped the Nazis' search and got word to the Swedish legation. Wallenberg and his assistants arrived in time to prevent the massacre of the remaining 160 Jews in the home."

From his home in Stockholm, Georg Libik related Wallenberg's fearless adventure during Christmas week. Now a civil engineer, Libik was a slalom champion in his native Hungary. His father was a commissioner in a Nazi war factory; his father-in-law, Albert Szent-Györgyi, was a Nobel laureate in medicine. During the war, Libik said, his father-in-law was a leader of the Hungarian resistance movement and a "personal enemy of Hitler." After the Arrow Cross came to power, the Nyilas raided a meeting of resistance leaders, at which Libik was present. The Arrow Cross seized his address book with its listings of underground workers. Libik managed to escape from the clutches of the Arrow Cross and warn all those in his address book.

At this time, Per Anger took Libik onto his staff under the pseudonym of Bela Ratkovsky, while sheltering Szent-Györgyi at his residence in Buda. Libik joined his father-in-law at the Anger residence around Christmas time.

Georg Libik reconstructed that memorable evening. "It was one night, some time after 10, when Wallenberg showed up at Per Anger's apartment. He looked like a student with his red scarf and black winter coat. He was bareheaded and looked very pale." Libik first thought that Wallenberg must be some sort of lunatic. "This fellow must be mad, I said to myself. It's suicidal to be out so late at night, with all the Nyilas roaming the streets."

Wallenberg and Anger went to a corner and began conversing in low tones, first in Swedish and then in German. "The situation was obviously very serious," Libik said. "The Arrow Cross had bullied their way into a protected house on Benczur Street, drove the people out into the courtyard, searched them, and treated them brutally. One could expect, Wallenberg said, that 'they would be shot in the Danube.'"

Wallenberg's car and chauffeur were missing, and for that reason he had come to Anger. "Wallenberg was afraid that he could not get to Benczur Street in time to stop the massacre from being carried out. There were many lives to be saved. Despite some misgivings about the recklessness of Wallenberg, Anger was agreeable and asked me to drive Wallenberg to Pest before the bridges over the Danube were blown up."

Libik left with a false identification and a gun at his side. According to Libik, "Wallenberg had a different outlook. 'I do not rely on power,' Wallenberg told me. 'My strength is that I can bribe or threaten the Arrow Cross.' We drove off with no lights on. It was a frightful scene on the streets of Pest. Everywhere there were houses on fire. It was my country, part of my life being destroyed. But with all the human corpses, all the dead horses strewn along the streets, there was no time for meditation."

Wallenberg entered the building on Benczur Street alone, telling Libik to park the car where the Nyilas could not see it. "I thought to myself," Libik said, "why is Wallenberg doing this? Why didn't he stay at home, even if the unfortunate people were to die. How could a foreigner—and a Swede—be more noble and a truer patriot than the Hungarians. If the Hungarians didn't care about their own people, why should a foreigner? My head was filled with such medieval, romantic wanderings while I thought of Wallenberg with admiration."

Libik waited an hour in the car for Wallenberg to return. "He came out and happily announced, 'Everything is okay. Everyone has permission to return to the house.' I never for a moment doubted the truth of Wallenberg's claim, but I admit it was difficult to believe."

An anonymous Hungarian Jew who was saved because of Wallenberg's refusal to be coerced, to give up, gave the following account in the March 6, 1945, *Dagens Nyheter* about a Nyilas armed patrol invading a protected house:

Wallenberg: "This is Swedish territory. You have got nothing to do here."

Chief of Patrol: "I have orders to take the able-bodied men away from here."

Wallenberg: "Nobody will get out. If you try to take anybody away from here you will get into trouble with me. As long as I am alive, nobody will be taken from here. You will have to shoot me first."

Tibor Vayda still vividly recalls the December rescue operation on Üllöi Street.

There were more than three hundred men and women at our office, which was also a Swedish protected house on Üllöi Street. The Nyilas stormed in and shouted, "Wallenberg is not here. Everybody, get out. Swedish protection means nothing. Protective passes mean nothing." People wanted to take their luggage, but the Nyilas sneered. "You don't need luggage because you will be dead soon." About noon we were marched to SS headquarters. We expected to be shot after being thrown into the Danube. Somehow—and I still do not know how—a message was gotten to Wallenberg. At 2:00 in the afternoon his car roared through the courtyard. Not one of the three hundred was lost. He simply put it straight to the SS commando: "You save these men, and I promise your safety after the Russians win the war."

Tibor Vayda never saw Wallenberg again. "He was a quiet hero. Few people got to know him on a personal level, except perhaps his secretary, Mrs. Falk, and our fellow worker, Vilmos Forgacz."

Per Anger describes his last meeting with his colleague on January 10, 1945. "I remember reminding him once again of the extremely dangerous position he was in, and advised him to move over with us on the Buda side from the Pest side. The Hungarian Nazis were especially at this point hunting for him and he endangered himself by continuing his rescue work. But he turned a deaf ear to this. He wanted to be near the Jews who needed his help."

During January, amid the infernolike fires in Budapest, Wallenberg received death threats in the mail. Stones were thrown against his car. Armed gangsters hunted him. Everything was done to make it impossible for him to visit his protégés, but nothing could make Wallenberg give up his work.

Although Wallenberg refused to give up his rescue work, he was neither naive nor foolhardy. He was fully aware of the dangers surrounding him. He continually changed apartments as well as his sleeping place for the evening. One of his last apartments was on the sixth floor of Madách Street. Lévai succinctly captured the historical charm and allure of the lodging: "He [Wallenberg] found a haven at the apartment of writer Magda Gabor. He had been there many times before and had spent much time with Baroness Kemény" (167).

But, while Raoul Wallenberg was a veritable Angel of Rescue, he was still a mortal possessing normal fears. After an encounter with the Nyilas official Vöczköndy, Wallenberg remarked, "I have never been closer to death." On January 10, Anger and Wallenberg were on a mission together.

Bombs fell continually. Proceeding with the car was most difficult, as the roads presented obstructions of human bodies, dead horses, fallen trees, and demolished houses. Anger turned to his colleague and asked whether he was frightened. The response tells the story of Raoul Wallenberg—as the Angel of Rescue, but equally as an ordinary mortal: "Sure, it gets a little scary, sometimes, but for me there's no choice. I have taken on this assignment and I would never be able to go back to Stockholm without knowing inside myself I had done all a man could do to save as many Jews as possible."

In explaining why Raoul Wallenberg could not return home, one of his protégés compared him to an obsessed, overworked violinist. "He was a driven man, unable to let go of what had become an obsession," according to Edith Wohl-Ernster, first violinist of the Stockholm opera. "He was like a violinist playing an extremely difficult concerto. His work sapped all his strength, but he refused to quit."

Wallenberg's nonprofessional counterpart at the nunciature, Tibor Baranski, recalled the Swede as an "extraordinary" person, but with the usual apprehensions of mortals.

> We were normal human beings. Certainly we both were afraid at times of the dangers in our path. What is important is that Wallenberg was able to rise above and defeat these fears and accomplish so many wonderful things. He saved 70,000 Jews when he prevented the central ghetto from being destroyed. More than 25,000 life-saving Swedish protection passes are the result of his initiative and actions. That's almost 100,000 lives saved by one man! What else is there to say?

7

The Last Days in Budapest

"Now the bad dream will soon be over; now we will soon be able to sleep."

These were the hopes – and even expectations – that Raoul Wallenberg expressed to his chauffeur Sandor Ardai, as the Russians pushed steadily towards Pest.

At the end of 1944 Marshal Fjodor Tolbukhin's forces controlled two-thirds of Buda, while the army of General Rodion Malinovsky occupied a large part of Pest. Conditions in Budapest were horrendous: neither electricity nor running water was available; the food supply was dangerously low; and fires raged throughout the city. The end of the war was near, and with that the advent of a new era.

Wallenberg's eyes were on the future of Hungary. According to Tibor Baranski,

I had heard that Wallenberg told an individual the following: "It is true that the Jews need my help now and will continue to do so after the war, but it is also true that the entire Hungarian nation will desperately need my assistance when peace comes." However, despite the hope that Raoul Wallenberg placed on Russia, it was obvious to me from his words that he had a certain fear and mistrust of the Russians.

Be that as it may, Wallenberg had decided to deal with Russia, the occupying power, through a secret plan. Wallenberg's coworkers were not allowed to discuss the plan for fear of its being frustrated by the Nazis and the Nyilas. Wallenberg hinted at one phase of the plan in a December 8 letter

97

to his longtime friend and business partner Kálmán Lauer. He writes that Lauer's relatives are on his staff at the Swedish legation, that the Nyilas have committed many atrocities, and that developments "in the last days have been overwhelming." The crucial paragraph in terms of Wallenberg's postwar plans is the following:

"After the Soviet occupation begins, I intend, since I won't at any rate be able to return home, to start an organization for the purpose of regaining the assets which were lost by the Jews." Wallenberg's thoughts are somewhat convoluted. One has to wonder what he means by the words "since at any rate I won't be able to return home." Interestingly, in a postscript of the December 8 letter to his mother, he wrote, "I will remain for a long time."

January 9, eight days before he disappeared from Budapest, was one important day in the life of Raoul Wallenberg. Minister Danielsson had earlier given instructions that anyone among the Swedish legation staff who was in the first part of the city to fall into Russian hands should enter into negotiations with the Russian commander, so that the legation activities would continue. Wallenberg decided to act on these general instructions. As his personal safety was becoming more precarious with each passing day, Wallenberg went into hiding and began making plans to contact the Soviet military authorities.

On the surface, Wallenberg's plan appeared to be plausible. The Swedes and the Russians enjoyed — or so it seemed — a cordial working relationship during the war. Russian prisoners of war were under the direct protection of the B-section of the Swedish legation. Wounded Russians were housed in a large hospital in Budapest under joint Hungarian and Swedish control. The guards were Hungarian, but the facility was managed by an employee of the Swedish legation, Count Michael Kutuzov-Tolstoy. Count Tolstoy was born in Russia, a member of the distinguished Tolstoy family. After fleeing Russia, he resided in Belgium for a long time and married a Belgian woman, who now helped him take care of the hospital. According to Berg, no one seemed to know what he was doing in Budapest during the war.

But his presence at the Swedish legation in Budapest seemed to imply that the Russians would amicably listen to Wallenberg's plans. Wallenberg's program, entitled the "Wallenberg Institution for Support and Reconstruction," could be likened to the European Recovery Program, more commonly known as the Marshall Plan. In addition to restoring Jewish assets, the plan had such goals as reuniting families, caring for war victims, distributing food, fighting epidemics, reestablishing business relations, creating employment opportunities, providing proper housing, and dealing with repatriation and emigration. Wallenberg felt that if the Hungarian government went along with the plan, then his assistance and that of his already existing social welfare network would be the bedrock on which the government could build. If the Hungarian authorities were cool to the idea, he would seek to form a company or foundation. To gain support for such a system, Wallenberg would appeal to the Hungarian people with a prepared text, excerpted below:

We have decided to create an organization . . . . It is not a purely humanitarian organization but also an economic one, since as we consider the situation, a humanitarian action without the corresponding economic organization for assistance would be limited and in many regards ineffective.

. . . It should be an organization which to some extent will give help to all participants to help themselves in a cooperative way.

I have an administration and a staff for this organization. I have come to know my collaborators during the largest of needs. I have had three viewpoints when I chose them: compassion, honesty, and initiative.

In our action we want to use rapid roads which are offered by private action and private command. We will accept government and national assistance and incorporate it in our activity, providing it will not cause delay in providing the assistance. I will only mention the more important areas of our activity:

Search for lost members of families, in particular returning the children to the parent, the reestablishment of existence, legal help to war victims, reestablishment and renewal of business relations, creation of employment, food distribution, help with housing, collection and distribution of furniture, repatriation and emigration (a special section for help to the Jews and a reestablishment of their means for existence), care of orphans, saving of cultural values, medical care for private persons and villages, fight against epidemics, establishing medical institutions and providing medicines, planning and construction of villages and industries, temporary housing, temporary hospitals, unemployment assistance and its international planning, a humanitarian and economic information service.

The Angel of Rescue, as the Master Rebuilder of Hungary, had formulated a most ambitious undertaking. Of course, Wallenberg realized that without the seal of approval of the Russians, the plan would remain on the drawing board. For this reason he hastened to Debrecen, to meet with Malinovsky and negotiate with the Hungarian government.

On January 10 Wallenberg, busying himself for the journey to Debrecen, met in the basement of the Home Bank with a Hungarian collaborator, Carl Szábo. Wallenberg asked Szábo to help him facilitate his mission in Debrecen. On January 11 Raoul Wallenberg went to 16 Benczur Street, the home of the International Red Cross, remarking, "I would like to spend a few days here. The Nyilas and the Nazis are trying their utmost to kill me." Wallenberg wanted to hurry to Debrecen before it was too late.

On January 12 Wallenberg went to the Üllöi Street headquarters for the last time. He signed protection passes and remarked with his customary good humor, "This is a moment for history. I have signed protection passes on the remains of Leningrad." His coworkers on Üllöi Street never saw him again. Later in a bunker Wallenberg met Pál Szalay, the Hungarian police chief he had befriended. "My apartments are not safe any more," Wallenberg told him. "I will be moving to a yet undetermined friend." After the liberation, Wallenberg promised to take Szalay to Sweden and introduce him to the king. Wallenberg's next stop was at the Swiss legation on Vadász Street. There he bid farewell to Miklos Krausz, the Zionist leader who worked closely with Wallenberg in his rescue activities. Krausz returned to Wallenberg the 200,000 pengös and the official papers that had been given to him for safekeeping when the Nyilas plundered the Swiss legation on Gyopár Street. Wallenberg briefed Krausz on his plans to meet Malinovsky in Debrecen. "I will be welcome in Debrecen since Sweden has represented Russian interests in Hungary." Although Wallenberg anticipated a cordial reception in Debrecen, his concern remained with the Jews in Budapest. He wanted to stress to the Russians that liberation of the ghetto was urgent, since the Nazis and the Nyilas still sought its destruction. Jews are dying daily, Wallenberg insisted to Krausz, while he urged Krausz to be vigilant and protect the ghetto's inhabitants.

Late that evening Wallenberg appeared at the Swiss legation, accompanied by his coworkers Paul Hegedüs, Hugo Wohl, and Otto Fleischmann and his Hungarian friend Carl Szabó. His colleague, Lars Berg, was the last Swede to see Raoul Wallenberg. Berg recalled the introduction of Szabó: "Be careful, Lars! He is a very important and influential Nyilas. And I think he will turn out to be very useful to us." Much of the discussion that evening centered on preventing the Nazis and the Nyilas from annihilating the ghetto before the Russians arrived. Berg remembered, "Szabó promised to keep Wallenberg informed about all homicidal intents, and he also promised active help by putting loyal gendarmes at Wallenberg's disposal."

Wallenberg left Gyopár Street at about 2 A.M. "I strongly urged Wallenberg to stay at the Legation and set up his headquarters there," Berg said. "In that way he would be a little safer at least. But he refused. His place was with his Jewish protégés in Pest."

Wallenberg tasted Russian occupation on January 13, as the troops pushed their way to 16 Benczur Street. A Soviet sergeant and several soldiers, acting civilly, surprised Wallenberg and his chauffeur Langfelder by knocking on their door. After showing the sergeant his diplomatic credentials, Wallenberg requested a meeting with the Russian commander. The Russians posted a guard and then left with Wallenberg and Langfelder. The group went to a site near the Varosligetbol amusement park where they were met by the Russian military officer Dimitrov Demcsinkov. Wallenberg was introduced to him by the translator Béla Révai, showed his identification papers in the Russian language, and was treated respectfully by the Russian officer, who was connected with General Tschernikov, the Russian commander in Budapest. After the meeting Wallenberg and Langfelder returned to Benczur and began packing. They left their money and valuables with Dr. György Wilhelm, a member of the "T" Group of the International Red Cross.

According to Dr. Wilhelm, as presented in Lévai (215), Wallenberg returned to Benczur Street on January 14 in a Russian car with Demcsinkov. He said that he had been staying on Queen Elizabeth Street and had come for a suitcase and package before leaving for Debrecen. He had ridden in a Russian car because his own was unusable. Wallenberg took a briefcase with money from Wilhelm and said goodbye in a carefree manner, without a hint or suggestion that he was in any way worried about his journey.

Dr. Wilhelm's narrative continues on January 15 when Demcsinkov returned to the Benczur office. The Russian amicably informed the workers that Wallenberg had left for the main Russian headquarters alone. (Wilhelm seems mistaken on the date, for it is generally agreed that Wallenberg returned on January 17, which would set Demcsinkov's appearance on January 18 or later.) Wallenberg's whereabouts are uncertain for the period between January 14 and 17, except that one can assume that he and his chauffeur were taken to a higher Russian command.

On January 17, 1945, Raoul Wallenberg's last day in Budapest, a number of friends and coworkers saw him for the last time. Dr. László Petö, a longtime friend of Wallenberg's as well as a leader of the Jewish community, had gone to 16 Benczur Street and met Wallenberg, who had a knapsack and sleeping bag. He had returned to gather his things and say farewell and is reported to have told Petö, "The Russians treated me fantastically." Wallenberg stated that a Russian officer Csernisev had given him permission to go to Debrecen, but before going there he wanted to see his protégés at 6 Tatra Street. As Petö and Wallenberg rode in the car driven by Langfelder, fully-armed Russian soldiers on motorcycles and in a sidecar followed. At Tatra Street, Wallenberg went to the first floor and talked freely with whomever he wanted, while a Russian soldier walked up and down the street in front of the house. Petö stressed the fact that a soldier, not a police officer or a member of the NKVD, a forerunner of the KGB, was on watch.

An ugly scene developed when Wallenberg, Petö, and Langfelder returned to their car. It collided with a truck filled with Russian soldiers headed for the front and the soldiers surrounded the car and began menacing Langfelder. A Russian officer then came to the rescue explaining that a "foreign diplomat" was involved, and Langfelder was freed from the angry soldiers.

In the car Wallenberg had told Petö those famous words: "I don't know whether I'm going as a prisoner or as a guest." If Wallenberg was really uncertain of his status, was he merely being flippant and humorous? An analysis of Petö's report has convinced Lévai that Wallenberg spoke freely in the car and was confident of a welcome reception in Debrecen. There were no Russians in the car, so Wallenberg could have confided in Petö if he were in trouble. While in the building on Tatra, the Russians showed no interest in what Wallenberg was doing or saying. Wallenberg also requested that Petö accompany him to Debrecen. If Wallenberg were a prisoner, Petö asked, "Could he have made such a request of me?" Petö turned Wallenberg down because his parents were hiding in Buda. It would soon fall to the Russians and he wanted to be near his parents. Wallenberg understood his friend's situation and had him driven to the corner of Aréna and Benczur Streets, where the friends parted. The car carrying Wallenberg and Langfelder then sped away.

The account of Rezsö Müller, a Wallenberg coworker who headed the Tatra Street office, indicates more uncertainty on Wallenberg's part. Müller reported that Petö, Wallenberg, and Langfelder, accompanied by a Russian officer, came to his office on January 17. Wallenberg related, "I will now be leaving with the Russian officer, so that I will be able to make the proper connections with the Russian officials and the Hungarian government. I hope to return soon; there is no certainty when I will return. Nothing is sure. Continue my work to the best of your ability." Wallenberg left 100,000 pengös for the continuation of social welfare activities and was given a receipt by Jenö Biró, the financial secretary. (Lévai, however, makes reference to a sum of one million pengös [217].)

While they said goodbye, Wallenberg asked Müller, "Am I correct in assuming that you know that in the Home Bank there are diamonds and other valuables?" Müller answered, "I am aware of this, but why do you ask?" Wallenberg replied, "I want to remind you because you are a witness to this." Petö had planned to go to Debrecen, which Müller corroborated, but as Petö told Müller, "I was to accompany him [Wallenberg], but after my mother's begging I refused." After the fifteen-minute visit, Wallenberg went down to the car and rode away.

The recollections of Ödön Gergely are somewhat at variance with the other reports. Gergely, another Wallenberg coworker at Tatra Street, states that Wallenberg seemed to be in a great hurry to get to Debrecen and did not expect to return from there for at least eight days. Wallenberg inquired about the liberation of the ghetto and about his protégés and seemed to be very pleased that the Jews were safe. During the relaxed fifteen-minute discussion, Gergely also noted that Wallenberg handed over a great deal of money.

The widow Elmérné Milkó and her son Gyula, two other observers on Tatra Street, noted that Wallenberg was wearing a sports suit and that he left hurriedly in a bluish car, headed for the Swedish hospital. Pál Névi, the manager, verified that Wallenberg left for the hospital accompanied by two men. Névi had greeted Wallenberg and informed him about the latest developments, especially the liberation of the ghetto. Wallenberg slipped on the icy sidewalk of Légrády Street and, as he picked himself up, three old persons still wearing the familiar yellow Star of David came out of a door. Although Wallenberg was in obvious pain, his thoughts were still on the Jews, and he remarked, "I am so happy that my mission was not in vain." Névi and Wallenberg walked up to a coffee house in Danube Park and parted. Wallenberg told Névi that he was going to Debrecen and would return as soon as possible.

All those who had seen Raoul Wallenberg, Petö, Gergely, Müller, Névi, and the Milkos, have all passed from the scene. But others still remember January 17, like Georg Libik, who met Wallenberg for only a minute or so as he was leaving the Swedish hospital, where he had gone to "snatch some beans" and other provisions. As Libik revealed to the author in May, 1980, Wallenberg had commented, "I am going to meet the Russians. I have money with me and will try to help the Jews." Reflecting on that remark thirty-five years later, Libik said, "It was certainly very naive on Raoul's part. Could one expect the Russians to do anything that was positive and humanitarian?"

Steven Radi, one of twenty-five prominent Jews who formed the "T" group and now a New York businessman, was also among the last to see Wallenberg. The group had been given refuge under the protection of the Hungarian government at 16 Benczur Street, a house that flew the flag of the International Red Cross, whose activities they had aided. Radi recalls,

It was January 11 when Wallenberg came to our house looking for shelter from the Nazis and the Arrow Cross. He stayed for several days. On January 13 the Russians had advanced to our house and came up through the basement. Wallenberg showed his papers to the Russians. He spoke to them about an hour. At no time did he seem nervous or give an indication that there was a problem. He did look thin and exhausted, but that was because of a super-human work schedule.

After the meeting, Wallenberg was offered the protection of two Uzbek soldiers and one captain. Radi continues, "The Russian soldier told me he was Jewish but begged me not to make known his religion. When the Russians announced on January 16 that Wallenberg and his possessions were under their protection, they were referring to the soldiers posted on Benczur Street."

Wallenberg left for about two or three days. Radi relates,

Before leaving he had indicated that he was going to headquarters. He returned on January 17 in a cheerful and good mood. He thanked me personally for the hospitality at Benczur Street since the building was under my care. He said that he was going to Debrecen and would call us when he returned. He took his things and left with the two Russian officers and a driver. That was the last I saw of Raoul Wallenberg. He was shy by nature—an unbelievable hero.

Certain conclusions are apparent from these various accounts. Wallenberg was determined to go to Debrecen and establish contact with the Russian authorities and with the new Hungarian government. As he prepared for the 137-mile journey east of Budapest, he was under constant military guard. Whether Wallenberg actually ever arrived in Debrecen or whether he ever met Soviet authorities will be discussed later.

Where is Raoul Wallenberg? This question has baffled and tormented diplomats, colleagues, friends, relatives, and concerned citizens throughout the world. At this point one important fact must be added to what has already been discussed. In a January 16 note to the Swedish minister in Moscow, Staffan Söderblom, Soviet Deputy Foreign Minister Dekanosov claimed that Wallenberg had been found in Budapest and identified himself as a member of the Swedish legation. The note concluded: "The Russian military authorities have taken measures to protect Raoul Wallenberg and his belongings." For twelve years this note was the only written Russian admission of its involvement in the fate of Raoul Wallenberg. This note provides the starting point for an investigation of the "case" of the whereabouts of Raoul Wallenberg. However, before the story can go further, we must return to Budapest after his disappearance. The actions and reactions of the Russian "liberators" in Budapest offers much insight in helping to piece together this mystery.

The Russians greatly suspected the Swedish diplomats; in fact, Lars Berg had great difficulty convincing the Russians that he was a member of the Swedish legation. Although he had a diplomatic passport, he had no Russian document. (Swiss diplomats, including Harald Feller, chargé d'affaires, were jailed because they had no Soviet documents.) On two occasions the NKVD interrogated Berg. When he showed the Russians his official passport, they were not moved. As Berg records their reactions to his documents in his book: "But how could they know it was genuine. It did not have any Russian text or any stamp from a Russian authority. If it were true that the Swedish Legation was in charge of the Russian interests, why did not I carry any document from a Russian authority proving that and my identity" (138). Before Anger had left for Budapest, he had asked the Swedish Foreign Office for an identifying document for the Russians. He was told that it was "completely unnecessary." Swedish diplomats on the Buda side were treated "correctly" despite such identifying documents. Anger wonders, "On the Pest side . . . it was considerably more difficult, and one can only guess how the Russians would have treated Wallenberg had he been equipped with an identification document issued by some Russian authority" (129). The Russian's skepticism about the Swedish diplomats no doubt partially resulted from the thousands of both legitimate and forged Swedish protective passes in circulation, from the Swedish flags flying over protected houses and buildings that had no official protection.

After seeing all the Swedish and Swiss flags flying over Budapest, Marshal Malinovsky reportedly remarked with sarcasm that he must be in a Swedish or Swiss city, certainly not a Hungarian one. "We already have come across thousands of so-called Swedes and at least ten Swedish Legations," one Russian told Berg as he interrogated him, adding, "Swedish papers don't mean a thing. You can be anybody, maybe even a German Nazi with a forged Swedish diplomatic passport" (138).

The "Swedenization" of Budapest became an acute problem after liberation and exasperated the Russians. According to Berg, the actions of the Hungarian Jews, although motivated by a desire to save their lives and possessions, was a factor in the Russians' distrust of anything Swedish.

Many Jews thought that the Russians would respect all Swedes and their property entirely and therefore established themselves as Swedish citizens at the arrival of the Russians. They adorned their houses with Swedish flags and wore yellow-blue badges. At one point the Russians came to the house on Üllöi Street, where Otto Fleischmann and some other sixty fellow-workers of Wallenberg had sought shelter. Fleischmann stepped forward and introduced himself as the Swedish Chargé d'Affaires in Budapest! "And who are the others in this house?" asked the Russians. "They are all Swedish diplomats," came the answer, and the identity cards from the Hungarian Foreign Ministry were shown.

After liberation, even more disheartening and revolting than their distrust of Swedes was the Soviet display of barbarity, a crudity that in certain aspects exceeded the Nazis. The cars of the Swedish legation were stolen by Russian officers. A Russian patrol had forced open the safes of the legation and stolen the legation's cash and silver, the money and valuables of its personnel, and the deposits entrusted to the legation for safekeeping by the Swedish citizens and the protégés of the B-section. Throughout Budapest Russian soldiers plundered banks.

Berg relates how the Russians forced Hungarians to smash up furniture, antiques, paintings, glassware, china—anything that smacked of Western civilization. A Hungarian citizen pleaded with Berg:

Lars, if you ever get out of this hell, try to tell people, try to explain to them what savages, what barbarians the Russians are! Try to make them understand that all this might also happen to their countries, to their homes, to their wives! People won't believe you. They did not believe what was said of Hitler. People never want to believe disturbing warnings, but try anyhow. If they could only see what is going on here (168)!

Berg, having sadly observed all the plundering, all the rape of both men and women, all the violations of accepted forms of behavior, concluded that neither Hungary nor the Soviet war allies could be free from the grasp of the Russians:

My visitors were still more amazed when I told them how the Swedish Legation had been ransacked. Was that not the height of ingratitude after the Legation had fought for years against the Nazis in order to protect the Russian interests in Hungary! At that time none of us had time to find out the Russians' basic tactic—to do anything from which they were not stopped by force.

Why not plunder and take away everything that could be moved? Why not rape the American girls in Budapest? Why not force the safes of the Swedish Legation? There were no policies to stop them, no court that would inflict punishment upon them. Why be so Westernly degenerated and pay attention to international customs, signed treaties or humanitarian principles. Let the stupid democratic countries feel themselves bound to such antiquated dogmas. One gains so much more by acting rapidly and without any moral scruples.

The doctrine of the Communist dictatorship, for which so many Eastern countries in Europe now have suffered, was by the time of the fall of Budapest not known yet by the world. So one could not blame the various Allied people in Budapest for being surprised and bitter at the Russian behavior. They could not possibly know already at that time that the Russians never had considered their Allies as their friends, but only as tools to help them to conquer their closest and strongest enemy, Germany. And far less could they suspect that Russia, as soon as Germany was taken, would turn against her Allies in order to carry on the number one Communist idea: to conquer the world, to make slaves of all free people, as they have made slaves out of the Russians" (180–181).

The Nobel laureate Albert Szent-Györgyi also had a bitter taste of the Russian liberators. He was a staunch foe of the Nazis, was in hiding during the Nazi takeover of Hungary, and looked forward to a new era in his homeland. Szent-Györgyi contacted Malinovsky's headquarters after the Russian conquest of Pest. He spent some time afterward in Moscow. His experiences left him sadder and wiser. He lashed out at the Hungarian Communist Party and at the Russian occupation forces, being especially censorious of their arrests and atrocities. Libik, his son-in-law, reported that the famed scientist had called Stalin "a bloodthirsty murderer, a thousand times worse than Hitler." The disillusioned Szent-Györgyi eventually left his homeland for the United States. Reflecting thirty-five years later on the Russian behavior and Wallenberg's trust in the Soviets, Libik commented, "Raoul Wallenberg was naive in expecting the Russians to be nice and hospitable and receptive to his ideas." Libik recalled that in the beginning of February, 1945, he had met Ernö Gerö, second in command of the Hungarian Communist Party. "He told me," Libik said, "that 'Wallenberg was in a good position.' You don't know anything, I told him. The Russians have no respect for values, for any form of decency."

Tibor Baranski, equally indignant over the Russian atrocities in Hungary that included the raping of 2.5 million women between 1944–45, gave a similar appraisal. While he did not dispute the fact that Wallenberg was concerned about the fate of Jews in postwar Hungary, Baranski insisted that the Swede planned to meet with the provisional Hungarian government and with the Russians because he was especially worried about the plight of the Hungarian people in general. Baranski said,

> I was told by a close contact of mine in Budapest that Wallenberg felt confident that the Jews in Budapest would not be harmed by the Russians. I cannot

name this individual because he may still be alive under Communist rule. Wallenberg was aware that Moscow had told its soldiers not to harm the Jews because it wanted to give a good appearance for the Allies. But the Hungarian people needed protection from the Russian beasts, for whom every woman was an object for sexual assault. The Russians were like troglodytes coming out of their caves.

When asked why Wallenberg was able to deal so successfully with the Nazis while his confrontation with the Russians turned out so tragically, Baranski replied that the "Nazis were so battered, so enervated, so frustrated in their war efforts that when Wallenberg came on the scene he brilliantly intimidated the Nazis every chance he had. With the Russians so victorious, so confident, what could Raoul Wallenberg do?"

Baranski also challenged the idea that Wallenberg's naivete in not realizing that the Russians were not the Germans brought on his tragedy:

I am often reminded—in connection with Wallenberg—of the fisherman in Hemingway's *Old Man and the Sea,* when to the fisherman's own question of what "beat" him he replied, "I went out too far." But like the fisherman Wallenberg did not go out too far. They did what they did because their mission had to be accomplished. When you are a Raoul Wallenberg, when you are humane, when you love people, you don't think or speak of naivete. If I can be sarcastic, for Wallenberg the Red Nazis were no different than the Brown Communists.

In light of the Russian distrust of the Swedes—with even greater suspicion directed toward the Allies—and in light of Russian barbarity, one can imagine the reception Wallenberg received at the hands of his Russian "hosts" and their attitude toward Wallenberg's reconstruction plan for Hungary.

Distrust of the Swedish diplomats in Budapest led to the suspicion that Wallenberg headed an espionage ring in the Hungarian capital. The Russians found it inconceivable that Wallenberg had endangered his life just to save Hungarian Jews. Berg reports,

The Swedish Legation had been accused of being a German espionage nest, and the leader of all German spies in Budapest must be either Wallenberg or myself. Wallenberg could not possibly have risked his life to help Hungarian Jews. As for myself, what reason did I have to help a bunch of foreigners, such as Dutchmen, Argentines, and Chinese.

Wallenberg's coworkers and those who worked in the B-section of the Swedish legation were arrested and interrogated about the work, private lives, and friends of the Swedish diplomats. While most of those were arrested and released, some never returned.

The Russians also questioned Count Tolstoy, who had instructions from the Swedish legation to see General Tjernysjov, the Russian town commander of Budapest. Tolstoy's dedicated work for the wounded Russian prisoners of war and his fluent Russian failed to ingratiate him and he was arrested, although treated well. Berg comments, "For several days, he was subjected to intensive questioning. The Russians wanted to know about his work and about the activities of the entire Swedish Legation. He had been ordered to tell the Russians everything he knew about Wallenberg, about myself, including our private lives." Whether willingly or unwillingly, Tolstoy was recruited as an employee of the Russian occupation forces and named the head of a Bureau for Foreigners, which was supervised by the Russian Town Command. All legations and consulates, including the Swedes, fell under the jurisdiction of the bureau. As a result of his new status, he behaved differently toward his former Swedish colleagues. When Berg visited Tolstoy unexpectedly, the latter was very uneasy and nervous. According to Berg, Tolstoy "begged me not to act independently on behalf of the Swedish Legation and not to do anything that might annoy the Russians." Tolstoy's link to the harrowing efforts to determine the status of Raoul Wallenberg and his involvement in the mystery will be discussed later.

Sweden had looked after the interests of the mighty Russian bear and devotedly cared for wounded Russian prisoners of war. As its reward, Sweden suffered Russian distrust, suspicion, and the arrests of its citizens.

The story of the Swedish rescue mission in Budapest, the saga of the Angel of Rescue, should not be terminated with Russia's wretched and treacherous thanklessness. It is well to remember Viola's words in Shakespeare's *Twelfth Night*:

> I hate ingratitude more in a man
> Than lying, vainness, babbling drunkenness,
> Or any taint of vice whose strong corruption
> Inhabits our frail blood.

Those saved by the devoted efforts, those with whom he worked, appreciated the selflessness of Raoul Wallenberg. Writer Rudolph Philipp has recorded the tribute to the Swede at a ceremony in the summer of 1945:

> The aura which surrounded him fascinated and enchanted his collaborators. In the middle of the hopeless dirt of a night hostel or in a moist dark cave he inspired thought towards the west, towards Sweden, where man was still considered a man. His protégés felt this magic, these refugees, who in desperation gathered around this Swede on their flight from the police; these unhappy souls whose sufferings sometimes broke the last limits of civilization, people who lived in utter anguish. By his presence they were calmed, not by calculation or in respect for Raoul's person — because he never tried to inspire respect — but only because they felt in his presence an inflexible personality, without fright, who did not recoil even from death . . . . He demanded of himself and of his collaborators complete self-sacrifice . . . . Hero worship was completely

foreign to him . . . . The waves of the war lifted him high, but at last these waves engulfed him, only a step from the victory. Wallenberg disappeared before the eyes of the people he had saved, like a hero in the legend. An unjust but a heroic end (161-162).

As an expression of thankfulness, a part of the Central Jewish Hospital was to be named Wallenberg Pavilion. This plan was never carried out, and a proposal to erect a monument in Saint Stephen's Park was postponed until he returns, at the request of Raoul's mother. As a token of appreciation for his work, a special book was produced in the summer of 1945 by the Hungarian Jewish community. North of Saint Stephen's Boulevard, in the middle of what once was the international ghetto, a four-block-long street was renamed for him—and still bears his name. At one corner a plaque reads: "Raoul Wallenberg, Secretary of the Swedish Legation, with courage and determination helped the escape of thousands during the reign of the Arrow Cross."

Praise was bestowed on Raoul Wallenberg during the summer of 1945 at a ceremony in the Israelite Congregation of Pest:

The time of horror is still fresh in our memory when the Jews of this country were like hunted animals, when thousands of Jewish prisoners were in the temple preparing for death. We recall all the atrocities of the concentration camps, the departure of the people who were to die, the sufferings in the ghettos and the attacks against the houses which had been placed under international protection. But we also remember one of the greatest heroes of those terrible times, the Secretary of the Royal Swedish Legation, who defied the intruding government and its armed executioners. We witnessed the redemption of prisoners and the relief of those who suffered when Mr. Wallenberg came among the persecuted to help. In a superhuman effort, not yielding to fatigue and exposing himself to all sorts of dangers, he brought home children who had been dragged away and he liberated aged parents. We saw him give food to the starving and medicine to the ailing.

We shall never forget him and shall be forever grateful to him and to the Swedish nation because it was the Swedish flag which warranted undisturbed slumber of thousands of Jews in the protected houses.

He was a righteous man. God bless him.

As Hungarians—both Jewish and non-Jewish—poured out their thanks to the Angel of Rescue, an incessant question troubled and challenged the mind and conscience of mankind: Where is Raoul Wallenberg?

8

Where Is Raoul Wallenberg?

In April, 1945, members of the Swedish legation arrived at the Stätsgard quay of Stockholm for a jubilant reunion with families who had just about given up hope of their kindred ever returning from Budapest. Among those who waited at the quay in hopeful anticipation was May von Dardel, the mother of Raoul Wallenberg. Lars Berg gave her a package that Wallenberg had deposited in the Home Bank of Budapest and which had been overlooked by the plundering Russians. "I gave her the package," Berg said. "She was in tears, tears of the deepest sorrow."

Because the other diplomats had returned, a strong hope still persisted that Raoul Wallenberg would be back in Stockholm soon; but as days went by, the distressing refrain became: Where is Raoul Wallenberg?

Various rumors or "reports" began to circulate about Wallenberg's whereabouts: one theorized that he had been killed in an air raid; a second concluded that he had been murdered by plundering Nazi or Arrow Cross soldiers. Hinshaw, in his book *Sweden's Neutral Policy in Two Wars*, argues that Wallenberg might have been kidnapped by the Nyilas before reaching Debrecen (182).

The Hungarian historian Lévai, still alive in his eighties in Buda, espoused the view that Wallenberg was never a captive or prisoner of Moscow. Writing in 1948, Lévai reviews the developments and testimonies to that date and with certainty concludes that the NKVD "had nothing to do" with Wallenberg's disappearance. Lévai picks apart the testimony and severely attacks the credibility of witnesses who maintain that they have seen Wallenberg in prison. According to Lévai, those who claim that Raoul Wallenberg was imprisoned are interested in extracting money from the Wallenberg family or are seeking to facilitate their immigration to Sweden. Those linking Wallenberg's disappearance with the NKVD do so for "political, economic, and sensationalistic reasons. There is a mother who suffers terribly. These people want to keep her hope alive, not caring, not having a conscience that they cause her pain and disappointment."

Lévai pledges that he will continue to attack the falsehoods in the Wallenberg case: "It is our duty to find out everything. It is our duty to refute lies and the sensation-seeking persons. That is the way Wallenberg would have wanted it. We consider every piece of information, even if it be little, because this is our obligation. We will not deal leniently with ruthless statements" (291-292).

Despite his expressions of concern for the mother of Raoul Wallenberg, Wallenberg's family found Lévai's position very distasteful. In a September 2, 1947, letter to Moses Leavitt, executive vice chairman of the American Jewish Joint Distribution Committee, Wallenberg's half brother, Dr. Guy von Dardel, says that Lévai "tries to sabotage the search for Raoul Wallenberg by stating without any proofs that he was probably killed by the Nazis." Wallenberg's stepfather, Fredrik von Dardel, wrote a letter to the editor of *Aufbau* on December 13, 1946, pointing out that reporting Raoul Wallenberg's death had a deleterious effect on the efforts to rescue his stepson:

> You must understand, dear sir, that our efforts as well as the efforts of the Swedish government to rescue my stepson, Raoul Wallenberg, are being counteracted if such a prominent newspaper as the *Aufbau* helps spread the news about Raoul Wallenberg's certain death. The consequences of such absolutely unfounded rumors—even if published entirely bona fide—can be outweighed by no monument.

Lacking concrete information, some of Wallenberg's workers, such as Mrs. Ernster, believed that the Swede had been killed in Budapest. "At first my father was influenced by the reports that Raoul Wallenberg was killed. We were aware that many people were shot in the streets, and the same could have happened to Raoul Wallenberg. As for our image of the Russians, in the beginning we looked upon them as liberators."

The rumors and reports of Raoul Wallenberg's death definitely impeded efforts to rescue him, according to Anger. "Certain powerful forces" tried to perpetuate the reports of his death. Anger writes that because of these rumors Staffan Söderblom

> delayed the official diplomatic representations to the Russians because he was loath to exclude the possibility that those rumors were true. The Foreign Office had to urge Söderblom not to fall into passivity. In April he was instructed to request careful investigation without further delay into what happened to Wallenberg (136).

Notwithstanding eyewitness accounts of Wallenberg in Soviet jails, his purported death in Hungary does not square with Russian actions. As mentioned previously, Soviet Deputy Foreign Minister Dekanozov had given Söderblom written assurance on January 16 that Wallenberg was under Soviet protection. And in February, 1945, Mme. Alexandra Kollontay, the Russian ambassador in Stockholm, told Mrs. von Dardel that her son was alive and well in the Soviet Union. "He will be back, but don't make too much noise about it." The Soviet authorities considered Mme. Kollontay's admission a diplomatic blunder and recalled her from Stockholm. (She had also passed on the information to the wife of Christian Günther, the Swedish foreign minister.) On March 8 Hungarian Radio Kossuth reported that Wallenberg had disappeared and had probably been murdered by Gestapo agents on January 17.

If we conclude that Raoul Wallenberg was taken to Russia, it is important to examine the possible reasons for his imprisonment in 1945 in an attempt to gain some insight into this thirty-seven-year-old mystery.

Because America had "sponsored" Raoul Wallenberg's mission to save Jews, the Russians looked upon legation members with distrust. When Berg was interrogated by the Russians, he thought he, as well as Wallenberg, was suspected and accused of being a German spy. "It was only after I returned to Sweden that I realized that the Russians considered the Americans at least as deadly as the Germans. I was unaware of the developing Cold War between Russia and America. I am sure that Wallenberg had no ideas of this whatsoever. After all, they were allies during the war." According to Berg, Wallenberg probably told the Russians that he "worked" for Roosevelt, surely thinking that this would make a favorable impression upon them. He continued: "Yet, when you think that Wallenberg did come to Budapest at President Roosevelt's personal request and that the funds at his disposal originated from the War Refugee Board in Washington, then one can understand why the Russians regarded Raoul in particular as an American spy! And in the eyes of the Russians that was considerably worse than working for the Germans!"

Wallenberg's spy status was further confirmed when the Russians examined the rationale for Wallenberg's activities in Hungary. Given the history of anti-Semitism in the Soviet Union, Russia certainly would not be favorably disposed to anyone engaged in helping Jews. Ambassador Malcolm Toon, who represented the U.S. in Russia from 1976 to 1979, sees anti-Semitism as a very potent factor in Raoul Wallenberg's arrest. "The Soviets have been terribly anti-Semitic, and they would certainly punish those who acted on behalf of the Jews. Yes, the imprisonment of Raoul Wallenberg was a deliberate act, although perhaps they may now feel that it was a mistake since it has caused such a flap."

In the context of Russian suspicions of any attempt to rescue Jews, one must mention the Joel Brand mission. In the spring of 1944 Eichmann, in negotiations with Dr. Rudolph Kasztner, a Hungarian Zionist leader, proposed that he would "sell" one million Jews to the Allies in return for one hundred thousand trucks for the German armed forces. The trucks would come from the British-American side and would only be used on the eastern front against the Russians. While on a mission to negotiate with British diplomats, the British Secret Service arrested Brand. Although the exchange failed, Eichmann's crude attempt to replenish German transport and divide the Allies through the Zionist-supported barter of Jewish lives could hardly have won Russian support for Wallenberg's activities in saving Jews.

Although Russian anti-Semitism probably contributed to Wallenberg's imprisonment, the possibility that anyone would undertake such an unselfish, humanitarian mission—especially one benefitting Jews—was a concept alien to the Russians. Such altruism would simply not be believed. His ambitious Nansen Plan for rebuilding Hungary—using his own independent organization to reconstruct Russian-occupied and controlled territory—probably seemed even more suspicious. Anger writes,

> Wallenberg was already compromised by having accepted American money for the aid operation. Would that financial support continue with new, mysterious purposes? These probably were the questions the NKVD asked themselves . . . . The Russians themselves usually use their humanitarian organizations as a cover for espionage, and probably considered it natural that other countries used similar methods . . . . Probably Wallenberg's reconstruction plan was to the Russians nothing more than an attempt at continued covert espionage. When he described his humanitarian efforts up to that time, and spoke of continuing, they probably did not believe him. Possibly the Russians have not to this day realized that they locked up an innocent person (148-149).

Another theory attributes Wallenberg's arrest—at least in the beginning—to a more limited decision by local or NKVD authorities; in fact, according to Hungarian journalists, Wallenberg was suspected of concealing bank notes, jewelry, and other Jewish property from the Russians.

It has also been suggested that Wallenberg was taken into custody as a hostage for the purpose of exchanging diplomats with the Swedes. Such exchanges took place with Switzerland and Italy, but Sweden was not interested in such exchanges.

Perhaps the most reasonable explanation for Wallenberg's arrest and continued imprisonment relates to the Soviet's world policy during the Stalin years. Certainly, Russia had a long tradition of anti-Semitism, has been locked in a cold war with America, and did not look favorably upon Wallenberg, a member of a "great capitalist family." As a hero of liberty and an exemplar of compassion, Raoul Wallenberg represented everything that the USSR detested. Stalin was monomaniacally determined to spread Communist rule. Bulgaria, Czechoslovakia, East Germany, Hungary, Poland, Rumania, and Yugoslavia all fell under the sway of the Russian bear using the same methods in all countries: oppression, police power, spies, prisons, deportations, and persecution of liberation movements. Could Russia afford to have such a person as Raoul Wallenberg on the loose? According to von Dardel, the Russians considered Wallenberg "a security risk, a person who could cause damage to the interests of the Soviet Union if he were released." Because Wallenberg fought the Nazis in Budapest, "he won a reputation as a hero for liberty, which made him suspect in the eyes of Russians" (33–34).

In the September 22, 1979, issue of the Hungarian-language newspaper *Menora,* Dr. Péter Gosztonyi develops a similar theme. After Russia occupied Estonia, Latvia, and Lithuania at the beginning of World War II, thousands of refugees found their way to Sweden, where they were aided by a relief network set up by the Swedes. Not only did Wallenberg help the refugees, but he asked those persons many questions and learned of the oppressive conditions in the Soviet Union. Gosztonyi continues, "Because of this Wallenberg was listed in Moscow as an imperialist spy. The Russians were familiar with Wallenberg's entire life. And this is the very thing that brought the downfall of the great Swedish diplomat."

Assuming that Wallenberg's acquaintance with Baltic refugees is true, it may be farfetched to relate this to his arrest in 1945, but Raoul Wallenberg had indeed become a symbol of freedom, embodying the hope of victory over repression and persecution. Before he left Budapest, Wallenberg reportedly remarked that he did not know whether he was leaving for Debrecen as a guest or as a prisoner; he soon found out that he was not a guest.

Wallenberg's potential value to the Russians could also have caused his imprisonment. According to Yuri Luryi, a lawyer before emigrating from the USSR and now on the law faculty of the University of Western Ontario and Osgoode Hall Law School,

> It is certainly conceivable that Russia wanted to draft him as a spy. With his knowledge of Sweden's upper class, he would have been an excellent choice for a spy mission in his native land. I feel that Wallenberg was kept alive by the Soviets with these hopes in mind. Incidentally, a KGB defector reached a similar conclusion after his own escape in the early seventies.

Ambassador Toon does not necessarily support this point of view, but he can visualize its possibility. "The NKVD could be described as simplistic and could be expected to say, 'if you don't work for us, we will take you.'"

Carl-Fredrik Palmstierna, private secretary of Swedish King Gustavus VI and a relative of the Wallenbergs, does not propound a theory for the imprisonment of Raoul Wallenberg, but he does feel that the young diplomat was a "bohemian who fell victim to his own methods. Wallenberg was too free and easy. When you deal with the Russians, you have to be formal, look and act like a diplomat."

Raoul Wallenberg's imprisonment leaves a number of legalistic questions unanswered. According to Professor Harold Berman, an authority on Russian law and member of the Executive Committee of Harvard University's Russian Research Center,

> The troika of the secret police might have been the ones who judged Raoul Wallenberg, who might never have been told why he was sentenced. This is not unusual. But let us say, for argument's sake, that he was accused of espionage, of conspiring to overthrow the government, or he was called "an enemy of the people." And as a foreign subject, he would have been subject to the same laws as a Soviet national. But then you have the question of diplomatic immunity.

Professor Berman said that the Soviets might have refused to honor diplomatic immunity, "but they would have been in violation of international law, something the Russians do not take lightly." If, however, the Russians violated diplomatic immunity, "what recourse did the Swedish government have: break off diplomatic relations?"

According to Professor Berman, a more serious question involves the circumstances surrounding the arrest of Raoul Wallenberg. "It seems hard to justify what happened. If Raoul Wallenberg was arrested on Hungarian soil, it perhaps could be justified under martial law, assuming that the Russian military authorities had been legally empowered to act. Another explanation might be that Budapest was in chaos, and in such situations one often acts out of expediency."

Regarding the sentence given Raoul Wallenberg, Professor Berman remarked that a twenty-five-year term was the norm in such cases. "However, it is possible to have years added on while in prison for crimes committed there."

The information recounting Raoul Wallenberg's odyssey through the Hades of the Russian prison system emerged through interviews conducted by the Swedish Foreign Ministry with former Russian prisoners. To ensure the veracity of the testimony, each former prisoner knew nothing of the testimony of the others. Only testimony coming from direct contact with Wallenberg was considered acceptable. Each interviewee confirmed his statement under oath, and it was then certified by a qualified notary.

On an uncertain date, the Russian staff officers that Wallenberg had contacted advised him to get in touch with Marshal Malinovsky, but Wallenberg never reached him. Instead Langfelder and Wallenberg were arrested by a Russian NKVD officer about three or four days after he had presented himself at the first Soviet headquarters. Some discrepancies have arisen concerning the arresting officer: von Dardel reports him to be a major (14), while Aleksandr Solzhenitsyn, in a 1975 interview with the Swedish publication *Russian Thought,* identifies him as a Jewish NKVD captain, Yefim Moshinsky. In later years Moshinsky was betrayed to the KGB, spent time on Wrangel Island, went to Israel after being released, reported seeing Wallenberg, and corresponded with Wallenberg's mother in 1975.

After the arrest, Wallenberg and Langfelder were briefly imprisoned in a provisional NKVD prison in Budapest. Guarded by a Russian officer and four soldiers, they were brought to Moscow by train via Rumania, with a stop at the Jasi station that included a meal in a restaurant named Luther. In both Budapest and Moscow they were told that they should not consider themselves as prisoners but only "under Soviet protection"; in Moscow they even briefly toured the city, including the underground railway.

Again, it is not certain when Wallenberg and Langfelder ceased being "under Soviet protection" and started being under arrest. But on January 31, Wallenberg and Langfelder walked to Lubianka Prison and were separated from each other.

The KGB reserves Lubianka Prison for those who especially interest them. The list of internees has included the executed KGB head Beria, Aleksandr Solzhenitsyn, and American U-2 pilot Gary Francis Powers. Another prisoner of Lubianka was Leopold Trepper, head of the Red Orchestra, a Russian spy network that infiltrated Nazi-occupied Europe during World War II. Trepper served part of his ten-year sentence in Lubianka during 1945, at a time that coincided with Wallenberg's stay. After his release, Trepper went to Poland, to Israel in 1974, and died in Jerusalem in January, 1982.

Trepper recalled that the prison had become a "symbol of police terror" worldwide. Located in the center of Moscow, the prison comprises a group of buildings that house the Ministry of Internal Security. "In the midst of these buildings, there is a relatively small prison set aside for a few hundred distinguished guests."

Joining the ranks of these "distinguished guests," Wallenberg entered cell 123, where he found Gustaf Richter, a former police attaché at the German legation in Bucharest, and an Austrian lieutenant named Scheuer. Langfelder shared his cell with Willi Roedel, former counselor of the German legation in Rumania, and a German interpreter, Jan Loyda. In early February Wallenberg wrote a letter to the director of the prison, protesting his incarceration, stressing his diplomatic status, and demanding to contact the Swedish legation in Moscow. The letter was not answered. While in cell 123, Wallenberg was interrogated once, for sixty to ninety minutes. The questioner told him, "You are well known to us. You belong to a great capitalist family in Sweden." Wallenberg was accused of espionage, a charge that had been made at least twice before, according to information Langfelder reported to his cellmates. On those occasions Wallenberg was accused of spying for the United States and Great Britain.

Although Wallenberg was not prepared to accept his imprisonment, he always maintained his humor, and in the midst of his troubles, he never stopped thinking of his family. Richter recalled that the Swede once asked him: "What will my relatives say when they learn that I am imprisoned?"

Despite all his personal torment, Wallenberg never lost his human dignity or his concern for his fellow man. Eduard Hille, a cellmate of Langfelder, testified that "Wallenberg was a very good comrade and asked the Soviet day officer to hand over his cigarettes to Langfelder."

On March 18 Langfelder was transferred to Lefortovo Prison in Moscow, and Wallenberg was put in Langfelder's former cell at Lubianka. After leaving the Soviet jail, Loyda testified that Wallenberg had told his Russian interrogators that as a member of the Swedish legation, he had watched over Russian interests in Hungary. In response, the Communists sneered at Wallenberg and asked why a wealthy Swedish capitalist would aid the Russians. In May, 1945, Wallenberg and Roedel were removed from Lubianka and placed in Lefortovo Prison. At this point Wallenberg came to the tragic realization that the Russians did not intend to release him.

Situated in the city of Moscow in Baumanskii's district, Lefortovo is a half-hour ride from Lubianka. One of the severest KGB prisons in the Soviet Union, it has accommodated such dissidents as Solzhenitsyn, Yuri Orlov, Georgi Vins, and Aleksandr Ginsburg.

Leopold Trepper, who was also in Lefortovo during 1945, described the facility:

> I had been imprisoned in the medieval fortress Saint Jean d'Acre as a result of my underground activities in Palestine. The Lefortovo Prison reminded me of that facility. Lefortovo was a military prison built during the czarist days. The conditions during the czarist period were so severe that inmates left in poor physical condition. With the October Revolution came the closing of that dreadful facility. However, the doors were once more opened by Stalin in 1937 to house Marshal Tukhachevsky and his circle.
>
> One can compare Lefortovo to a stadium: three stories of circular galleries on which the cells opened and in the center a huge, empty space making possible observations at every level.
>
> The guards were much more offensive [than at Lubianka]. Prisoners were never given a moment's peace. The guards continually slammed the doors of the spy holes. They were in and out of the cell all day with every imaginable complaint: "you have been sitting down too long"; "you have slept too much"; "you are walking too much." As for the food, I thought that there could be no worse than Lubianka. I was proven wrong at Lefortovo.

Abraham Shifrin, a former Russian prisoner closely following the Wallenberg case, gives a meticulous description of the prison. In his *First Guidebook* to the prisons and "concentration camps" of the Soviet Union, Shifrin writes of prisoners who "exhausted by the endless interrogations and otherwise driven to utter despair committed suicide by throwing themselves into the stairwell" (45). The deathlike, torturous darkness and other horrid conditions were graphically recorded by Russian dissident Anatoli Shcharansky and also presented in the *First Guidebook*:

I spent 28 days in solitary confinement cell no. 3 in the basement of Lefortovo Prison. Not having a bed, I had to stand up to my ankles in water the whole time. I was given a daily ration of 300 grams of bread, twice a day a mug of water. After a few days in a standing position, I began to fall over. Soon I found myself sitting in the water and filth on the floor of the cell (54).

The KGB at Lefortovo uses many methods to extract "voluntary confessions," according to Shifrin. In addition to total isolation, the prisoners may be subjected to "exhausting interrogation, intimidation, threats to their family, and placement in a room with ruffians who have been incited to attack them."

Wallenberg found Lefortovo to be a forbidding four-story, K-shaped prison in which prisoners could only see their cellmates. A guard on each floor was positioned so that he could see the entrances to all cells. A system of flag signals enabled guards to move prisoners without their being observed by other inmates. Wallenberg and Roedel were put in cell 203. Like the other cells, it had a peephole, and every few minutes a guard could inspect the two prisoners. Their tiny room contained a toilet and a small table, and a barred window allowed the distribution of food. Isolation was also maintained outside the cell in the courtyard, where eight walled sections separated and secluded prisoners during their daily twenty-minute exercise period. A prison library had only books in the Russian language. No writing implements were allowed the prisoners; however, once in two weeks they were permitted materials for sending a written message to the prison administration. Such were the wretched conditions in which Raoul Wallenberg found himself—a man who loved humanity, who loved being with people, now shut off from them in the Soviet abyss.

Communication was possible through the "knocking" system. Prisoners used their toothbrushes and other hard objects as wall-tapping instruments in a simple but time-consuming system. One knock indicated the letter *a,* two, the letter *b,* and so on through the alphabet; thus, the word "espionage" involved eighty knocks. But time was plentiful in Lefortovo. A modified form of knocking is the "5 × 5 system" or the "square system," in which a prisoner knocks a certain number of times to indicate the row, and then a certain number of times to designate the column for each letter. For example, to indicate the letter *n,* the prisoner would knock three times, then take a short break, and knock four times. To hide the sound from the guards, a prisoner would sit on a bed with his back against the wall and a book on his lap, and knock with the hand farthest from the cell door.

Actual conversation was also possible, but the opportunities for it were more limited. Only those on the prison's top floors could communicate in this way. In the summer months, when the water pipes were often empty, the prisoners on the top floors could open the taps and speak through them. Wallenberg and Roedel began "knocking" with cell 202 and with cells 149–152 on the second floor.

The Square System of Knocking

	1	2	3	4	5
1	A	B	C	D	E
2	F	G	H	I	J
3	K	L	M	N	O
4	P	Q	R	S	T
5	U	V	X	Y	Z

Willi Bergemann, who occupied cell 202, often communicated with his third-floor neighbors through knocking and through the pipes. Bergemann told the Swedes of Wallenberg's agonizing story:

> Raoul Wallenberg was a very eager knocker. He spoke and knocked fluent German. He called us by knocking five times in a row. I learned that he had gone on January 13, 1945, to the Russian headquarters to negotiate for better conditions for the Jewish people in Budapest. On this occasion Raoul Wallenberg was arrested and sent to Moscow suspected of espionage. While he was in cell 203, he asked repeatedly for information from the commissar about his fate.

The only point in this testimony that can be challenged, based on other reports, is the date, January 13. All information presented in the previous chapter pinpoints January 17 as Wallenberg's last day in Budapest.

Wallenberg's fellow prisoners also testified that he frequently appealed to prison officials to permit him to contact the Swedish embassy. After many unsuccessful efforts, he decided to appeal to the top — Joseph Stalin.

Ernst Wallenstein, in cell 150, had been a career diplomat and advised Wallenberg on appropriate phraseology. The letter was written in French, with a salutation of "Monsieur le President," and closed, "Agréez, Monsieur le Président, l'éxpression de ma très haute considération." According to a prisoner named Bernard Rensinghoff, the letter mentioned Wallenberg's diplomatic status, his desire to be interrogated, and his request for contact with the Swedish embassy in Moscow. A guard named Starji received the letter, and he later confirmed that it had been sent. Not long after the letter was dispatched, Wallenberg was summoned for further questioning by an inspector. He repeatedly protested against his imprisonment and demanded to communicate with the Swedish embassy. During his testimony Rensinghoff reported:

> The inspector had informed him that his case was quite clear, that his was a "political case." If he considered himself innocent, it was his responsibility to prove it. The best proof of his guilt was the fact that the Swedish embassy in Moscow had done nothing to help his case. "Nobody cares about you. If the Swedish government or its embassy had any interest in you, they would long ago have contacted you."

One would hope that Wallenberg never for a moment believed that nobody cared about him. Could the world have so soon forgotten about a man who devoted all his energies and risked his life countless times to save some one hundred thousand persons? Could the country of his birth have failed to care about an individual whose humanitarianism and heroism showed the world a spark of righteousness amid the hellish fires of Nazism? If nobody cared about Raoul Wallenberg, could one imagine a more unspeakable expression of ingratitude? Wallenberg never succeeded in communicating directly with the outside world; but, even more tragic, Sweden and the outside world have never been able to communicate their concern to Raoul Wallenberg.

Rensinghoff also testified that he learned from Wallenberg that he had once asked a Russian officer whether he would ever be tried and sentenced. "For political reasons you will never be sentenced," the officer answered.

In testimonies concerning Wallenberg, the prisoners showed their amazement at a neutral diplomat's confinement in prison. For example, Karl Supprian, secretary-general at the German Scientific Institute in Bucharest, spoke of his "surprise" at learning of Wallenberg's arrest. The Italian diplomat Claudio de Mohr and his cellmates could not at first believe that a Swedish official was in prison: "We were so surprised that a Swedish diplomat had been arrested that we many times asked for confirmation."

In February, 1947, Wallenberg and Roedel were taken out of cell 203. Mysteriously, on July 27, 1947, at both Lubianka and Lefortovo Prisons, every prisoner—ten in all—who had been a cellmate of either Wallenberg or Langfelder was brought for special interviews by secret police officials. (Langfelder had been removed from cell 105 at Lefortovo in December, 1945, and nothing has been reported about him since that time.) They were forced to reveal the names of those prisoners with whom they had discussed Wallenberg, and to disclose everything that Wallenberg had told them. Richter, Wallenberg's first cellmate, was interrogated most intensely, and was put in solitary for seven months.

The Swedish officials who later questioned the prisoners concluded that "the treatment received by the questioned prisoners after the examinations shows that the Russian authorities wished as far as possible to prevent information about the Swedish diplomat from spreading."

On August 18, 1947, Russia's Deputy Foreign Minister André Vishinsky sent a note to the Swedish Minister Söderblom that began, "As a result of a careful investigation it has been established that Wallenberg is not in the Soviet Union, and that he is unknown to us." After making this point, the Soviet had to void its previous admissions, and so the note continued:

It is correct that the Foreign Office on January 14, 1945, received a short message, based on indirect information from one of the commanders of a unit engaged in the fighting in Budapest that Wallenberg had been found at the Benczur Street. Later thorough investigations and research was carried out in order to confirm this information, but did not lead to a positive result. The Russian officer who gave the information has not been found. Wallenberg has also not been found in the prison and internment camps. The member of the Collegiate of the Foreign Office, Novikov, has on the basis of this informed Minister Hägglöf that the attempts of the appropriate authorities to find Wallenberg has been without success.

The obvious question, then, is: Where is Raoul Wallenberg? In its conclusion the note suggests "the only remaining possibility . . . that Wallenberg perished in the street-fights in Budapest or was captured by Szálasi's followers."

The Vishinsky note is authentic in form and terminology, according to Mark Popovsky, the Russian emigré writer who, despite nonmembership, had access to KGB files while researching a book on the morality of Soviet science.

While the message is a total fabrication, the writing is intended to answer a question previously raised. One does get a clear picture of Vishinsky's personality: an inflexible Stalinist, not given to human emotions. For that reason the letter is cold and dry. Vishinsky shows himself as unyielding and decisive. Undoubtedly, he wrote the note himself.

Vishinsky's note was intended to lay to rest all assertions that Raoul Wallenberg was still alive, but it was also necessary, wherever possible, to eradicate the memory of Wallenberg as symbol of humanitarianism. A memorial statue in Budapest met the same fate as Wallenberg himself. After the war, his surviving Jewish protégés formed a Wallenberg Committee in Budapest to honor their rescuer. The famed Hungarian sculptor Pal Patzay, in gratitude to the Angel of Rescue for saving Patzay's friend, and fifteen others, from the cattle cars, undertook to create a monument. The monument took two years to complete. Standing six meters high, a bronze figure of Saint George fighting a serpent, symbolic of Wallenberg's successful fight against Nazism, topped a support. The support itself bore a relief of Wallenberg's face. Underneath a poetic text spoke of "silent and eternal gratitude to him," a reminder "of the eternally lasting humanity in an inhuman period."

The mayor of Budapest, the Wallenberg Committee, and representatives from the Swedish legation were invited to the unveiling ceremony in April, 1948, in Saint Stephen's Park. When the long-awaited day came, the invitees stared in shock. The monument had disappeared—as had Raoul Wallenberg. According to witnesses, the Russians had removed the monument during the night with ropes and horses. The support with the relief of Wallenberg and the inscription has never been found. The statue was located some years later in a Budapest cellar and put on a new support in front of a state factory for penicillin, in Debrecen. Now the statue is used to symbolize the triumph of medical science over disease. How ironic it is: Raoul Wallenberg never made it to Debrecen, but his statue did.

The years 1947-1950 brought no new information clarifying Raoul Wallenberg's status. Evidence began to accumulate in 1951, as political prisoners from Italy, Germany, and other countries gained release from six and seven years of Soviet imprisonment. Dr. Claudio de Mohr, an Italian cultural attaché in Bulgaria, was exchanged in 1951 for Communists in Italian jails. At a cocktail party in Rome, de Mohr told a Polish lady that he had had daily contact with Wallenberg by "knocking" at Lefortovo from April, 1945, until the beginning of 1948. Another former Italian diplomat, Giovanni Ronchi, issued a sworn statement that he had been in contact with Wallenberg at Lefortovo. A third diplomat Roland Gottlieb, a Swedish citizen who was the consul at the German embassy in Sofia before being captured by the Russians in 1944, had learned about Wallenberg's imprisonment from a coprisoner at Lefortovo at the end of 1947. General Moser testified that from Christmas, 1947 until the midsummer of 1948 Wallenberg was held in the same section of Lubianka as he. Georg Libik testified that a fellow Hungarian, Horvath, had informed him that in 1953 he had knocked with the Swede, who asked him to inform Stockholm about his imprisonment.

As the years have passed, concern for the fate of Langfelder has steadily dwindled. A Hungarian survivor pleaded to us: "Please don't forget Wilmos Langfelder. He was a faithful worker of Wallenberg. He has scarcely any family left to take up his cause. Remember that Langfelder played a role in helping his fellow Jews." Langfelder's fate has been tragically echoed by other instances in which the Communists have "punished" chauffeurs and bodyguards along with their bosses. In Hungary, for example, the chauffeurs of Foreign Minister Lászlo Rajk and Communist Party First Secretary János Kádár received long jail sentences after their bosses had been found "guilty."

But the Russians never changed their official line: Wallenberg had never been in Russia. To maintain their false claim, they isolated prisoners who knew Wallenberg and Langfelder from other inmates; however, the Russians failed to take into account the knocking system at Lefortovo.

On February 6, 1957, the Soviet government stunned the world diplomatic community. In an about-face, it admitted, by implication, that it had deceived the world for twelve years. In a memorandum to Ambassador Rolf Sohlman in Moscow, Deputy Foreign Minister Andrei Gromyko said, it is true that Wallenberg has been a prisoner in the USSR, but he is now dead! According to the note, an exhaustive investigation revealed a handwritten document dated July 17, 1947, and signed by Colonel A. L. Smoltsov, chief of the prison's medical department, in the archives of the medical department of Lubianka Prison. The document was addressed to State Security Minister Viktor Abakumov and read:

> I report that the prisoner Walenberg [sic], who is known to you, died suddenly in his cell last night probably as the result of a myocardial infarction [heart attack]. In connection with your instructions that I maintain personal supervision of Walenberg, I request instructions as to who shall make the postmortem examination to establish the cause of death.

Smoltsov's signature and date are followed by a handwritten notation: "Have personally informed the minister. Order has been given to cremate the corpse without postmortem examination." The Gromyko statement blamed Wallenberg's death on former State Security Chief Viktor Abakumov, who allegedly kept the Swede in jail and lied to the government about the case. The Supreme Court of the Soviet Union condemned and executed Abakumov in 1954 as a "tool of Beria" (Lavrenti Beria, minister of interior and chief of the secret police, was executed in 1953). The memorandum closed with an expression of "sincere regrets for what has happened" and "deep sympathy with the Swedish government and with Raoul Wallenberg's relatives."

The Gromyko memorandum was hardly convincing. All Soviet reports, including the petitions Wallenberg submitted to Russian officials, were gone, with the exception of the Smoltsov document. The persons who "protected" Wallenberg on the trip from Budapest to Moscow seem to have disappeared. Can anyone believe that Dekanosov and Vishinsky were unaware of Wallenberg's diplomatic status? Wallenberg allegedly died on July 17, 1947; yet his cellmates were interrogated ten days later and Vishinsky denied any knowledge of him in the following month. As for Abakumov, he was executed for complicity with Beria in the so-called Leningrad Affair, a purge in the Communist Party, and not for any involvement with Wallenberg. Moreover, at a time when Soviet prisoners died as a matter of course, the head of a prison medical department did not need permission to perform an autopsy. In addition, neither document mentions Wallenberg's chauffeur, Langfelder, and Wallenberg's name is misspelled, appearing with only one "l." As students of the Russian prison system know, the Soviets strive to be precise in their record keeping. Von Dardel sees this inaccuracy as a possible hope that in the future the Russians may reverse their position and claim that they had been referring to another prisoner (38).

However, Dr. von Dardel is not convinced of the importance of the misspelling.

I am not sure how much weight should be given to the fact that Wallenberg is spelled with one "l" in the famous death certificate note of 1947. It is true that names of foreign origin are usually transcribed letter for letter in the Russian alphabet. On the other hand, it should also be stated that the pronunciation of the name according to the Russian rules rather corresponds to the spelling with one "l."

The evidence of former prisoners, pinpointing Raoul Wallenberg as a prisoner still alive in the 1950s, still offers the best proof of the falsity of the Gromyko note. Their testimony indicated that Wallenberg had been transferred to the prison in Vladimir, one hundred twenty miles northeast of Moscow, and detained in an area called Corpus II. He spent part of this time in an isolation ward for the sick. A German prisoner, Mulle, in Vladimir in 1956, met a Georgian prisoner, Gogeberidse, who was well versed on the status of prominent prisoners. Gogeberidse told Mulle that Wallenberg had been isolated in the prison during 1948–53, although he was not certain whether Wallenberg was sick or just isolated. Another prisoner at Vladimir, Rehkampf, has given testimony whose main points are nearly identical with the report of Mulle.

A Swiss citizen, Brugger, who had been in Russian prisons from 1948–58, had "knocked" with Wallenberg while in Corpus II during the summer of 1954. According to Brugger, Wallenberg made him promise that if the Swiss were released he would go to the Swedish embassy or consulate and tell officials that Wallenberg was not permitted to write or receive letters. Brugger reported this conversation to a French Major Lucica Gouazé, who conveyed this information to the French embassy in Moscow after his release from prison in the spring of 1958.

Another account came from an Austrian prisoner who was released on condition that he become a Soviet agent. At the time of his release, he refused to meet this condition, and so his testimony was given anonymously. In a prison cell in Corpus II, he met Wallenberg who charged him to go to the Swedish embassy if he were released and tell the officials that he had met Wallenberg. If he forgot the name he should say that he had met "a Swede from Budapest." When a political officer discovered that the Austrian had been in Wallenberg's cell, he transferred the Austrian to another cell. The Austrian dated his meeting with Wallenberg around January or February, 1955. The credibility of the testimonies is enhanced by the fact that Brugger and the Austrian, as far as is known, had never communicated with each other.

In separate interviews with two former German prisoners, each swore that he had learned about Wallenberg's incarceration in Corpus II from a Soviet coprisoner on different occasions.

Throughout the 1950s Sweden continued to receive testimonies from persons returning from Soviet prisons. All indicated that Wallenberg had been transferred to Vladimir and confined to a hospital and isolation ward.

In 1960, fifteen years after his disappearance, the world community had good reason to believe that the Angel of Rescue was still alive, although perhaps languishing as a Russian political prisoner.

The Swedish government considered itself on top of the Wallenberg case: officials were questioning former Russian prisoners to determine Wallenberg's status. But was Sweden doing enough to free him, or was the world idly standing by while a hero wasted away in the Gulag?

9

A Victim of Swedish Neutrality

"Nobody cares about you."

With a sneer in his voice, one of Raoul Wallenberg's inquisitors told the Swede that the world had turned its back on the Angel of Rescue. His homeland had no interest in his fate.

Nothing was further from the truth! Sweden continually communicated with Russia from the time Wallenberg disappeared. In 1957 Sweden published a White Book about the Wallenberg case. The eighty dossiers contain, among other things, most of the official correspondence between the Swedish and Soviet governments in the Wallenberg case. The file has more than seven thousand documents today, Sweden's largest file on any one person.

The Swedish White Papers on the Wallenberg case reveal that the government had been concerned with the protection of its diplomats in Hungary before the abduction of Wallenberg. During 1944, Stockholm had told Moscow the names of the staff of the Swedish legation in Budapest and asked the Russian military leaders to ensure proper protection for those officials.

However, Palmstierna has told the writer about reports that Wallenberg's passport had expired in December, 1944. "If that were true, how can one excuse such negligence? The Russians would never recognize such a passport."

Palmstierna also criticized the inaction of Danielsson. "On the way back to Sweden, Danielsson went via Russia. Why didn't he ask about the welfare of his Legation associates, especially Wallenberg?"

But the attitude of Valdemar Langlet and his wife, Nina, coworkers of Wallenberg in Budapest, remained Palmstierna's biggest "disappointment."

In his book *Verk och Dagar i Budapest,* Dr. Langlet is critical of Wallenberg's methods, Palmstierna noted. "One may assume that there was a certain degree of jealousy involved. After all, the Langlets were doing a very commendable job in aiding victims of Nazi persecution, and then this young Wallenberg comes to Budapest, and their humanitarian activities become overshadowed. More than this, one must be aware that Mrs. Langlet was a Russian. Perhaps this is the reason they tried to convince people that Wallenberg died in Hungary."

Palmstierna pointed out that Mrs. Langlet was a close friend of Queen Louise, who was very unsympathetic to the plight of Wallenberg. "It is very strange that Mrs. Langlet was recently on television in connection with the commemoration of the Holocaust, and she never once mentioned Raoul Wallenberg."

Despite the personal criticisms of parties intimately concerned with the rescue mission, the Raoul Wallenberg affair teaches us one thing: a government's "neutral mentality" can be woefully ineffective. While one can sympathize with Sweden's determination to remain a neutral nation, and while the "weak" actions of Sweden have been preferable to no action at all, one must say with sorrow that a more aggressive approach could conceivably have led to Raoul Wallenberg's freedom.

If Raoul Wallenberg had been "neutral" and less militant in his approach, the outcome for the Jewish community of Budapest would have been dismal.

In the beginning Sweden kept a low-keyed approach, not only because it considered itself a neutral country, but also because it hoped that Wallenberg would be released in good time. After all, his colleagues in Budapest had come home. Moreover, Mme. Kollontay, the Soviet ambassador to Sweden, had hinted that prudent diplomacy was advisable. A cousin of Wallenberg, Gösta Nisser, was told by a Swedish citizen, Mrs. Ström Salveotti, that a member of the Soviet embassy in Stockholm had related: "Raoul Wallenberg lives and is well. He is not directly arrested but must be kept since he had committed some faults after the liberation."

Statements in the Swedish press that Wallenberg had been murdered before arriving in Russia complicated efforts to obtain Wallenberg from the Russians. On November 27, 1945, newspaper correspondent Emil Langlet reported in the newspaper *Stockholmstidningen* that if a Russian officer had accompanied Wallenberg on January 17, it is a likely possibility that Nazi sympathizers in the vicinity of Cegled had attacked the car and murdered both the Russian and Wallenberg. In interviews with the Swedish press, Vilmos Böhm, the former Hungarian ambassador to Sweden, declared that objects had been found that belonged to the Russian officers who had escorted Wallenberg. The Hungarian diplomat concluded that Wallenberg and the Russian officers had been murdered on their way to Debrecen.

Although these reports were transmitted through Hungarian and Swedish sources, they played into the hands of the Russians, who did not admit to Wallenberg's being in their country.

A Swedish Foreign Ministry official assigned to the Wallenberg case wished to remain anonymous in describing the Swedish government's attitude in 1945: "The government's interest centered on Anger and Berg. No one knew what had happened to them. The government felt that Wallenberg was safe because the Russians had told us that he was under their protection. What reason was there to worry. After all, even the Nazis respected diplomatic immunity."

The 1946 publication of Rudolph Philipp's book, *Raoul Wallenberg: Diplomat, Kampe, Samarit (Raoul Wallenberg: Diplomat, Fighter, Samaritan)*, spurred both the Swedish government and citizen groups to actively work for the release of Wallenberg. According to Nina Lagergren, Philipp "had an enormous passion for the truth, for liberty, for justice, and for democracy." The Austrian-born author who had spent some time in Russia compiled an exhaustive account of Wallenberg: his life, his heroic achievements, and his disappearance. He based his work on interviews with the Wallenberg family, with Wallenberg's coworkers, persons saved by Wallenberg, and an examination of appropriate documents. Dr. Paul Hegedus, Wallenberg's coworker who moved to Prague after the war, also generated greater interest in the case. According to the dedicated Dr. Guy von Dardel, Hegedus went to Hungary to gather information on Wallenberg "although warned that he and his relatives risked their lives." He presented his findings to the Swedish government. In 1947 Anders Örne chaired a special committee to look into Rudolph Philipp's findings; it agreed that his conclusion that Wallenberg was imprisoned in the Soviet Union had solid basis. The same year Wallenberg Action, a coalition of thirty national organizations representing 1,600,000 Swedes, petitioned the USSR on behalf of the Angel of Rescue. There was no response to the petition.

Although there were doubts about the success of these efforts, a commitment had been made to conduct a relentless campaign. Dr. von Dardel crystallized these sentiments in an April 9, 1947, letter to the American Jewish Joint Distribution Committee:

Whether all these mutual efforts and expenses will succeed to give Raoul Wallenberg back to his country and his family, back to normal life, back to the honor and estimation which he deserves, we do not know. But as long as we know or hope that he is alive and can be saved, we can not spare any trouble or work or grudge any expenses which have the slightest prospect of success and we are not going to let any failure or other difficulty change our determination.

But had the Swedish government done enough? Had it acted wisely? At the time of the Vishinsky note, Sweden had contacted Russia at least twenty times but never received a clarification of Wallenberg's status. However,

Sweden was timid in its approach. The reason why Wallenberg had not been returned, Dr. von Dardel said in the 1947 letter, was "due to the fact that Sweden is a small country which is very much afraid of its neighbor." Ambassador Söderblom did gain a private audience with Stalin, but the meeting was ill fated. As the Swedish press recently pointed out, it seemed more of an opportunity for the ambassador to make an impression upon the Russian dictator. One can feel the ambassador's sense of "achievement" as he noted in his report that although the Russian rarely receives ambassadors, he was amiable and respectful toward him.

Stalin began the conversation by telling Söderblom, "You know that we ordered the Swedes to be protected." In response, Söderblom not only made no attempt to "deal" or negotiate the matter, but he told Stalin, "I personally believe that Wallenberg was the victim of an accident or robbers in Budapest." Taking note of Söderblom's attitude, Stalin jotted down Wallenberg's name on a piece of paper and promised his further attention to the matter. Of course, that was the end of that. In a recent television interview, Sweden's former prime minister, Tage Erlander, said that the Söderblom meeting with Stalin was unfortunate, and that Soviet officials who might have acted felt restrained, because Stalin had already involved himself in the case.

The Swedish press and those involved in the effort to free Raoul Wallenberg have been especially censorious of Söderblom. He has been accused of seeking accommodation with the Soviets at the expense of recovering a fellow Swedish diplomat. The editor of *Expressen,* Sweden's largest circulation paper, has called Söderblom a victim of *ryssräck,* or fear of Russia. *Ryssräck* is not to be taken lightly in a country where children are warned to act properly or "the Russians will get you!" After 1945 *ryssräck* was associated with Sweden's position of neutrality in the war while millions of her Russian neighbors died.

An awareness of *ryssräck* does not resolve the question of Swedish-Soviet relations. Historical developments and attitudes through the centuries have shaped relations between the countries and are important in trying to formulate intelligent theories about the Wallenberg case. At this point it is necessary to be conversant with the centuries-old Swedish policy of neutrality.

Those Foreign Ministry officials who displayed a nonaggressive approach in the Wallenberg case were, to some extent, carrying out what they saw as Sweden's historical role as neutral. The uninterrupted tradition of Swedish neutrality can be dated from the end of the Napoleonic wars when Jean Louis Bernadotte, a talented marshal of Napoleon, became Sweden's crown prince. In his book *Sweden's Foreign Policy* Abrahamson cites 1809 as the year Sweden changed its direction. Czar Alexander I compelled Sweden to cede Finland and the Swedish-speaking islands of Åland, which had been in Swedish hands for centuries. The policy of neutrality has remained unchanged through the remainder of the nineteenth century, through both World Wars, and through the postwar period.

Beyond the desire to keep away from confrontations of the big powers, Swedish leaders see the policy of neutrality as affording Sweden the invaluable privilege and power of acting as international mediator, of serving justice and freedom, and of advocating the cause of tolerance and high ideals. Foreign Minister Östen Undén, a key figure in the Wallenberg story, firmly believed that neutrality was as valid after World War II as the policy had been in the nineteenth century. Undén stressed that the policy had worked well during both wars, ensuring that Sweden remained free and independent. In a full report to the Riksdag in 1949, Undén outlined the virtues of neutrality:

"A common misunderstanding is also that a policy of neutrality means an obligation to maintain spiritual neutrality . . . . Neutrality in the political sense and in the meaning of international law implies by no means that a nation renounces the right of its citizens to take sides in the debates on international problems or the right to plead the case of international democracy and freedom."

Is not the case of Raoul Wallenberg worthy of being pleaded in the international arena by Sweden? While Swedish officials do not deny the moral importance of the Wallenberg case and while the policy of neutrality does not exclude governmental activity to protect the diplomatic immunity of a member of its legation, the neighboring presence of the Soviets has obviously been a deterrent for Undén and others who have performed timidly in the Wallenberg case.

Dr. von Dardel commented on the weak-kneed attitude of Sweden during 1945-47 in a January 25, 1980, interview in the *Jerusalem Post*:

My government was not always forceful enough during the first years of Raoul's disappearance, 1945 to 1947—particularly on one occasion when against their will we handed back to the Russians over 150 soldiers belonging to the Baltic nations who had served in the German army. There was a scandal over that at the time. We could have pressed for an exchange with Raoul then.

The timidity of the Swedish government has been contrasted with the bold initiative of the neutral Swiss. At the war's end, Swiss diplomats, including Harald Feller, secretary of the legation in Budapest, were taken away and interned by the Russians. The Swiss quickly retaliated by seizing Russian diplomats at the Berne embassy. The matter was resolved with an exchange of the diplomats. "One had to admire the action of the Swiss," Palmstierna said. "They acted quickly and with much care. The names of those they took hostage were never revealed. In such situation, both action and silence are important. Unfortunately, all Sweden showed was silence."

Some sharp criticism was also directed at Stockholm's actions by Per Anger, who has played a major role in the efforts to free his Budapest colleague. His book on the Hungarian mission and its aftermath was published after his retirement service, enabling him to be more candid in his appraisal of the government's actions. His comments deal with the government's activities during the first years of Wallenberg's disappearance and relate to a meeting of the Wallenberg Action:

> But when time passed and nothing happened, it would have been natural for the new Social Democratic government, which had come in during the summer, to take more forceful action.
>
> It seems as though the new government soon came to feel that the Wallenberg matter was unpleasant, an especially disturbing factor in our relation with the Soviets. One almost gets the impression that Foreign Minister Undén willingly accepted Vishinsky's answer that Wallenberg was not on Russian territory . . . . In Undén's view, which was supported by Vishinsky's words, Wallenberg could have been killed in connection with the final struggle, for Budapest. When . . . Guy von Dardel reported that evidence existed that Wallenberg was alive in a Russian prison, Undén wondered what reason the Russians would have for locking him up. Mrs. Birgitta de Wylder-Bellander, who was then the prime mover in the so-called Wallenberg Action, answered that the Russians seem to have suspected Wallenberg of being a spy. Undén then put the question that gave him away: "Mrs. Bellander, do you think Vishinsky is lying?" The answer was affirmative. "But this is terrible, this is terrible!" Undén burst out. Yet Mrs. Bellander was right (139–40).

One wonders at Undén's naivete—if that be the correct word—since Vishinsky had achieved world notoriety as the prosecutor during the bloody Stalin purges of the 1930s.

The Vishinsky note did not mollify an already agitated Swedish public. Further investigation was demanded by the press and members of the Riksdag.

The Russians were contemptuous of such efforts. On January 21, 1948, an article appeared in *New Times,* the Soviet semiofficial weekly of international affairs. The biting article is the only lengthy treatment ever given Wallenberg in the Soviet press. Entitled "The Wallenberg Legend" in a column known as "Spotlight on Slander," the article got to the heart of the matter in the first sentence:

> A new campaign of slander against the Soviet Union has been unleashed in Sweden. Delving into the rubbish heap of anti-Soviet fabrications, the servitors of Swedish and foreign reaction have dragged out and revived the so-called Wallenberg affair.

The article then rebukes the responsible parties:

> Fables about the "Soviet secret police," which is allegedly holding Wallenberg in its fearsome clutches were persistently disseminated by the press. It is interesting to note that the circulation of these absurd inventions in print coincided

with a visit to the United States of Wallenberg's step-brother, an engineer named von Dardel.

Behind this anti-Soviet propaganda, the article concluded, was the ulterior motive of poisoning Russian-Swedish relations:

> It is obvious that the people who circulate vicious fabrication about Wallenberg are least of all interested in his fate. The whole affair is utilized as a pretext for anti-Soviet provocation by those Swedish circles that cannot reconcile themselves to the development of friendly relations between the Soviet Union and Sweden and are doing their utmost to damage these relations. The Soviet public views such provocatory endeavours with profound indignation and hopes that Swedish democratic circles will draw the correct conclusions, giving a merited rebuff to the despicable activities of the Swedish "step-brothers" of the American warmongers.

To keep the Wallenberg case alive, three deputies of the Swedish Riksdag, Bertil von Friesen, Ture Nerman, and Vilhelm Lundstedt, nominated the Swede to the Nobel Committee of the Norwegian Storting for the Peace Prize of 1948. The Swedish legislators pointed out that Wallenberg, like Fridtjof Nansen, the Nobel laureate of 1923, had contributed to alleviating the horrors of war and eliminating hate between peoples, at continual risk to his life. In its article, *New Times* scornfully took note of this proposal:

> The people who have fabricated the "Wallenberg affair" stop at nothing in their choice of means . . . . Three Riksdag deputies—Friesen, Ture Nerman, and V. Lundstedt—turned to the Nobel Committee of the Norwegian Storting with the suggestion that the Nobel Peace Prize for 1948 be awarded to Wallenberg.

Anger was assigned to the Wallenberg case during 1949–50. He was constantly frustrated by Undén's refusal to accept the fact that his former colleague was in Russian hands. Proposals to help bring Wallenberg out of captivity went unheeded at the highest government levels. One day Svén Dahlman, who headed the political section, assured Anger that he would get the opportunity to confront Undén. Anger told the prime minister that he was convinced that Wallenberg was in Russian hands, and "the only language the Russians understand in a situation such as this is: meet force with force, or offer something in exchange." Sweden was in a favorable position for barter, because during trade negotiations in 1946, Sweden had given the Russians a billion dollars in credit without getting anything in return. Sweden had also had some spy cases that implicated Russian citizens. Anger thought it a natural and morally proper thing to exchange the spies for Wallenberg, instead of merely kicking the Russians out of the country.

Anger got a sharp rebuff from the prime minister. "The Swedish government does not do such things," Undén responded and put an end to Anger's hopes. Given the prime minister's intractable stance, Anger could no longer act as government spokesman to the Wallenberg Committee, whose plans were more in line with his own. Consequently, Anger resigned after two years on the Wallenberg case (140-142).

The way the Swedish government handled information reported by Edward Sandeberg well illustrates its stagnation. A Swedish journalist covering the war scene in Berlin, Sandeberg was the only correspondent from a neutral country to remain after the Russians entered the country. He was arrested on June 13, 1945, and was put in Butyrka Prison, where his cellmate was Eduard Hille, a former cellmate of Langfelder. Hille asked the Swede whether he knew Wallenberg. Having been away from Sweden for several years, Sandeberg did not know Raoul Wallenberg or the story of his disappearance. Upon his release in April, 1946, Sandeberg met other released prisoners from foreign countries who said they had seen Wallenberg while they were in prison.

Now retired and still living in Stockholm, Sandeberg recalled that the Foreign Ministry had contacted him following his return home. "I told the ministry that I had never heard of Wallenberg. I had forgotten. The experience of a Russian prison, with its inadequate food and harsh conditions, tends to weaken you and brings on a weakening of the memory." However, Sandeberg remembered shortly afterward. "When I told the government that Wallenberg had been imprisoned by the Russians, I was told: 'It was pure fantasy.'" For five years, the Swedish government failed to act on Sandeberg's report, the first account that Raoul Wallenberg had been brought to Russia. Sandeberg reflected, "If the government had acted at once, the Raoul Wallenberg case might have turned out differently."

Not only did the Swedish government refuse to act vigorously and creatively, but when given the opportunity it averted situations that might cause contention with the Russians. After returning to Stockholm, Berg left governmental service for a while and wrote about his experiences in Budapest under the title *Vad Hände i Budapest*. Many pages are severely critical of the Russians and their suspicions of Wallenberg. "Several thousand books were published," Berg said, "but they all seemed to disappear quickly in Sweden, to the point where it became very difficult to find a copy."

The Swedish government's reluctance to aggressively pursue the Wallenberg case affected other worldwide attempts to bring back the Angel of Rescue. Mrs. Bellander of the Wallenberg Committee had written to the secretary-general of the United Nations in 1948, and asked him to intervene in the matter. William H. Stoneman, special advisor to the secretary-general, responded:

I have been asked by the Secretary-General to reply to your letter . . . referring to the case of Mr. Raoul Wallenberg. After making enquiries he has found that in view of the very clear and definite reply made to the Swedish

authorities by Mr. Vyshinsky, it would serve no good purpose for him to intervene personally in the question.

While the government showed little initiative, individuals explored all
leads and contacts to free Wallenberg. Karl Ivan Westman, the Swedish
minister in Paris, had made contact with Dr. A. Coen, a Polish diplomat
before the Nazi occupation. In his letter of July 22, 1947, Coen locates
Wallenberg in Lwów, offers the reason for his imprisonment, and puts
forth a plan to force Russia to admit his imprisonment and eventually to
release him:

> I am sorry I have nothing to add to our last conversation. However, knowing
> the Communist system and ways of dealing, I have reason to believe that my
> advice could be instrumental in securing the release of Mr. R. W. From the
> various conversations I had with Mr. R. W., I have come to the conclusion
> that the only reason for which the NKVD (formerly the GPU) is still keeping
> him is that they took a large amount of money from him during his imprison-
> ment, as well as jewelry which had been given to him by some friends, for
> safety's sake . . . . The only way to prove the fact that Mr. R. W. is impris-
> oned in Lwów would be for you to arrange to send somebody from your Lega-
> tion in Moscow — an employee or a newspaperman . . . . Once in Lwów he
> might get sick, pro forma, and interrupt his journey for one day and go with a
> parcel of laundry for Mr. R. W. to the prison. Laundry parcels are usually
> accepted even for strictly isolated prisoners. The dirty laundry is taken from
> the prisoner and returned with receipt. Having such an irrefutable evidence in
> his own handwriting, the Russian authorities will then be helpless and confirm
> his existence in prison in Lwów. It may be that they will force him to sign a
> false statement to the effect that he had Fascist money in his possession and
> was collaborating with the Fascists. However, one will be able to prove that
> they violated international law by arresting someone of the diplomatic service.

A report by Stig Engfeld, a bureau director in the Foreign Ministry,
dated April 29, 1949, and entitled "Concerning the Search for Wallenberg,"
highlights the intrigue involved in the case. The report points out that Engfeld involved himself in the search "privately" at his "own risk and expense."
The key person discussed in the report is "Mr. B.," who eventually is revealed
as an impostor and a Russian spy. Excerpts of this fascinating report follow, dealing with events in the spring of 1948:

> With two sets of clothes and a sum of money, B. went to the jail in East Slo-
> vakia, where he had seen Wallenberg, in the city of Poprad. He expected to
> come back shortly, together with Wallenberg . . . . I met with B., who was
> very tired and said that he was forced to return without success. Wallenberg
> had been moved to another jail in Ilava in Slovakia, between Bratislava and
> Zilina . . . . We left the same day with the car from Prague to Bratislava. My
> wife came to help me but also to make us look like tourists . . . . Next day we

continued the trip past Ilava, where B. got off to investigate the situation. I stayed in Zilina, where B. arrived in the evening by car together with some less trustworthy types, whom I never came in contact with. B.'s companions were personnel from the jail whom B. had befriended. B. needed two nights to prepare an escape for Wallenberg if it could be confirmed that he was among the prisoners. So as not to draw attention from the police, I took a two-day round trip and returned April 25 to Bratislava, where I was to meet B. to make the necessary plans.

According to Ukrainian partisans, Wallenberg was again in jail in Poprad. B. had lied to the personnel of the jail in saying that he was on a secret mission for the Americans, who wanted to use the Ukrainians for underground activity in Russia. He asked the jail personnel whom he befriended to help free Wallenberg. He promised to give them travel permits to America. This action needed two to three additional days in which to get a car and to make sure the proper jail keeper would be on duty. The turn of events made us feel uncomfortable and uncertain. From the beginning, B. had been counting on doing it alone, with only the affidavit from NKVD that gave him the right to take some prisoners from jail and transport them to the Prague. Since he had already used his papers on the trip to Poland, he was afraid to use them one more time.

During our meeting in Bratislava that evening, we felt very uneasy since the hotel my wife and I checked into was being watched. We agreed that we should return to Prague and continue our actions from there. Not wanting to take unnecessary risks, we left that same night for Prague. During our night trip we found out that we had some new problems. B. told us that he was forced to show that his actions were legitimate by promising the five jail wardens $100 each before the action to free Wallenberg took place.

I decided to continue at my own risk and spoke with B. about ways to get the needed money. I went with B. to five or six different addresses in the city, where he collected money. Since he could only obtain half of the needed money, I gave him the rest.

It was decided that B. and my wife should go to a city in Mahren on the border of Slovakia, from where B. would travel to Ilava for the release of Wallenberg. After the release we were supposed to meet B., who had a special plan to get rid of the helpers. That afternoon I went to Bratislava by plane and was met by my wife. We went to a prearranged meeting place, but nothing happened.

I met with B. again later, but it is unnecessary to go into detail about these meetings. B. told an unbelievable story. The release succeeded, but he could not get rid of his helpers. They were suspicious of Wallenberg, guarded him the whole time, and took him to a place close to Prague. The helpers disputed among themselves. Some of them had relatives in Slovakia who were accused of spying. They wanted to make use of Wallenberg to free their relatives.

As has been stated, there is no doubt that B. is an impostor and that he was in the service of NKVD. He had no morals, was insolent and naive, and did whatever he liked.

Obviously, the efforts of government officials working on their own could not succeed if the official government policy was working in an opposite direction. Anger has called the period after the war the "lost years," a time in which Sweden missed the opportunity to get Wallenberg back. According to Anger, one gets the feeling that even the Russians expected Stockholm to offer some proposal for the exchange of Wallenberg.

The appointment of Arne Lundberg in 1951 as undersecretary for foreign affairs seemed to mark an upward turn in the Wallenberg case. Lundberg was an energetic and skillful diplomat who was determined to find out the truth about the missing hero. The interrogation of returning prisoners from the USSR was resumed with rigor. For the first time since 1947, a Swedish representation was made to the Soviets. However, the Russian "answer" of April 16, 1952, was a six-line reference to the Vishinsky note of 1947. A similar response was given August 5, 1953, by Soviet Ambassador K. K. Rodionov.

While the Swedish government was making its diplomatic approaches, Swedish citizens were showing that they cared about Raoul Wallenberg. A petition signed by 1.6 million Swedes was sent to Stalin, requesting him to return the Angel of Rescue to Stockholm. In November, 1952, King Gustav VI Adolf of Sweden awarded Raoul Wallenberg the Illis Quorum decoration "for his humanitarian work in Budapest in 1944 and 1945." Clearly it was not a posthumous award, since the Foreign Ministry believed that Wallenberg was still alive.

In June, 1954, Foreign Minister Undén made a private nine-day visit to Russia to discuss the Wallenberg case with Soviet authorities, but was unsuccessful in his efforts.

Undén's attitude seems somewhat perplexing. Although the minister journeyed to Russia to bring up the Wallenberg case, he seemed determined not to do anything that would upset the Russians. In his memoirs Carl-Fredrik Palmstierna directs attention to Undén's ideological leanings. Formerly a Marxist professor of law, Undén "followed with benevolent interest the great socialist experiment in Russia and allowed nothing to interfere with Sweden's friendly relations with the Soviets." Gromyko, then Soviet vice minister of foreign affairs, realized Undén's pivotal role in Swedish affairs during his visit to Stockholm, in which Gromyko had a private audience with the king of Sweden. Palmstierna saw this as the perfect opportunity to bring up the Wallenberg affair, and he describes the result in his memoirs, *The Feather in My Hand*:

> But my optimism had been premature. In a quarter of an hour His Majesty returned, declaring that, having pondered the suggestion, he thought he had better talk to Undén before seeing Gromyko. The disappointment was great: the issue of the conversation was only too easy to guess.

Indeed, it was easy to guess how Undén would respond. In the early fifties Ulf Brack-Holst, a Swedish chargé d'affaires, had reported that the Soviets were interested in reclaiming certain persons in Sweden. Stockholm again had the opportunity of trading for Wallenberg; however, Undén let the opportunity pass and meekly returned the persons to Moscow, except for five who were seriously ill. Sweden got absolutely nothing in the transaction.

Palmstierna is not convinced, however, that Undén was responsible for the king's lack of initiative. Even if the king had gained nothing, it would have been worthwhile for the ruler personally to have raised the matter with Gromyko: "If . . . the King had overcome himself and spoken to the Russian Foreign Minister, he would, anyhow, have felt satisfaction in knowing that he at least—in his position—had done something." Then who is to blame? Palmstierna accuses the queen, who had become convinced that the attack on the Russians was motivated by writer Rudolf Philipp's desire to reap financial gains from the Wallenberg family.

> It may be indiscreet, but in the name of historical truth the person who saw to it that the King should not take any personal initiative in this matter was Queen Louise. I do not know what persons could have persuaded her to believe that the Austrian Rudolf Philipp . . . who had devoted years of research in order to reveal the Russian lies was using the Raoul Wallenberg case as "a means of living" (at the expense of the latter's family).

The spring of 1956 was a propitious period for the Swedish government to launch new efforts for the return of Wallenberg. Stalin had been dead since 1953 and the Soviets sought improved relations with the Scandinavian countries. A Swedish government delegation made an official visit to the USSR. During the talks with Prime Minister Nikita Khrushchev and other top officials, Swedish Prime Minister Tage Erlander presented the Soviet authorities with the material compiled by the Foreign Ministry on the Wallenberg case. In order to facilitate improved Russian-Swedish relations, the Soviets consented to review the Wallenberg case. On April 3, 1956, a joint communiqué was issued and published as a front-page story on April 4 in *Pravda*. This was only the second time that Wallenberg's name appeared in the Soviet press. The following paragraph was included in the communiqué:

> The Swedish Ministers had stressed the great importance attached by them to the fate of Mr. Raoul Wallenberg. The Swedish Ministers had handed to the Soviet side the material collected concerning Mr. Wallenberg with the request that the Soviet authorities should study and examine it, to which the Soviet Ministers had agreed. It had also been agreed that if Mr. Wallenberg was still alive in the Soviet Union he would be permitted to return, and that the results of the Soviet investigation would be notified to the Swedish Government through diplomatic channels.

Also during the spring of 1956, an effort was made for the intervention of Dag Hammarskjöld, the Swede who in 1953 had been named secretary-general of the United Nations. Hammarskjöld was scheduled to make his first visit to Moscow in June. The Wallenberg Committee asked Palmstierna to approach the king with a suggestion that he ask Hammarskjöld to raise the Wallenberg case with the Soviets. The king asked his secretary to discuss the proposal with the secretary-general but to omit any mention of the king. Palmstierna was unaware of the secretary-general's previous remarks on the case. On the very day he was named to the U.N. post, he had promised that if Swedish representations proved fruitless, he himself would work "heart and soul" for the release of Wallenberg. However, Palmstierna writes that he was also unaware of the secretary-general's response to an appeal of the Wallenberg Committee in 1955. Hammarskjöld said that "officially he was unable to interfere unless he had been formerly charged to do so by the U.N.—a measure which he, however, would not recommend." To his regret, Palmstierna discovered Hammarskjöld's attitude for himself: "The fact that he himself was a Swede made it doubly difficult for him to put the case of a compatriot to the Russians. If matters had been different, he would of course . . . ." The king's secretary was unconvinced and bitter about the response:

I wondered, however, in my heart of hearts how the matter could have been different. If Hammarskjöld had assumed the case of a non-Swedish citizen, he would probably have been snubbed by an answer that as Secretary-General to the United Nations, he had no right to meddle with internal questions in other countries! The indifference of H. did not surprise me. Again the Foreign Office spirit! Of course, there was no question of "declaring war on Russia for the sake of Wallenberg," as he repeated on a later occasion, quoting Undén. But was it not to be feared that the Russians would consider such lack of official interest in one of our own people, this anxiety to avoid anything which might be unpleasant, as a touchstone of Swedish weakness?

Another futile attempt to have Hammarskjöld intervene was made in 1959 when Khrushchev came to New York. The response was short and dispiriting: "An intervention would be of no avail before the end of the 'Swedish-Russian exchanges of opinion.'"

It took the Russians ten months to respond in "fulfillment" of their promises, and even that answer came after Sweden had sent pointed notes and reminders to the Russians. After having "studied and examined" the Swedish material given them by Erlander, the Soviets issued the Gromyko memorandum of February 6, 1957.

As previously mentioned, the memorandum admitted that Wallenberg had been kept prisoner in the USSR until his death on July 16, 1947. An "exhaustive investigation" had only revealed a handwritten note addressed to State Security Chief Viktor Abakumov, dated July 17, 1947, and signed by Colonel A. L. Smoltsov, chief of the Lubianka Prison medical department. The document reported that Wallenberg died suddenly in his cell the

Newly arrived women prisoners from Hungary, their heads shaved, at Auschwitz. (Courtesy: Yad Vashem.)

Wallenberg commemorative monument; original design by Pal Patzay.

Stripped of plaque and support by the Soviets, original sculpture stands in Debrecen.

Hungarian woman and her children walk to their death in Auschwitz. (Courtesy: Yad Vashem.)

A Budapest street named in honor of Wallenberg.

Battered Budapest.

Lubianka Prison in Moscow. Wallenberg's first stop in the Gulag.

Nyilas in pursuit of Wallenberg outside the Swedish legation, January, 1945. (Courtesy: Per Anger, *Med Raoul Wallenberg i Budapest.)*

Adolf Eichmann.

May von Dardel and Raoul Wallenberg.

White House signing of bill granting Wallenberg honorary U.S. citizenship. From left to right, Nina Lagergren, Congressman Lantos, President Reagan, and Dr. Guy von Dardel.

Raoul Wallenberg, 1935.

O L T A L O M L E V É L.

A Római Szentszék Apostoli Követe igazolja, hogy
Spitzer Gábor László, született Budapesten 1944 janu-
ár 1.-én, anyja Dr Szekeres Hedvig, lakik Budapest VII.,
István ut 17.sz., a Budapesti Apostoli Nunciatura /Pá-
pai Követség/ védelme alatt áll.

Budapesten, 1944 november. 5..

Nunzio Apostolico.

The Apostolic Nunciatura   No.1772/44

S A F E   C O N D U C T

        The Apostolic Nuncio of the Holy See at Rome
attests that Gábor László Spitzer was born in Budapest
on January 1-st 1944, his mother is Dr.Hedvig Szekeres,
he resides at 17 István Road Budapest VII., He is under
the protection of the Apostolic Nunciatura (Papal Embassy)
at Budapest.

Budapest, November 5,1944   Signature of
                                         Angelo Rotta
                                         Apostolic Nuncio

                        Round Seal
                          affixed

Papal safe-conduct pass, in Hungarian and in English translation. (Courtesy: Tibor Baranskic.)

Red Army advancing into Budapest.

Raoul Wallenberg in Budapest.

M. kir. rendőrség sárvári Kisegitő Tolonchása

........13.24........./944

M. kir. Rendőrkapitányságnak

Főszolgabirói Hivatalának

.....rt sitem, hogy ...7.233.....944 ... számu véghatározattal intern-
nált 1.439 évbeli születésű ...Treitel Rachele..............
zsidót, kine anyja Landmann Hale............1944 julius hó ..4. a,
átadta ....tor ..nek németországi munkára.
Sárvár, ...44 ... julius hó 1 . ...ddén.

A tolonchás vezetője:

m. kir. rendőrfőfelügyelő.

139

Deportation of Hungarian Jews for forced labor was never concerned with age. **Top**—deportation order for Rachele Treitel, age 10; **Bottom**—deportation order for Abrahamne Szerebrenik, age 74.

M.kir.rendőrség sárvári Kisegitő Tolonchása.

1.224....../944.

M.kir.Rendőrkapitányságnak

Főszolgabirói Hivatalának.

Értesitem,hogy..7.233......1944.számu véghatározattal internált
..1879..évbeli születésű Szerbrenik Abrahamné.....zsidót,kinek
anyja Koruj Johanna ......1944 julius hó ..4..in átadtam a német
katonaságnak németországi munkára.

Sárvár,1944 julius hó 14-in

A tolonchás vezetője:

m.kir.rendőrfőfelügyelő.

141

night before and asked who should do the autopsy. Following Smoltsov's signature was a further handwritten notation: "Have personally notified the minister. Order has been given to cremate the corpse without postmortem examination." This evidence alleged that former State Security Chief Viktor Abakumov was to blame for keeping Wallenberg in jail and lying to the Soviet government about it. Unfortunately, Mr. Abakumov had been executed for his crimes in 1954 and thus could shed no light on any possible motives for his actions. Gromyko expressed his "sincere regrets for what has happened" and "deep sympathy with the Swedish government and with Raoul Wallenberg's family."

Compared to the Swedish response to the Vishinsky note—which was practically nil—the government's reaction to the Gromyko memorandum at least showed that Stockholm was not prepared to accept Moscow's word without further proof. In a special declaration on February 7, 1957, Sweden expressed its displeasure that there was so little available information on Wallenberg and it hoped that Russia would present more evidence: "It must be deeply regretted that the answer contains such short information. Nothing is said about the reasons why Raoul Wallenberg was imprisoned or about his fate during those years." Lundberg, secretary-general of the Foreign Ministry, in a speech prepared for the radio, declared the government's intention of finding out the truth: "Since the Russian materials are incomplete, it is reasonable to assume that the conclusion based on the materials are uncertain. For the Swedish Foreign Ministry it will therefore be necessary even in the future to investigate all clues in the Wallenberg case."

The official Swedish answer to the Gromyko memorandum was delivered by Ambassador Sohlman on February 19. For the mild-mannered government, the remarks certainly pulled no punches:

> If the Soviet security police was able to act in such an autocratic manner as to make a diplomat of a neutral country a prisoner and to keep him in prison for two and a half years without reporting it to the Soviet Government or the Foreign Ministry, this is in itself a situation for which the Soviet Government cannot disclaim responsibility.
>
> Expressing its regrets, the Soviet Government has admitted its responsibility. To this is added the fact that, while Wallenberg was confined in a Moscow prison, the Soviets cannot, considering the numerous Swedish appeals, have been unable to obtain reliable information in the matter, if they had really undertaken the thorough investigations which they repeatedly assured the Swedish Government that they had made.

The Swedish response also reminded the Russians of the many representations by Stockholm, including one by Sohlman a day before the reported death of Wallenberg. With this in mind, the note continues, "The Swedish Government finds it difficult to believe that all other documentation regarding Wallenberg's stay in Soviet prisons, except the report mentioned in the

Soviet Memorandum, should have been completely obliterated." The Swedish government, the note goes on, has the right to pursue its investigation of the case and calls upon Moscow to look further into the matter and give fuller information to Stockholm.

The Swedish government did not stop in its representations to the Russians. On February 9, 1959, the Swedish Foreign Office informed the Russians that it had testimonies from former prisoners in Russia that indicated that Wallenberg had been transferred after 1947 to a prison in Vladimir, where he was in a prison and isolation ward. Sweden asked Russia to determine whether Wallenberg was in the Vladimir prison.

The Soviet Foreign Office responded on March 6. The note firmly declared that the Gromyko memorandum of 1957 was conclusive: Wallenberg had died in July, 1947. Moreover, a new investigation had not changed the veracity of that memorandum.

However, the Soviets were still nettled by Sweden's continued interrogation of former Russian prisoners. Ambassador Rodionov, now with the Soviet Foreign Office, told Swedish Ambassador Sohlman that the Russians were concerned about the articles in the Swedish press that cited the testimonies of witnesses who had seen Wallenberg after 1947. Rodionov hoped that the Swedish government would step in and not allow certain elements to exploit the Wallenberg case and endanger relations between Russia and Sweden.

Rodionov's request went unheeded. Sweden continued to press the Wallenberg case. On July 18, the Foreign Office sent a detailed memo with the testimonies it had received and stated that it placed great importance upon these accounts. The note pointed out that these testimonies were given independently of each other. All pointed to Wallenberg's continuing imprisonment in Russia in the 1950s. As for the Soviet concern that continued attention to the Wallenberg case would poison relations between the two countries, Sweden made it clear that it had only one purpose in mind: to find out once and for all the entire truth in the Raoul Wallenberg affair. Once this was accomplished, a serious, disturbing element in relations between the two countries would be eliminated.

So, witnesses continued to be interrogated and the evidence given was carefully studied. The government assigned two former members of the Swedish Supreme Court, Gyllensvärd and Santesson, to examine the new materials and testimonies. Gyllensvärd and Santesson completed their report on April 25, 1960. Their investigation had found that while there was no absolute proof in accordance with Swedish law, it was certainly probable that Raoul Wallenberg had been alive at least in the early 1950s. After that period, one could make a strong assumption that he had been transferred to the prison in Vladimir — where he still might be found.

On the record the 1950s, especially before and after the Gromyko memorandum, seem to reflect a great amount of activity on the part of the

Swedish government in dealing with the Wallenberg case. From February, 1952, through February, 1957, the Foreign Office had given the Russians fifteen written and thirty-four oral reminders about Wallenberg. Compared to its actions in the years immediately after Raoul Wallenberg's disappearance in 1945, the Swedish government now could be described as persistent and even aggressive in dealing with the Soviet Union.

Despite what might be perceived as a more hard-hitting approach toward the Russians, the actions of the Swedish government, even in the 1950s, still had very serious critics.

Palmstierna even goes as far as saying that certain Swedish officials would not have been overjoyed if Raoul Wallenberg were to come home: "To my mind some people in the ministry [Foreign Ministry], having for reasons of career or prestige, staked on the death of Wallenberg, might feel uncomfortable if he was returned. I thought in the first hand of our representatives in Moscow since 1945."

Ambassador Per Anger is equally censorious of the attitudes and actions of the Swedish government. He is not convinced that the diplomatic approaches and the many investigations represented a genuine commitment to free Raoul Wallenberg:

> A tremendous responsibility weighs upon the postwar Social Democratic governments, including the coalition ministry of Erlander and Hedlund in the 50's. They have deliberately lain low and been unwilling to take any action they feared might have serious consequences for our relations with the Soviet Union. Were they, at first, so anxious to preserve our neutrality in the Cold War then starting, that Wallenberg was sacrificed on the altar of neutrality? True, the government cannot be blamed for passivity during the years that followed. Countless are the clues that have been investigated and the diplomatic approaches that have been made to the Soviets, especially since 1952. But one asks oneself if a real will existed behind all the inquiries and appeals that have been made? Has it not been merely a game of make-believe in which the government, for the benefit of domestic Swedish opinion, made a show of sparing no effort in a case that they neither believed in nor wanted to believe in? Because it was most comfortable that way (145).

To be fair to the Swedish government, it must also be reported that it was faced not only with official Russian statements that Wallenberg was not alive, but also with what Fredrik von Dardel called "unofficial emissaries." One of these emissaries was the former member of the Swedish legation in Budapest, Count Tolstoy, later employed by the Soviets.

Before Gromyko came to visit the Swedish foreign minister in Stockholm on March 25, 1955, he was preceded by a letter from Danielsson, the former minister in Budapest. That letter enclosed another letter from Tolstoy, which stated that during the four years he had remained in Budapest after the liberation, he sought to find out about Wallenberg's status. His conclusion was either that Wallenberg had been killed by the Nyilas or the Germans because he established contact with the Russian army, or that he had been shot accidentally by the Russians because he was dressed in a German uniform.

Throughout the years Swedish officials and journalists closely involved in the search for Raoul Wallenberg continued to see Tolstoy as a crucial link in the puzzle. *Aftonbladet* correspondent Anders Hasselbohm visited Tolstoy in 1979. Hasselbohm related,

> Tolstoy had been living in Ireland for many years in the employ of the Russians. There has always been good reason to believe that Tolstoy turned Wallenberg in. It is strange that Tolstoy, who fled Russia as an enemy of the state many years before the war, did not run away when the Russians liberated Budapest. How could such an individual suddenly become a town commander of Budapest without having made some sort of deal with the Russians or without having given them any information? In the 1950's there were disclosures from the Swedish and British secret services that Tolstoy was a spy for the KGB.

Hasselbohm said that at first Tolstoy received him cordially. The Russian told the correspondent that not only did he dislike Wallenberg, but that the young diplomat had also found disfavor with other Swedish officials:

> I didn't like Wallenberg because I disliked his methods. He did not act like a diplomat. He tempted the patience of the Hungarian officials when he tried to save all the Jews. He tried to do the impossible. Danielsson had told me that Wallenberg was a danger to all our officials: "That young guy will sink the boat we are sitting in." By making out far too many passes, Wallenberg had made trouble for the other diplomats.

After listening to Tolstoy's tirade against Wallenberg, Hasselbohm turned to the Russian: "There are things written about you in Sweden." Tolstoy turned white, and the visit was over. Tolstoy died in 1980 at the age of eighty-five.

In the spring of 1956, an Estonian named Temvelius became the next Russian emissary to bring news of Wallenberg's death. A prisoner in the Inta camp in Russia, Temvelius wrote a letter to the Swedish government asking for an entry permit. He stated that he thought of writing when the name of Wallenberg came up during Erlander's visit to Moscow. Temvelius claimed to have met Wallenberg in the Inta camp, but he had reliable information that Wallenberg had been transferred to Butyrka Prison, where he died in 1947. An interview with Rudolph Philipp exposed Temvelius's deceit when he could not properly identify a picture of Wallenberg. Commissar Danielsson of the Swedish State Police later interrogated Temvelius and concluded that he had concocted the story, either because the Russians ordered him to do it or because he hoped that it would gain him entry into

Sweden. Von Dardel writes that an Estonian priest who knew Temvelius told Philipp that two top GPU officers had visited Temvelius at Inta and questioned him at length. "It is possible," von Dardel continues, "that he was then liberated and granted an exit permit from the Soviet Union on the condition of telling his story about Wallenberg" (37).

Another intriguing emissary of falsehood was the supposed Baron von Wetschl. On February 21, 1960, the *Svenska Dagbladet* of Stockholm carried an article by an anonymous witness who maintained that he met Raoul Wallenberg in Lubianka Prison in June, 1945, in Lefortovo Prison in March, 1946, in the Pervoja camp in 1949, and at Kasgobol near Archangel'sk in 1950. Von Wetschl claimed to have been present at Wallenberg's deathbed at Kasgobol.

After the article was published, the Hungarian impostor came to Stockholm in an attempt to induce another newspaper to publish his story. He also planned to meet with Raoul Wallenberg's mother; however, she refused to see the baron. As reported by von Dardel, there was, in fact, a Hungarian named von Wetschl who had been imprisoned in Russia. This information was presented in the book *In Beria's Camps* by a Finnish author Parvilathi.

Not only did the baron claim to have been with Wallenberg in prison, but he also claimed to have been transported together with Wallenberg from Budapest to Moscow in January, 1945. They were separated in Moscow but reunited again at Lubianka Prison.

When the Finnish author was given a picture of the supposed baron, Parvilathi was certain that it was not the von Wetschl he had met in the Soviet Union. Rudolph Philipp, once again sent to sniff out deceit, visited the masquerading baron in a rather modest apartment outside Hamburg, West Germany. Philipp was introduced to the "mother," who seemed more of an ordinary peasant than Baroness von Wetschl. The "baroness" inadvertently told Philipp that mother and son were living on social welfare.

Philipp continued his investigation of the baron. A neighbor told Philipp that von Wetschl was often seen driving a new Opel car. The German police, also mentioning the new Opel car, informed Philipp that von Wetschl kept in contact with government leaders in Budapest. The police were of the opinion that his income far exceeded his apparent life style. He used the alias Wentzel or Wehdern; the police were fairly certain that von Wetschl was not his real name.

If that be the case, what was the Hungarian impostor doing in West Germany? It is the opinion of von Dardel that the impostor was Hungarian by birth. He had been allowed to leave the Soviet Union—whether he was ever a prisoner there is not known. It seems likely that the Hungarian managed to obtain the identification papers of von Wetschl and smuggle himself into West Germany. Once in West Germany, according to von Dardel, the Hungarian served as a Soviet agent (37).

Von Dardel sees an orchestrated scheme in these emissaries. The "messages" of Tolstoy and Temvelius, Dardel writes, "may have been intended to counterprove the testimonials about Wallenberg's imprisonment in Moscow, which the Swedish Foreign Office refers to in their notes to the Russians during the first half of the 50's." As for the Hungarian baron, that episode occurred after the Russians admitted that Raoul Wallenberg had been imprisoned and died. The von Wetschl article is therefore intended to refute Wallenberg's imprisonment in Vladimir, which the Swedish Foreign Office referred to in their notes to Russia in 1959 (38).

These emissaries of deceit, while each had been challenged and proven false, still represented a complicating factor in the effort to bring the Angel of Rescue back home. But for those who refused to be cowed by the Russians and for those who saw in the rescue of Raoul Wallenberg the sacred fulfillment of justice, no complications, no obstacles were too great to overcome.

10

American Efforts Rebuffed

Raoul Wallenberg was not only of Sweden; he was of the world. The War Refugee Board of the United States both advocated and financed his mission in Hungary. While this American support could not be openly acknowledged during the war, the United States government clearly had a moral responsibility towards Wallenberg, especially since Soviet mistrust of his American connections may have been the real reason that the Russians imprisoned him. Why didn't the United States do something to secure his release from its Soviet ally after the war?

A study of the available materials clearly shows that the American government kept itself well informed about Raoul Wallenberg's activities in Budapest and took an active concern about his fate after the war. A communiqué from the U.S. legation in Stockholm to the secretary of state shows that America was closely following the reports of Wallenberg's disappearance. An April 9, 1945, communiqué from the secretary of state to the U.S. representatives in Moscow and Budapest instructed them "to give all support possible to Swedish Legation in securing information regarding Wallenberg's fate." Similar instructions were given on May 8 from the Department of State to the War Refugee Board. In April U.S. Ambassador to Moscow Averell Harriman and Secretary of State Edward R. Stettinius, Jr., offered their services in the Wallenberg case to Swedish Ambassador Söderblom. Stockholm said, no thank you. On April 12, the U.S. embassy in Moscow reported the Swedish response to the secretary of state. Stockholm felt "that Soviets are doing what they can to locate him [Wallenberg] and they [Sweden] do not feel that approach on our part to Soviet Foreign Office would be desirable."

A letter from Chris M. Ravndal of the American legation in Stockholm, dated August 21, to Sven Grafstrom of the Swedish Ministry of Foreign Affairs not only points up the continued concern of American officials, but also indicates that there were Swedish officials who were deeply concerned about Wallenberg. In his letter, Ravndal speaks of the Department of State's inquiries in the case and its promises to inform Sweden of any pertinent information it obtains.

The Final Summary Report of the U.S. War Refugee Board on September 15, 1945, is a very revealing document. Signed by the board's Executive Director William O'Dwyer, later mayor of New York City, the report spells out the relationship of the board and Wallenberg and cites the achievements of the Swede. It also takes note of his disappearance and his "reported death," but gives no source for that information:

Raoul Wallenberg, a young Swedish businessman, volunteered to proceed to Hungary for the War Refugee Board to aid in the rescue and relief of persecuted Jews. The Swedish government granted him diplomatic status and stationed him in Budapest for the purpose of providing protection to these people. The Board furnished Wallenberg with detailed plans of action, but made it clear that he could not act in Hungary as a representative of the Board. Wallenberg, supplied with funds from the Board and the American Jewish Joint Distribution Committee, carried on a relentless campaign in Hungary on behalf of the Jews. He issued Swedish protective passports by the thousands and hired extra buildings as official Swedish quarters to house several hundred rabbis and communal leaders under the protection of the extraterritoriality which attached to such buildings. He constantly pressed the Hungarian authorities for better treatment of Jews and succeeded in having thousands brought back from forced labor marches. In all, approximately 20,000 Jews received safety of Swedish protection. As a measure of the devotion of Wallenberg and as proof of the risks involved in his activities, the Board received word on April 14, 1945, that he was missing. Despite repeated attempts to trace his whereabouts, he was reported dead early in June, 1945.

The man who selected Wallenberg for the mission, Iver C. Olsen, special attaché to the War Refugee Board, was interviewed for the *Jewish News* of New Jersey on March 28, 1947, and mentioned the U.S.'s role:

I feel terribly concerned about Wallenberg's disappearance because it was I who selected him for the Budapest mission. So far as the United States is concerned, while it is not accurate to describe Wallenberg as an undercover agent for this country, the government fully recognized his remarkable activities on behalf of the War Refugee Board and on several occasions has paid high tribute to him. From the start this government has been concerned with his disappearance and would undoubtedly undertake any measure which might offer hope of finding him.

Olsen felt that changing conditions inside Russia might make Wallenberg's return possible. "Now that internal conditions and communications are more normal than heretofore," Olsen said, "one could hope that Wallenberg might return to Sweden."

However, concerned officials were not sitting back and letting the situation develop on its own. Exchanges throughout the fall of 1945 (e.g., November 2, 16, 19) between officials in the Swedish Foreign Ministry and their counterparts at the American legation show that information was being sought about Wallenberg and Langfelder—who was not being forgotten—from friends, former coworkers, and other Hungarian citizens. Káláman Lauer and Hugo Wohl told what they knew. Professor Albert Szent-Györgyi and M. Takacsy, of the Hungarian National Bank, were not able to provide new clues but indicated "their belief that Mr. Wallenberg, if still alive, was taken prisoner by the Russians without being given the opportunity to establish his identity."

With no breakthroughs taking place and with Swedish inaction an unfortunate reality, Wallenberg's mother and half brother sought the assistance of American government officials, including President Truman, U.S. Senator A. H. Vandenberg, and Mrs. Franklin D. Roosevelt. The responses from the first two officials crystallize the crux of the problem at that point: America recognized the achievements of Wallenberg and was ready to help, but had been stymied up to now and, given the stone-wall attitude of the Russians, successful action was difficult. Actually the letter to Truman was answered by George L. Warren, advisor on refugees and displaced persons:

I have received by reference from the White House your undated letter concerning the effort to locate Raoul Wallenberg, who disappeared in Budapest in January, 1945. The heroic efforts of Mr. Wallenberg as Secretary of the Swedish Legation in Hungary in 1944 in collaboration with the War Refugee Board are well known to this Government and are appreciated.

The efforts which this Government has made in the past to determine Mr. Wallenberg's whereabouts through diplomatic channels have unfortunately not succeeded. However, we are continuing our interest in the matter and will advise you if any new information is brought to light.

Michigan's U.S. Senator Vandenberg, the powerful chairman of the Committee on Foreign Relations, responded with genuine concern and practical realism:

Certainly you present a thrilling summary of your brother's record and I completely agree with you that he has richly earned any helpful interest which this Government can express in him. I do not need to remind you, however, of the difficulties which we confront in dealing with Soviet Russia in respect to missing persons. It is a well-nigh imponderable situation until such time as we can have a *total* showdown with the Soviet Union. But I shall be very glad to bring your present letter to the personal attention of the Secretary of State to see whether it is possible to make a *special* effort in your brother's behalf in view of the fact that his record obviously deserves it.

Acting Secretary of State Dean Acheson responded directly to Senator Vandenberg. Acheson informed Vandenberg that those in the State Department familiar with the case had discussed the matter with the senator's office. The secretary of state acknowledged Wallenberg's achievements and the involvement of the War Refugee Board. But while the U.S. stood willing to help, "the initiative" must be taken by Sweden:

Because of Mr. Wallenberg's heroic service, inspired in part by representatives of the War Refugee Board in Stockholm, the Department has participated in efforts to locate him and has recently sent an inquiry through the United States mission in Stockholm to determine the latest developments in the efforts of the Swedish Government to do so. In view of the fact that Mr. Wallenberg acted as a member of the Swedish diplomatic mission in Budapest, *the initiative* in inquiries directed toward the Soviet Government rests with the Swedish authorities. The Department is willing, as it has in the past, to support the initiative of the Swedish Government whenever the collaboration of the Government is desired and will prove helpful.

Nearly two years later, in the winter of 1949, Dr. von Dardel reminded Acheson of the State Department's willingness to help. Von Dardel had a stunning proposal. Fully aware that Sweden was not interested in trading with the Russians, von Dardel suggested that the Americans exchange a Soviet prisoner for Wallenberg. At that time, the Soviet official Valentin Gubitchev was arrested by the Americans for espionage in the Judith Coplon episode. Even though he is not an American, Wallenberg is deserving of American intervention, according to von Dardel: "There may be missing American citizens claiming priority. However, in my opinion few if any are more worthy of regaining their liberty than my brother by virtue of his courageous humanitarian work. The fact that he set out on his dangerous mission chiefly on the initiative of the American War Refugee Board certainly makes him entitled to all possible help from the American side, even if he is not an American citizen himself." Although Acheson did not respond to von Dardel's proposal for the exchange of prisoners, the secretary of state did promise "any assistance that U.S. can give."

The Swedish government still reacted to all American offers with the same response: no, thank you. Ambassador Sohlman set the tone with his statement, "We cannot drive tandem with the Americans."

Anger reflects on these missed opportunities with sadness: "As is now known, the Americans showed through their embassy in Moscow great interest in the Wallenberg case as early as 1945. But the Swedes never followed up on this, and no cooperative effort on this matter was ever established between the American and Swedish missions in Moscow. Still another example of the paralysis that characterized the Swedish behavior in the beginning!"

In the 1950s the Wallenberg family seemed to make few approaches to the American government. In reality, America could do little without appropriate action by Stockholm. The author requested the file on Raoul Wallenberg from the Federal Bureau of Investigation, under the Freedom of Information Act. One item in the file, dated June 15, 1954, came from New York public relations man Maurice Feldman. Mr. Feldman had prepared news notes for Walter Winchell. The lead item was the Russian "vacation" of Swedish Foreign Minister Undén to try to "liberate Wallenberg and bring him back to Sweden." In an interesting piece of misinformation, Raoul Wallenberg is described as the "son of one of the world's richest men."

If the U.S. government felt a responsibility to Raoul Wallenberg because it was a partner to his mission, American citizens, especially those in the Jewish community whose family and brethren were rescued through the dedicated efforts of the Swede, had a much greater obligation. An examination of the archives of the American Jewish Joint Distribution Committee (JDC) shows that the Wallenberg family felt that the American Jewish community was not as responsive as it could have been. On May 3, 1945, the JDC, convinced of the death of Wallenberg, cabled its condolences to Stockholm and expressed its gratitude to him: "Please express to Minister Danielsson our grateful appreciation for extraordinary humanitarian efforts on behalf of Jewish victims [during] German persecution which resulted in saving lives of thousands of Jews in Budapest. Please extend our heartfelt condolences at great loss of Raoul Wallenberg, who died a true martyr in cause of suffering humanity."

However, the Wallenberg family was looking for more than gratitude; it was seeking financial support for the campaign to rescue Raoul. Before V-J Day $50,000 in unused funds from the rescue mission was returned to the JDC. In correspondence during 1947 with Dr. Joseph Schwartz and Moses Leavitt, director and executive vice chairman of JDC respectively, Dr. von Dardel asked the organization for assistance. In particular, he requested $20,000 to support the writing and research of Rudolph Philipp. "Until his book appeared," von Dardel wrote to Leavitt, "the whole matter was surrounded by a veil of diplomatic secrecy, uncontrolled rumors, and unfounded theories." What made the situation difficult to accept for the Wallenbergs was their feeling that the JDC had given "support" to Lévai, whose book was "to a great extent based on the facts and investigations" of Philipp. In addition, Lévai's suggestion that Wallenberg was killed by the Germans or the Nyilas made the search for him more difficult.

J. W. Pehle, former executive director of the War Refugee Board, sent a very stinging letter concerning the American Jewish organizations to U.S. Treasury Secretary Henry Morgenthau, Jr., in November, 1947. The Wallenberg family, Pehle writes, feels that the American Jewish organizations are no longer interested in Raoul Wallenberg now that they don't need him. The postscript is also very revealing in its description of the "wealthy" Wallenbergs:

> Wallenberg's family has, on several occasions, requested American assistance in the search for Raoul Wallenberg . . . . I get the impression that Wallenberg's family are afraid that Americans, particularly the American Jewish organizations, were interested in Wallenberg only to the extent that he could bring credit and distinction to their various European organizations, which he undeniably did, but are now disposed to forget the whole matter.
>
> I am very anxious . . . that the Wallenberg family has every possible assurance of our interest and concern in Raoul Wallenberg's whereabouts, as well as a continuing appreciation of his remarkable contribution to a critical humanitarian mission . . . .
>
> P.S. While Raoul Wallenberg bears the name of a prominent and wealthy Swedish family, his problem and those of the immediate relatives are of no concern to the more prominent Wallenbergs.

The letter notwithstanding, the JDC decided not to support the work of Philipp because the nature of the organization was to support overseas relief programs, not individual projects.

However, one cannot accuse the JDC of indifference to the fate of Wallenberg. After his disappearance, Herbert Agar relates in *Their Brothers' Keepers,* the JDC hired a detective to find out the status of Wallenberg. However, the detective could not gain entry into Russia, and as a result nothing was learned (104).

The JDC sought to establish an appropriate memorial for Wallenberg. One plan was to name a hospital or home for the aged in Israel for him. Specifically, the JDC's Malben Program had such facilities to be named in Rishon or Nahariya. The Wallenberg family was not interested in memorials. As Leavitt reported on August 26, 1957, "Nothing can be done until the family is prepared to accept death [Raoul Wallenberg's]."

In looking back at the attitude of the American Jewish community to the rescue of Wallenberg, Mrs. Lagergren said, "The American Jewish community was indifferent to the fate of Raoul. I have never understood why it should have been so."

Mrs. Lagergren was also critical of those Israelis associated with *Encyclopaedia Judaica* for not having a "positive" attitude about the chances of Raoul Wallenberg's being alive. An article by Livia Rothkirchen of Yad Vashem lists Wallenberg's birth as 1912 and "death" as "1947?" After speaking of the Swede's exceptional courage and devotion, Rothkirchen says that "the circumstances of his final disappearance were regarded by many as unsolved."

Pursuing a line of thought similar to Mrs. Lagergren's, former Wallenberg aide Thomas Veres expressed pleasure at all the recent "sudden interest" in the Swede, but asked, "Where was the Jewish community for the past thirty years?" Despite these criticisms, Mrs. Lagergren was quick to add that there were individuals who contributed money and who spoke out about the achievements of Raoul Wallenberg and who sought avenues of helping to bring him back.

A very fervent plea to U.S. Vice President and Labor Party leader Henry Wallace was made by Dorothy Thompson in an open letter in the Boston *Daily Globe* on April 18, 1947.

The Wallenberg Affair May Seem Small, but You Would not Call It Insignificant

I see you are going to Sweden. While there, you might inquire whether anything has been heard officially about Raoul Wallenberg. Until April 1, I believe, nothing had. Your reputation as the champion of the common man and the four freedoms together with the confidence you deservedly enjoy from the Soviet Union, may enable you to accomplish something for the ends you desire.

The Wallenberg Affair may seem small, but you would not call it insignificant . . . . Wallenberg managed — by pleas, bribes, threats, intrigues, and by his influence on the amorous wife of a Nazi minister — to save 100,000 Jews. He issued papers of protective Swedish citizenship to several thousands. He organized rescue missions in all neutral legations. He snatched victims from the Gestapo, even at the railroad stations where they were being deported. Seldom in the course of human history has so much been accomplished by one man . . . .

Since official channels have failed, your personal intervention with the Russian government might succeed. Sweden — small, and so near Soviet frontiers — finds it hard to do more for her citizens, especially since the new type, jet-propelled, radio-directed robot bombs were tried out over her territory from the German station at Peenemunde, now in Russian hands. With your passion for peace, you might — at the same time — obtain permission to visit this station and set international fears at rest . . . .

But if this is too difficult, you can surely obtain news of and justice for a man who responded to a plea from President Roosevelt, in whose name and for whose policies you claim to speak. The USSR is greatly indebted to you. I am sure that on issues that must command your humanitarian sympathies and sense of honor you will not prove less intrepid in facing the leaders of the Soviets than in facing the President of the United States.

Undoubtedly, Albert Einstein, who came to America to escape Nazi persecution, provided the most inspiring story of an American's support for Raoul Wallenberg during the postwar years. Einstein's involvement in the Wallenberg case is related in the series of letters between him and fellow physicist Dr. von Dardel. In a letter of June 6, 1947, Einstein tells how important it is — especially for Jews — to help the Swede: "There is no doubt that your brother is a man of extraordinary merits and there is no doubt too that it is a duty for everyone, especially for a Jew, to do everything possible to help him in his situation."

Einstein shows great incisiveness in understanding the Russian mentality in this matter:

One has to try to understand an attitude of the Soviets which shows itself quite systematically in all those cases where foreigners are prevented from leaving and the Russians refuse (mostly by passive resistance) to give any information about the status and fate of the people concerned. In my opinion the explanation might be as follows: Through their experiences in the past 30 years and recently through the aggressive attitude of the American government towards Soviet Russia the Russians are living in a perpetual persecution complex. They are suspecting every foreigner to be a spy, so they are trying to prevent any communication to the outside world about Russian life and happenings. For this reason, so it seems to me, they are preventing all persons from leaving Russia who they believe might be able to give information considered dangerous. In the case of people whose right to leave Russia cannot be contested it is not quite easy to predict how they will react if pressure is brought on them.

In order to avoid pressure, Einstein proposed a "personal" approach by means of a short and simple letter to Stalin. Einstein and von Dardel agreed to Einstein's letter: "As an old Jew I appeal to you, Generalissimo Stalin, to do everything possible to find and send back to his country the Swede Raoul Wallenberg, who was one of the very few, who during the bad years of Nazi persecution on his own accord and risking his own life worked to rescue thousands of my unhappy Jewish people." The letter was sent to S. Tsarapkin, the chargé d'affaires of the Russian embassy in Washington, for transmittal to Stalin. In the letter of November 18, 1947, Einstein informs Tsarapkin: "The letter concerns no political matter; I am sending it in obeyance to moral obligation."

The answer was quick and negative. The undated letter of December, 1947, was written by Tsarapkin and informs Einstein that "necessary measures were taken by appropriate authorities to search for Mr. Vallenberg [sic], but they have not produced any positive results."

Inspired by the compassion and heroism of Raoul Wallenberg, Albert Einstein favored the Swede's winning the Nobel Peace Prize of 1949. It is ironic that Raoul Wallenberg never received the Nobel Prize, even though nominated in two successive years, while Dag Hammarskjöld, who turned his back on his heroic countryman, won the award in 1961.

In terms of the Wallenberg case, the year 1961 was much more momentous than any comparison of the relative merits of Wallenberg and Hammarskjöld in regard to the Nobel Peace Prize. Wallenberg was almost fifty and had already spent sixteen years in Russian jails. After years of presenting a continual stream of information to the Russians that only met with consistent denials, perhaps the most startling development in the Raoul Wallenberg drama unfolded.

11

Hope and Despair in the Gulag

The parents of Raoul Wallenberg, May and Fredrik von Dardel, waited in agony but also with hope. His mother was under the care of Dr. Nanna Svartz, an internationally renowned internist and researcher. In January, 1961, she was invited to a scientific conference in Moscow, where she met a Russian colleague, Dr. Alexander Miasnikov, the head of a number of hospitals. After a lengthy discussion of scientific matters, Dr. Svartz, who had known the Russian for seven years, inquired whether Miasnikov had heard about the Wallenberg case. As always, the discussion between them was in German — a fact that later proved significant. Svartz describes Miasnikov's response: "My informant then suddenly said that he surely knew about the case and that the person I was asking about was in very poor condition. Asked what I wanted, I replied that the main thing was that Wallenberg be brought home, no matter in what condition. My informant said in a very low voice that the person inquired about was in a mental hospital."

What a stroke of fortune, thought Svartz. After all these years of frustration, Raoul Wallenberg had finally been located — alive! Miasnikov even asked her whether she would like to see him. Unfortunately, Svartz declined; her only interest was to get Wallenberg back to Stockholm as soon as possible. Miasnikov called in another Soviet doctor whom Svartz had known for twenty-five years. He promised to do all he could for Wallenberg. This doctor advised her to contact Russian Deputy Foreign Minister Vladimir Semyonov and ask that Wallenberg be sent home for medical treatment.

Svartz was unable to reach the foreign minister by phone; instead, she wrote to him and left for Sweden. Palmstierna wonders whether the golden opportunity was lost because Svartz did not stay in Moscow and take advantage of the unforeseen development: "It is now to be regretted that Professor Svartz did not postpone her return in order to devote herself wholeheartedly to the matter. But could she in that case have counted on help from our embassy?"

However, Svartz relentlessly pursued the matter once she returned to Sweden. She quickly reported to Prime Minister Erlander and the Foreign Ministry. The government decided that any public disclosure of the news might doom Wallenberg's chances. No one else was to know, not even Wallenberg's mother. Erlander wrote to Premier Khrushchev on February 9, detailing what Svartz had learned and specifying the sources. The Swedish leader proposed that he be permitted to send a doctor to Moscow who, along with a Russian colleague, would decide on the best means to have Wallenberg brought home.

The euphoria was short-lived. The Russian premier read the letter and assailed the contents. The Swedish Ambassador Sohlman was summoned and brusquely informed that nothing had changed: Wallenberg had died in 1947; any other information was false. According to Palmstierna, Erlander's letter "was both belated and over-hasty." Palmstierna writes that Khrushchev had already known of the conversation between Miasnikov and Svartz — perhaps that information had been passed along by Semyonov.

In fact, the Russian foreign minister never responded to Svartz. The Swedish doctor returned to Moscow in March and sought out Miasnikov. He told her that she should not have reported their previous talk to the Swedish authorities. Although he did not deny that Wallenberg had been discussed, he did deny that he had ever heard of Wallenberg. There had been a misunderstanding, according to Miasnikov, because of his bad German. The Russian scientist added that after Erlander's letter had been received, an incensed Khrushchev had called him on the carpet.

Fredrik von Dardel saw this sudden reversal by Miasnikov as a clear but shocking illustration of conditions in Russia.

> After Khrushchev had made him [Miasnikov] the object of his wrath, probably without much restraint, the Russian scientist feared that his impudence could lead to a catastrophe for him. This highly educated man, who at many conferences had talked German without difficulty with Professor Svartz, now blamed his bad German, to explain how such a misunderstanding could have arisen. One may ask oneself, however, how a word as "Mentalkrankenhaus" could have been misunderstood (36).

In the spring of 1963 Swedish governmental circles learned that not only had Erlander's letter never been answered, it had not even been opened. According to Palmstierna, this disclosure necessitated a visit to Moscow by the new Foreign Minister Torsten Nilsson. However, Nilsson was turned away empty-handed, as Khrushchev labeled new Swedish claims and testimonies as "rumors propagated by evil-minded people." Erlander had two opportunities to state his case in person to top Soviet officials. In March, 1964, Soviet Foreign Minister Gromyko came to Stockholm. When Erlander referred to the Wallenberg affair, Gromyko restated the Soviet line that the report of Svartz had been the result of a misunderstanding. In fact, Miasnikov was ready to confront Svartz with this fact.

Khrushchev came to Stockholm that June for a visit that had been delayed for five years. The outcome was a downright disaster for Erlander. Palmstierna describes the meeting between the two leaders: "Our Prime Minister Erlander then went far to extort from his guest straightforward information regarding Wallenberg. When Khrushchev heard that evidence that the former was still alive were so strong that the case could not be cancelled, the great man had one of his outbursts of fury. Disappointed the Swedes gave way. The only result of this 'state visit' was a communiqué which not even mentioned the name of Raoul Wallenberg."

In his memoirs Erlander also mentions Khrushchev's anger. The Russian leader told Erlander that if he had known that the Wallenberg matter would be raised, he would not have come to Stockholm. Erlander notes, however, that Khrushchev did understand Sweden's concern because his own son had disappeared in Germany during the war and was never seen again.

The veil of secrecy that surrounded the Svartz discovery and its aftermath was even more astounding than the failure of Swedish diplomacy. Palmstierna suggests the reason for the secrecy: "These encounters were not made public; neither was the report of Nanna Svartz. The worst vituperations of the Russian guest were never interpreted. We know today that they had been caused by our disbelief regarding Wallenberg. Once again the latter was made a victim."

Meanwhile, in a letter to Dr. Svartz in May, 1964, Dr. Miasnikov referred to information he had given her about Wallenberg during her 1961 visit to Moscow. Miasnikov made it clear that he had told her that he knew nothing about Wallenberg and did not know if he were alive; in fact, he had never even heard of Wallenberg before she brought up the name.

After Sweden held its parliamentary elections in the fall of 1964, the government could safely inform the opposition of the three-year developments in the Wallenberg case. Another relevant development was the ouster of Premier Khrushchev in October, 1964. However, before the Swedish government considered revealing the Vladimir testimonies or the Svartz report, it appealed to the new premier, Aleksei Kosygin. Not surprisingly, Kosygin replied that the Soviet position still rested with the Gromyko memorandum that Wallenberg died in 1947. However, Kosygin finally consented to a meeting between Dr. Svartz and Dr. Miasnikov in the presence of Swedish and Russian representatives.

The moment of truth arrived for the two internationally acclaimed scientists on July 6, 1965, three and one-half years after the startling revelation by the Russian doctor. Svartz and Miasnikov were joined by Swedish Ambassador Gunnar Jarring and two members of the Soviet Foreign Office. It was a tense three-hour meeting. Miasnikov was ashen and uneasy throughout the confrontation. He repeated the now familiar line that there had been a misunderstanding because of language difficulties. Svartz challenged this assertion by reminding the Russian that they had discussed complex and highly technical medical questions in German many times before. Miasnikov would not budge from his position. One should not be surprised at his actions, Dr. von Dardel said in a recent interview. "We know that Miasnikov had been given a dressing down for his indiscretion by Khrushchev in person." In November, 1965, the Soviet press reported that Miasnikov had died of a heart attack. Despite Miasnikov's subsequent denials, Dr. Svartz has never wavered in her conviction that her original report is totally correct.

Now retired from government service, Palmstierna remains convinced of the "total accuracy" of Svartz's report. "The central question in the Svartz episode," he said, "is the fluency of Miasnikov's German. While serving in Russia, I was treated in a Moscow hospital. And one thing I noticed: the excellent German of the Russian doctors."

Fredrik von Dardel writes that the mental hospital referred to in the Miasnikov-Svartz conversation might be a type of facility for isolating political prisoners, even if they are sane. Dardel cites an article in *Svenska Dagbladet* by a Russian journalist, Valery Tarsjis, who lectured in Gothenburg, Sweden. The Russian related

> the existence of a big hospital in the neighborhood of Moscow, where more than 80 percent of the patients are undesired former Communists . . . . These patients are sane and sound, and there is no treatment except for mental and physical narcotic. If this account is true there exist hospitals in Russia which at the same time are institutions for isolating political prisoners. It does not seem excluded that the mental hospital of which the contact of Professor Svartz told her is such an institution (31).

Now that the Svartz incident had finally come to a close, the Swedish government felt "safe" in speaking to the public after a silence of four and one-half years. On September 16, 1965, the Vladimir and Svartz revelations were disclosed to the press. Erlander and Svartz appeared on television to discuss the new evidence.

Dr. von Dardel added a fresh piece of information to the Svartz-Miasnikov episode. Svartz, now in her nineties, recently revealed that her Russian colleague not only had known of the Wallenberg case, but also had personally examined the Swede in a Soviet mental institution in 1961. The Svartz-Miasnikov episode is part of the classified section of the Wallenberg file that the government had been expected to open in 1981.

Semyonov, the Russian official involved in the 1960 drama, is presently the Soviet ambassador in Bonn. The author was in East Berlin in the fall of

1980, as a guest of the German Democratic Republic, on a study mission of its Jewish communities. The author unsuccessfully sought to meet Semyonov in an attempt "to hear the Russian point of view."

Although for practical purposes the Svartz incident had come to a close in 1965, further evidence was forthcoming. In 1965 Mogens Carlson, a Dane, reported that during February, 1951, he had shared a cell in the Butyrka Prison with Professor Zoltan Rivo. The Hungarian had told him that in the first week of 1951 he had a Swedish diplomat for a cellmate. Carlson's account was presented in a September 26, 1955, interview with the Swedish newspaper *Dagens Nyheter*. According to Rivo, Wallenberg had been intensely interrogated; yet, he was accorded special treatment. The guards gave him extra rations and cigarettes, and took him out to be shaved. This surprised Rivo, because most prisoners were simply cut bald by a machine. One day, Rivo saw that the diplomat had been given civilian clothes; the next day, he was no longer at Butyrka. Von Dardel writes that no one had been able to make direct contact with Rivo, but it is fairly evident that the Swedish diplomat must have been Raoul Wallenberg (35-36).

More difficult, however, is the material that appeared in a 1966 book by a Finnish citizen, Björkelund, who had been a commodore in the Russian marines. In the summer of 1955 he was detained in a prison camp at the railroad station of Poime near Irkutsk. One day in August, an elderly German told him that in the camp hospital there was a very sick patient by the name of Wallenberg. The German asked the Finn to inform the Swedish embassy of this fact when he was released. The Finn asked the German to tell him the details of Wallenberg's imprisonment. According to the old man, Wallenberg had been with the Swedish Red Cross in Budapest in 1945. He was arrested on charges of spying for the Americans and sentenced to ten years. Two days after meeting the elderly German, the Finn saw another German coming out of the hospital. When the Finn asked about the Swede's condition, the German responded, "I think there was one there, but he died yesterday and was brought to the morgue." To convince himself of that fact, the Finn asked the German if he were absolutely certain. "Yes, of course," was the answer. "I was two beds away from him."

When Björkelund returned to Finland at the end of 1955, the Finnish police interrogated him without mentioning Raoul Wallenberg. Björkelund never gave more thought to Wallenberg until he wrote his book in 1966. No one has been able to fault the integrity of Björkelund: he is not a Baron von Wetschl. How should his account be interpreted? Unanswered is why it took the Finn eleven years to bring up the question of Wallenberg, especially since the German prisoner had asked him to do so upon his release from prison. Although not answering this question, von Dardel has a plausible explanation for Björkelund's experience. Aware that the Finn's prison sentence was to expire at the end of 1955, Russian authorities instructed the camp director to arrange for two Germans to pass on information about

Wallenberg. Upon his release, the Finn would present this information to the Swedish embassy in Helsinki. The accounts of Tolstoy and Temvelius were circulated during 1955–56, and the Russians hoped that the Finn's report would lend further credibility to their insistence that Raoul Wallenberg was dead: "All these messages may have been intended to counterprove the testimonials about Wallenberg's imprisonment in Moscow, which the Swedish Foreign Office refers to in their notes to the Russians during the first half of the 50's" (38).

If von Dardel's explanation is true, then the Russians cared little about the compatibility of the emissaries' reports: Tolstoy said that Wallenberg was killed in Budapest; Temvelius placed Wallenberg's death in 1955; von Wetschl indicated that Wallenberg died in 1950; Björkelund told of Wallenberg's death in 1955.

Although the Swedish government still looked into every driblet of new information about Wallenberg, hopes of freeing the Angel of Rescue had been dashed with the closing of the Svartz episode. Stockholm did not make any fresh approaches to Moscow; however, the public had been made aware of the Wallenberg odyssey, and their interest did not die out. The Wallenberg case was introduced into the history curriculum at the University of Stockholm, under the supervision of Svén Palme. Discussion of the case remained a major concern of the press.

It seemed as if the Swedish government was anxious to close the books on the Wallenberg affair. Palmstierna relates a meeting of the newly established Swedish chapter of Amnesty International. The major purpose of the organization was to defend human rights by working for the release of so-called political prisoners. Palmstierna wrote to Ambassador Alva Myrdal, who was scheduled to address the Stockholm chapter on January 17, 1966. The king's secretary pointed out to the ambassador that Sweden also had a political prisoner — Wallenberg. "Much, but not everything, had from Swedish quarters been done to have Raoul Wallenberg set free," Palmstierna told Myrdal. He asked her to mention the name of Wallenberg "as a striking example" of a political prisoner. Myrdal did not mention the name of Wallenberg at the meeting of Amnesty International. When Palmstierna later confronted her, she refused to explain why she did not mention Raoul Wallenberg's name. "This I considered rather feeble," Palmstierna sadly noted. "Who prohibited her?"

As the Swedish public was learning more about Raoul Wallenberg, the accomplishments of the Angel of Rescue were being recorded in Israel. Although thousands of survivors, many of them rescued through the Wallenberg mission, had made their way to Israel, the retelling of the Holocaust was not popular with much of the Israeli public. As the Jews were building their own state, they preferred to look ahead to a brighter future, not back to a tragic past. But the Eichmann trial in 1961 focused the world's attention on the atrocities of the Holocaust. With that Israel realized that the rebirth of a people could not be separated from a remembrance of its past. In recalling Eichmann and his plans for the annihilation of Hungarian Jewry, it was inevitable that the story of Raoul Wallenberg would be told.

One of those who knew Raoul Wallenberg through working directly with his staff as well as the Swedish legation was the lawyer Arie Breslauer. On January 6, 1961, in response to Israeli Solicitor-General Gavriel Bach's question: "Will you tell the court who is this Wallenberg?" Breslauer testified:

> I shall come to that. He was one of the men sent there. He was perhaps the man who had the greatest influence in Budapest. He was sent by the king of Sweden. I met this man in the course of common work later on several times and I was with him together on our way to the Austrian border. His rescue operations were on the greatest scale. There was a lot of rescue work, but he gave courage and showed a personal example. He was in complete contrast to what was happening in Budapest then.

After the Eichmann trial Wallenberg's achievements were recorded through testimonies given at Jerusalem's Yad Vashem, the Central Archives for the Disaster and the Heroism. In fact, the accomplishments of Raoul Wallenberg are recorded in a monograph "The Actions of Foreign Diplomats in Hungary for the Rescue of Jews," by Dr. Alexander Bronowski of Tel Aviv, a member of Yad Vashem's Commission for the Designation of the Righteous. Bronowski concludes his narrative of Wallenberg with these lines:

> All this was accomplished by a brave individual who had the strength to act according to his consciousness and belief. These acts, like those of the Danish King Christian, bring a wondrous feeling to the heart: how many more people could have been saved in those devastated countries if there had been more like Raoul Wallenberg among those persons who had the power to act, whether openly or secretly.

Another Israeli who witnessed the heroism of Raoul Wallenberg was Dr. László Antal, a lawyer from Bat Yam, whose father-in-law, Miklós Kertesz, was a member of the Hungarian parliament before the Nazi occupation. Antal's testimony, given in December, 1969, speaks of the Wallenberg protective pass and the "novelty" of the document in the eyes of the Hungarian Jews. Kertesz had given Wallenberg a list of some 90 former members of the Social Democrat Party who were to be given protection passes. According to Antal, "People looked at the protection passes as something new" and did not know what to make of them. Some thought the documents were useless because they were not able to travel to Sweden; others wanted to see how the situation developed in Hungary. Antal recalled that Swedish Minister Danielsson was at first reluctant to sign the passes, and Wallenberg arranged a meeting between the minister and Kertesz. Danielsson told Kertesz that the passes were a very political matter and could jeopardize his career. But failure to sign these passes could cost people's lives, Kertesz quickly answered. Danielsson agreed to sign the passes if the situation worsened. Kertesz soon called upon the minister and asked him to make good on his promise. Danielsson signed the passes, whose number had been increased to 130.

Referring to the protection pass as but one of Wallenberg's accomplishments, Antal gave full praise to the Swede: "All who knew Raoul Wallenberg and became familiar with his work have come to know his deep level of humanity and his self-sacrificing nature. The saving of so many Jews was the nearest thing to his heart."

In testimony in June, 1970, Yitzchak Younger of Tel Aviv dealt with the provision of food for the persecuted Jews, especially the children. Mr. Younger and nine others were were hiding in the basement of a locksmith shop that also housed a Jewish children's home. Mr. Younger told Wallenberg that the children, as well as those in hiding, desperately needed food. Without delay Wallenberg sent canned foods, sweets, and other provisions to that house and always made sure that its inhabitants had the supplies necessary for survival.

The testimonies of Antal, Younger, and other Israelis were significant not only in giving deserved praise to Wallenberg, but also in helping stimulate an awareness among the general Israeli population. During the 1970s, this awareness grew to the point that an Israeli prime minister involved himself in the battle to free Raoul Wallenberg, and Israeli citizens stepped forward to report that they had seen Raoul Wallenberg while they were in Soviet prisons.

However, there seems to be disagreement on the efficacy of the Israeli government's involvement in the Wallenberg case. At a 1974 Yad Vashem conference on Rescue Attempts During the Holocaust, Professor Béla Vago, of Haifa University, said that Israel was withholding "publication of certain diplomatic documents," whose revelation would make clear that Gromyko lied when he stated that Wallenberg died in 1947. The author wrote to Professor Vago, asking for a clarification of his statement and a listing of the withheld documents. The history scholar replied:

> In the past the Swedish government asked the Israeli authorities to locate and contact Jews living in Romania and in Hungary who allegedly possess information about Wallenberg. In one concrete case a Jewish citizen of Communist Romania (Transylvania) had personal information about Wallenberg, whom he had allegedly met when he was a prisoner of war in the Soviet Union (a former member of a forced labor battalion sent to the Eastern Front). I am sure time is not ripe yet for disclosing these inquiries.

When asked about Professor Vago's 1974 comments and his letter of July 28, 1980, Dr. von Dardel replied that he was unaware of the prisoner mentioned or of the documents to which Professor Vago alluded.

Nevertheless, beginning with Sweden, then Israel, and later the United States, interest in Raoul Wallenberg's fate was especially keen among the citizenry during the decade of the seventies. At the beginning of the decade the Swedish government did its best to dampen interest in the Wallenberg case. At a press conference in Vienna in 1972, Foreign Minister Krister Wickman stated that the government had consigned the case of Raoul Wallenberg to oblivion. The efforts to rescue Wallenberg had been "spent," to use a favorite expression of Swedish officials.

The diagnosis was premature. In March, 1973, Palmstierna asked the Swedish section of Voices of Martyrs, headed by anti-Communist Richard Wurmbrand, if there was any hope for determining the status of Raoul Wallenberg. Yes, there was news, Palmstierna was told. An "official" American publication included testimonies by former Russian prisoners. Raoul Wallenberg had been alive as late as 1962!

The Voices of Martyrs referred to the hearings of February 1, 1973, before the U.S. Senate. The subject was "USSR Labor Camps" and the hearing body was the Subcommittee to Investigate the Administration of the Internal Security Act and Other Internal Security Laws. It is a horrifying, chilling, blood-curdling document. Twenty years after the death of Stalin, thousands of Russian camps and prisons still held millions of political prisoners, under conditions as savage as they had ever been. The major witness was Abraham Shifrin, now of Zichron Yaakov, Israel, who spent ten years in the Russian camps and four years in exile. Shifrin, who had been chief legal adviser of the Contract Division of the Ministry of Defense, was originally arrested in 1953 as part of the Stalin-inspired anti-Jewish terror (although Stalin had died before the arrest was made). He remained imprisoned on charges of spying for Israel and America, a charge the Russians supported with the fact that his father had been imprisoned in Siberia, where he died after a ten-year sentence.

Shifrin was last incarcerated at Camp Number 7 in Potma (Dubravlag). There he stealthily completed a Russian translation of *Exodus* and smuggled it out in his baggage—a story in itself. At Camp 7 Shifrin first heard of Wrangel Island, a camp above the Arctic Circle. A group of prisoners who had recently returned from Wrangel Island told about their experiences, to Shifrin's amazement. He had never heard of the island before and had not known that there were three camps there. Shifrin concluded that the existence of the camps was "top secret." In the spring of 1963, the new arrivals told Shifrin that the camps contained only "fascist generals" and high-ranking foreign officers.

Shifrin was still not convinced that there was a Wrangel Island. But in 1972, having already settled in Israel, Shifrin received confirmation from a most unlikely source—another Israeli immigrant and former Russian prisoner, Yefim Moshinsky. Irony of ironies! The same Russian officer who had arrested the Angel of Rescue in Budapest in 1945 was his fellow prisoner some fifteen years later, in frigid hell, at the Arctic Circle.

The notary of the American embassy in Israel certified Moshinsky's story, and it was incorporated into the Senate testimony under the name "KOZLOV," because Moshinsky still had close relatives in Russia. His problems began in 1948, on the day that Andrei Zhadanov, the powerful Soviet political figure, died. That day also marked the arrival in Moscow of Mrs. Golda Meir, Israel's first envoy to the Kremlin. At the time Moshinsky was a translator for the Ministry of Internal Affairs. He was sent to the Metropol Hotel disguised as a waiter and "instructed to eavesdrop on everything Mrs. Meir would say in Yiddish." Moshinsky was unaware that someone had also been sent to keep tabs on him. Sensing the conviviality of the occasion, Moshinsky decided to ask Mrs. Meir about her newly independent country. According to Moshinsky, "She replied in Yiddish that it was the first Jewish state in history for Jews throughout the world." That was it for Moshinsky: he was denounced to the KGB as a Zionist. Moshinsky was arrested, released after a long period, harassed and persecuted for ten years, imprisoned and sent to Amurskaya, and finally to Wrangel Island, where he remained until 1962.

Situated 30 miles within the Arctic Circle and some 100 miles north of the Siberian mainland, Wrangel Island has a colorful history. It was discovered in 1867 by an English whaling crew and named for Baron Ferdinand von Wrangel, a Russian Arctic explorer who was governor of Alaska from 1829 to 1834. The U.S. laid claim to the island in the 1880s, but over the next four decades Russia and Great Britain also contested for it. The Soviets closed the matter in 1942 when a gunboat landed. Russia's *Great Encyclopedia* describes Wrangel as a mountainous island with small lakes and a "very bad climate," whose median temperature is −21.3 to −23 degrees centigrade. There is much snow in the "very short" summer season.

While written reports are scarce about life on Wrangel Island, there are many detailed presentations about existence in the area known as Kolyma, called by Solzhenitsyn "that pole of cold and cruelty in the Archipelago." In the *Gulag Archipelago* Solzhenitsyn relates the experiences of a Kolyma resident, Ivan Semyonovich Karpunich-Braven, former commander of the Fortieth Division. Their hunger was so severe that prisoners ate the week-old corpse of a horse that was covered with maggots. Other prisoners ate large amounts of lubricating grease and Iceland moss. They worked in temperatures of 50 degrees below Fahrenheit but were forbidden to light fires to warm themselves. In the winter, those who did not meet the work quotas were punished by being stripped, having cold water poured over them, and being forced to run naked back to the compound; in the summer they were tied to a pole under a cloud of mosquitoes, beaten with the butt of a rifle, and thrown into an isolation cell. The ultimate punishment, the death carriage, was for those who persisted in not fulfilling their work quotas. The carriage was a frame on a tractor sledge with a small door, no windows, and nothing inside. Condemned prisoners were jammed into the carriage and hauled off by a tractor to a vale several miles from the camp. After one day the carriage was unlocked and their corpses thrown out to be buried in the wintry storms.

Another account of Kolyma is presented in *Journey Into the Whirlwind* by Eugenia Ginzburg, who was in Siberia during her eighteen years of imprisonment:

> I cannot remember, and perhaps I never knew, what rational purpose this "improvement" was supposed to serve. I only remember the ferocious wind, the forty-degree frost, the appalling weight of the pick, and the wild, irregular thumping of the heart. At one o'clock we were marched back for dinner. More stumbling in and out of snowdrifts, more shouts and threats from the guards whenever we fell out of line. Back in the camp, we received one longed-for piece of bread and soup and were allowed half an hour in which to huddle around the stove in the hope of absorbing enough warmth to last us halfway back to the field (367).

Under conditions similar to these, Moshinsky testified, Wallenberg was still imprisoned in 1962.

There is some doubt if Stockholm knew about Moshinsky's testimony. In the spring of 1973, diplomatic relations between Sweden and the United States had been suspended because of American involvement in Vietnam. Only Chargé d'Affaires Leif Leifland represented Stockholm in Washington. Palmstierna is convinced that Leifland did not have immediate knowledge of the hearing and thus could not inform the government to move quickly and make an approach to the Soviets. "In other words," writes Palmstierna, "our then government had deprived itself of the possibility of using these expedients without delay." Once more, the neutrality of Sweden had worked to the detriment of Raoul Wallenberg.

However, Palmstierna is quick to emphasize that private Swedish citizens could easily have gotten the Senate report and forwarded it to top Swedish officials. But Prime Minister Olof Palme did not learn the latest news about Wallenberg until July, 1973, and the source was not the Foreign Ministry. Once again, Palmstierna lashes out at the callousness and deceitfulness of the Swedish government:

> It was, however, an easy matter for a private Swede to get this upsetting reading matter a few weeks after publication, and equally easy to forward it. But not until July, 1973, did our Prime Minister Olof Palme hear about it—not through the channels of our Foreign Ministry. It is hardly surprising that he turned pale—not from sympathy for the fate of Wallenberg, but rather from fear for the reactions of the press if before the elections of 1973 it was informed of the way these matters had been dealt with.
>
> But Mr. Palme could feel reassured. Our leading papers did not understand or did not dare to use this weapon.

That much can be stated. Ignorance of the information contained in the hearings of the Senate was not in accordance with Palme's dictum that "every trace and every clue regarding Wallenberg had been closely followed up"—a dictum that he repeated in 1974. This was simply not true.

Moshinsky is certain that Raoul Wallenberg was at Wrangel Island in 1962—fifteen years after the Russians had certified him as dead. Moshinsky pinpointed Wallenberg's imprisonment in the Dwelling Zone, one of three units in Wrangel, the others being the Working Zone and Hospital Zone. More than that, Moshinsky had firsthand knowledge because he exchanged many messages with Wallenberg. The following testimony of Moshinsky, although not totally accurate, clearly attests to the fact that he had been in contact with Raoul Wallenberg:

There were also many others, including Italian war prisoners. There was also Raoul Wallenberg, who had been Swedish consul in Budapest during the war and who under the German occupation, aided by money, helped Jews escape from Hungary, through Switzerland, into other countries. When the Russians entered Budapest, Raoul Wallenberg was immediately arrested at the request of the military commandant of the city of Budapest and sent by special train to Moscow. He was then 27 years old and was a handsome, educated young man.

Moshinsky continued, describing Wrangel as a place for those who were "legally" dead but still alive—prisoners like Wallenberg. It was a place for human experimentation, in the despicable pattern of the Nazis:

The camp on Wrangel Island was an experimental camp, where experiments were conducted on living people. The experiments were in the form of injections, diets, oxygen tests on people who were long declared dead but were alive at that time [1962] and were working very hard in the camp. The guards and the administrative staff were former convicts.

The Wallenberg family is not convinced of the truth of the Wrangel Island testimony. Dr. von Dardel said:

I attach very little weight to the reports from Wrangel Island. The major witness is Moshinsky, and he does not personally make a very credible impression. When he left Wrangel he produced letters of personal greetings supposedly written by Raoul, which had been smuggled out of Russia. The letters are not authentic. There is no possibility that Raoul wrote them. It is possible that the Russians sent Moshinsky out in an attempt to frustrate our search. . . .

[It is] very improbable that Raoul Wallenberg, who is considered an important prisoner of the Soviets, should be exposed to the rigors of that Arctic island. Secondly, except in the first year of imprisonment, Raoul was never together with foreign prisoners. If he were in Wrangel, he would have been with foreign prisoners—a very unlikely situation.

Nothing has shaken Shifrin's trust in the veracity of the original testimony of Moshinsky, who presently works in an Israeli hospital. According to Shifrin, those who maintain that the Russians would not place Wallenberg in "such severe conditions" as Wrangel Island do not understand the Soviet system. Shifrin also feels that Moshinsky has compromised his trustworthiness, in part, by being misled by the press. However, the essence of his testimony still remains believable. As Shifrin told the author in October, 1981:

> Those who think the Soviets could not place Raoul Wallenberg in such severe conditions simply know nothing of the essence of the system ruled by these gangsters . . . . Concerning Moshinsky I can say that I was the first to find him and take testimony from him. I have checked every little detail of his *original* testimony in many ways and am absolutely sure that he *originally* said the truth. Later on when he saw that the newspapermen demanded new and new details and paid money for the "news," he started inventing new details, which was quite stupid on his part . . . . However, those who know the matter real well know what is true in his testimony and what belongs to the imagination.

The Wrangel Island testimony is quite important to the Wallenberg case. First, it establishes that Wallenberg was alive fifteen years after the Russians claimed him to be dead. Secondly, and perhaps more critically, it prompts the question: Can an individual, especially a Westerner, survive the rigors of the Arctic Circle camp? And if one can survive, what is his condition?

With the new information that came from Moshinsky and Shifrin, one could assume that following the Svartz disclosure, Wallenberg had been transferred to Wrangel Island. There was no information about what happened after the close of the Svartz case, but the Wallenberg family was not going to sit back and wait for the government to act.

Two months before the Swedish prime minister was aware of the Wrangel Island information, Mrs. von Dardel, then in her eighties, wrote a moving, personal appeal to U.S. Secretary of State Henry Kissinger, asking him to find out the truth about her son, and if he was alive, to help him gain his freedom. The letter of May 4, 1973, and the subsequent developments were first revealed in 1979 by Svén Stromberg, correspondent for the Swedish radio in London, after he had researched the documents under the U.S. Freedom of Information Act.

Mrs. Dardel's brief letter makes its points clearly:

> I ask you, who by virtue of your extraordinary efforts have liberated thousands of prisoners, against the background of my tragic ignorance of what really happened to my son after he was arrested, to inform me if you have the possibility to undertake something which can throw new light on my son's fate, and if he still is alive to return him to liberty.

After researching the case, a panel of five State Department officials recommended that Kissinger undertake appropriate action. The panel drafted a letter for the secretary's approval and taped coded instructions requiring U.S. envoys in Moscow to initiate an inquiry with the Russians. The proposed letter to Mrs. Dardel was as follows:

"Against the background of the humanitarian nature of the case and your son's efforts for the Hungarian Jews during the last war, the United States government is prepared to ask the Soviet government via the American Embassy in Moscow what has happened to your son."

The letter was never sent. On October 11, 1973, the proposal's doom was noted with three words, "rejected by Kissinger." Kissinger gave no explanation for his rejection. In fact, queries to his office received a response of "no comment." When pressed for an answer by Lena Biorck Kaplan, head of the American Wallenberg Committee, Kissinger maintained that he never knew the letter was disapproved; in fact, his staff members were authorized to use his signature. Stromberg feels that Kissinger's refusal to aid a mother in distress was based on his animosity to Sweden's criticism of America's involvement in Southeast Asia, and especially its bombing of Cambodia.

Kissinger's refusal was by no means taken as a signal that all was hopeless twenty-eight years after the disappearance of Raoul Wallenberg. Late in 1973 a television team from Sweden came to Israel to interview Abraham Shifrin. Following its broadcast in Sweden, a letter arrived at the Swedish television center from a Hungarian national who had been a political prisoner in the Russian camps. He wrote that in 1967 he was briefly held captive with Raoul Wallenberg at a large camp for foreigners, situated east of Irkutsk, in Zabaikal'e. To the best of the prisoner's knowledge, Wallenberg had been brought to the camp from Wrangel Island. And so Raoul Wallenberg, certified as dead in 1947, had been traced alive at least until 1967.

Hopes were rekindled. Among those joining the search for Raoul Wallenberg was the famed Nazi-hunter Simon Wiesenthal, whose Vienna-based Jewish Documentation Center had helped bring more than one thousand former Nazis, including Eichmann, to justice. Wiesenthal's dedication to the search for the missing Swede was conveyed in a letter of February 12, 1975, to U.S. Senator Henry Jackson: "To millions of Swedish citizens and to thousands who have survived Soviet Russian barbarity, the case of Wallenberg has become a sort of trauma. To know that we can do nothing to bring light into the fate of a man who fell victim to his own good deeds is almost unbearable." In 1975 Wiesenthal located a former prisoner who reported that while he was serving a sentence on Wrangel Island in the 1960s, he had heard talk of "a Swede" being in the same camp. Wiesenthal, whose interest in Wallenberg dates to 1970, also located an Austrian Jewish doctor, former Communist Menachem Meltzer, who maintained that he treated Wallenberg while they were both prisoners in the summer of 1948, at camp Khal'mer-Yu, located in the subpolar Komi republic. According to Shifrin, Khal'mer-Yu has been described as a group of three "special strict-regime camps," where some nine hundred prisoners are assigned to mining duties. A former prisoner at a nearby camp in Syktyvkar reported being threatened by the camp commander: "This is an ordinary-regime camp. If you get into trouble here, you'll be sent to Khal'mer-Yu." Shifrin relates that prisoners at Khal'mer-Yu, north of the Arctic Circle, often joke, "Twelve months of the year we have winter. The rest of the time we have summer" (205).

Wiesenthal's involvement in the Wallenberg affair was heartening; however, a more exciting happening related to Aleksandr Solzhenitsyn, the 1974 Nobel laureate in literature, whose imprisonment in the Gulag Archipelago is reflected in the sordid details in the novel by that name. While in Sweden to receive the Nobel Prize, he visited Raoul Wallenberg's mother and urged her not to stop trying to find her son. During the visit he held a press conference, at which he answered questions on a wide range of subjects, e.g., Amnesty International, his reputed contempt for democracy, his plans to return to Russia. He also spoke at length in response to questions from a correspondent of *Russian Thought.* The interview, which appeared in its edition of January 16, 1975, was translated from the Russian by Albert and Tanya Schmidt.

The correspondent asked Solzhenitsyn two questions about Wallenberg: "What can you say about the fate of Raoul Wallenberg? Did you hear about him when you were in the camps?"

Solzhenitsyn replied,

No, I heard nothing of him when I was a prisoner, or for many years after that. This just shows how vast is the Gulag Archipelago, and how many hidden places there are. There are many such secret places, where prisoners are isolated forever, where no word ever trickles out, so that no one knows about these people.

I happened to meet another Scandinavian who called himself Erik Arvid Andersen. When I tried to find out something about him here in Sweden, and to learn who his relatives are, I came across the Wallenberg story.

From Solzhenitsyn's response, it is quite clear that he never actually met Raoul Wallenberg. He did meet a Scandinavian called Erik Arvid Andersen, on whom he based a character in his book *Gulag Archipelago.*

Solzhenitsyn then describes his meeting with Raoul Wallenberg's mother, noting the impact and reality of a twenty-nine-year sentence:

Yesterday I saw Wallenberg's mother. It was heartbreaking to see this old lady, who has been waiting for her son for twenty-nine years. Please weigh and consider the full meaning of what I am saying — twenty-nine years! Wallenberg was arrested at almost the same time I was. I served my entire sentence, both imprisonment and exile, was set free for a number of years, as you know from my published writings . . . . But this man has been in prison for twenty-nine years and is still there today!

Although Solzhenitsyn does not challenge the accounts of the witnesses who claim to have been in prison with Wallenberg, he stresses that because of the nature of the Soviet system, these reports can only be "indirect testimony":

> Wallenberg's mother has information on who was in prison with her son, and when. I do not for a minute doubt the authenticity of her data. In the Gulag Archipelago, if a man said he was in prison with someone else, that is the truth. Fourteen witnesses are listed here, and it is evident that he has been kept in secret confinement, but occasionally someone or other saw him briefly and this is how the information seeped out.
>
> But here is the difference: if a man is arrested in the West or the Third World, it is open knowledge in what prison he is held and how he is being treated . . . . But Wallenberg is in a Soviet prison, so all we have is this kind of indirect testimony from people, some of whom conceal their identity either because they are still in Eastern Europe or because they have relatives there . . . . And so, since they are all so well hidden in Russia, since prisoners are so well concealed and kept incommunicado, no one tries to free them; I have heard that your Prime Minister Olof Palme considers that there is too little information to justify spoiling relations with the Soviet Union on account of Wallenberg.

In his lengthy response Solzhenitsyn mentions the "amazing story" of Yefim Moshinsky:

> Wallenberg's mother is currently in correspondence with a certain Yefim Moshinsky, the former KGB captain who arrested Wallenberg. Now in Israel, he tells what a nice man Wallenberg was, the man he was ordered to arrest. Ordered to arrest a Swedish diplomat! Well, all right. The State Security captain summoned him amicably from the Embassy, drove off with him in his car, then arrested him. Wallenberg was then sent from one Soviet secret prison to the next.

At the close of his response, Solzhenitsyn reviews the Soviet's efforts to close the case in 1957 through falsifying records and stating that Wallenberg died in 1947. Evidence after 1957, according to the Soviet author, shows that Wallenberg was still alive as late as 1970. Action must be taken immediately, and Solzhenitsyn suggests Jewish activism in Raoul Wallenberg's behalf:

> Much of the information in the possession of Wallenberg's mother dates from later [after 1957], and even very recent times . . . from fellow prisoners who said he was still alive in 1970. He is now sixty-two years old. We must hurry, hurry to have him released. What is needed for that is a powerful public opinion movement able to force your government to save this man. And here I think that Jewish world opinion could be very helpful. Here is why I say this: you probably know that Wallenberg, as an official of the Swedish embassy in Budapest, rescued Jews from death by getting them to the West. According to that data, he saved over twenty thousand Jews in this manner, and I think that

Jewish public opinion, which has been so effective in defending Jewish people in the Soviet Union imprisoned for one, three, or five years, could come out strongly for Wallenberg and save him.

Having given hope to the Wallenberg family and having publicly voiced his sentiments, Solzhenitsyn felt that he had done everything he could. In order to rouse world opinion for Wallenberg, members of the family and members of the Free Wallenberg Committee communicated with the Nobel laureate. He replied that he could do no more.

"We appreciate that Solzhenitsyn stepped forward when he did," Mrs. Lagergren said. "He did show that he cared about the fate of Raoul Wallenberg. But he is no longer part of the effort to free Raoul Wallenberg."

In any event, the involvement of Solzhenitsyn and Wiesenthal, as well as the reports of new witnesses, served to keep the Wallenberg case open and sustained the hopes of those who refused to give up; but for all practical purposes, Stockholm had ceased to act. Foreign Minister Anderson said in May, 1974, that in the past the government had tried many times to speak to the Russians. However, all the talk led nowhere and now any further attempt "seems useless."

When the author asked Dr. von Dardel what he would have done differently during the thirty years of his half brother's imprisonment, he quickly responded: "The family should have been more aggressive in pushing the Russians for an exchange of prisoners. The father of Francis Gary Powers, the American flyer shot down by the Russians, was aggressive in seeking his son's release, and the result was an exchange for Rudolf Abel. Perhaps we missed out because we weren't aggressive enough."

Three decades had passed since Raoul Wallenberg was abducted by the Russians in Budapest. Those who returned from the Gulag Archipelago testified that they had seen him alive at different times, and at different places during those thirty years. How long could one man survive imprisonment by a merciless, totalitarian power? A vigorous, intensive campaign had to be set in motion worldwide before it was too late.

12

The Decisive Years

The year 1977 marked a turning point in the bizarre story of the disappearance of Raoul Wallenberg. No one single incident or development— such as the Svartz discovery—that dramatically raised hopes for the freeing of Raoul Wallenberg appeared in 1977; yet, there were no agonizing setbacks, no Vishinsky-like notes, no Gromyko-like memoranda. Taken together, everything that has occurred since 1977 has given rise to the feeling that if Raoul Wallenberg is to be brought back alive from Russia, it will have to be accomplished soon. If Raoul Wallenberg is no longer living, conclusive proof will be given during this period. If the years after 1945 were the lost years, then the period starting with 1977 can be considered the decisive years.

A clearer focus on human rights, a greater awareness of the Holocaust, further involvement of dedicated individuals and groups, and new accounts by former Soviet prisoners are the major elements of these decisive years.

The widespread advocacy of human rights has created a climate more conducive for demanding the release of prisoners such as Raoul Wallenberg. U.S. President Jimmy Carter's 1977 call for the affirmation of human rights throughout the globe buoyed up those seeking freedom for Wallenberg. U.S. Ambassador Arthur Goldberg reportedly brought up the Wallenberg case at the Belgrade sequel to the 1978 Helsinki Conference on Human Rights. In 1979 the Carter administration exchanged two Soviet spies for five leading Soviet dissidents. Speaking before the U.S. Senate in 1979, U.S. Senator Claiborne Pell called the Raoul Wallenberg case "a human rights question that should be resolved." The senator added: "The Soviets have been asked repeatedly for fuller information concerning Raoul Wallenberg

170

and, most important, to give him his freedom if, as many of us believe, he is alive." According to Per Anger, "The worldwide attention which has been placed on human rights has been a very significant development in giving us hope that we will win the freedom of Raoul Wallenberg."

Mrs. Lagergren feels that the world has become more sensitized to the Raoul Wallenberg case through a greater awareness of the Holocaust, accomplished, in particular, through the television showing of "Holocaust." She noted that the series, first shown in 1978, has been seen by more than 300 million persons, introducing them to the horrors of the final solution. After becoming aware of the atrocities committed by the Nazis, she said, one can better appreciate and be grateful for the heroism of Raoul Wallenberg and want to do something to help him gain his freedom.

Although the human rights issue and public awareness of the Holocaust and the heroism of Raoul Wallenberg were welcome and helpful, the campaign to free the Angel of Rescue needed positive information about his survival to sustain its momentum. Such reports were forthcoming. In November, 1977, Wiesenthal spoke at international hearings in Rome on alleged violations of human rights in Russia and Eastern Europe. According to Wiesenthal, Wallenberg was seen in a mental hospital in Irkutsk, Siberia, as late as 1975.

This information, carried as a small news item in the *New York Times,* had a personal significance for Mrs. Annette Lantos, of Hillsborough, California. Mrs. Lantos, who was twelve years old during the terrifying Nazi takeover of Hungary, feels that she owes her life to Raoul Wallenberg. Armed with Portuguese papers, the teenage girl and her mother managed to get out of Hungary. However, her father was snatched from a safe house by the Arrow Cross and murdered on the street.

When she began lecturing on the Holocaust several years ago, Mrs. Lantos tempered the atrocities of the Holocaust with a recital of the heroism and humanity of Wallenberg. When she read the item in the *Times,* she recalled, her mind "just went blank." Mrs. Lantos continued: "The horror of it! That this man might be languishing, alive, in prison—this hero! My mind began to race. What could I do? I knew I could not go on living my own little life without doing something."

She hardly could have done more. She contacted the media, wrote to the Wallenberg family, and organized a national campaign. Joining in her efforts was her husband Dr. Thomas P. Lantos, a professor of economics at the University of California in San Francisco, who survived in a Swedish protected house during the Nazi takeover of Hungary. The Lantos's campaign led to the 1979 formation of the U.S. Free Wallenberg Committee, which then included U.S. Senators Rudy Boschwitz, Frank Church, Daniel Moynihan, and Claiborne Pell. Committees in the U.S. and Sweden have coordinated their efforts with similar groups working on behalf of Raoul Wallenberg in England, France, Israel, Switzerland, and West Germany.

Speaking of her determination to work for the release of Wallenberg, Mrs. Lantos said that her hero "saved not only our lives, but our faiths, our beliefs. He was a shining example of the triumph of the human spirit. Seeing this courage, in the midst of the unspeakable brutality, somehow enabled us to rise above ourselves, too."

Following the appearance of a December 19, 1977, article in *New York* magazine, indicating that Wallenberg might still be alive, Mrs. Lantos suggested to Senator Church that he write to Soviet Ambassador Anatoly Dobrinin. In 1978 Peter Fenn, the senator's executive assistant, had a meeting regarding Wallenberg with Nikolay D. Smirnov, attaché of the Soviet embassy. Mr. Fenn filed the following memorandum on his meeting with Smirnov:

> I inquired as to why there was not a written response and Mr. Smirnov replied that the Soviet Union had responded already to the Swedish government and we were a third country. He stated that we should contact the Swedish Embassy if we desired further information on the case.
>
> According to Smirnov, Wallenberg was taken into custody by the Russian military in 1945. In July of 1947 Wallenberg was found dead in the Lubianka prison outside Moscow. For a number of years the Swedish government made inquiries concerning Wallenberg without success. On February 6, 1957, the Swedish Ambassador in Moscow was given a note by the Swedish official which indicated that Wallenberg was imprisoned with no charges and died in prison. There was evidence of wrongdoing, and the Chief of the Internal Security Division (KGB), Mr. Abakumov, was held responsible. He was later executed for committing atrocities during the Stalin era. However, since his trial was closed, it was impossible to know the specific charges against him, and, therefore, to substantiate the involvement with Wallenberg.
>
> Smirnov said that the note that was given to the Swedish diplomat expressed the condolences to the family of Raoul Wallenberg.
>
> Finally, Smirnov maintained that the Swedish White Book, published in 1965, devoted a major section to the Wallenberg case, and the Soviet Union considered it closed.

In 1977, the release of Gunnar Rode, who had been imprisoned for fifteen years for anti-Soviet activities in Latvia, brought forth new information on the whereabouts of Raoul Wallenberg. Rode was told by a copassenger in a 1973 prisoner transport that he had recently shared a cell with a Swedish diplomat in Mordvinia, a prison complex in the Moldavian republic.

In 1981, Rode, now a resident of Stockholm, recreated the conversation during the 1973 transport:

> I was at a train station leaving for Mordvinia when I met another prisoner who was leaving the station, headed for another destination. Suddenly the man shouted, "Are there any political prisoners here?" While it may seem strange that a prisoner can shout, there are certain conditions when it is possible,

especially if there are guards who are sympathetic. Because he spoke what sounded like Yiddish, I assumed he was Jewish.

The man continued his conversation: "I am not important, but that other person is. He is a Swedish diplomat. That other person can do something for me. Tell the people in Sweden."

Rode thought the incident was "peculiar" because he could not understand how diplomats could be in prison. But during his imprisonment in Vladimir during 1974-77 he confirmed the fact that a Swedish official was in prison. Rode cited Yaakov Suslansky, now in Israel, who corroborated the information.

However, the name of Raoul Wallenberg still meant nothing to Rode, until he held a press conference after his release in Stockholm, and the name of the missing Swede was mentioned. He didn't make the immediate connection between Wallenberg and the 1973 transport, but finally, after making contact with the Sakharov Committee, Rode was able to piece the facts together.

While the Rode testimony seems credible, and it does establish that Wallenberg was alive some twenty-five years after his supposed death, members of the Wallenberg Association do not stress the significance of Rode's account.

According to a spokesman for the association, "The testimony of Gunnar Rode seems to vary, depending on the questions put to him by different reporters. It is also difficult to visualize a Russian prisoner shouting on a train and no guard stopping him. Since Rode didn't speak Yiddish—and had no common language with the other prisoners—it is hard to explain how Rode got the message. What occurred to Rode illustrates some of the problems we have with second-hand testimony."

Rode, however, still reiterates his basic point: he had been told by another prisoner of the continued imprisonment of a Swedish diplomat.

Those working for the release of Raoul Wallenberg were more encouraged by the appearance of Avraham Kalinski, a former Soviet prisoner who became the sixteenth witness known to the West who claimed to have seen Wallenberg after the USSR certified him as dead. Kalinski, a Polish Jew who was a former army captain, arrived in Haifa, Israel, in 1976. He had spent fifteen years in the Gulag Archipelago, from 1944 through 1959. In two postcards from a Russian prison to his sister in Haifa, Kalinski mentioned that in 1959 he had met a Swede who had saved Jews in Rumania. According to Dr. von Dardel, "The mixup between Hungary and Rumania is understandable. We have seen these postcards, and we have no doubt they are genuine."

According to Kalinski, he had first heard about Wallenberg through the Russian author Vendrofski, who shared a cell with the Swede in Verchneuralsk in 1951.

Kalinski's testimony further states that Wallenberg was interned in the Verchneuralsk Prison in the Cel'abinsk region from the late 1940s until 1953; from 1953 to 1955, he was imprisoned in Alexandrovski Central Prison in the Irkutsk region; in 1955 he was transferred to the Vladimir Prison and placed in cell 23, Corpus 2, where Kalinski last saw him in late 1959 before his own release and rehabilitation.

According to Shifrin, the Cel'abinsk region, located on the eastern slopes of the southern Urals, includes eighteen camps, among them Verchneuralsk. Prisoners at the camp labor under hazardous health conditions in the construction industry or in metallurgical plants (341). Shifrin can provide little information about Alexandrovski Prison in the Irkutsk region, an area about which precise data are lacking; however, some of the camps include many foreigners and operate under brutal conditions (154–157).

Much is known about Vladimir Prison, which was built during the reign of Empress Catherine II and later renamed the Special Political Isolation Prison. The facility is said to be the most rigorous under KGB rule, making it very difficult to learn the identity of one's neighboring inmates. Former inmates have included Vasili Stalin, son of the late Soviet dictator; Francis Gary Powers; and Anatoli Shcharansky. The newer buildings, including Corpus 2, have been constructed to deny the prisoners sunlight. The windows are sealed off halfway up and are barred. Prisoners are prevented from looking out onto the courtyard by translucent screens on every window, producing a constant twilight illumination. According to Shifrin, the newer structures "are built of reinforced concrete, which represents a serious hazard to the health and lives of the inmates" (248–249).

The terrifying conditions at Vladimir are detailed in Shifrin's *Guidebook* by an eyewitness, A. V.:

> Upon arriving in 1970, we were told by the prison authorities that we would first be put into quarantine. This meant living on starvation rations in a cell without personal possessions or books. We were subsequently placed under strict regime for six months. The first of these six months was spent under isolation-cell conditions (approximately 800 calories).
>
> All this was done to break the spirit of the inmates at the outset of their imprisonment. After six months of stupefying hunger, you could hardly think about anything except a piece of bread. The people were reduced to humiliation, torpidity, and brutality. I witnessed a few prisoners who cut open a vein in order to dip bread in their blood as a means of satisfying their hunger. I once even saw a prisoner who cooked a piece of flesh that he had cut from his own leg. He started a fire with the use of pages torn from a book by Karl Marx that he had obtained from the library.
>
> Except for the herbs that the inmates were allowed to eat in the camp in the summer and from which at least a few vitamins could be gotten, I was never given any vegetables or greens during my whole three years in Vladimir prison (249–250).

Former prisoner Kalinski said that it is possible that Wallenberg was still alive, even under such horrendous conditions, and the only way to gain his freedom would be for the Swedish government to be more aggressive. "The Swedes have tried quiet diplomacy . . . and it has got them nowhere."

Kalinski presented his suggestions in a March, 1979, interview in the Swedish magazine *Veckojournalen*: "If Wallenberg is to be saved, Sweden must make a fuss all over the world. With the Russians, one must be forceful! This is the only language they understand in questions of this kind. Had the Swedish government pounded on the table earlier, you would have had Wallenberg in Stockholm long ago!"

In his book Anger maintains that "because of the commotion that arose" from the Kalinski testimony, the Russians "were anxious to show accommodation"—but not concerning Wallenberg. In 1978 Lajmonis Niedre was jailed for espionage in his former Latvian homeland. After being released early in 1979, Niedre returned to Sweden and revealed to the press that a high official in the Soviet Ministry of the Interior had told him the Russians saw four possible ways to "close the [his] case": an exchange of Niedre for someone else; a plea from Sweden for humanitarian considerations; a release of Niedre because of physical disability; Niedre's retrial in Russia. The Russian official said that the preferable choices were the prisoner exchange and release on humanitarian grounds. Because of Niedre's failing health, it seems that he was released for humanitarian reasons.

However, Anger feels that Niedre may have been released to avoid an unpleasant incident with Sweden, and by freeing Niedre the Russians did not have to be concerned about Wallenberg: "Did they want to avoid creating still another irritating factor in their relations with Sweden? In that case, did this happen at Wallenberg's expense" (144-145)?

The Swedish press kept a close watch on developments in the Wallenberg case—and it was getting very restless, demanding openness on the part of the government. This could be achieved in part, Ulf Brandell suggested in the February 12, 1978, *Svenska Dagbladet,* by opening the Wallenberg files to the public: "It is certainly time for Sweden to open all the Wallenberg archives. All secret information should be open to the public. At the least, an impartial, trustworthy person should go through the extensive files and then report what has been done and what has been neglected." The government met that request and in 1979 began to disclose the documents in the Wallenberg case.

However, the public could not be satisfied when it read a remarkable article by Svén Stromberg in the March 18 edition of *Dagens Nyheter.* Having researched the U.S. State Department Archives on documentation relating to Wallenberg, he wrote that the U.S. aided Wallenberg's efforts to save Hungarian Jews and that the U.S. offered to intercede with the Russians, but Sweden declined to accept the American offer.

Stromberg concluded his article with these bitter remarks: "If the U.S. had been allowed to intervene earlier, Raoul Wallenberg's fate would most probably have not remained a riddle. The American commitment was strong and passionate. The sad truth is that it was the actions of Swedish politicians which caused Wallenberg's long suffering."

In 1979, thirty-four years after Raoul Wallenberg disappeared, his mother and stepfather both died within two days of each other. His mother was eighty-eight; his stepfather, ninety-three. Mrs. von Dardel, the most dynamic force behind the movement to free her son, never allowed the family to forget about Raoul, commenting at every family event, "If only Raoul could be with us." She never wavered in her belief that her son was still alive. Before her death she wrote to Soviet President Leonid Brezhnev, but as with previous letters sent to the Kremlin, she received no reply. After the deaths of Mr. and Mrs. von Dardel, the direction of the Wallenberg campaign passed on to the von Dardel children, who had promised their parents on their deathbeds that they would never give up the fight to find Raoul. Dr. Guy von Dardel, a physics professor at Lund University in Sweden who spends half the year doing research in nuclear physics in Switzerland, has circled the globe following leads about his half brother. His sister Mrs. Nina Lagergren, whose husband Gunnar is chief of protocol at the Swedish royal court and a judge at the International Court at The Hague, has been indefatigable in working with Wallenberg committees throughout the world.

Dr. von Dardel spoke with much admiration about the role played by his father in the search for Raoul Wallenberg: "My father deserves full credit for the magnificent work in searching for Raoul. The search occupied a major part of his life. My sister and I have been involved, but it has been an incidental undertaking, interspersed with the more mundane matters of living: in the case of my sister, raising a family; in my case, developing a scientific career."

The efforts of Dr. von Dardel and Mrs. Lagergren resulted in a U.S. approach to the Soviets — thirty-four years after Raoul's disappearance. The Swedish government was not involved and, in fact, a third country served as an intermediary. Von Dardel and Mrs. Lagergren flew to Jerusalem to meet with Menachem Begin after the Israeli prime minister had privately expressed an interest in the case. In response to an appeal by the Wallenberg family, Begin instructed Israel's Ambassador to the U.S. Ephraim Evron to ask President Carter to raise the Wallenberg case with Soviet Premier Brezhnev when the two leaders met in Vienna in June, 1979.

In the summer of 1979 U.S. Senator Frank Church, chairman of the Senate Foreign Relations Committee, asked the Soviets to make a full disclosure of its files on the Wallenberg case. Later that summer a Department of State spokesman reported that Secretary of State Cyrus R. Vance had told members of the Wallenberg Committee, "We have recently raised this case with the Soviet government and we are awaiting a Soviet reply." No reply ever came.

However, the case was far from closed. In 1979 the Wallenberg case reached another peak of hope with the case of Jan Kaplan, a Jewish prisoner in the Gulag Archipelago. The facts of the case were presented on August 10 in a *Boston Globe* article by John Bierman.

Kaplan, a former administrator of an operatic conservatory in Moscow, had been jailed in 1975 on currency charges. He was released eighteen months later for health reasons. Upon his release he phoned his daughter, Dr. Anna Bilder, an immigrant dentist in Tel Aviv, to tell her the good news. Kaplan, then sixty-six, told her, "It wasn't so bad. When I was in the prison infirmary at Butyrka in 1975 I met a Swede who'd been in different prisons for thirty years and he was in pretty good condition."

Mrs. Bilder did not catch the significance of the remark because she had never heard of Raoul Wallenberg. Subsequently, however, the story was related to Kaplan's relatives in the United States who were familiar with the Wallenberg affair. They relayed the information to the Swedish embassy in Washington. Stockholm sent a note to Moscow that pointed to the new information that Wallenberg was alive as late as 1975. The Soviets responded in January, 1979, with the usual comment: nothing had changed since the report of 1957.

Unfortunately, the Swedish government never had a chance to establish direct contact with Kaplan. The former Russian prisoner had carried a letter about Wallenberg on his person for a long time, in the hope of sending it out of Russia via a foreign tourist. One day he succeeded in giving the letter to a foreign tourist at the Moscow synagogue. Unfortunately, the letter was intercepted by the KGB, who quickly rearrested Kaplan on February 3, 1978, and sent him to Lubianka.

That seemed to be the end of the Kaplan incident, but as the thirty-four-year-long Wallenberg case had shown, the unexpected often happened. In the first week of July, 1979, Dr. Bilder received a letter from her mother Eugenia Kaplan, dated June 14. The letter had been smuggled out of Moscow by a new Israeli immigrant. Mrs. Kaplan wrote:

> I write this letter but I am not sure it will reach you and that the same thing will not happen because of the letter about this Swiss or Swede Wallberg [sic] whom he met in the prison infirmary . . . .
>
> Father wrote a long letter about this Wallberg and for a long time he carried it around with him looking for a chance to send it to you through a foreign tourist. Every Saturday he went to the synagogue where many tourists visit, but for a long time he had no success . . . .
>
> One Saturday, father came back in a very good mood and told me that at long last he had succeeded in giving the letter to a young foreign tourist who promised to send the letter from Vienna or Germany, I don't remember which.
>
> A few days later, it was on Friday night, February 3, 1978, there was a meticulous search at home and they took father away . . . . When I was called in May to the Lubianka a very angry colonel screamed at me. The Soviet authorities behaved humanely and released him [her husband] because of his sickness, but he ungratefully decided to send out illegally through a foreigner

anti-Soviet spy letters to Israel. "And your daughter," he screamed, "started there in Israel anti-Soviet propaganda . . . ."

I don't know if it is better to keep quiet as some people advise or the opposite, that some American Senators and other important people should start campaigning for father because many people were released through complaints to American Senators, and even the President himself. And some people say that only a fuss in the papers and on the radio will help.

I don't know the answer myself. Here we are like blind puppies. You can see better there. But I'm afraid he won't ever see you again or your little Daniella.

Why did your father have to interfere in this business? He never had anything to do with politics and wouldn't even listen to political jokes. Because of that letter about a poor prisoner they arrest a man and kept him for a year and a half, so what good can you expect here?

According to Dr. Bilder, the letter is authentic; the handwriting and the manner of expression are both her mother's.

Although Kaplan has never been interrogated by the Swedes, Dr. von Dardel feels that the story "smells credible." There is "something honest and unadulterated" about the Kaplan episode, he said.

However, the Kaplan story points up the difficulty of charting more than three decades of Raoul Wallenberg's imprisonment. The Kaplan story places Wallenberg at Butyrka in 1975. Previous reports had Wallenberg in that prison in the 1950s and 1960s. Other former prisoners testified that Wallenberg was in other prisons during those years. Dr. von Dardel said,

It is virtually impossible to know with absolute certainty where Raoul has been throughout these thirty-five years. The only people who have the answers are the Soviets. One of the difficulties is that many of the prisons are transition prisons. For example, Raoul was taken from Lubianka in 1946 and brought to Odessa for interrogation, according to a witness, Sigmund Mannheim. He was then returned to Lubianka. As for Butyrka, the special character of that prison as a transition prison does not cast doubt on the accuracy of the Kaplan story. Raoul may well have been transferred to Butyrka for a short period, for example, for medical treatment. He then might have been brought to Lubianka for interrogation, and then he might have been taken back to wherever he was before.

Dr. von Dardel's analysis is disputed by Cronid Lubarsky, an authority on the Soviet prison system who himself served four years. Disputing the Bierman report and subsequent Raoul Wallenberg Committee announcements, Lubarsky, now living in West Germany, said that his investigations showed that it is impossible for Kaplan to have met Wallenberg in Butyrka.

If indeed Wallenberg was at Butyrka in 1975, it might be helpful to know the character of the facility that Dr. von Dardel has called a "transitional" prison. The prison dates back to Catherine II when it served as a barracks. For Trepper, Butyrka was much more tolerable than either Lubianka or Lefortovo. As he writes in *The Great Game*: "The prison in Butyrka . . . left me with the least unpleasant memory, with its huge, light, well-ventilated rooms" (370).

Shifrin describes Butyrka as one of the largest prisons in Moscow, a complex of some twenty-five large buildings. Although spacious, seventy to one hundred inmates are often in a single cell. One building is reserved for political prisoners, with an adjacent edifice for those sentenced to death. Despite Trepper's cheerful recollection, notorious Pugachev Tower provides the setting for nightly executions by firing squad (42).

On August 22, 1979, Sweden's Prime Minister Ola Ullsten made a strong representation in a letter to Soviet Premier Alexei Kosygin, asking that a member of the Swedish embassy in Moscow be permitted to be present at a talk with Kaplan. The Swedish official also raised the issue again in the spring of 1980 when he paid an official visit to Foreign Minister Gromyko. These approaches have proven unproductive. According to official sources, Gromyko replied "coldly and was unmoved" and reaffirmed the Soviet reply already given to Sweden on January 24, 1979: "There is and cannot be anything new in the case of Raoul Wallenberg."

The *National Review* reported on August 17, 1979, that Jan Kaplan had been sent to a camp in Komi in the northern Urals, six hundred miles from Moscow. His daughter in Israel was threatened and admonished to stop talking about her father's discovery.

While Jan Kaplan may have been silenced, a Russian officer made an inadvertent disclosure on May 1, 1978, which was reported by a recent Soviet émigré to Israel in November, 1979. While still a Russian citizen, he attended a May Day celebration at the home of a friend whose father is a high official in the KGB. After a few drinks, his defenses down, the young Russian—who desires anonymity—remarked, "Wouldn't it be good to get out of this place [Russia]." The KGB official, also somewhat intoxicated, quickly retorted: "Just don't be in such a hurry; I have under me a Swede who has been trying to get out of here for over thirty years and he is still in jail." Only after the Russian had immigrated to Israel did he realize the momentous implications of the KGB official's remark. He informed Thorsten Orn, the Swedish ambassador to Israel, and publicly announced the dramatic, heartening news. The KGB official has since been ousted from his position, according to Swedish diplomatic sources.

Not all information, not all new leads are made public, however. Some of the prisoners reported to have been in a cell adjoining Raoul Wallenberg or to have known others who were his cellmates remain silent. "Some of these prisoners are still alive and free today," Dr. von Dardel said. "We hope to contact them. There is one Russian general, Kupriyanov, but I'd rather not say any more . . . ."

Unfortunately, General Gennadi N. Kupriyanov did not remain silent.

Kupriyanov had been arrested in 1949 in connection with an alleged plot known as the Leningrad Affair. He was sentenced to the Gulag, where he served until his pardon in 1956. On January 1, 1979, an article appeared in *The New Russian Word,* the American Russian immigrant paper, detailing a story of the general and his coprisoner Wallenberg.

The general said that he had been with Wallenberg in 1953, 1955, and 1956. In 1953 they had been together for three weeks during a transport between the prisons of Verchneuralsk and Alexandrovski Central. Two years later the two met again during a transport from Verchneuralsk to Vladimir lasting several weeks. In Vladimir the general was kept in Corpus 3, while Wallenberg was imprisoned in Corpus 2. Their final meeting, in 1956, took place at a dentist's office, where guards prevented their communicating with one another.

A month after the *New Russian Word* article appeared, the general was ordered to KGB headquarters and interrogated. He was reminded that he had promised, upon release from prison, never to mention the name of Wallenberg. At that meeting the general first learned that Wallenberg had never returned to Sweden. As later recorded in his notes, brought to light in 1981 by a Western acquaintance known as "I.L.," Kupriyanov "knew that he [Wallenberg] was sentenced to 25 years in 1945 or 1946 and should have been released in 1970 or 1971."

Problems intensified for Kupriyanov. In May, 1979, an article discussing his meetings with Wallenberg appeared in the Swedish newspaper *Svenska Dagbladet.* The general was immediately ordered to report to the KGB, who accused him of collaborating with Western journalists. "You who have been rehabilitated," the interrogator cried out, "must help refute the American-Israeli provocations." The general responded quickly: "We have already acknowledged the crimes of Beria. Why cannot we, then, also acknowledge the crime against Wallenberg?" Infuriated, the KGB colonel shouted, "We are not here to discuss the possible crimes of Beria but the crimes of the American and Israeli intelligence agencies against the Soviet Union." The general was directed to formulate a denial of the article in the Swedish paper, but at a second session with the KGB, he refused to disclaim that he had met Wallenberg. A third and final questioning with the KGB followed several days later. The general would not give in.

According to "I.L.," the general became sick after the third meeting and was taken to the hospital. Five days later Mrs. Kupriyanov received a call from the hospital requesting that she visit her husband. When she arrived, he was already dead and in the morgue. She was not even allowed to identify him. The cause of death was given as "infarctus of the heart." While Mrs. Kupriyanov was at the hospital, the KGB searched her apartment and removed all papers and documents.

While the disheartening Kupriyanov episode offers no new, conclusive information on Wallenberg's whereabouts, it reinforces past reports of his imprisonment during the fifties in Vladimir and also underlines the Soviet's determination to suppress discussion and airing of the Wallenberg case.

Silence has become essential in the Wallenberg case. To disclose the names of witnesses at too early a stage may result in the spiriting away of people like Jan Kaplan. Toward the end of 1980, the Wallenberg Association in Stockholm announced that in previous months unidentified prisoners leaving the Mordvinia prison complex in the western autonomous republic of Moldavia had reported seeing Wallenberg. He was in relatively good health, in a special prison for those inmates who have been declared officially missing or dead.

All past criticism of the Swedish Foreign Ministry notwithstanding, the government has spoken of its commitment to be closely involved in the search for Raoul Wallenberg. Perhaps this resulted from public access to the Swedish White Papers on Raoul Wallenberg and their current careful examination by scholars. In May, 1980, the writer interviewed an official in the Foreign Ministry who wished to remain anonymous. He said,

There was not much official activity from 1965 through 1978. In 1978 interest dramatically increased with the worldwide campaign for human rights. And late in 1978 Kalinski appeared with his important testimony. Uri Belov, a secondhand witness, came to our attention in 1979.* Many people contact the Foreign Ministry with new information, and we try to follow all these leads. At the moment we are looking into information from witnesses in Southern Europe and in Israel. Of course, one can not be sure, but he [Wallenberg] still might be alive. When we have solid information from new witnesses, we will bring the matter up again with the Russians. The history of the Wallenberg case has shown that such things do happen, that surprising developments can take place.

Another surprising development in 1979 was the Swedish proposal of a prisoner exchange with the Soviets—a sharp departure from previous Swedish policy. Stig Bergling, a former Swedish Defense Ministry employee, was convicted as a KGB agent and sentenced to life imprisonment in November, 1979. The Bergling affair was the biggest Swedish spy scandal in recent times. Bergling was offered to the Soviets for Wallenberg, but the Russians were not interested.

While everyone waits for the next startling development in the Wallenberg case, the name of Raoul Wallenberg must remain before the public so that work will continue to secure his liberty—or to receive a true, final determination of his status.

---

*On December 5, 1979, Belov was questioned by the Swedish embassy in Vienna after being released from Soviet prisons, where he had been held for fifteen years. He was ill and was taken to the camp hospital in Baraschevko. There he met an American, Cecil August Stowner, who told him that he had been with Raoul Wallenberg in 1961 in Butyrka Prison for a few days. Stowner stressed how pleased he was to have someone talk to him in English.

One of the interesting notes on this aspect concerns Yad Vashem, the Israel Holocaust remembrance in Jerusalem, where trees are planted to honor the "righteous gentiles." Although many of those honored are still alive, Mrs. von Dardel had always felt such an honor would connote that her son was no longer living. Moshe Bejski, an Israeli judge who is chairman of the Yad Vashem Committee for the Designation of the "Righteous Among the Nations," mentioned Mrs. von Dardel's position at a 1974 conference in Jerusalem on rescue attempts during the Holocaust: "Wallenberg's aged mother has so far refused to accept the medal granted by the Commission for the Designation of the Righteous because of the lack of certain knowledge about his fate. We have honored her wish. Nevertheless, Raoul Wallenberg stands in the front rank of the nobleminded individuals whose actions to rescue Jews surpassed all expectations." After the von Dardels died, the children decided to accept the Yad Vashem tribute as a means of sustaining public interest in the fate of Raoul Wallenberg (actually, he had been granted the title of Righteous Gentile in 1960, one of the first so designated). On January 17, 1980, the thirty-fifth anniversary of Raoul Wallenberg's arrest, an evergreen carob tree was planted in Raoul's name on the Street of the Righteous Gentiles. In a special area behind the memorial of Yad Vashem, Hungarian Jews residing in Sweden planted a woodland of 10,000 trees.

The Jewish community in Stockholm also marked the anniversary of the disappearance of the Angel of Rescue by packing the Great Synagogue to hear tributes by the bishop of Stockholm and the president of the Stockholm Jewish community.

At the beginning of 1980 the Free Wallenberg Committee announced that international hearings would be held in Stockholm May 2–3 to focus worldwide attention on the fate of Raoul Wallenberg. The Sakharov Human Rights Committee of Copenhagen had agreed to cosponsor the forum. Scheduled to participate were Eichmann prosecutor Gideon Hausner; Member of Parliament Grenville Janner; the French Nobel laureate in medicine Dr. André Lwoff; famed Holocaust writer Elie Wiesel, chairman of the U.S. Holocaust Memorial Council; and Simon Wiesenthal. By this time Wiesenthal was referring to Wallenberg as a "holy man" and said that locating Raoul Wallenberg had priority over finding former Nazi war criminals.

Unfortunately, Raoul Wallenberg was once more victimized by developments within Sweden. As fate would have it, the hearings were postponed to the winter of 1980 because of a crippling strike of public employees. The writer, who was in Stockholm during the strike, found great interest and sympathy among the Swedes for their fellow countryman. Although members of the Wallenberg family and government officials have frequently repeated the adage "You can not be a prophet in your own country," a great deal of citizen interest in the fate of Raoul Wallenberg and much pride in his accomplishments still persist. Many Swedes were perturbed that Raoul Wallenberg's "day," with its international spotlight, had to be postponed because of an "unnecessary" workers' strike.

Plans were quickly made to reschedule the international conference for early 1981. In the fall of 1980, the Wallenberg case was raised at a follow-up conference on the Helsinki agreement on security and cooperation in Europe. The Madrid conference heard a presentation of the Wallenberg case in an address by Swedish Foreign Minister Ola Ullsten. Other officials, including those from the United States, also raised the subject at meetings on human rights issues.

An international tribunal met in Stockholm on January 15-16, 1981, almost thirty-six years to the day after Raoul Wallenberg was last seen in Budapest. "We have every reason to believe that he is still alive," read the resolution adopted by the panel chaired by Ingrid Garde Widemar, a justice of the Swedish Supreme Court and chairman of the Swedish Raoul Wallenberg Association. Testimonies and speeches were given by Wiesenthal, Hausner, Janner, Lwoff, and Wiesel. Reports of the tribunal were featured in the world press.

The Russians gave a chilly response to the proceedings. The Soviet ambassador to London refused to receive the British Foreign Office minister who asked to see him about the Wallenberg case. The Russian embassy also refused to accept a petition bearing some 15,000 signatures that called upon Brezhnev to reopen inquiries into the fate of Wallenberg. Following the hearing, the Soviet embassy in Stockholm spurned the resolution and turned away Justice Widemar when she sought to see the Soviet ambassador.

In addition to providing an international forum and mobilizing world opinion for Wallenberg, the hearing presented new witnesses and reports about his status. Perhaps the greatest eye-opener was the statement of Cronid Lubarsky. Now living in West Germany, Lubarsky is the editor of *USSR New Brief.*

Citing a "reliable source in Moscow," Lubarsky reported that in 1978 an aged Swedish prisoner had been in Blagoveshchensk Special Psychiatric Hospital, situated in the Amur region close to Manchuria. The prisoner's "physical state was very bad," according to informants, and "he was in confinement for a long time." Lubarsky feels that if the prisoner were in fact Wallenberg, he is no longer in Blagoveshchensk. This conclusion is based on a report of a transfer of a large group of political prisoners to the hospital on November 22, 1980. "The Soviet authorities will never put Wallenberg together with well-known dissidents," Lubarsky said.

(Following the hearing, a bulletin was smuggled out of Russia by dissidents, which gave more precise information on the health of the aged Swede. He was described as being "on his last legs.")

Another remarkable report was presented by André Lipchitz, stepson of the late Jacques Lipchitz, the world-renowned Jewish sculptor. Speaking under the assumed name of André Shimkevitch, he said that he was Wallenberg's cellmate for two days in Lubianka Prison, before Christmas, 1947. "I met Raoul Wallenberg in December, 1947," Shimkevich said. "Nothing is forgotten in prison." Now living in France, he said that Wallenberg had told him that he was a diplomat who was being held on spy charges.

Luryi expanded on Shimkevitch's remark that "nothing is forgotten in prison." "What Shimkevitch said may be very eloquent, but to most people it may not be convincing. But keep in mind that Shimkevitch saw the date on the papers he was asked to sign when he was interrogated. Prisoners also have the ability to note changes in time by such seemingly minor things as changes in their menu. For example, they are given more sugar as the New Year approaches."

According to Shimkevitch, Wallenberg appeared "healthy," although he was "depressed" because he had not been "sentenced" and his situation was "most uncertain." When asked why he had waited nearly twenty-five years after his release from prison to come forward with this information, Shimkevitch said that in 1958 he had attempted to tell the Wallenberg family that he had seen Raoul. Aside from refuting the Soviet contention that Wallenberg died at Lubianka on July 12, 1947, Shimkevitch's testimony enhances the credibility of witnesses who claim to have seen Wallenberg long after that date. Shimkevitch's testimony takes on additional importance because he is one of only two or three still living witnesses who claim to have seen Wallenberg.

While not an eyewitness, an American, Marvin W. Makinen, who served twenty-eight months in Soviet prisons in the early sixties, testified that a fellow prisoner had told him of meeting Wallenberg in the Vladimir prison. A professor of biophysics at the University of Chicago, Makinen shared a cell in Vladimir with Zygurd Kruminsh, a Latvian who had been the cellmate of American U-2 pilot Gary Powers until his release. Kruminsh told Makinen that several years earlier he had met a Swedish prisoner, whose name "he did not learn," who was no longer at Vladimir. When Makinen was transferred to a labor camp in the Mordovian Autonomous Republic, a prisoner inquired about his former cellmates in Vladimir. Upon telling him of Kruminsh, he instantly replied, "He got to sit with all the foreigners. He sat with you. And he sat with the Swedish prisoner van den Berg."

Makinen estimates that Kruminsh had contact with the Swedish prisoner in the period from 1956 to 1959. This would coincide with the testimony of Kalinski, who had seen Wallenberg for the last time in the fall of 1959.

Worldwide interest in the fate of Raoul Wallenberg continues to grow. The concern for the heroic Swede and appreciation for his accomplishments have been manifested in varying ways. A dozen major streets in Israeli cities, including Jerusalem, are being renamed Raoul Wallenberg Street. A park in Jerusalem has been named for Raoul Wallenberg. Israeli schools cite the heroism of the Angel of Rescue as part of their history courses.

The Board of Deputies of British Jews cited Wallenberg's "courage and devotion far beyond the call of duty" in proposing him as the first winner of a human rights prize to be awarded every three years by the Council of Europe. As a means of directing international attention to the fate of Raoul Wallenberg, suggestions that his name be placed in nomination for the Nobel Peace Prize have come forth once again. Philip Slomovitz, editor of *The Jewish News* of Detroit, wrote in an April 25, 1980, editorial, "A Nobel Prize for Raoul":

> In 1949, Dr. Albert Einstein nominated Wallenberg for the Nobel Peace Prize. It was an unsuccessful presentation of the name of one of the greatest heroes of the cruel war.
>
> Now, therefore, let the nomination be renewed. In the present tasks, conducted internationally to secure Wallenberg's release from Russian imprisonment, the most appropriate means of inspiring these efforts would be recognition accorded him in the form of the Nobel Peace Prize . . . .
>
> The least that can be done to honor the name of the man who truly acted as a Saint as well as Hero is to award him the Nobel Peace Prize. Let this become a major undertaking for all lovers of justice.

The proposal of a Nobel Peace Prize for Raoul Wallenberg continues to gather momentum. According to a report in the *International Herald Tribune,* a U.S. Senate committee and a British Parliamentary Wallenberg Committee planned to propose the Swede for the 1981 Nobel Peace Prize. In its editorial of November 8-9, 1980, the *Tribune* spoke of the significance of a Nobel Prize for the heroic Wallenberg:

> If Mr. Wallenberg were to get the Nobel award, the effect would be double: the entire world would learn of the moral significance of the man's struggle against the Nazis and his punishment by the Communists, and it would double the number of Nobel Peace Prize laureates banished by the Kremlin. The other one, of course, is Andrei Sakharov, restricted to the city of Gorki.
>
> And even if this gesture would not bring back Mr. Wallenberg, it would serve to shake the men in the Kremlin, who have never been able to understand that men do exist who are ready to risk their lives for humanitarian goals.

Raoul Wallenberg was honored as Man of the Year by the Judaic Heritage Society, which dedicated its annual award medal of 1980 to the Swede. According to its president Robert Weber, the society sought to participate in the intensified effort to learn the fate of Wallenberg. "The Holocaust had hosts of martyrs and victims, but not too many heroes," he said, "and here was a chance not only to spotlight one such hero, but also to be a part of the rather belated attempt to learn his fate."

At its annual ordination ceremonies in 1981, the Hebrew Union College-Jewish Institute of Religion honored Wallenberg with its prestigious $10,000 Roger Joseph Prize.

Interest in the fate of Raoul Wallenberg today continues even in Hungary, a Russian satellite and the setting for both Wallenberg's heroism and his subsequent abduction. Despite the Communist renaming of many Budapest streets, Wallenberg Street remains. At one corner of the four-block street, a plaque still endures proclaiming that Wallenberg saved "victims of fascism" and that he himself was executed by the fascists before Budapest was liberated by Russian troops. Fresh flowers are often found at the plaque. During a visit to Budapest in the summer of 1979, the writer discovered that Raoul Wallenberg's name is well known among the residents of Budapest—both Jewish and non-Jewish. Although the plaque does not specify Jewish victims, the people of Budapest are quite knowledgeable about the exact purpose of the Wallenberg mission.

Budapest's Jews were quite interested in the fate of Raoul Wallenberg. They indicated that *Uj Elet,* the Hungarian Jewish newspaper, occasionally carried stories about the Swede, always stressing the Russian position that he was dead. However, a surprising number of people voiced both hope and belief that he might still be alive.

Wallenberg Street, located in what in 1944 was the heart of the international ghetto, still bears remembrances of the war. Many buildings are visibly scarred by bullet marks, but one can still find the safe houses organized by Wallenberg. The heart of the Budapest Jewish community—which totals some eighty thousand throughout Hungary—centers around Sip Street, the home of the Central Board of Hungarian Jewry. We met Yitzchak, a student at the rabbinical seminary, who not only knows of Raoul Wallenberg, but also keeps himself informed of the latest developments in the case by speaking to tourists. "Nobody in my family was saved because of Wallenberg," Yitzchak said, "but as Jews and as Hungarians we should forever be grateful for the heroic acts of that man. He will always be in my prayers."

Gabriel, whose father is a leader in the Jewish community, remarked that the achievements of Wallenberg are not forgotten among Hungarian Jews: the story of Wallenberg is taught in Jewish schools.

Although Wallenberg's achievements are familiar to the Jewish community, the writer could not locate even one person who was saved by the Swede. The overwhelming majority of survivors had long since left Budapest; most of those who remained had died. No one mentioned the name of Jeno Lévai, who found refuge in one of the safe houses and in 1948 wrote a biography of Raoul Wallenberg. After our visit we learned that Lévai, now in his eighties, lives in Buda. A friend of ours was in Budapest in June, 1980, and called the Lévai home. Mrs. Lévai told him that her husband had been very sick since October and was not accepting any calls. Our friend asked whether her husband, after thirty-five years, still believed that Raoul Wallenberg was murdered in Budapest. Mrs. Lévai responded: "If you have any questions about Raoul Wallenberg, please refer to my husband's book."

Even more surprising than not finding a Hungarian Jew who had heard of Lévai and his book was the lack of historical references at the Jewish Museum. The museum, on Dohany Street at the birth site of Theodor Herzl, founder of Zionism, receives government support. Open only during the summer, the museum features an "exhibit" on the Holocaust, including a display case about Raoul Wallenberg and his mission in Budapest. The Swedish protection pass is the dominant item in the display. We asked Dr. Ilona Benoschofsky, the director, if the museum had any written materials in Hungarian on Raoul Wallenberg. She answered in the negative and said that she was unaware of any book in Hungarian on Wallenberg.

The National Library in Budapest did contain materials on Wallenberg, among them books in Hungarian and Swedish by Lévai and Philipp, respectively, an article by Marion C. Siney in the January, 1964, *Michigan Quarterly Review,* and the program and texts from the First Annual Raoul Wallenberg Lecture in 1972 at the University of Michigan. When we told the librarian we were writing a book on Raoul Wallenberg, there were no raised eyebrows. We were serviced very quickly and efficiently.

The Hungarian government was not as cooperative. Before leaving for Hungary we communicated with N.Y. Congressman Jack Kemp about our desire to meet government officials in connection with our research on Raoul Wallenberg. In response, Congressman Kemp said that he had asked Ambassador Ferenc Esztergalyos to provide us with advice and assistance. When we arrived in Budapest, we called the ambassador's office, but found no one available to help us. We then called on James Bodnar, the first secretary of the American embassy, whose efforts were also unsuccessful. Abandoning efforts to meet with Hungarian officials, we next called the Swedish embassy and spoke with First Secretary Jan Karlsson. Everytime this writer mentioned Raoul Wallenberg, the conversation was cut off and it became difficult to dial from our apartment. Obviously, our phone was being tapped. After several attempts to speak with Karlsson about Wallenberg had proven unsuccessful, he invited me to the embassy, where he proved himself to be very knowledgeable on the subject and provided many useful contacts.

Throughout 1981 an intense campaign was conducted in Washington to pass a bill conferring honorary citizenship upon Wallenberg, a distinction previously granted only to Winston Churchill. This action enjoyed the support of President Ronald Reagan, who told Secretary of State Alexander Haig, "This is a very important matter and I want to back it all the way."

The United States Congress soon passed a bill bestowing honorary citizenship upon Raoul Wallenberg. On October 5, 1981, in signing ceremonies at the White House, President Reagan spoke of the Swede's mission in Hungary: "The United States supplied the funds and directives, and Raoul Wallenberg supplied the courage and the passion." His accomplishment, the president continued, "was of Biblical proportions."

The bill states in part:

"Section 1. Raoul Wallenberg is proclaimed to be an honorary citizen of the United States of America.

"Section 2. The President is requested to take all possible steps to ascertain from the Soviet Union the whereabouts of Raoul Wallenberg and to secure his return to freedom."

Congressman Kemp called the signing of the bill, attended by Wallenberg's half brother and half sister, "a tremendous international statement," which will "shake up some diplomats in the Soviet Union. The Soviet Union will have to account for the whereabouts of Raoul Wallenberg."

Even more effusive about the future impact of the bill was the sponsor Congressman Lantos, who called honorary citizenship "a profound commitment on the part of Congress and the White House. Our President and our Secretary of State now have the moral authority of this nation behind them in demanding an accounting by the Soviets for Raoul Wallenberg's fate."

The signing of the bill, Lantos added, "does not conclude the Wallenberg saga. It begins a mandate to free Raoul Wallenberg from the Soviet Gulag, or should he have died, it demands that the Soviets make an accounting for his fate. If Raoul Wallenberg is alive, he is now an American citizen and a hostage. He must be freed."

Sweden attached great hopes to final passage of the honorary citizenship legislation. "It may make all the difference," according to Ingrid Widemar. Eric Sjöquist, the *Expressen* correspondent who had been a powerful voice in the Wallenberg campaign, said that "with honorary citizenship for Raoul Wallenberg, the U.S. could talk to the Russians on another level, and not be bound to accept a no to their questions."

While members of the Free Wallenberg Committees saw honorary citizenship as providing leverage for the U.S. in making approaches to the Russians, the Reagan administration made it clear that this was not so. Assistant Secretary of State for Congressional Relations Richard Fairbanks told Congress that giving Wallenberg honorary citizenship "does not confer on the United States any new international legal right, duty, or privilege on which basis to confront the Soviets on their indefensible incarceration of Wallenberg." What honorary citizenship does, according to Fairbanks, is "underscore the seriousness in which the American government and people view Soviet behavior in the Wallenberg case."

Ambassador Toon had a similar appraisal of honorary citizenship. "America is not given any additional rights in the Wallenberg case because of the honorary citizenship," he said. "What it does give us is a further rational basis for discussion."

The U.S. recently sought to advance discussion of the Wallenberg case in Geneva before the United Nations Human Rights Commission. Following a suggestion by the author to Congressmen Kemp and Lantos, the U.S. delegation raised the Wallenberg case during a debate in the Human Rights

Commission on persons who have disappeared under circumstances that could be considered political. Supported by Sweden, the U.S. asked that a special United Nations working group investigate the Wallenberg case. The Soviet delegation did not react to the proposal.

The nonreaction of the Soviets has become the typical response. The author has written several letters to Valentin Kamenev, first secretary and counselor of the Russian embassy in Washington, D.C., seeking to meet him to learn the "truth," to get the "Soviet view." Approaches on our behalf were also made by Charles Allen, Jr., the noted journalist who has worked closely with the Soviets in the identification of former Nazi war criminals. Kamenev has yet to respond to our request.

Worldwide momentum in the search for Raoul Wallenberg that was spurred by the signing of the citizenship bill received a temporary setback with the publication of the book *Lost Hero: The Mystery of Raoul Wallenberg* by Werbell and Clarke. They conclude that, following torture, Wallenberg died in 1965 in a Moscow hospital. According to their findings, Wallenberg came to the hospital following the Svartz episode and the Wrangel Island incarceration. The authors base their conclusion on exclusive interviews with former Prime Minister Erlander and Dr. Svartz, who allegedly knew about Wallenberg's death since 1965.

This gives rise to two obvious questions: Why did Erlander and Svartz give their statements now? What compelled them to keep quiet for so long? According to Werbell and Clarke, this revelation was made at the 1981 international conference on Wallenberg. Dr. Svartz, quite irritated at what she considered a senseless gathering convened "to perpetuate what she considered to be falsehood," told Werbell of Wallenberg's death. Erlander also made known that he was convinced of Wallenberg's death in 1965 and had learned of it from Svartz.

Werbell and Clarke report that Erlander held back the information for sixteen years in "deference" to Wallenberg's mother and stepfather, despite the fact "that he [Erlander] had been shown factual information concerning his [Wallenberg's] death." Perhaps Erlander swore Svartz to secrecy, suggest the authors, because he feared that announcing Wallenberg's death "would have led to a serious rift with the Soviet Union." They support their contention that Wallenberg is dead with details of a "secret meeting" on April 14, 1980, between Wolfgang Vogel, an East German attorney, and Rabbi Ronald Greenwald, an intermediary in international prisoner exchanges who directed Richard M. Nixon's presidential campaign in the Jewish community in 1972.

Although explanations of Russian actions may seem to defy logic, there seems to be no iota of plausibility in Werbell and Clarke's report that the Russians told a Swedish official that Wallenberg died after being tortured in a Russian hospital. What Russian would admit to such atrocities twelve years after the death of Stalin?

The Wallenberg Committee quickly responded to the reports of Werbell and Clarke. Erlander and Svartz categorically denied telling Werbell and Clarke that they knew of Wallenberg's death in 1965. Even before the book was officially released, the Wallenberg Committee released the following statement from Erlander, dated December 29, 1981:

> When I read Werbell's description of my conversation with him, I was upset. There are in his report hardly any traces of truth. He is right in one respect only. In 1965 I met with Premier Kosygin in Moscow and brought up the case of Raoul Wallenberg, as I used to do in talks with Soviet leaders in order to clarify his fate. There is no truth either in the authors' assertion that Nanna Svartz should have mentioned to me anything about Raoul Wallenberg's having died in 1965. Professor Svartz and I have met and talked many times about this remarkable man and his fate, but on no occasion did she say anything about his having died.

A follow-up letter signed by Sonia Sonnenfeld, executive director of the Wallenberg Association, was sent to the book's publisher asking for "rectification" of the "serious errors" that would be "most harmful" to the cause of finding Raoul Wallenberg.

The most incensed person was Nina Lagergren. She was "absolutely horrified" by the actions of Rabbi Werbell, who was an active member of the N.Y. Wallenberg Committee when he began researching his book. Alluding to the professor (mentioned in chapter 13), a friend of the family who, in 1966, wrote a book siding with the Russians, Mrs. Lagergren said that "Werbell is another Villius" who is seeking to "take advantage of the agony of our family."

But Wallenberg's half sister will not be discouraged by "absurd" reports. "Raoul has been dead at least twenty times, supposedly found in forests, in camps, and the like. But remember one thing: a person cannot die in so many places, but a person can be alive in so many places." (Actually, the Wallenberg Association has listed the "fourteen deaths" of Raoul Wallenberg, all of which have been proven false.)

On October 27, 1981, a golden opportunity to recover Raoul Wallenberg presented itself to the Swedish government. A diesel-powered Soviet submarine ran aground on the Swedish coast, inside several barrier islands in restricted waters near the Karlskrona naval base. Swedish naval vessels surrounded the ship and demanded to know what it was doing there. For several days the Soviet captain discussed his predicament by radio with Moscow, but refused to speak to the Swedes. A sizable Soviet fleet gathered outside Swedish waters and demanded permission to pull their sub free of the rocks before it broke up from the force of a coming storm. The Swedish government refused to allow any more Soviet vessels into the restricted area or to order Swedish tugs to pull the sub free until naval investigators had questioned her captain and inspected the ship.

Raoul Wallenberg committees, both in Sweden and abroad, appealed to

Stockholm to intern the Russian submarine crew until Moscow released Wallenberg. Telegrams poured into Swedish embassies around the world as many concerned citizens expressed the same theme, but to no avail. Foreign Minister Ola Ullsten refused their pleas: "No, the Swedish government is not going to link these cases together."

Swedish experts examined the submarine from the outside with sophisticated radiation detection gear. They discovered the characteristic radiation emitted by uranium 238 coming from the area of the torpedo room. Weapons experts interpreted this to indicate that the vessel probably carried nuclear torpedo warheads. Finally, under orders from Moscow, the Soviet captain left his ship to present his well-prepared story to the Swedes. He claimed that he had gone off course during a storm because of a faulty gyrocompass. He also permitted Swedish investigators to inspect the navigation area of his sub and see the allegedly malfunctioning gyrocompass (that somehow allowed the sub to navigate unerringly through the narrow passage between two barrier islands during a storm in order to reach its current position). The captain denied the investigators access to the torpedo room. Despite the evidence provided by naval investigators, appeasement (or perhaps *ryssräck*) prevailed. The "neutral" Swedish government ordered Swedish naval tugs to pull the sub free of the rocks and escort it out of their territorial waters.

"We are terribly disappointed," Nina Lagergren told the author. "Mr. Ullsten said that there could be no link between Raoul Wallenberg and the Russian submarine. However, his refusal to link the two made it clear that the two should not be separated."

Her point is well taken, since this ironic episode illustrates a fundamental difference in attitudes between the "neutral" Swedish government and the "paranoid" Soviet government.

The captain of a Soviet submarine, obviously carrying nuclear weapons on what must be interpreted as a spy mission, is caught "red-handed" in inaccessible, restricted Swedish waters. While the whole world watches the incident on television, the Swedes demand an explanation. For several days the Soviet captain communicates with his superiors, but refuses to answer Swedish questions about this serious breach of international law. Finally, the captain submits to polite interrogation. After eleven days of pressure from the Soviet Union, he and his crew are released unharmed.

In contrast, Raoul Wallenberg, carrying a Swedish diplomatic passport in Budapest to rescue Hungarian Jews from Nazi and Arrow Cross murderers, voluntarily approaches the Russians with a plan to ease the suffering of Hungarian war victims. In direct violation of international agreements on diplomatic immunity, the Soviets secretly arrest him, repeatedly interrogate him, deny him access to Swedish diplomats, imprison him in the Gulag, and brutally subject him to untold horrors for perhaps more than thirty-seven years without trial or explanation. All requests by Sweden for his release are rebuffed, as the Soviets deny even holding Wallenberg, despite reams of evidence to the contrary.

After this shameful episode, the feeling in Sweden is that the government, weakly neutral with a woeful record in the Wallenberg case, can do little in the future.

The government has "spoiled" the Wallenberg case, according to Palmstierna. "As far as Sweden is concerned, the case is closed," Sjöquist said. "Those who seek to have Raoul Wallenberg returned must turn to America." Yoran Berg, a Foreign Ministry official whose responsibilities include the Wallenberg case, admits that "we like pressure that comes from America."

One thing still remains certain: the granting of honorary citizenship has brought forth heightened activity to call attention to the case. For example, in November, 1981, some twelve hundred prominent personalities in the entertainment and business worlds gathered in Hollywood as the Simon Wiesenthal Humanitarian Laureate was presented in absentia to Raoul Wallenberg. Cochairpersons of the gala evening were Elizabeth Taylor and Jon Voight.

One has to be concerned whether the search for Raoul Wallenberg has lost its original and true fervor. Undoubtedly there are totally dedicated and determined individuals in the Wallenberg effort. But, one of the dynamic workers of the Wallenberg Committee in Stockholm has told us that meetings and deliberations of the group have, unfortunately, become mere social get-togethers. What keeps the campaign together is the singlemindedness and perseverance of Nina Lagergren.

Dr. von Dardel describes the present strategy: to keep the Wallenberg case alive until U.S.-Russian relations improve and offer an opportunity to exact concessions from Russia. He feels that top-level Soviet officials who claim no knowledge of his brother are "honestly misinformed" by lower-level officials who are covering up the case.

"We have always been very careful never to get mixed up with professional anti-Soviet groups," Dr. von Dardel said. "For that reason we have kept a distance from Shifrin and his group. We always make it clear that we do not want to harm the Soviets. We simply want Raoul back with us."

Throughout the years Dr. von Dardel and others have sought to keep the U.S. closely involved with the Wallenberg case, but disappointments have occurred. For example, certain officials of the Wallenberg Association had spoken to Armand Hammer, the new U.S. ambassador to Peking, who has been a friend of Leonid Brezhnev. However, Hammer only achieved one more "nyet."

It is not wise to count on American involvement, according to Ambassador Toon. "Because of America's interest in the Wallenberg case, I felt entitled to raise the issue with the Russians. But Brezhnev and Gromyko were very reluctant to discuss the case with me because Wallenberg is a Swedish official. Technically the Russians were right."

But those who devote their energies to the Wallenberg campaign refuse to be discouraged. They cite the words of one of its most dedicated workers, Simon Wiesenthal: "We Jews believe in miracles."

13

The Raoul Wallenberg Case in Perspective

Politics of Caprice or Politics of Reason?

Damnant quod non intelligunt — They condemn what they do not understand.

This ancient Roman saying is easily applicable when one seeks to understand the actions of the Soviet Union: the veil of secrecy and the networks of bureaucracy confound attempts at scientific analyses of Soviet policies. Students of Soviet politics speak of the seemingly illogical, nonordered nature of Russian policy as the politics of caprice. Eugenia Ginzburg, herself a victim of the Communist system that led to her years of imprisonment in the Gulag, spoke of the difficulties in being forced to confront "that reversal of logic and common sense." It was "the height of bad form" to ask questions "dictated by common sense, for we were all supposed to pretend that syllogisms invented by sadists reflected the normal processes of the human mind" (33).

However, the tendency to label the Soviet modus operandi as capricious can bring very unproductive results, for within the Soviet system certain courses of action are formulated on the basis of systematic thought, although to those outside the system there seems to be no logic. This is the difficulty the Western mind encounters in looking for a systematic explanation and understanding of the Raoul Wallenberg case. Indeed, it seems nigh impossible to comprehend all the intricacies in the thirty-seven-year case of the missing Swedish hero. But certain pieces in the puzzle can be put together on the basis of historical attitudes and developments. Specifically, some of the answers to the Wallenberg mystery can be traced to the history of relations between Germany and the Soviet Union and between Sweden and the Soviet Union.

The surprise invasion by German troops on June 22, 1941, marked the beginning of a nearly three-year German occupation of western Russia, another chapter in the centuries-old paradoxical relations between the two countries. The nineteenth-century anarchist Mikhail Bakunin eloquently enunciated the Russian hatred of the Germans when he wrote his sister-in-law: "I say, as Voltaire said of God, that if there were no Germans we would have to invent them, since nothing so successfully unites the Slavs as a rooted hatred of Germans." On the other hand, Russian intellectuals who admired Kant, Schilling, and Goethe idealized the Germans. Major diplomatic appointments in the Russian foreign service were given to those of German descent. Before World War I, the Germans had become a significant element in Russia, with more than one hundred thousand former Germans living in Moscow, Saint Petersburg, Odessa, and Saratov.

The Russian-German Alliance of 1939–41 continued the appearance, if not the spirit, of good feeling between the two countries. V. M. Molotov, Russian foreign affairs minister, referred to the friendship as being forged in blood. However, the uneasy alliance abruptly ended when Hitler gave orders for the German army to begin Operation Barbarossa, the invasion of Russia. The Russians were caught off guard not only by the attack, but also by the behavior of the German occupiers. The Germans had occupied a large portion of Russia during World War I, but they had acted neither more civilized nor less decently than the other occupiers. Such was not the case in World War II. In a famous *Untermensch* brochure, of which hundreds of thousands of copies were distributed, Germany told the world that it was the savior of Western civilization against the new Asian savages, the *Untermenschen,* whose goal was world domination. If the Asian Bolshevik beasts triumphed, Western civilization would be destroyed.

In his book *Nauka Nenavisti,* Mikhail Sholokhov described the Russians' trauma when they found that the German occupiers did not live up to their traditional image as civilized and cultured people. The Soviets reacted with disbelief to the first reports of mass murder, mass pillaging, and mass oppression. Disbelief turned to anger and then to hatred. Russian intellectuals lashed out at the Nazis. Aleksey Tolstoy urged his fellow Russians: "Kill the beast, this is your holy duty." The most acerbic commentary was articulated by the famed writer Ilya Ehrenburg. As Walter Laqueur writes in *Russia and Germany,* Ehrenberg told his people that "for the first time the Russians were facing not human beings, but evil and vile creatures, savages, equipped with all the most recent technical achievements, who had transformed the killing of babies into a matter of political philosophy." References to traditional Germanophobia enflamed the anti-Nazi spirit even more.

During World War II, the Soviet Union suffered more loss of human life than any other European country. These losses have been estimated as high as 21 million, with a sizable proportion of deaths attributed to the Germans. As is to be expected, the Nazi occupation left a psychic imprint on the Russian mind. On one level, the Russians, contrary to worldwide Nazimania, ignored the Third Reich for years. No books were written on the Nazi regime, on Hitler or the other leaders, or even on the history of the Third Reich—to this day, the Russian curse word for German is "Nemetz," which is also a derogative term for foreigner.

A wariness of Germans is part of the general Soviet suspicion of foreigners. In his *Memoirs,* former U.S. Ambassador to Russia George F. Kennan writes that the USSR has "no conception of permanent friendly relations between states" and views all foreigners as "potential enemies." The occupation experience heightened Soviet suspicions, both of its own citizens and of foreigners who took part in the war.

Hitler once proposed to Stalin that both sides provide access to their POW camps for Red Cross parcels. Stalin refused stating, "There are no Russian prisoners of war. The Russian soldier fights on till death. If he chooses to become a prisoner, he is automatically excluded from the Russian community."

To avoid the barbaric conditions of German POW camps, thousands of former Red Army soldiers enlisted in special units of the German Army. There was little incentive to remain loyal to a government that viewed surrender as an act of treason.

The Soviet Union was in no mood to forgive any of its citizens who collaborated with the Nazis, not to mention those who took up arms for them. Aside from being traitors whose punishment was essential as an example to others, they also represented a security risk. While many of these dangerous elements were killed outright, the Stalin regime considered imprisonment to be the best solution.

As the victorious Red Army drove through Eastern Europe in late 1944 and 1945, thousands of suspicious persons were swept off the streets. Whenever the Russian armies liberated a Nazi concentration camp, they took into custody those whom they thought might be dangerous. While conducting a project on the oral testimony of ghetto survivors, Prof. Henry R. Huttenbach, a Russian history scholar, interviewed a former Jewish policeman in a Nazi-established ghetto who was denounced as having collaborated with the Germans and was then sentenced to a long term in the Gulag. This policeman, the scholar said, like thousands of others, disappeared at the war's end and later turned up in Soviet prisons and camps, and was released in 1955.

Raoul Wallenberg also disappeared into the Gulag. "His case was not unique in terms of his disappearance," according to Vladimir Kozlovsky, a reporter for the BBC who had worked in the India Department of the Young Communist League before emigrating several years ago, "The numbers of people who were lost at the war's end might approach and surpass one million. As for Wallenberg himself, he might have looked suspicious just by virtue of the fact that he was walking the streets of Budapest, seemingly without any cares."

But what relation is there between the imprisonment of Raoul Wallenberg and the relations between Russia and Germany? He was a Swede, a diplomat from a neutral country sent on a rescue mission with the support of the United States. While this may seem obvious to a Western-oriented mind, the same can not be said for the Russian mind that decides not only capriciously, but also on the basis of a logical system that may make sense only to Russian decision makers. Although Raoul Wallenberg may have told the Russians of American support for his mission in Budapest, there is no conclusive proof that he was in fact suspected and sentenced as an American agent or spy. As suggested in a previous chapter, would the Russians be convinced that a Swede would undertake a dangerous mission for America in Hungary for the sole purpose of saving Jews? What does seem plausible, however, is that Wallenberg was suspected of having collaborated with the Germans. To the Russian way of thinking, such a theory has a basis in the career of Raoul Wallenberg, in the activities of his family, and in the dealings of German leaders in Sweden during the war.

Wallenberg was fluent in the German language, and, in fact, wrote much of his correspondence from Budapest in that language. But this is of little importance when compared to reports that Wallenberg was a friend of Allen Dulles, who headed the U.S. Office of Strategic Services during the war. The German underground contacted the Allies at neutral points, such as Switzerland and Sweden, mainly through Dulles. In conversations with Eric Downton, foreign affairs specialist with the *Vancouver Sun* in Canada, the former Reuters war correspondent recalled that he had met Wallenberg in London at the suite of Vincent Massey, the Canadian high commissioner to Britain. "I was very impressed by the word being passed around," Downton said, "that Wallenberg was a friend of Allen Dulles, the American spymaster."

However, it was Wallenberg's uncles, the bankers Marcus and Jacob, who maintained especially close contacts with Dulles. For the German underground, led by Karl Goerdeler, the mayor of Leipzig, the Wallenbergs were the most valuable contact in Stockholm. From 1940 to 1944 the Wallenbergs and Goerdeler constantly discussed his plans for the overthrow of Hitler in return for more favorable peace terms from the Western Allies. All the discussions proved abortive. The SS arrested Goerdeler in September, 1944, and executed him in February, 1945.

Gerhard Ritter points out in his book *The German Resistance* that Goerdeler continually stressed the dangers of a Russian victory. He told the Wallenbergs that a powerful Russia would seek to impose a Bolshevik revolution on the European continent, thereby threatening the democratic government of Sweden, among others. In a letter smuggled out of prison, Goerdeler asked Jacob Wallenberg to urge that Stockholm mediate between the Germans and the Western Allies in order to rescue Europe from Bolshevism. In his book *Heusinger of the Fourth Reich,* Charles R. Allen, Jr., notes that Goerdeler was determined to retain the 1939 boundaries of Hitlerian Germany.

It is believed that Heinrich Himmler delayed the Goerdeler hanging in order to exploit his contacts in Switzerland and Sweden should the head of the SS supplant Hitler — a thought that was very much on his mind. In fact, in November, 1944, Jacob Wallenberg was invited to visit Himmler, but the Swede refused because of the possibility that Himmler would ask him to negotiate with the Allies, a position he would not undertake. As Wallenberg told Dulles: "I do not consider it unlikely that Himmler might have asked me to perform for his account the assignment which I had accepted for Goerdeler. The fact that I was, of course, not willing to do anything of the sort reinforced my decision not to go."

While the Wallenbergs discontinued their discussions with German resistance leaders and preferred to stay away from Himmler, the SS chief developed his own contacts in Sweden. As with Goerdeler, Himmler's major theme was that a negotiated peace with the Western Allies would prevent the Russian armies from overrunning Eastern Europe. The prime contact was Dr. Felix Kersten, Himmler's masseur, who moved with his family to Stockholm in 1943. Traveling frequently between Sweden and Germany, Kersten was as adept at working on Himmler's conscience as he was at working on the Nazi's body. Commissioned by the Swedish government during 1944–45 to negotiate with Himmler, Kersten initiated plans for the removal of Swedes and other Scandinavians from German-occupied territory and worked for the release of Dutch, French, and Jewish prisoners. Perhaps the most remarkable meeting Kersten arranged took place on April 21, 1945, and included himself, Himmler, SS General Walter Schellenberg, and Norbert Masur, director of the Swedish section of the World Jewish Congress, who had a pivotal role in the selection of Raoul Wallenberg for his mission in Budapest. Masur flew incognito to Germany to negotiate with Himmler, who was in charge of the implementation of measures to annihilate the Jews, thus becoming the first Jew that the SS chief had met on equal terms. After the meeting, during which Kersten had achieved what best he could for the release of the remaining Jews in German camps, Himmler seized his masseur by the sleeve and said in desperation:

"Have you any access to General Eisenhower or the Western Allies? If so, use them! I am ready to concede victory to the Western Allies. They only have to give me time to throw back the Russians. If they would let me have the equipment, I can still do it. They must join us, to continue the war against the Bolsheviks! It is their war as well as ours."

A few days later, on April 23, Himmler met with another Swede, Count Folke Bernadotte, vice president of the Swedish Red Cross. A recollection of the Himmler meeting in the Swedish consulate at Luebeck is presented by Bernadotte in his book *The Curtain Falls:*

HIMMLER: In order to save as great a part of Germany as possible from a Russian invasion I am willing to capitulate on the Western front in order to enable the Western Allies to advance rapidly towards the East. But I am not prepared to capitulate on the Eastern front. I have been, and I shall always remain, a sworn enemy of Bolshevism. At the beginning of the · World War, I fought tooth and nail against the Russo-German pact. Are you willing to forward a communiqué on these lines to the Swedish Minister for Foreign Affairs, so that he can inform the Western powers of my proposal?

BERNADOTTE: It is in my opinion quite impossible to carry out a surrender on the Western front and to continue to fight on the Eastern front. It can be looked upon as quite certain that England and America will not make any separate settlement.

HIMMLER: I am well aware how extremely difficult this is, but all the same I want to make the attempt to save millions of Germans from Russian occupation.

If the proposals were rejected, Himmler told Bernadotte, "I shall take over the command of the Eastern front and be killed in battle." The proposals were rejected. Himmler was arrested by the British in May and committed suicide.

The Himmler dealings, the continued discussions of the Wallenbergs, and other negotiations between German leaders and their contacts in Stockholm all came to light after the war. When Raoul Wallenberg presented himself to the Russian command at Debrecen with plans for a new order in Hungary, one can assume that his case was scrutinized, and a plausible conclusion for the suspicious, paranoid Russian mind was that Raoul Wallenberg collaborated with the Nazis. Following the war, Russian prisons were filled with many former German officials. In fact, Wallenberg's first cellmate at Lubianka was Gustaf Richter, police attaché at the German legation in Bucharest, while Langfelder shared a cell with Willi Roedel, consul of the German legation in Rumania, and another German, Jan Loyda.

Some of the cellmates and neighbors of Wallenberg and Langfelder were among the fifteen hundred German prisoners sent back to West Germany on June 19, 1953.

During his interrogation by the Russians, Lars Berg told the Swedish government, "I and Raoul Wallenberg were pointed out as leading German spies."

In testimony given after his release, Wilhelm Mohnke, the major general who was commander of the government quarters in Berlin, said: "During my imprisonment in the Soviet Union, I often heard of an imprisoned Swedish diplomat who had been active in Budapest. The Russian authorities were said to have accused him of espionage for the Germans."

In many of its approaches to the Russians, the Swedish government sought to dispel the idea that Raoul Wallenberg was acting on behalf of the

Nazis, a thought perhaps adopted by the Russians because of the Swede's dealings with Eichmann and other Nazi leaders. For example, in a memorandum of September 29, 1954, to the Russian Vice Minister Zorin, Ambassador Sohlman speaks of the possibility that the Russian police might have found protective passes on the persons of Arrow Cross members and other Nazi sympathizers. This may have led the Russians, according to Sohlman, to get "the wrong impression that Raoul Wallenberg protected fascist elements."

Although all these German "involvements" surround the Wallenberg case, the fact still remains that Sweden was a neutral country during the war and, as such, the diplomat Wallenberg should have been treated differently. In actuality, however, Sweden was not fully a neutral country. When Russia declared war on Finland in November, 1939, Sweden declared herself not a neutral but a nonbelligerent. Making use of this status, Sweden permitted some twelve thousand volunteers and large shipments of arms to pass through the Gulf of Bothnia to fortify the Finns. Through Swedish diplomatic aid, Russia and Finland ceased fighting in March, 1940. But one major irritant still remained. Nearly thirty-five thousand refugees from Latvia, Estonia, and Lithuania, many of whom had taken up arms against Russia, fled to Sweden in 1944.

"While Sweden might have looked upon herself as a neutral," Kozlovsky commented, "Stockholm was not well liked by the Allies, especially for her continued trading with Germany during the period."

However, the problem between Sweden and Russia lay deeper. While neutrality had been an official policy of Sweden since the nineteenth century, it had existed alongside a deep Russophobia. The first articulate spokesman of this virulence was the nineteenth-century poet Esaias Tegnér, who voiced the anger of so many Swedes after their loss of Finland to Russia in 1809. Abrahamson points out in his book *Sweden's Foreign Policy:* "One must keep in mind that the place of Finland in Swedish foreign policy cannot be overemphasized. Sweden's concern for Finland must be viewed in terms of her traditional distrust of Russia, whether Czarist or Communist."

Hatred for Russia also led to the cultivation of close ties with Germany. There were distinct pro-German tendencies in Sweden's foreign policy in the early 1900s, helped along by renewed czarist persecution in Finland, as well as by the favoritism of King Gustav V, who married a granddaughter of the first kaiser. When World War I broke out, however, Sweden remained true to its tradition of neutrality; yet, considerable sentiment for the Germans still remained, especially among the upper class, who saw the Germans as the major guardian against Slavic inhumanity.

When the Communist revolution raised its flag in 1917, Stockholm waited until 1924 to recognize the new regime. In contrast, when Finland declared its independence shortly thereafter, Sweden quickly recognized the new government.

Throughout the interwar years, Sweden maintained close economic ties with Germany, even supplying iron ore for Hitler's rearmament program. Although the Nazi regime received little support from the people, the Swedes were more worried about the Russians. The absorption of Estonia, Latvia, and Lithuania, as well as the attack on Finland, proved to the Swedes that the Communists were even more dangerous than the czarists. Students of Swedish-Soviet relations point to several major wartime espionage cases directed by the USSR against Sweden as indicative of the suspicion and tension that existed between the two countries.

With the war's end, Russia never took its eyes off Sweden and looked askance at Sweden's proposal of a Scandinavian defense alliance. Russia expressed its disapproval of Swedish policy by such measures as the harassment of Swedish Baltic fisheries and the shooting down of two unarmed Swedish military aircraft.

The aircraft incidents in June, 1952, were a low point in Swedish-Soviet relations. On June 17, two Russian MIG-15 jet fighters shot down a Swedish Catalina plane. The Soviets charged that the Swedish plane had violated its territory and had fired first on the Russian aircraft. Sweden denied these charges, maintaining that its aircraft was unarmed and had been flying over international waters. The confrontation followed another Soviet downing of an unarmed Swedish aircraft.

While hot words were being exchanged between the two countries, Stockholm had tried Fritiof Enbom, leader of a Communist group, and seven accomplices on charges of espionage. Enbom was accused of gathering military secrets, over a period of ten years, for the Soviet embassy in Stockholm, and of organizing fifth-column activity in northern Sweden in case Russia attacked.

As a consequence, Sweden was very cautious in its dealings with the Russians. Sweden acceded to Soviet demands for forced repatriation of Baltic and German refugees who fought against the Russians. Sweden also refused to join the other Scandinavian nations—Denmark, Norway, and Iceland—as original members of the North Atlantic Treaty Organization (NATO). Commenting on Swedish behavior in his book *Sweden's Foreign Policy,* Abrahamson points to the "Russian threat to Finland, who, with its large Communist Party, might yet become part of the Soviet bloc." This has put Stockholm "in a particularly difficult international situation which was not fully appreciated either at home or abroad."

Whenever the occasion presented itself, the Russians would always remind Sweden of its tradition of neutrality. When Khrushchev visited Sweden in 1964, the Soviet premier "joked" about this tradition with Rolf Sohlman, Swedish ambassador to Moscow from 1947 to 1964, whose wife Zinaida was Russian by birth. The conversation is recorded in *Khrushchev Remembers*:

> "Well, Mr. Sohlman, . . . relations between our countries are all right now, but we haven't forgotten our history. We have to keep an eye on you, lest you make another march on Poltava."

"You know, Mr. Khrushchev, . . . after the lesson your Peter I taught our Charles XII at the Battle of Poltava, not only have we never again waged war against Russia—we've never waged war at all. We've been neutral ever since."

Perhaps Sohlman was convinced of the viability of a policy of neutrality; those outside of Sweden, particularly in America, were not. In two incisive columns in the *New York Times* on July 25 and 27, 1949, James Reston was amazed at the Swedish practice of neutrality. In discussing Sweden's abstention from NATO, Reston expressed surprise that Sweden "is afraid of open discussion" and insisted on "staying aloof from the moral debates" on this vital issue.

Reston saw a remarkable contrast between the neutrality of America in the years before it entered World War II and the neutrality practiced by Sweden. Whereas America had practiced neutrality in an atmosphere of war, Sweden for centuries had disrupted times of peace with its tradition of militarism. And, whereas our stance of neutrality was in harmony with the beliefs of Washington and Jefferson, Reston felt that the neutrality of Sweden clashed with the "romantic tradition of Charles XII and Gustavus Adolphus, whose interventionist theme of foreign policy would have made Thomas Jefferson and George Washington squirm."

The aircraft shootings of 1952 brought more wonderment about the efficacy of Swedish neutrality. Writing in the *New York Times* of July 18, Ann O'Hare McCormick saw the policy as a "miracle," not that Sweden could practice it, but that "their neutrality has been respected." The outcome of the incidents, McCormick states, "must be to set the Swedes and other neutrals to pondering on the uses of neutrality."

Sweden, however, looked upon its policy of neutrality as a positive factor in international politics, the Russians did not, and the Khrushchev incident should be viewed in that light. Moreover, Swedish neutrality proved detrimental to the Wallenberg case. According to Professor Jonathan Sanders, assistant director of the Russian Institute at Columbia University, "Russian diplomats laugh at a policy of neutrality. For the Russians, neutrality is not a practical policy at all. They expect other countries to be hostile and are prepared for tough dealings in the international arena." Writing in his *Memoirs,* Ambassador Kennan's advice to America in its dealings with Russia can be applied to any country, including Sweden:

"We must be prepared to undertake a 'taming of the shrew' which is bound to involve a good deal of unpleasantness. On the other hand, we need not fear that occasional harsh words will have permanent bad effect on our relations. The Russian is never more agreeable after his knuckles have been sharply rapped . . . . The Russian governing class respects only the strong. To them, shyness in dispute is a form of weakness."

While there have been questions and criticisms concerning the Swedish policy vis-à-vis the Wallenberg case, many of the comments on and analyses of Russian actions center on the Gromyko memorandum of 1957. Why was the memorandum written in 1957, twelve years after Wallenberg's disappearance? Why did the Russians choose 1947 as the date of Wallenberg's death in Lubianka? Why did the Russians issue a document whose credibility has been questioned?

A Swedish government delegation visited Russia in the spring of 1956 for the purpose of urging the Soviets to review the Wallenberg case. With improved relations between the countries a potential benefit, the Russians reviewed the case. But there is more involved in the official Russian review.

The Russian review was undertaken about two months after the historic "secret speech" of Khrushchev in February, 1956, at the Twentieth Party Congress. The Russian leader attacked Stalin for his one-man rule and for his immoderate actions, especially the arbitrary punishment and imprisonment of millions. The congress also attacked two other villains: Beria and Abakumov. After Stalin died, Beria controlled the entire centralized machinery of repression as head of the Ministry of State Security and Ministry of the Interior. From 1946 to 1951 Abakumov had been the minister of State Security. For their dictatorial decisions that sent millions to the Gulag, the congress condemned the "Mafia of the Caucasus" in scathing terms such as these:

> Everywhere and in everything he [Stalin] saw "enemies," "two-faces," and "spies." Possessing unlimited power, he indulged in great wilfulness and choked a person—morally and physically . . . . Meanwhile Beria's gang, which ran the organs of state security, outdid itself in proving the guilt of the arrested and the truth of materials which it falsified . . . . And how is it possible that a person confesses to crimes which he has not committed? Only in one way— because of application of physical methods of pressuring him, tortures, bringing him to a state of unconsciousness, deprivation of his judgment, taking away of his human dignity.

According to A. Medvedev and Roy Medvedev, one of the most significant outcomes of the congress was the return of millions of former prisoners and the posthumous rehabilitation of additional millions. The Medvedevs estimate that by the summer of 1957, five million prisoners returned home from the camps.

"The Secret Speech and the Congress inaugurated a new era for Russia," Kozlovsky said. "Russia opened itself up to the outside world. One example was the International Youth Festival in 1957. This was obviously an opportune time, as far as the Russians were concerned, to clear the air on the Wallenberg case."

The Russians took ten months to announce their findings on the Wallenberg case. This can perhaps be explained in terms of the tertiary importance the Russians assigned to the Wallenberg case, in light of all the developments and changes in Russian society following the Twentieth Congress. A further explanation of the Russian attitude can be understood, according to Yoran Berg, by realizing that "Sweden and Russia talk at different levels." The Russians lost so many people in the last war, Berg continued, "that they could not grasp the importance of the Wallenberg case to Sweden."

In addition, Professor Sanders explained, "The Swedish government has certainly not been an important factor in the international camp. Its diplomats have not exerted a powerful influence in the international community."

But once the Russians announced their findings, why did they "decide" on 1947 as the year of Wallenberg's death? Professor Sanders does not feel that there is necessarily any logic in the choice of 1947: "There is a gray bureaucratic mass in Russia. Decisions are very often made without concern for systematic thought. In the case of Wallenberg, who knows, perhaps two bureaucrats assigned the Wallenberg case were faced with the problem of pinpointing Wallenberg's death. One said, 'how about 1947, the year of my son's birth.' And this whimsical choice found its way into the final document."

Kozlovsky had similar thoughts: "Decisions in the Russian bureaucracy are made in a very arbitrary manner. Little thought is involved as decisions are made in an unsophisticated, carefree manner, perhaps even over a drink."

However, Kozlovsky added that in the case of Wallenberg the Russians did not want the world to think that they had held the Swede for as long as twelve years—even if Beria and Abakumov could be blamed. Therefore, Kozlovsky said, the choice of 1947 seemed adequate as a response for the Swedes and for the world. Of course, one does not know why the years 1948 or 1949, were not chosen instead.

Yuri Luryi, who was a lawyer before emigrating from Russia to Canada in 1974, also saw no logical reason for the choice of 1947.

> I see no reason why the Gromyko memorandum indicated Wallenberg died in 1947. However, you must remember that around 1957 thousands of prisoners, many of them foreigners, were to be released from Soviet prisons, and they were reporting to embassies in Germany, France, and Italy. So the Soviets were somewhat pushed to give an answer on Wallenberg. If the Soviets said that Wallenberg died in 1956, for example, the world might have asked, "where is the grave" or "let us have better proof." But ten years elapsed since 1947, so the Soviets might have felt that they did not have to say or do more.

Mrs. Lagergren comments, "Since the Swedish government in its White Papers and in its presentation to the Russians dealt primarily with prisoner testimonies prior to the summer of 1947, the Russians chose July 17, 1947, very conveniently." However, this explanation does not account for testimonies in the White Paper, such as de Mohr's, which went beyond 1947.

Luryi, now on the faculty of the University of Western Ontario and Osgoode Hall Law School, has examined the Russian version of the Gromyko memorandum and finds it a "phoney" document. He lists his reasons in a recent interview in *Maclean's* magazine:

> The letter included the full text of the medical report of Wallenberg's death, which begins "Report on the prisoner known to you as Walenberg." It is very important that there is no first name in that phrase and that Wallenberg here has one "l." In the report the chief of Lubianka's medical section asks the state security minister who should conduct the autopsy on "Walenberg." Now that is very strange, since it was the medical chief's *job* to assign such autopsies. And I really doubt that he would send such a report to bypass the man responsible for the jail and send it straight to the minister. I believe it is a phoney document.

Even if the letter were "true," Luryi went on, the world is still left with a very unsatisfactory document. "So we know that someone whose name is Walenberg, with no age, nationality, or first name, died. We do not know how many Walenbergs were jailed in the USSR. They could be of any nationality and it does not suggest that it was our Wallenberg."

One can only wonder why the Russians did not release a more credible document. Luryi notes, "When the Gromyko letter was written in 1957, nobody cared how plausible it looked because no one expected the Swedish government to check the veracity of the document. Things are different now. Who could have foreseen the wave of emigration from the Soviet Union in the 1970s, which has included specialists who are qualified to make a judgment on the plausibility of the 1957 document."

One thing is certain about the Gromyko memorandum: it has become the crux of the Wallenberg case. "The Russians will always refer to the note," according to Sjöquist. Is the document genuine? According to Mark Popovsky, "The document looks authentic when one considers the terminology. Some of the details are plausible. For example, everybody who died in prison had an autopsy, and Smoltsov had a reason to be concerned because Abakumov held the prison director personally responsible."

Popovsky said there is a marked change in style between the Vishinsky and Gromyko documents. "The Gromyko memorandum, without a signature, represents the amorphous bureaucrat, faceless, impersonal, a reflection of how times have changed since the days of Stalin."

Despite the stamp of authenticity given to the document, Popovsky is totally convinced that the basic thrust of the memorandum can not be true. "It is impossible that there can only be one piece of paper on the Wallenberg case. There has to be myriads of papers encompassing every action, every interrogation in the case."

Harald Wigforss, former editor of *Göteborgs Handelstidning,* reaches a similar conclusion. "The fact that the Russians have only one piece of paper on Raoul Wallenberg is absurd, and it is certainly to be doubted that only Abakumov and Beria were familiar with the case."

Despite the many questions raised about the truthfulness of the facts in the Gromyko memorandum, some Swedes are convinced that Raoul Wallenberg died in Lubianka in 1947, and they cite the memorandum as proof. The most noted Swedish supporter of the claims made in the Gromyko memorandum is Professor Hans Villius, who, along with his wife Elsa, wrote a book in 1966 entitled *The Raoul Wallenberg Case.* An authority on Swedish history, Professor Villius is also a prominent television producer. Nothing that has happened since 1966, including the Kalinski testimony and the Kaplan report, has changed Villius's opinion.

Villius concedes that the Smoltsov note is "not done well," and that the handwritten document may not answer all questions. "However because it is not perfect," Villius stresses, "this is proof that the Smoltsov note is not a forgery."

Villius presented his hypothesis of what lay behind the information contained in the Gromyko memorandum:

> In response to the Swedish approach to the Russians in 1956, the Russians made a thorough search of its prisons, in a sense asking "Is Wallenberg here?" All that was found was the Smoltsov note. A logical question would be: why was there no more material on Wallenberg? Well, Beria and Abakumov had been responsible for the imprisonment of Wallenberg, and to avoid all chances of being blamed for the action had destroyed all the files and to further sweep away all evidence had ordered the interrogation and later the isolation of all prisoners who had shared a cell with Wallenberg or Langfelder.
>
> The next obvious question is: why was the Smoltsov note not destroyed? Since Smoltsov had been entrusted with such an important prisoner, it is natural that he would ask Abakumov what to do with the corpse. And so Smoltsov prepared to send the note, but before the note was actually forwarded, Smoltsov met Abakumov and personally informed him. And this can be seen in the postscript, which states that an order has been given that there should be no autopsy. It is this postscript, incidentally, which makes the memorandum so authentic. Abakumov did not know that Smoltsov has written the note, so when the Russians look for a file on Wallenberg, all they find is the Smoltsov document, which Beria and Abakumov did not destroy.

Villius discounts all evidence and reports of Wallenberg's being alive after 1947 because all testimonies "are vague and second-hand in nature. As a scholar, one must look at reliable and authentic evidence, and this is exactly what you find in the Gromyko memorandum."

Sweden has refused to accept the death of Wallenberg, according to Villius, "because it needs a hero, having gone through World War II without such a personality. It is to be regretted that in the tragic episode of Wallenberg he has been made a Messiah and a Christ figure."

Before Villius and his wife wrote their book, he had prepared a documentary on the missing Swede and concluded that Wallenberg was still alive. Since Wallenberg's parents had closely cooperated with him on the production, his later conclusions were very discomforting for the entire family.

What accounted for Villius's change of opinion? "When I made the documentary, I had little chance to look at the entire picture intensively. However, upon a thorough study of the facts at hand and upon examining the evidence in the Gromyko memorandum, I concluded that Raoul Wallenberg died in 1947," Professor Villius said.

Fredrik von Dardel responded to Hans and Elsa Villius in his *Facts Around a Fate,* and, according to Mrs. Lagergren, her father wrote the book "primarily to refute the Villiuses."

Von Dardel challenges a key point in the Villius hypothesis: Wallenberg had died in July, 1947, because all prisoners who shared a cell with Wallenberg or Langfelder were interrogated in July, 1947, and then isolated. Von Dardel raises the name of a prisoner named Huber, who shared a cell with Langfelder. Huber was interrogated in April, 1947, and then sent first to Siberia, from where he was transferred to Lubianka. Obviously, concludes von Dardel, someone other than Abakumov wanted to cover up the Wallenberg case—before the supposed death in July, 1947:

"If Abakumov, as the Villiuses seem to want to imply, became nervous for being charged with concealing Wallenberg's imprisonment because of what happened around July, 1947, and tried to remove the traces, it cannot have been Abakumov, who already in April, 1947, started to cover up by sending Huber from Siberia to Moscow . . . . There must have been somebody else who ordered this transfer of Huber, who is probably to be found in the Soviet Foreign Office."

Von Dardel's argument does not impress Villius. According to him, Huber's transfer prior to July, 1947, has no relevance or relation to Wallenberg:

> Fredrik von Dardel's argument is not very clever. The fact that a single prisoner or two is transferred from one place to another at one time or another does not say anything at all. You can't decide who did it and why it was done. We don't even know if it had any connection with Raoul Wallenberg. The opportunity to draw conclusions comes when you can see a lot of prisoners being interrogated at the same time, about the same subject, and after that being treated in the same manner. That is what happened at the end of July, 1947.

And so, despite von Dardel's refutation, Villius continues to be a thorn in the side of those who feel that Raoul Wallenberg did not die in 1947, and that he may be still alive today. Some members of the Raoul Wallenberg Association are convinced that Professor Villius was "paid off" by the Russians to "change his mind" and write his book. "We who are fighting for the release of Raoul Wallenberg," Mrs. Lagergren said, "were very displeased when Professor Villius's remarks were carried in papers throughout the country on the eve of the 1981 international hearing on Raoul Wallenberg. Because Professor Villius has a certain scholarly standing, his remarks are sadly taken as truth by many people."

What surprisingly has received scant attention is the fact that no Swedish official has ever seen or asked to see a "true copy" of the handwritten report from Smoltsov to Abakumov, which includes a postscript by the head of Lubianka's medical service. According to Yoran Berg, "It wasn't appropriate to ask Russia to see a copy of the report. Besides our government had other questions, more serious, about the contents of Gromyko's memorandum." Berg added that even if such a request were made, one could not rule out a "fabrication" on Russia's part.

Dr. Adam B. Ulam, Gurney Professor of History and Political Science at Harvard University, sees nothing untoward in one country asking another, even if that country be Russia, to show a copy, or even an original, of a document of an important nature. "It certainly would not have been bad form for Sweden to have asked Russia to see a copy of the Smoltsov report. Even today Sweden could make that request. The fact that no such request has ever been made should be attributed to Swedish timidity."

The oft-used name of the document—the Gromyko memorandum— suggests another question: What is the importance, if any, of Andrei Gromyko in the future Soviet approach to the Wallenberg case? He signed the memorandum as deputy foreign minister and in March, 1957, replaced Dmitri T. Shepilov as foreign minister. A leader in the Communist Party for more than four decades, Gromyko is a member of the Politbureau, among the five most powerful officials in the Soviet Union. Although Westerners are unclear about Gromyko's contributions in shaping foreign policy, he has frequently accompanied Khrushchev, Brezhnev, and Kosygin on state visits. When named foreign minister, Gromyko was already known for his stony silence and for his hard-line stance. In analyzing the appointment in *Reporter* magazine, Isaac Deutscher described Gromyko as "a cold war veteran" who is "second only to Molotov in inexhaustible capacity for patient maneuvering, for tireless obstructiveness, and for all those interminable contests at mudslinging and pettifogging which belong to the Cold War." While Khrushchev gives only scattered references to Gromyko in his memoirs, he does note that the foreign minister accompanied him on all state visits and deems him a "real craftsman" in foreign affairs, a "good civil servant who always went by the book."

While Gromyko is undoubtedly a mighty figure in the Communist hierarchy, there seems to be no consensus on the importance of his role or involvement in the Wallenberg case. Professor Sanders said,

> You must keep in mind that the Wallenberg case has not occupied that important of a place in Russian politics, as had the Powers case, for example. It is not applicable to say that Gromyko can be embarrassed personally by the

Wallenberg case, and that it could lead to his removal from power and then to a change in the Soviet approach to Wallenberg. To make a comparison, could one say that America's Secretary of State would step down because of his actions in the Berrigan case?

But Palmstierna remains convinced that even in 1982 one has to be aware of the centrality of Gromyko in the Wallenberg case: "It was Gromyko who first said that Raoul Wallenberg was not alive and it was Gromyko who has been twice received in Sweden and asked about Wallenberg."

Kozlovsky, uncertain of Gromyko's role in the 1957 memorandum, comments, "Perhaps he actually signed the document himself, but he just may have been a conduit for the foreign department of the Central Committee." However, Luryi considers Gromyko's involvement to be more crucial.

In the eminent struggle for political survival in the Soviet Union, Gromyko does not want any fatal mistakes to happen. As a member of the Soviet Mount Olympus, Gromyko is one of the gods who never errs. I would say that there is a 50-50 possibility that if Gromyko were no longer on the scene, things could be different. In fact, one of the panelists at the Wallenberg hearing in Stockholm said that until Gromyko falls from power there can not be any positive change in Russia's approach in the Wallenberg case.

Late in the summer of 1981 the name of Soviet President Leonid Brezhnev took on new meaning in the Wallenberg case. A former Soviet army officer now living in Israel, Yaakov Leontevich Menaker, revealed that Brezhnev was responsible for the kidnapping of Wallenberg. Menaker was a lieutenant in the 571st battalion of the Eighteenth Army, whose political section was headed by Brezhnev. The Soviet emigré told the Israeli paper *Yediot Aharonot*: "The head of the political section of the Soviet 18th Army, Leonid Brezhnev, who is today the president, initiated, planned, and was responsible for the kidnapping of Wallenberg in Budapest in 1945."

Further information was forthcoming from Anders Hasselbohm, the correspondent for *Aftonbladet*, who disclosed the story to the Swedish public. According to Hasselbohm, Menaker was a guard in the "window operation," better described as a spy activity, during the liberation of Budapest.

Menaker came to Israel two years ago. While visiting Yad Vashem he read of the destruction of the Jewish communities during the Holocaust. He also noted details of the Hungarian episode, including the heroics of Wallenberg. But he didn't make any connection until he met Shifrin and others who have been involved in the Wallenberg campaign. In other words, Menaker had known that his fellow officers had participated in the arrest and abduction of a famous person, but he had never known or heard of Wallenberg while in Russia.

Hasselbohm identified the commander of the 571st battalion as a Captain Aminayev who had been decorated for his part in the Wallenberg abduction. "Menaker once attended a reception at which Aminayev was present," Hasselbohm continued. "When questions were asked about Aminayev's decoration, there suddenly was silence and no answer."

Hasselbohm said that Menaker had "reliable" information from his fellow officers that "Brezhnev's soldiers confiscated Wallenberg's money, jewelry, and diamonds which he had used to finance the release of Jews from the Nazis."

While the role of Brezhnev in the Wallenberg abduction was first revealed by Menaker, Hasselbohm indicated that the story of the Eighteenth Army in Budapest was never hidden, but nobody had taken the trouble to check the historical records. The details of the Eighteenth Army can be found in a recent biography of Brezhnev, published by Simon and Schuster.

Although it can be accepted that the Eighteenth Army liberated Budapest and perhaps actually arrested Wallenberg, the facts of Brezhnev's involvement are very disputable. Officers of the Raoul Wallenberg Association in Stockholm have told of their knowing of Brezhnev's heading the political section of the Eighteenth Army months before the story made headlines in the Swedish papers. They didn't want to publicize the information lest it be inimical to the Wallenberg campaign. As an official in the association states, "We do not have reliable information that President Brezhnev was personally involved in the arrest of Raoul Wallenberg. All we do know is that he was with the Eighteenth Army and might know more about Wallenberg than he will admit."

Ambassador Per Anger does not exclude the possibility that Brezhnev played a major role in the arrest of Wallenberg, but he expresses surprise that it has taken almost thirty-six years for the information to surface.

Expressing the view of the Foreign Ministry, Yoran Berg said that the Brezhnev developments may "shed new light on the Wallenberg case, but it is certainly amazing that after untold numbers of witnesses have returned from Hungary, we should now, in 1981, have first heard the story." Yoran Berg does not see any possibility of "a de-Brezhnevization along the lines of de-Stalinization," so in other words, "the death or removal of Brezhnev should not be expected to produce any change" in the Wallenberg case. However, Harald Wigforss sees no possibility of change in the Russian approach as long as Gromyko and Brezhnev are alive. But Hasselbohm does not rule out the possibility that the death of Brezhnev would allow Gromyko to "pin the blame" for the Wallenberg case on the Soviet president.

Former Soviet prisoner Gunnar Rode feels that the involvement of Brezhnev would have been to Wallenberg's advantage in the past. "If Brezhnev arrested Wallenberg, then Brezhnev would have seen to it that Wallenberg was well treated since he didn't know whether Wallenberg would be used in an exchange with the Russians."

Mark Popovsky says that it is not possible that Brezhnev plotted the arrest of Wallenberg. Popovsky feels that the action undoubtedly involved SMERSH, the acronym for Soviet counterintelligence.

One can say with certainty that Raoul Wallenberg was alive well beyond the date of his supposed death in 1947 as specified in the Gromyko memorandum. The Svartz testimony appears to be solid, thereby establishing his presence in the Gulag in 1961. The Svartz testimony is preceded by very credible reports by General Kupriyanov, which places Wallenberg alive at the end of the fifties. After the Svartz episode, there is the Wrangel Island testimony. As Moshinsky has testified that Wallenberg was in the Arctic camp as late as 1962, one must be concerned whether the Westerner Wallenberg could survive the rigors of such a setting. The sixties, seventies, and the early eighties have produced witnesses, none impeccable individually but, nevertheless, impressive in their total number. But, again, one has to confront the question, for which the answers are not satisfying. Can a Westerner, or anyone, survive thirty-seven years of servitude in the Gulag? Can Raoul Wallenberg still be alive in 1982? It would be extraordinary and nearly impossible for the answer to be in the affirmative. However, Raoul Wallenberg is an extraordinary individual whose deeds were seemingly impossible.

"People often tell me that I am indulging in wishful thinking to imagine my brother is alive," Nina Lagergren said. "They are totally wrong. It is wishful thinking to imagine that he is dead, to feel that he has been spared these years of being alive. That is wishful thinking."

It is for precisely this reason that the search for Raoul Wallenberg must go on until there is incontestable evidence . . . that he lives or that he has died.

14

Survival in the Hells of Russia

In his poem "The Law of the Yukon," the twentieth-century Canadian writer Robert William Service describes the "Will of the Yukon," the northwest territory whose severity of climate has its counterpart in Siberia. In the Yukon, Service writes, "surely the Weak shall perish, and only the Fit Survive." But in the frosts of Canada, man has only to contend with the natural elements, not with repressive systems and mechanisms of totalitarianism.

Can anyone, then, survive a long-term sentence in the Gulag, a network of more than two thousand penal institutions that, as Leopold Trepper observes, "are all part of a system where terror is the driving force"?

Is it possible for Raoul Wallenberg to survive for more than thirty-seven years in these prisons and camps where, Shifrin estimates, more than 60 million persons have been tortured, murdered, or otherwise have perished during the past sixty years? And, if he still survives, what can his physical and psychological condition be?

In the twentieth century, man's ability to endure the unendurable, to survive the unsurvivable has been put to the test in the death and labor camps of Nazi Germany and Communist Russia. In addition to countless accounts of survivors of the Nazi Holocaust, Terrence des Pres has written an eloquent testimony to the resolute human will to survive in these crude conditions of living. *The Survivor,* however, makes little distinction between Dachau-Auschwitz and Khal'mer-Yu-Wrangel Island. True, the human spirit can overcome the hells of Treblinka and the Gehenna of Kolyma, but working in the temperate, mild-weather labor camps of Nazi Germany, even over an extended period, could be rather "tame" compared to laboring in the severity of the Arctic climate found in many camps of the

211

Gulag. All depends on the individual involved, emphasized Prof. Henry R. Huttenbach, a Russian historian at City University of New York who has also written extensively on the Holocaust: "The Nazi and Russian camps are categorically distinct in terms of the political, social, penal, and psychological perspectives underlying their establishment and operation."

While doing research in Moscow from 1964 to 1965, Professor Huttenbach met several dozen prisoners released during the post-Stalin years. He noted, "It was obvious that the labor camps of the Nazis and the Russians were in no way comparable. Most of those who survived in Russia were sturdy peasant types, hardy manual laborers, true believers, and, of course, the young. Few survivors came from comfortable middle-class backgrounds."

Most of the ten thousand German prisoners who returned home in 1954, according to Professor Huttenbach, had been "well schooled in the skills of survival by military training." As part of his project in collecting oral testimony from Jewish survivors of the Riga ghetto, Professor Huttenbach encountered several Jewish survivors who, after liberation, suffered still more years in Russian camps. According to their testimony, they credited their survival to two factors: the lessons of survival they learned during the Nazi years and the support they received from other inmates.

Since "Raoul Wallenberg is of an aristocratic background, with few basic survival skills, with minimal exposure to the physical rigors of the camps, who would not have had much opportunity for developing rapport with the types of prisoners the Soviets would have chosen for his companions," Professor Huttenbach sees little hope for Wallenberg's survival.

Professor Huttenbach's opinion is but one of many on the subject of survival in the hells of Russia. The family and former colleagues of Raoul Wallenberg, former Russian prisoners and citizens, as well as scholars and writers, have given much thought to the possibility of Raoul Wallenberg's survival in the Gulag.

Dr. von Dardel said that the struggle to find and free Raoul "gave meaning" to the lives of his parents and "kept them alive." Both died still convinced that Raoul was alive. The father, called by Dr. Dardel "the brain behind all our efforts over the years," in 1970 reflected on the question "Is Wallenberg alive?":

Wallenberg . . . is when this is written 57 years old if he is still alive. He had a very good health and good constitution, both physically and mentally. He is not known to be seriously ill or liable to illness. Under normal circumstances he would be expected to outlive the normal average Swedish age of about 70 years old, and probably more. It is hard to judge how his life in prison, which must have been very trying, can have influenced his health. During his stay in the Lubianka and Lefortovo prisons he was interrogated and reported to his coprisoners about them. He does not seem to have been mistreated or tortured in any way . . . . The Russian prisons are in general equipped with hospital wards, and the doctors and nurses seem to be in general competent and considerate. To some extent the prisoners are more protected from some of the dangers of life in liberty, traffic accidents, and other accidents, stress, etc., and it is therefore possible that imprisonment does not by itself shorten the life expectancy. This is proved by the case of Hitler's minister Rudolph Hess, who in spring, 1941, flew to England to transmit a peace proposal and ever since has been in prison, first in England and then in Spandau outside Berlin. He is now 75 after 28 years in prison (38).

(In 1982 Hess still remains in Spandau—the only inmate of that prison.)

In an interview with the *Jerusalem Post Magazine* on January 25, 1980, Dr. von Dardel echoed some of the same themes as his father, stressing the ability to survive life in a Russian camp, in both physical and mental terms:

"People exaggerate the risks of life in Russian prison camps. One can adjust after a few years. After all Raoul is not in a death camp. He always had robust health. And we are a long-lived family . . . .

"Even the most miserable life is worth living. I've met other released Russian prisoners. They're active and happy—even after 10 and 15 years in the camps."

In a recent interview with the author, Dr. von Dardel spoke of the value of Raoul's knowledge of Russian:

Raoul studied Russian in high school. As far as we know he did not have much occasion to practice before his captivity. However, it seems very likely that his knowledge of Russian, acquired during his most receptive years, must have been a very good foundation for becoming fluent in the language in the Soviet prisons. This fluency may have been important in keeping up his morale through the possibilities for human contact which would be open through this language fluency. We know that Raoul was never put in prison with Westerners, but always with Soviet prisoners—presumably because of the much smaller risk that these Soviet prisoners would eventually be able to report about him.

Ambassador Per Anger, Wallenberg's colleague in Budapest, contrasted the Russian and German treatment of those whom they accused of being spies. "The Germans killed those whom they accused of spying. In Russia if you are sentenced as a spy, it is not intended that you die—that is your punishment. Of course, the Russian bureaucracy is more complex than that. You can not murder such a prisoner because it could lead to trouble for the one responsible for the decision. In short, a prisoner such as Raoul Wallenberg cannot be simply released and cannot be murdered."

As Anger writes in his book, the physical and spiritual strength of Wallenberg has convinced him that his colleague may well be alive: "I have met German diplomats who sat in Russian prisons for about 10 years and came through it. True, that is not so long a period as in Wallenberg's case: However, he had an unusually strong physique and an impressive strength of spirit" (156).

And, as Anger told the U.S. Senate in 1979, at this point it is of the utmost importance to learn the truth about Raoul Wallenberg, and if he is alive to have him returned to Sweden:

"It has become a question of decency, a legitimate claim to learn what happened to a man who on an official Swedish mission saved tens of thousands of lives and if he is still alive, which we believe, to get him back to Sweden.

"We Swedes have the right to demand this and so have all those he saved as well as all men in this world who are fighting for human rights."

Wallenberg's extraordinary qualities lead another former colleague, Lars Berg, to believe that the Angel of Rescue is still alive. "Raoul Wallenberg impressed me as an exceptional person. He must have studied and mastered the Russian language while in prison. And most important, he set out and never has wavered in his determination to save his own life."

A career diplomat now serving in Brazil, Berg feels that "we must give the Russians an opportunity, an opening whereby they can say that they themselves have found Raoul after all these years." However, a face-saving formula is not absolutely essential, according to Berg. "With the Russians, one does not have to expect explanations or resolution of contradictions." In 1949 Berg concluded his book with the belief that one day Raoul Wallenberg will return to his homeland. Thirty-three years later Berg still clings to the lines of 1949:

"And one day Raoul Wallenberg will be back. He was neither a German nor an American spy in Budapest. He had other and greater duties to attend to. The Russians know that, and one day they will let Raoul return to Sweden. When Raoul is home again, no excuses, no explanations will be asked for. It is sufficient that he does come back" (196).

Although the Wallenberg family and former colleagues point to the ability of former prisoners to come out of the Russian camps with a sound body and a sound mind, former inmates stress the physical and mental devastation of long-term sentences. Tibor Baranski was arrested by Hungarian Communist forces in 1948 and sentenced to nine years in prison for spying and conspiracy. He was released after Stalin's death in 1953. According to Baranski, who worked together with the Swede in 1944, "There is very little hope for Raoul Wallenberg. I know the Communist mind. The Communists feel that Raoul Wallenberg has to know too much. Even should he be alive after all these years, his condition would tragically be like that of a scrambled egg."

Although he has not served any time in the Gulag, Professor Jonathan Sanders has met emigrés who have familiarized him with the difficulties of survival in the camps. "This is especially true," he said, "if you look German. The danger would not come from the guards, but from the camp criminals who would react adversely to Wallenberg." Professor Sanders thought it unlikely that Wallenberg received any special treatment. "What special skills does Wallenberg have that could be put to use in the prisons. Of what value could his banking background be?"

Rabbi Albert Belton, who was spiritual leader of the Budapest ghetto, cites personal experiences for his view that Raoul Wallenberg will never be seen again as a free man: "I personally know the Russians quite well for I have 'enjoyed' their 'hospitality' twice in 1945, although thanks to the good Lord, for short periods on both occasions. Without doubt the Russians lie to their teeth. Once they arrested him, they will not let him go for fear he saw, he knew too much. In short, all is futile and to no avail as far as freedom for Raoul Wallenberg is concerned."

Russian emigré Mark Popovsky is very pessimistic about the likelihood of Wallenberg's surviving decades in the Gulag. "I would be the first man to rejoice if Wallenberg were found alive in the Gulag, but the chances are very slim, especially for a Westerner who is not used to the Russian prison diet and for a nonproletariat who is not conditioned to meet the rigors of the camps."

Another expert on the Soviet prisons is Aleksandr Solzhenitsyn, the Nobel laureate who has served many years in the Gulag. In seeking to shed light on the status of the unaccounted American prisoners in Vietnam, the *National Review* of August 21, 1981, cites previously made remarks of Solzhenitsyn. These comments perhaps offer a bleak prognosis for Wallenberg:

> There is a law in the Archipelago that those who have been treated the most harshly and who have withstood the most bravely, who are the most honest, the most courageous, the most unbending, never again come out into the world. They are never again shown to the world because they will tell tales that the human mind can barely accept . . . . These are your best people. These are your foremost heroes who, in a solitary combat, have stood the test. And today, unfortunately, they cannot take courage from our applause. They cannot hear it from their solitary cells where they may either die or remain for thirty years.

The Ukrainian dissident Leonid Plyushch offers another explanation— perhaps one not readily understandable to the Western mind—for the Russians' keeping prisoners "forever." In a society where God does not exist, nothing is disallowed, according to Plyushch.

However, the Free Wallenberg Committee quickly points out instances of prisoners who have come out unscathed after thirty-five years in the Gulag Archipelago. A Rumanian Jew was released in 1978 after a thirty-five-year term. The committee located a Spaniard who was released in sound condition after completing a thirty-five-year sentence.

Simon Wiesenthal reported at the Stockholm hearings that one German was freed after spending thirty-seven years in the Gulag; another returnee had served twenty-eight years. According to Khronica Press, which issues a Soviet affairs journal called *Chronicle of Current Events,* the longest term in the Gulag for a dissident freed and now in the West was that of Sviatsolav Karavansky, who served thirty years. Currently residing in Columbia, Maryland, the former Ukrainian said that it is "difficult to survive a long-term sentence in the Gulag, but it is not impossible." Karavansky cited the cases of Danylo Shumuk, a Ukrainian who served nearly forty years, although the sentence was not served consecutively, and other Ukrainians whom he knew, such as Tarka Husak, who was at Vladimir eighteen years, and Katryn Carytsky, incarcerated at Vladimir for twenty years.

Karavansky maintains, "An important factor in survival is isolation. If you are with other prisoners, you are exposed to vicious, criminal elements. While I can not say that a foreigner receives any better or any worse treatment at the hands of prison authorities, I can say that the foreigner will be at a great disadvantage if pushed among other prisoners, especially if they be sadistic."

Another Russian emigré, Vladimir Kozlovsky, has known prisoners who served forty or more years, beginning their sentences under Polish and German authorities. "It is true that you can physically survive the rigors," he said, "but there is no doubt that you do age considerably."

Abraham Shifrin, who spent fourteen years in Russian jails and camps, now operates a documentation center in Tel Aviv on the Gulag Archipelago. In an interview with John Bierman, presented in the *Boston Globe* on August 10, 1979, Shifrin related the case of Leonid Berger, who spent thirty-four years in the Russian camps. "He is now 57 but looks 45. I will explain. It's not a miracle. Three times a day you have a very bad meal, but it is a meal, and you always get it at the same time. It is very healthy. After the interrogations, when you are very tense, you have no problems — only how to get more food and less work."

Shifrin's attitude was shared by another long-term prisoner, Avraham Kalinski, who was incarcerated for fifteen years in the Gulag. Now living in Tel Aviv, Kalinski looks ten years younger than his actual age of sixty-three. "You see, all those years I was never able to take alcohol, never able to overeat. It preserves you." He believes that Wallenberg can still be alive. As late as 1959, he had seen Wallenberg regularly and had observed him as a determined and intelligent person. "I saw Wallenberg on an average of five times a week during our twenty-minute walking exercise in the yard. We would talk to one another through the cell walls or knock on the water pipes in a code we made up. Wallenberg speaks fluent Russian, and is a very intelligent and energetic knocker."

While the physical condition and background of the prisoner are stressed in discussion of survival in the Gulag, one must not overlook the mental attitude, the determination of the prisoner to survive. Eugenia Ginzburg survived her "journey into the whirlwind." From the start, she was determined to stay alive; "I must live! In prison, if needs be, but I must at all costs live!" (174).

The internationally famous psychologist Bruno Bettelheim has studied the Holocaust survivor in *Surviving and Other Essays,* and his conclusions certainly have application for those in the Gulag. The will to live, the maintaining of one's self-respect, and the keeping up of one's hope in the future — all these are necessary for survival in the camps. According to Bettelheim, "If one could maintain one's self-respect and will to live despite the utter exhaustion, physical mistreatment, and extreme degradations one had to endure, then one could continue to hope that one had not been forsaken by the rest of the world." In Wallenberg's case, one has to wonder what effect the words of the Russian inquisitor had upon the Swede, "Nobody cares about you."

Bettelheim's accent on self-dignity is also echoed by Erving Goffman in *Asylums,* who sees "recalcitrance" as a way of retaining one's selfhood. Human dignity is realized, Goffman writes, in "the practice of reserving something of oneself from the clutches of an institution . . . very visible in mental hospitals and prisons."

Dr. Boris Zoubok, a Russian émigré psychiatrist now with Columbia Presbyterian Hospital in New York, also considers the "special qualities" of Wallenberg. He himself has seen prisoners who have come out of the Gulag after serving for long periods of time and has pronounced these people physically and mentally fit. "I have examined a good number of old-time prisoners, those who were arrested in the 1950s and 1960s. These prisoners received different treatment than today's prisoners, for example, as the Soviet Jewish dissidents. The place of confinement for the old-time prisoners was such that they were set apart from the other prisoners. In many cases these prisoners were set aside in readiness for being exchanged."

According to Dr. Zoubok, who has examined more than one hundred long-term prisoners after their release, these special prisoners were assigned to perform badly needed professional services in the camps, such as teaching the children of prison personnel or taking care of the books and financial records of the camps. Given the skills of Raoul Wallenberg, Dr. Zoubok said, it is reasonable to conclude that he would have been given special tasks in the camps. He continues,

In addition to the nature of the consignment and the health of the individual, both of which seem favorable in Wallenberg's case, one must also look at the special qualities of the individual. Raoul Wallenberg was an extraordinary person with great determination. It is reasonable to expect that he has sought to recreate the life he led before being imprisoned. He could then act in prison in what can be called an adaptive mode. In the case of Wallenberg, he would choose to act altruistically, whereby he could help others, perhaps working with the medics or with the religious personnel. The point to be made is that by acting in a manner consistent with his former existence, the prisoner can go on living even under adverse situations.

Dr. Zoubok has never met Raoul Wallenberg, but his opinions do lend more credibility that Raoul Wallenberg still lives. In all the testimonies of returning Russian prisoners who saw Wallenberg, there is no mention of his being mistreated; some even mention the privileged status of the Swede.

If anything is certain, it is that the Russians were not telling the truth in the Gromyko memorandum. Raoul Wallenberg was definitely alive after July, 1947. From the Svartz episode and the Shifrin and Moshinsky testimonies, it is clear that Raoul Wallenberg was alive as late as 1962. Other reports, such as the account of Jan Kaplan, which places Raoul Wallenberg's being alive at a date after 1962, can not be accepted as prima facie evidence because the prisoners have never been interrogated by an official government or judicial body.

On the other hand, Malcolm Toon, who was the U.S. ambassador to Russia from 1976 to 1979, feels that the overwhelming evidence in the Wallenberg case is of a "secondary" nature. According to Ambassador Toon, "There is no credible evidence that Raoul Wallenberg is alive. I vacationed in Israel after leaving Russia and was approached by three emigrés about the case. I told them that the evidence that Wallenberg is alive is flimsy and we should recognize it as such."

Aware that there are certain weaknesses in the evidence, Luryi looks at the evidence not as individual strands, but as a totality. "Certainly much of the evidence is not only hearsay, but secondhand hearsay. But firsthand evidence is difficult to bring forth when Wallenberg was kept so often in isolation. Therefore so-called hearsay evidence is important, especially when there are so many accounts — some twenty all told. They are independent, but they are corroborated." As he told *Maclean's,* "Together they cry, they shout."

Kozlovsky sees the question of whether Wallenberg is alive not in terms of the evidence presented, but rather in light of the evidence not revealed. "There are many leaks in the Soviet Union. With so many emigrés throughout the world, one must ask and wonder why there has not been more information in recent years about Wallenberg."

Luryi explained the relative scarcity of information coming out of the Soviet Union. "The KGB has never been as strong and skillful as it is now. In the sixties it was nearly disbanded under Khrushchev. Because it is so powerful, people have become more circumspect in passing information."

And, according to an official of the Wallenberg Association, "Because of the world attention, information has become more difficult to come by.

It is reasonable to assume that Raoul is being put with Russians who are not expected to come out. It is, therefore, even more surprising that we get any new, important details at all."

Those active in the Wallenberg campaign continually investigate reports of his whereabouts. In the past few years, they have been given accounts of his imprisonment in Mordovia during 1964, in Zadivovo near Irkutsk during 1966–67, in Vladimir during 1968–70, in Irkutsk during 1973–74, in Spets Corpus, Gorki, during 1976–77, and in a prison in the Leningrad area during 1980. Sources for such information are Russian dissidents, emigrés, tourists, Swedish doctors and other professionals who visit Russia. Israeli security has interviewed emigrés and has made use of sources inside Russia. According to Mrs. Widemar,

> We admit that much of the information we have been receiving is of a second-hand nature. But if Raoul Wallenberg is dead we would know that. And there is no reliable information that he is dead. What is important is to locate him, but we have to make sure that the source is reliable. When we locate him, we can then go to the Americans and ask for their assistance. But we can't wait much longer, perhaps two years or so. How long can one man survive in Russian prisons and camps?

Although severely criticized for its ineffective performance in the Wallenberg case, the Swedish government states that it will not abandon the campaign, but it is aware that the search is difficult. Yoran Berg says,

> We have made mistakes in the past but we are not giving up. We will continue until we know for certain that Raoul Wallenberg is dead. When the government receives testimonies and reports as solid as the accounts of Kalinski and Kaplan we will approach the Russians and demand an explanation. Unfortunately, in most cases we get second- or third-hand information or contradictory evidence. Because of the worldwide publicity in the Wallenberg case, people coming out of the Russian prisons suddenly remember Wallenberg. But since their memories are weak they only imagine they saw him.

While Stockholm seems determined to press on, the Swedish stance vis-à-vis the Russian is simplistic and unrealistic. "Our approach to the Russians," Berg said, "can be looked at in this manner. We are asking them: 'Can we cooperate? We don't want to accuse you. We want to help you find Raoul Wallenberg.' Perhaps all this sounds naive."

Assuming that incontrovertible evidence is presented to the Russians that Raoul Wallenberg is still alive, how can the Russians reverse their position and admit to the world that they have lied for more than thirty-seven years. For that reason, Ambassador Toon sees little likelihood that the Russians will adopt a new line, even if a tempting deal were offered them. And, according to Professor Sanders, the worldwide campaign has aggravated the problem. "While an international campaign for Wallenberg brings attention to the case, the worldwide spotlight makes it almost impossible for the Russians to change their position."

Professor Luryi disagrees. "The more noise that is made, the better it will be. We must cause the Russians so much difficulty that they will look ridiculous. The Wallenberg campaign has two goals. If he is still alive, we must save him. If he died recently, not as the Russians say, then we must stop the Russians from saving face. To do this would be a spiritual monument to the Swedish hero and humanitarian Raoul Wallenberg."

It is one thing to cite case histories of prisoners who have survived long terms in the Gulag, and it is another thing to have Raoul Wallenberg returned to freedom. If American involvement is of little value, if honorary citizenship confers no added rights, what practical approach can be taken? "It is necessary," advised Ambassador Toon, "to have absolutely firm evidence and then confront the Russians. If Sweden would at that moment happen to have, for example, a top KGB official in its hands, perhaps a deal could be made." Pointing out that Sweden has little to offer the Russians, Professor Sanders suggested that the initiative could come from West Germany. "Russia has been significantly aided by West German technology. A very favorable pipeline deal is in effect. By making a representation for Wallenberg, the West Germans would be fulfilling the proper moral role since they had been guilty during the Holocaust."

And so the world waits for an answer to the question "Where is Raoul Wallenberg?" Perhaps he will one day return to his homeland and personally accept not only the gratitude of those whom he saved but also the gratitude of humanity whom he served.

The efforts to find him, to free him must never cease. Yet, of equal importance is telling and retelling the story of Raoul Wallenberg: how one man transcended the basest conditions in the atmosphere of World War II; how one man realized his fullest potential and became an Angel of Rescue — and more. The grandeur of Raoul Wallenberg amid the horrors of Nazism recalls the eloquent lines of *Hamlet*:

> This goodly frame, the earth, seems to me a sterile promontory; this most excellent canopy, the air, look you, this brave o'erhanging firmament, this majestical roof fretted with golden fire, why, it appears no other thing to me than a foul and pestilent congregation of vapours. What a piece of work is a man! how noble in reason! how infinite in faculty! in form and moving how express and admirable! in action how like an angel! in apprehension how like a god!

Afterword

During the last three years, interest in the fate of Raoul Wallenberg has spread like an explosion all over the world. Not only in Sweden but also in many other countries like the United States, Canada, Britain, France, Austria, and Israel, action groups have been formed to work for Wallenberg's liberation. More books than ever before have been written, and plays and films are being produced about his heroic rescue work during World War II for the Hungarian Jews. In newspaper articles his story has been told over and over again, and Jewish immigrants in many countries have testified how they were miraculously saved by Wallenberg.

With this book Harvey Rosenfeld has contributed in a very valuable way to the picture of Wallenberg and his work. The book is comprehensive and well documented. It is a very good description of "the Swedish Angel of Rescue," his early background, and how he was assigned to the mission in Budapest. It tells accurately about Wallenberg's humanitarian action during "Hungary's darkest hour," how he became the savior of tens of thousands of Jewish people. Without losing himself in too many details the author puts Wallenberg into the historical perspective of that time. Through his book you learn to know a man who through his heroic, unselfish efforts to save human lives has become a legend.

Surprisingly enough, Wallenberg did not give the impression of being a hero. He was not a superman type. We met in Stockholm some years before he came on his mission to Budapest in 1944 and we became very good friends. I learned to know Raoul more as an intellectual, almost weak person. He spoke with a soft voice and sometimes looked like a dreamer. At heart he was no doubt a great idealist and a warm human being. It did not

221

take long, however, till you discovered that he had a remarkable inner strength, a core of fighting spirit. Furthermore, he was a clever negotiator and organizer, unconventional and extraordinarily inventive. I became convinced that no one was better qualified for the assignment to Budapest than Raoul.

In my book I recall the day in July 1944 when he arrived at our legation in Budapest — where I was serving as young attaché at that time — equipped rather oddly for a diplomat. He was carrying two knapsacks, a sleeping bag, a windbreaker, and a revolver. But this equipment would be put to good use in the months ahead. "The revolver is just to give me courage," he said to me in his typically joking way. "I hope I'll never have to use it," and he never had to. He grew with his task and the bravery he showed in many dangerous situations became legendary.

I still remember rather vividly my last meeting with Raoul on January 10, 1945. I tried to persuade him not to risk his life any longer and to hide on the Buda side with the other members of the legation. The Hungarian Nazis were especially on the lookout for him and he was in great danger. The increased bombing of the city had also made it more and more difficult to continue the aid work for the Jews. But Raoul did not listen. His words are still ringing in my ears: "For me there's no choice. I've taken on this assignment and I'd never be able to go back to Stockholm without knowing inside myself I'd done all a man could do to save as many Jews as possible."

Why has the interest in Wallenberg's cause taken such proportions during this recent time when it is over thirty-five years since he was arrested by the Soviets? Well, his fate has of course preoccupied Swedish public opinion from the end of the war to this very day. From the sixties to 1978, however, there was a long period when nothing more was heard about Wallenberg, when no new witnesses appeared, and people tended to forget about him. Suddenly, then, Kalinski's and Kaplan's stories reached the public: Wallenberg is still alive. As late as 1975, he had been seen in a prison in the Soviet Union.

This new information caused great excitement all over the world; based now on the principles of human rights laid down in the Helsinki agreement, voices were raised in a number of Western countries for his release. Not only the Swedish government but also the leaders of other countries — among them President Carter — intervened in Moscow for him. Many people all over the world have acted for his cause, directly or through the different national action groups or Free Wallenberg committees. The Soviet government has been bombarded with letters, cables, and telephone calls requesting Wallenberg's release. The fight for him is continuing and is not going to stop until the Soviets have realized their mistake in imprisoning an innocent person.

Through his saving of tens of thousands of Jewish lives Raoul Wallenberg has himself become a symbol for the fight for human rights.

Per Anger
Ambassador
Stockholm
January, 1981

Appendix

A. Chronology of Events Relating to Wallenberg's Mission in Hungary

1944

March	18	Hitler summons Horthy to Klessheim and holds him incommunicado.
	19	The German occupation of Hungary begins.
	19	Eichmann assembles his cadre in Budapest to plan the liquidation of Hungarian Jewry.
	22	Horthy appoints the Sztójay government.
	22	Von Clages orders Jewish leaders to set up a Judenrat or Jewish council in each area of Hungary to carry out German orders.
	29	Horthy grants the Sztójay government full discretion in the handling of the Jewish question.
	31	Jews are forced to wear the yellow star.
April	7	Baky issues a secret decree regarding Jewish deportations.
	7	Nazis begin to "ghettoize" the Jews in camps near rail stations.
	16	Government issues decree on the registration of Jewish assets and on the sequestration of Jews.
	26	The Council of Ministers puts 50,000 Jews and their families at German disposal "for labor service."
May	15	Jewish deportations from rural provinces begin.
June	7	289,357 Jews have been deported from Carpatho-Ruthenia and Transylvania—completion of first phase.

225

	24	Budapest Jews are relocated into buildings marked with a star.
	25	Pope Pius XII sends open telegram to Horthy.
	28	Archbishop Spellman appeals to Hungarian Catholics to help and protect Jews.
	30	92,304 more Jews have been deported from northern Hungary and southern Hungary east of the Danube.
July	1	Horthy replies to the pope's telegram.
	8	55,741 more Jews have been deported from Transdanubia and suburbs of Budapest, completing Eichmann's plan for liquidating Hungarian Jews in the provinces.
	8	Horthy stops the deportations.
	9	Wallenberg arrives in Budapest.
	17	Wallenberg files his first report on the condition of the Jews in Hungary.
	19	Wallenberg outlines rescue plans in letter to Káláman Lauer.
August	12	Horthy receives Wallenberg and agrees to honor his new Swedish protective passports.
	23	Rumania makes peace with the Soviet Union.
	24	Horthy orders Eichmann and his Sondereinsatzkommando to leave Hungary three days before the deportation of the Budapest Jews is scheduled to start.
September	7	American Jewish Joint Distribution Committee authorizes check for Wallenberg's mission.
	29	Wallenberg's letter to Lauer details accomplishments of mission.
October	15	Horthy attempts to surrender and quit the Axis.
	15	Skorzeny and Szálasi stage coup d'etat.
	17	Eichmann returns to Budapest.
	23	Interior Minister Vajna issues decree on the Jews that invalidates protective passes issued by the neutral legations.
	29	Foreign Minister Kemény broadcasts that the validity of protective passes is restored.
November	2	2nd Ukrainian Front breaks through defenders south of Budapest and advance elements reach the city's outskirts.
	3	Eichmann begins sending Budapest Jews on death marches to Hegyeshálom.
	7	Ferenczy demands 15,000 Jews with protective passes relocate to international ghetto.
	15	Jews protected by neutral legations finish moving into the

		international ghetto.
	17	Neutral legations send sharply worded memorandum to the Szálasi government.
	29	Ministry of Interior and Home Defense signs agreement with Gestapo to deliver 17,000 Jews for forced labor.
December	8	Red Army lays seige to Budapest.
	8	Wallenberg writes "Report on the Situation of the Hungarian Jews."
	8	Wallenberg writes last letter to his mother.
	23	Eichmann and his commando escape from Budapest
	23	Szálasi government relocates to Szombathely.
	23	Vöczköndy demands that Swedes leave Budapest.
	24	The Red Army completely surrounds Budapest.
	25	Nyilas invade the Swedish legation.

1945

January	4	Government orders Jews in international ghetto to move into the central ghetto.
(approx.)	6	Wallenberg trades food to Vajna to stop the movement of more Jews into the central ghetto.
	10	Wallenberg last meets with colleague Per Anger. Wallenberg prepares for trip to Debrecen.
	11	Wallenberg prevents the SS and Nyilas from massacring the Jews in the central ghetto.
	12	Wallenberg goes to Üllöi headquarters for last time.
	13	Wallenberg meets with colleague Lars Berg, the last Swede to see him.
	13	Red Army captures the ghettos.
	17	Wallenberg spends his last day in Budapest.
February	13	All of Budapest falls to the Red Army.

B. Designation of Jewish Accommodation

Hungarian Ministry of Foreign Affairs.
No. 6163/1944. res.

Subject: Designation of Jewish Accommodation.

The Royal Hungarian Government intends to rid the country of the Jews. On my instructions this operation will take place district by district. The Jews will be taken to pre-arranged assembly centres regardless of age and sex. In towns and larger localities a part of them will later be transferred to Jewish houses, respectively ghettos, which will have been prepared by the police. Jews employed in war essential factories, mines, agriculture and larger concerns, as well as highly-trained technicians, whose dismissal would adversely affect the production of the factory concerned, will be exempted. In the case of firms not essential for the prosecution of the war, dismissal will be immediate and replacements will be found from among the most suitable members of the staff of the firm concerned.

The Jews will be assembled by the police and/or gendarmerie responsible for the district affected. If necessary, the gendarmerie will assist the Royal Hungarian Police with their arms in townships. The German "Sicherheitsdienst" (Security Police) will be represented in an advisory capacity. Particular importance is attached to closest co-operation. The Provincial authorities will prepare a sufficient number of assembly centres, bearing in mind the proportional strength of the Jews. The location of these assembly centres must be reported to the Secretary of State for Public Security. In all towns and in the larger localities, where the number of Jews justifies the institution of special Jewish houses, the police will immediately take steps to ensure that suitable houses are earmarked for this purpose without delay, as only Jews considered dangerous to the safety of the State will be retained in the assembly centres, whereas the others will be sent to the Jewish houses. Houses, in which the larger part of the occupants are of Jewish descent will be described as "Jewish Houses". Non-Jews resident in these houses will have to be evacuated at least 30 days before the date fixed for the conclusion of the operation. The police authorities will provide them with flats evacuated by Jews, taking care to ensure that size, rent and locality correspond to those of the flats evacuated by the non-Jews. The municipal authorities will appoint special commissions at the time the Jews are collected and assembled. The job of these commissions will be to lock and seal the flats and shops of Jews about to be evacuated and they will be assisted by the police and/or gendarmerie. The keys will be marked with the name and address of the owners and handed to the Administrative Officers i/c Camps in sealed envelopes. Perishable food-stuffs and non-productive animals are to be handed over to the municipal authorities. Cash and valuables (gold, silver, shares etc.) will be handed over to the police authorities, who for their part will acknowledge receipt to the municipal authorities. These valuables will then be transferred to the nearest branch-office of the National Bank.

Jews earmarked for deportation may take with them no more than clothes they are actually wearing, two changes of under-clothes, food sufficient for 14 days and 50 kilos of luggage containing bedding, blankets, palliasses etc. They will not be in possession of cash, jewelry and other valuables. The Jews will be assembled in the following order: VIII., VI., IX., X., II., III., IV., V., VII., I. Gendarmerie District.

All active formations and their training companies will be subordinated to the competent gendarmerie headquarters and the police authorities. Gendarmerie and Police will maintain close liaison in order to ensure the success of the operation.

I would draw the attention of the authorities to the fact that all Jewish refugees from other countries are, without exception, to be treated in the same way as Communists, i.e. that they are to be detained in the assembly centres.

These instructions are to be treated as strictly confidential. Heads of departments and Officers Commanding will be held responsible in case news of this operation leaks out prior to its commencement.

Budapest, April 7th, 1944.

László BAKY
e.h.
Secretary of State.

C. Open Telegram from Pius XII to Regent Horthy

Vatican, June 25, 1944

Intervention in favor of those persecuted due to nationality or race.

We have been implored, from many sides, to work on the problem of mitigating the suffering, already so burdensome, endured by a large number of unfortunates because of their nationality or race, in your noble and chivalrous nation. Our Father, unable to remain insensible, especially in view of our record of ministry of charity which embraces all of mankind, We personally address Your Highness, calling on your noted noble sentiments, in full confidence that you would like to do all in your power to see that the many unfortunates are spared additional sorrows and suffering.

D. Regent Horthy's Reply to Pope Pius XII

Budapest, July 1, 15h. 30
received July 2, 12 h. 49

I have just received the wire from Your Holiness with a most profound under-standing and gratitude, and beg that Your Holiness be convinced that I am doing all that I possibly can, especially to follow the humanitarian principles of Christianity. I beseech Your Holiness again to hold the Hungarian people, during their hour of painful trial, in his graces.

E. Archbishop Spellman's Radio Address
to the Hungarian People

Following is the text of a radio address of His Excellency, Most Rev. Francis J. Spellman, D.D., Archbishop of New York, to the people of Hungary delivered for transmission by the Office of War Information, June 28th.

Almost on the feast of Pentecost, the day on which the Church of Christ emphasizes the supernatural, supraracial character of her mission, we learned that the Government of Hungary had agreed to enforce against the Jewish people a code of discriminatory laws. We were told that this unhappy segment of Israel in Hungary is being herded into Ghettos after its homes and its shops had been systematically looted and pillaged.

This announcement has shocked all men and women who cherish a sense of justice and of human sympathy. It is in direct contradiction of the doctrines of the Catholic Faith professed by the vast majority of the Hungarian people. It is a negation of the noblest pages of Hungarian history and cultural tradition.

Through stormy ages, the Hungarian Catholics have been loyal to the lofty principles of justice, mercy and charity proclaimed by Our Divine Lord in the Sermon on the Mount. They have been steadfast whether under attack by the Mongols and the Turks in centuries past or in our own times under the bitter persecution of Bela Kun and his cruel cohorts.

It seems incredible, therefore, that a nation which has been so consistently true to the impulses of human kindness and the teachings of the Catholic Church should now yield to a false, pagan code of tyranny because of blood and race. How can they not heed those solemn words of Pope Pius XI: 'Abraham is called our patriarch, our ancestor. Anti-Semitism is not compatible with the sublime reality of this text. It is a movement in which we Christians cannot share. Spiritually we are Semites.'

One of the great lessons to be learned from the life of Hungary's King and patron saint is that no minority should be oppressed. For injustices of whatever kind can weaken and destroy the integrity of any nation's life.

Nearly a thousand years ago, St. Stephen, King of Hungary, received his crown from Pope Sylvester II. He realized that Hungary was destined by the very exigencies of geography to be the crossroads of Europe where diverse racial stocks would necessarily meet. St. Stephen pledged himself and his people to live as common children of a loving mother country.

This same saintly national hero dreamed always of Hungary as a 'regnum Marianum' as a realm of Mary. To this day, the coinage and the postage stamps of the country bear the figure of Mary, the Mother of Mankind. It would be all the more tragic, therefore, if a people so devoted to Mary, the Jewish maiden who was the mother of the Messiah, should freely countenance cruel laws calculated to despoil and annihilate the race from which Jesus and Mary sprang.

It is incredible that a people with such profound Christian faith, with its glorious history, with the oldest parliamentary tradition on the Continent, will join in a hymn of hatred and willingly submit to the blood lust and brigandage of tyranny.

No one who hates can be a faithful follower of the gentle Christ: and no man can love God and hate his brother.

F. Deportations of the Hungarian Jews

Dates of the reports	Interval between two successive reports	Total number of deportees on the dates indicated	Number of deportees between two successive reports	Average number of deportees each day
4,28 and 29-1944	2 days	3,800		1.800 2.000
5-18-1944	19 days	23,363	19.563	1.030
6-7-1944	20 days	273,949	250.586	12.529
6-13-1944	6 days	303,499	29.550	4.925
6-14-1944	1 day	316,803	13.304	13.304
6-15-1944	1 day	324,005	7.202	7.202
6-25-1944	10 days	351,850	27.845	2.784
7-1-1944	6 days	377,601	25.751	4.292
7-6-1944	5 days	381,661	4.060	801
7-9-1944	3 days	429,028	47.367	15.789
	73 days			5.877

(According to the secret reports of Veesenmayer, German Ambassador to Budapest).
(Archives of the Center of Contemporary Jewish Documentation of Paris, classification numbers CLXXXIX-22, 25-28, 33, 37, 39 40 et 46)

G. Correspondence between Papal Nuncio Rotta and Vatican

365. Mgr. Tardini to Papal Nuncio Rotta

Vatican, 21 October 1944

According to news which has arrived, Jews in Hungary may be once more threatened with deportation and persecution.

I urgently ask your Most Reverend Excellency to send me any information concerning this.

The Holy See relies upon your constant action, Excellency, and episcopate for every possible protection for the persecuted.

370. Mgr. Tardini to Papal Nuncio Rotta

Vatican, 23 October 1944

I have received telegram no. 302.

The Holy Father has received the news [of the atrocities] with sorrow. He is happy with the diligence with which you keep the Holy See informed. He sends special Apostolic Blessing.

Weighty appeals continue to reach here imploring the intervention of the Holy See in favor of so many persons who are exposed to persecution and violence because of their religious faith, their race, and political beliefs. May Your Excellency continue with the well-known zeal your beneficent activity, enjoying at the same time the collaboration of your episcopacy—supporting as much as possible the paternal preoccupations of the August Pontiff and showing to all that the Catholic Church leaves nothing untried in order to accomplish its universal mission of charity, even in the difficult conditions of the present.

371. Nuncio Rotta to Vatican Secretary of State

Budapest, 23 October 1944

I have received telegram no. 326.

In my telegram no. 302 concerning recent events I alluded also to the resumption of the fight against the Jews; all the exceptions conceded by the preceding government have been revoked, and [the new government] even wants to go so far as the dissolution of mixed marriages with Jews. There will not be deportations but forced labor in Hungary; numerous acts of cruelty have been committed by members of the party.

On the 18th of this month I conferred with the Minister of the Exterior and on the 21st with the President of the Council of Ministers Szálasi; I insisted vigorously in the name of the Holy See on the amelioration of the conditions of the Jews, especially that it not proceed to the declaration of the nullity of marriages, and that concessions previously obtained remain in force; I had good promises. The President of the Council of Ministers seems to me well disposed, although I don't have much confidence, considering the great influence of the extremists of the party. In the aforesaid conversation I interrogated the President of the Council of Ministers concerning the attitude of the new government towards the Catholic Church; the President of the Council of Ministers made a satisfactory enough declaration, but it cannot be relied upon.

408. Nuncio Rotta to Vatican

Budapest, 27 November 1944

I consider it appropriate to send to you there [in Rome] a copy of the Memorandum presented on the 17th of this month to the head of state, Mr. Szálasi, so that its memory may be preserved in case the Archive of the Nunciature should be destroyed.

The said memorandum, which was mentioned in my telegram no. 324, was presented by me and by the Minister of Sweden in the name of the representatives of the united neutral nations twice for this object to the Nunciature. In it is summarized the real state of things, more minimized than exaggerated. Not that any practical result can be expected, given the demonstrated mentality of religious ignorance and fanatical hatred against the Jews of the majority of the Arrow Cross, who in the execution of their given directives proceed with a truly incredible brutality. But it is an act that is required by a civilized and Christian conscience.

The Nunciature for its part has made it possible to alleviate much suffering, by insisting to various concerned Ministries and by releasing more than 13,000 letters of protection. These to some extent have helped at least to impede—for a certain time —the deportation of many Jews and especially baptized Jews.

When this report reaches you there [in Rome], perhaps substantial changes in the political situation of Hungary will have put an end to this type of barbarism against the Jews. But may God forbid that, through reprisal, similar systems unworthy of a civilized people should then be put into practice against Hungarian Christians, as unfortunately is to be feared.

Note of Mgr. Tardini

1-3-45. Bravo Mgr. Rotta!

H. Memorandum from the Neutral Legations

The representatives of the neutral countries accredited to the Royal Hungarian Government have the honour of presenting the Royal Hungarian Government with following demands:

It will be remembered that in August half a million Jews were deported from Hungary. As the Governments of the neutral countries have positive knowledge of the real meaning of deportation, the representatives of the above-mentioned powers took a joint diplomatic step in approaching the Royal Hungarian Government with the request to prevent all further deportation. This step was favourably received and resulted in several hundred thousand lives being saved.

Shortly after October 15th, the new Government and His Excellency Prime Minister Szálasi himself stated clearly and solemnly that there would be no more deportation or extermination of the Jews. Nonetheless the representatives of the neutral powers have been informed by an absolutely reliable source, that the deportation of the Jews has again been decided on, and that this action is being carried out with such inhumane severity that the whole world is witness of the atrocities accompanying its execution. (Babies are separated from their mothers, the old and sick are exposed to the rigours of the weather, men and women are left without food for days, thousands of persons are herded into a single brick works, women are violated, and innumerable persons are shot for the slightest offence.)

In the meantime, just as in the past, it is alleged that there is no question of deportations and that the persons concerned are only sent abroad for labour service. The representatives of the neutral countries, however, are fully aware of the cruel reality hidden behind this word and the sorry plight facing the majority of the unfortunate victims. It is enough to remember that babies and old and sick people are amongst those dragged from their homes, to realise that there is no question of labour, but the end of this tragic journey can be foreseen from the cruelties committed in the execution of the transport.

In view of these cruelties, the representatives of the neutral powers cannot escape the obligations dictated by humanity and Christian love in expressing their most deeply felt sorrow to the Royal Hungarian Government and to ask:

1) That all decisions appertaining to the deportation of the Jews be withdrawn and the measures in progress be suspended, thus rendering it possible for the unfortunate persons dragged from their homes to return there as soon as possible.

2) Proper and humane treatment to be accorded to those compelled to live in concentration camps through being eligible for compulsory labour service. (Adequate food and shelter, sanitary conditions, religious care, etc.)

3) Full and loyal execution of the decrees issued by the Royal Hungarian Government in favour of Jews accorded the protection of the legations accredited to the Royal Hungarian Government, as the number of cases, in which subordinate authorities ignore the orders issued by their superiors, is surprisingly high.

The representatives of the neutral powers hope that the Royal Hungarian Government will perfectly understand this diplomatic step and will honour the statements and promises made by His Excellency, Prime Minister Szálasi. This diplomatic step is dictated not only by sympathy for the persecuted Jews, but also by the deep affection the representatives of the neutral powers have for Hungary, a country which they would like to see unsoiled by a stain, which would forever mar its glorious history, furthermore by the desire to see the Government responsible for the future fate of the Hungarian people freed from a heavy responsibility, as the reprisals imposed on Hungary by the countries at war with her would be continued unless the deportation and extermination of the Jews did not cease. (To say nothing of the possibility of an eventual Army of Occupation in Hungary applying the same measures against the Hungarian nation.)

The representatives of the neutral powers as well as their Governments have no other motive than the mitigation of human misery and the amplification of relief institutions for the victims of war. No matter what reception this diplomatic step is accorded by the Royal Hungarian Government, it will certainly not fail to greatly influence the Hungarian public opinion.

The representatives of the neutral powers take it for granted that the noble Hungarian nation, returning to its age-old Christian traditions, will in these difficult times remain faithful to the principles and methods, which made Hungary a civilised country and deserving of the admiration of the whole world.

Budapest, November 17th, 1947.

Sgd.: Carl Ivar Danielsson,   Angelo Rotta,
        Swedish Minister.   Apostolic Nuntio.

        Harald Feller,   Jorge Perlasca,
        Swiss Chárge d'Affairs.   Spanish Chárge d'Affairs.

        Count Pongrac,
        Portuguese Chárge d'Affairs.

I. Losses of Hungarian Jewry

| Specification: | Actual Territory | | | Pre-Armistice Terr. | |
	Budapest	Province	Total	Lost Territory	Total
According to 1941 Census:					
1. Of the Jewish faith	184,453	216,528	400,981	324,026	725,007
Non-Jews considered as Jews	62,350	27,290	89,640	10,360	100,000
Total Number of Jews	246,803	243,818	490,621	334,386	825,007
Loss Prior to German Occupation:					
2. Labor service-men	12,350	12,500	24,850	17,150	42,000
Deported foreign* Jews (7,1941)	3,000	2,000	5,000	15,000	20,000
Ujvidek/Novisad/massacre (1,1942)				1,000	1,000
Total:	15,350	14,500	29,850	33,150	63,000
No. of Jews on March 19, 1944	231,453	229,318	460,771	301,236	762,007
During German Occupation:					
Deported, killed, deceased	105,453	222,318	327,771	290,236	618,007
Fled abroad	2,000	1,000	3,000	2,000	5,000
Total:	107,453	223,318	330,771	292,236	623,007
Remnant	124,000	6,000	130,000	9,000	139,000
3. Liberated:					
As labor-service men on Hungarian territory.	5,000	6,000	11,000	9,000	20,000
In Budapest	119,000	—	119,000	—	119,000
No. of Jews at Liberation:					
4. Returned from deportation up to the end of 1945	20,000	40,000	60,000	56,000	116,500
No. of Jews on 31/12/45	144,000	47,000	191,000	65,500	255,500
Jewry's loss:	102,803	196,818	299,621	268,886	569,507
No. of Jews of the Jewish faith 31/12/45	96,500	47,124	143,624	No data available	
5. Israelite loss:	87,953	169,404	257,357	No data available	
Israelite loss: %	47.68	78.00	64.20	No data available	

*I.e. having been found with adequate proof of their Hungarian citizenship.

‡WORLD JEWISH CONGRESS. *HUNGARIAN SECTION. Hungarian Jewry Before and After the Prosecution.* Budapest, n.d., p. 2.

J. Table of Organization of Wallenberg's Staff

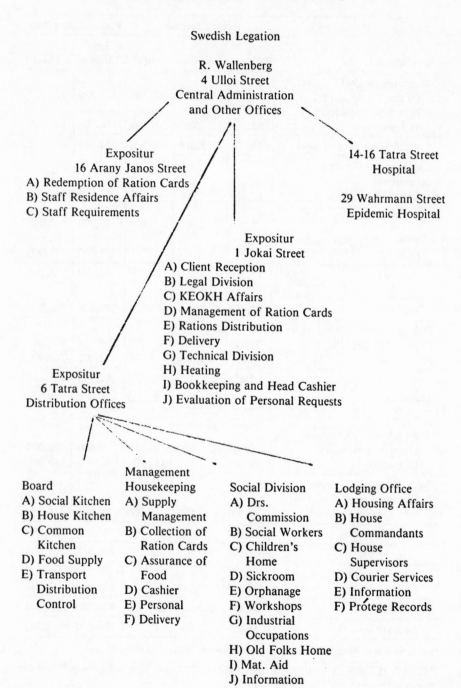

Swedish Legation

R. Wallenberg
4 Ulloi Street
Central Administration
and Other Offices

Expositur
16 Arany Janos Street
A) Redemption of Ration Cards
B) Staff Residence Affairs
C) Staff Requirements

14-16 Tatra Street
Hospital

29 Wahrmann Street
Epidemic Hospital

Expositur
1 Jokai Street
A) Client Reception
B) Legal Division
C) KEOKH Affairs
D) Management of Ration Cards
E) Rations Distribution
F) Delivery
G) Technical Division
H) Heating
I) Bookkeeping and Head Cashier
J) Evaluation of Personal Requests

Expositur
6 Tatra Street
Distribution Offices

Board
A) Social Kitchen
B) House Kitchen
C) Common
Kitchen
D) Food Supply
E) Transport
Distribution
Control

Management
Housekeeping
A) Supply
Management
B) Collection of
Ration Cards
C) Assurance of
Food
D) Cashier
E) Personal
F) Delivery

Social Division
A) Drs.
Commission
B) Social Workers
C) Children's
Home
D) Sickroom
E) Orphanage
F) Workshops
G) Industrial
Occupations
H) Old Folks Home
I) Mat. Aid
J) Information

Lodging Office
A) Housing Affairs
B) House
Commandants
C) House
Supervisors
D) Courier Services
E) Information
F) Protege Records

K. Gromyko Memorandum

A word-by-word translation of the Russian memorandum, handed over oy V. Foreign Minister Gromyko to Ambassador Sohlman in Moscow, on February 6, 1957

Upon the Swedish Government's request, the Soviet Government has ordered the respective Soviet Organs to examine and verify the material referring to Raoul Wallenberg, received from the Swedish Side at the Soviet-Swedish discussions in Moscow in March-April 1956 and also in May 1956.

When examining and verifying this material, the Soviet Organs did undertake a careful investigation of the 'Archives for the Registration of Prisoners and Subjects of Investigation' in order to find possible information about Wallenberg. Also many persons were interrogated, who possibly could have any connection with those circumstances, mentioned in the material that was received from the Swedish Side.

As a result of these measures, however, no information whatsoever about Wallenberg's being in the Soviet Union was found. At this occasion it came forth that none of those interrogated knew any person by the name of Wallenberg.

In this connection the respective Soviet Organs have searched, at several prisons, all Administrative Departments' archive documents, page by page. As a result of such examination of the Ljubjanka prison's archive documents one came across one document, which there is reason to look upon as referring to Raoul Wallenberg. This document has the form of a handwritten report directed to the former Minister for State Security in the USSR, Abakumov, and written by the Head of the Medical Service at this prison, A.L. Smoltsov, as follows:

"I report that the prisoner Walenberg, who is known to you, died in the cell last night, probably because of a sudden myocard infarction.

According to your instructions that I personally look after Walenberg, I ask you to inform me who is to be ordered to carry out the post-mortem examination, to establish the cause of death."

17 July 1947

Head of the Medical Department of Prison
Colonel of Medical Service - Smoltsov.

On this report there is added in Smoltsov's handwriting: "I have personally informed the Minister. Order was given to cremate the body without examination.

17 July, Smoltsov"

It was not possible to find any other information in form of documents or testimonies, the more as the a.m. A.L. Smoltsov died 7 May 1953. Because of what is said above, the conclusion ought to be drawn that Wallenberg died in July 1947. ...

L. The Odyssey of Raoul Wallenberg in the Gulag

Prison	*1945-50	1950-55	1955-60	1960-65	1965-70	1970-75	1975-81
Lubianka	•a •b	•c					•d
Lefortovo	•e						
Khal'mer-Yu	•f						
Verchneuralsk	•g	•g1					
Vladimir	•h		•i		•j		
Butyrka	•k	•l		•m			•n
Irkutsk		•o			•p	•q	
Mental Hospital				•r			
Wrangel Island				•s			
Zabaikal'e					•t		
Mordvinia					•u	•v	
Blagoveshchensk							•w
Gorky							•x
Moscow Region							•y
Leningrad Region							•z

*The dates in parentheses refer to the year(s) of Raoul Wallenberg's imprisonment

a.   Testimony of Lipchitz (1947).

  a1.   Testimony of Mannheim (1946).

b.   Testimony of Moser (1947-48).

c.   Testimony of Libik (1953).

d.   Report by Soviet emigre of conversation with Soviet KGB officer.

e.   Testimonies of de Mohr (1945-48), Ronchi (1947-48), and Gottlieb (1947).

f.   Testimony of Melzer (1949).

g.   Testimony of Kalinski (late forties-1953).

  g1.   Newspaper interview with Kupriyanov (1953, 1955).

h.   Testimonies of Mulle and Rehkampf (1948-53), Brugger and Gouazé (1954), Schoggle (1954), an anonymous prisoner (1955).

i.   Testimonies of Kalinski (1955-59), Makinen (1956-59), and newspaper interview with Kupriyanov (1956).

j.   Report by Raoul Wallenberg Association, Stockholm (1967).

k.   Testimony of Karl Kraemer (1949).

l.   Testimony of Carlson (1951).

m.   Testimony of Belov (1961).

n.   Report of conversation with Kaplan by Bilder (1975).

o.   Testimony of Kalinski (1953-55).

p.   Report by Raoul Wallenberg Association, Sweden (1966-67).

q.   Report by Raoul Wallenberg Association, Sweden (1973-74).

r.   Testimony of Svartz conversation with Miasnikov (1962).

s.   Testimony of Moshinsky (1962).

t.   Report by Shifrin (1967).

u.   Letter of Spira (1964).

v.   Testimony of Rode (1973-74).

w.   Report by Lubarsky that names an "old Swede" (1978).

x.   Report by Raoul Wallenberg Association Sweden (1976-77).

y.   Report by Raoul Wallenberg Association, Sweden, of imprisonment in Moscow region (1979).

z.   Report by Raoul Wallenberg Association, Sweden, of imprisonment in Leningrad region (1980).

M. Letter from May von Dardel to Sol King

Mrs. Maj von Dardel
Auravagen 25 . 182.62. Djursholm.
Sweden.

Mr. Sol King, F A I A.
President, Albert Kahn Associates, Inc.
The university of Michigan. Ann Arbor

Dear Mr. Sol King.

I am deeply touched by your friendship to my beloved son Raoul and the warm-hearted and admiring lecture you held March the 15, 1972. The lectures gave such a beautiful portrait of Raoul. He was always the most wonderful and loving son. He has never been allowed to write to me. But through many prisoners from Sovjet we know about his tragic fate until 1961 when professor Myasnikov in Moscow told my friend Professor Svartz, on her question, that Raoul was in a mental hospital. In 1966 I was told by an hungarian that Raoul was in Siberia.

Though he wrote it on oath, we have not been able to make any researches. It can be true and it might be a lie.

In February 1957 the Sovjet Government represented by Gromyko sent a note to the swedish Government "that it ought to be concluded that Wallenberg died in the prison of Ljubljanka in July 1947."

I am sending you a little pocketbook, written by my husband Fredrik von Dardel "Raoul Wallenberg—facts about a fate", as I am sure that somebody can help you to read it.

With gratitude and friendly regards sincerely yours

Maj von Dardel

Bibliography

Page numbers in the text refer to the following books:

Anger, Per. *Med Raoul Wallenberg i Budapest.* Stockholm, 1979.

Berg, Lars G:Son. *Vad hande i Budapest.* Stockholm, 1949.

Björkman-Goldschmidt, Elsa. Ur den Varld Jagmott. Stockholm, 1967.

Freed, G.B. "Humanitarianism vs. Totalitarianism: The Strange Case of Raoul Wallenberg." *Papers of the Michigan Academy of Science, Arts, and Letters* 46 (1961): 503-528.

Ginzburg, Eugenia. *Journey into the Whirlwind.* Translated by Paul Stevenson and Max Hayward. 1967. Reprint. New York, 1975.

Hinshaw, David. "Sweden's Neutral Policy in Two Wars." In *Sweden: Champion of Peace.* New York, 1949.

Lévai, Jenö. *Black Book on the Martyrdom of Hungarian Jewry.* Zurich, 1948.

———. *Raoul Wallenberg.* Budapest, 1948.

Philipp, Rudolph. *Raoul Wallenberg: Diplomat, Kämpe, Samarit.* Stockholm, 1946.

Shifrin, Abraham. *The First Guidebook to Prisons and Concentration Camps of the Soviet Union.* Berne, 1980.

Trepper, Leopold. *The Great Game: Memoirs of the Spy Hitler Couldn't Silence.* New York, 1977.

Von Dardel, Fredrik. *Facts Around a Fate.* Stockholm, 1970.

Wallace, Ralph. "Raoul Wallenberg, Hero of Budapest." *Reader's Digest,* July 1947, pp. 96-100.

Of related interest:

Agar, Herbert. *The Saving Remnant: An Account of Jewish Survival.* New York, 1960.

Allen, Charles R., Jr. *Heusinger of the Fourth Reich: The Step-by-Step Resurgence of the German General Staff.* New York, 1964.

American Federation of Labor. *Slave Labor in Russia.* New York, 1949.

Arendt, Hannah. *Eichmann in Jerusalem: A Report of the Banality of Evil.* rev. ed. New York, 1965.

Bailey, Ronald H., and the editors of Time-Life Books. *Prisoners of War.* World War II. Vol. 30. Alexandria, Va., 1981.

Barron, John. *KGB: The Secret Work of Soviet Secret Agents.* New York, 1974.

Barta, Stefan. *Die Judenfrage in Ungarn.* Budapest, 1941.

———. "Die Judenfrage in Ungarn." *Volk und Reich* 18 (1942): 408-412.

Bauer, Eddy. *Illustrated World War II Encyclopedia.* Edited by Peter Young, James L. Collins, and Correlli Barnett. New York, 1978.

Bauer, Yehuda. *American Jewry and the Holocaust: The American Jewish Joint Distribution Committee, 1939-1945.* Detroit, 1981.

Béreczky, Albert. *Hungarian Protestantism and the Persecution of the Jews.* Budapest, n.d.

Berend, Béla. "The Hungarian Dreyfus Affair." Ms., 1982.

Berman, Harold J. *Justice in the USSR: An Interpretation of the Soviet Law.* rev. ed. Cambridge, 1963.

Bernadotte, Count Folke. *The Fall of the Curtain.* London, 1953.

Bethell, Nicholas. *The Last Secret.* New York, 1974.

Bettelheim, Bruno. *Surviving and Other Essays.* New York, 1979.

Bierman, John. *Righteous Gentile: The Story of Raoul Wallenberg, Missing Hero of the Holocaust.* New York, 1981.

Birenbaum, Halina. *Hope Is the Last to Die.* Translated by David Welsh. New York, 1971.

Biss, Andreas. *Der Stopp der Endlosung,* Stuttgart, 1966.

————. *A Million Jews to Be Saved.* Cranbury, N.J., 1975.

The Black Book: The Nazi Crime against the Jewish People. New York, 1946.

Bloch, Sidney and Reddaway, Peter. *Psychiatric Terror: How Soviet Psychiatry Is Used to Suppress Dissent.* New York, 1977.

Braham, Randolph L. "The Holocaust in Hungary: An Historical Interpretation of the Hungarian Radical Right." *Societas* 2 (1972): 195-220.

————. *The Hungarian Jewish Catastrophe; a Selected and Annotated Bibliography.* Joint Documentary Projects Bibliographical Series, no. 4. New York, 1962.

————. "The Kamenets Podolsk and Delvidek Massacres: Prelude to the Holocaust in Hungary." *Yad Vashem Studies* 9 (1973): 133-156.

————. *The Politics of Genocide: The Holocaust in Hungary.* 2 vols. New York, 1981.

————. "The Rightists, Horthy, and the Germans: Factors Underlying the Destruction of Hungarian Jewry." In *Jews and Non-Jews in Eastern Europe, 1918-1945,* edited by Béla Vago and George Mosse. New York, 1974.

————, ed. *The Destruction of Hungarian Jewry: A Documentary Account.* 2 vols. New York, 1963.

Bronowski, Alexander. *The Action of Foreign Diplomats in Hungary for the Rescue of Jews.* Jerusalem, 1973.

Broszat, Martin. "Das deutsch-ungarische Verhältnis und die ungarische Judenpolitik in der Jahren 1938-1941." *Gutachten des Instituts für Zeitgeschichte.* Vol. 1. Munich, 1958, pp. 183-200.

————. *German National Socialism, 1919-1945.* Translated by K. Rosenbaum and Inge P. Boehm. Santa Barbara, 1966.

Brugger, Emil. *Ein Schweiser erlebt die Sowjetunion: elf Jahre in Sowjetgefanguissen und Zwangsarbeitlagern.* Solothurn, 1960.

Brzezinski, Zbigniew K. *Ideology and Power in Soviet Politics.* 1962. Reprint. Westport, Conn., 1976.

Buber-Neumann, Margarete. *Under Two Dictators.* Translated by Edward Fitzgerald. New York, 1949.

Carmilly-Weinberger, Moshe. *Memorial Volume for the Jews of Cluj-Kolozsvar.* New York, 1970.

Childs, Marquis. *Sweden: The Middle Way.* 1936. Reprint. New Haven, 1961.

Churchill, Winston S. *The Gathering Storm.* New York, 1948.

Cianfarra, Camille. *The Vatican and the War.* New York, 1944.

Ciszek, Walter J., and Flaherty, Daniel. *With God in Russia.* New York, 1964.

Cohen, Stephen F., ed. *An End to Silence: Uncensored Opinion in the Soviet Union. From Roy Medvedev's Underground Magazine* "Political Diary." Translated by George Saunders. New York, 1982.

Cohn, Norman. *Warrant for Genocide: The Myth of the Jewish World-Conspiracy and the Protocols of the Elders of Zion.* New York, 1969.

Conquest, Robert. *Kolyma: The Arctic Death Camps.* London, 1978.

Conway, J.S. "Between Apprehension and Indifference: Allied Attitudes to the Destruction of Hungarian Jewry." *The Wiener Library Bulletin* 28 (1973-4): 37-48.

Dallin, Alexander. *German Rule in Russia 1941-45.* London, 1957.

Daro, Michael. "Report on Hungary: What Has Been Happening Behind the Censorship." *Harper's Magazine,* February 1942, pp. 308-313.

Dawidowicz, Lucy S. *The War Against the Jews 1933-1945.* New York, 1965.

———. "Dehumanization in Soviet Concentration Camps." *Intellect* 106 (January 1978): 263-265.

Derogy, Jaques. *Le Cas Wallenberg.* Paris, 1980.

Des Pres, Terrence. *The Survivor: An Anatomy of Life in the Death Camps.* New York, 1976.

Deutscher, Isaac. "Who Shall Decide, When Planners Disagree." *Reporter*, 16 March 1957, pp. 11-14.

Druks, Herbert. *The Failure to Rescue*. New York, 1977.

Dulles, Allen W. *Germany's Underground*. New York, 1957.

Eastman, Max. "The Truth About Russia's 14,000,000 Slaves." *Reader's Digest*, April 1947, pp. 140-146.

Ehrenburg, Ilya. *Memoirs, 1921-1941*. New York, 1966.

Ekart, Antoni. *Vanished Without Trace*. Translated by Egerton Sykes and E.S. Virpsha. London, 1954.

Feingold, Henry L. *The Politics of Rescue: The Roosevelt Administration and the Holocaust, 1938-1945*. New Brunswick, N.J., 1970.

Fenyo, Mario D. *Hitler, Horthy, and Hungary: German-Hungarian Relations, 1941-1944*. Russian and East European Studies, no. 11. New Haven, Conn., 1972.

Flannery, Edward H. *Anguish of the Jews: Twenty-Three Centuries of Anti-Semitism*. New York, 1965.

Foley, Charles. *Commando Extraordinary*. New York: G.P. Putnam's Sons, Berkeley Publishing Corporation, 1967.

Forstrom, Annette. *Collection of Documents*. Stockholm, 1966.

Friedlander, Saul. *Pius XII and the Third Reich: A Documentation*. New York, 1966.

Friedman, Philip. "The European Jewish Research on the Recent Jewish Catastrophe in 1939-1945." *Proceedings of the American Academy for Jewish Research* 17 (1949): 179-211.

———. *This Was Oswiecim: The Story of a Murder Camp*. London, 1946.

Frischauer, Willi. *Himmler: The Evil Genius of the Third Reich*. London, 1953.

Gilbert, Martin. *Auschwitz and the Allies*. New York, 1981.

Gliksman, Jerzy. *Tell the West*. New York, 1958.

Goffman, Erving. *Asylums*. Chicago, 1972.

Gollancz, Victor. *The Case of Adolf Eichmann*. London, 1961.

Gutman, Yisrael and Rothkirchen, Livia, eds. *The Catastrophe of European Jewry.* Jerusalem, 1976.

Handler, Andrew, ed. *The Holocaust in Hungary: An Anthology of Jewish Response.* University, Ala., 1982.

Hashomer, Hatzair. *The Massacre of European Jewry: An Anthology.* Israel, 1963.

Hausner, Gideon. *Justice in Jerusalem: The Eichmann Trial.* New York, 1966.

Hayes, Carlton J.H. *Wartime Mission in Spain, 1942-1945.* 1945. Reprint. New York, 1976.

Hegedüs, Sándor. *A tiszaeszlári vérvád.* Budapest, 1966.

Herling, Gustaw. *A World Apart.* Translated by Joseph Marek. 1951. Reprint. Westport, Conn., 1974.

Hilberg, Raul. *The Destruction of the European Jews.* New York, 1961.

―――, ed. *Documents of Destruction: Germany and Jewry, 1933-1945.* Reprint. New York, 1971.

Hirschfeldt, Lennart. "Swedische Aussenpolitik nach dem zweiten Weltkrieg." *Schweizer Monatshefte* 32 (1952-3): 143-151.

Hoffman, Peter. *The History of the German Resistance, 1933-1945.* Cambridge, Mass., 1977.

Horthy, Admiral Miklós. *The Confidential Papers of Admiral Horthy.* Edited by Miklos Szinai and László Szucs. Budapest, 1965.

―――. *Memoirs.* New York, 1957.

Hough, Jerry F. *Soviet Leadership in Transition.* Washington, 1981.

―――, and Fainsod, Merle. *How the Soviet Union Is Governed.* Cambridge, Mass., 1980.

Huber, Max. "Krise der Neuteralität?" *Schweizer Monatshefte* 37 (1957-8): 1-13.

Hull, Cordell. *The Memoirs of Cordell Hull.* 2 vols. London, 1965.

Institute of Marxism-Leninism, CC CPSU. *Great Patriotic War of the Soviet Union, 1941-1945.* Translated by David Skvirsky and Vic Schneierson. Moscow, U.S.S.R., 1974.

Israel. *The Attorney General of the Government of Israel vs. Adolf, the Son of*

Adolf Karl Eichmann. Transcripts. Jerusalem, 1961.

Italy. *Actes et Documents du Saint Siège Relatifs a la Seconde Guerre Mondiale.* Vol. X. Rome, 1980.

Jukšinkij, V.I. *Sovetskie Koncentracionnye Lageri v 1945-1955.* Munich, 1958.

Juna. *Die Judenverfolgunen in Ungarn.* 6 parts. Geneva, 1944.

Kallay, Miklós. *Hungarian Premier.* New York, 1954.

Katzburg, Nathanial. "Hungarian Jewry in Modern Times: Political and Social Aspects." In *Hungarian-Jewish Studies.* Edited by Randolph L. Braham. Vol. 1. New York, 1966.

Kempner, Robert Max Wasili. *Eichmann und Komphzen.* Zurich, 1961.

Kennan, George F. *Memoirs 1925-1950.* Boston, 1967.

Kersten, Felix. *The Kersten Memoirs 1940-1945.* New York, 1957.

———. *The Memoirs of Doctor Felix Kersten.* Edited by Herma Briffaut. Translated by Ernst Morwitz. New York, 1947.

Kertész, Stephen D. *Diplomacy in a Whirlpool: Hungary Between Nazi Germany and Soviet Russia.* 1953. Reprint. Westport, Conn., 1974.

Khruschev, Nikita S. *Khruschev Remembers: The Last Testament.* Edited and translated by Strobe Talbott. Boston, 1974.

Kimche, Ion. "The War's Unpaid Debt of Honor: How El Salvador Saved Tens of Thousands of Jews." *Jewish Observer and Middle East Review* 41 (1955): 10-14.

Klarsfeld, Serge, ed. *The Holocaust and the Neo-Nazi Mythomania.* Translated by Barbara Rucci. New York, 1978.

Kleist, Peter. *Zwischen Hitler und Stalin.* Bonn, 1950.

Kogon, Eugene. *The Theory and Practice of Hell: The Concentration Camps and the System Behind Them.* 1950. Reprint. New York, 1972.

Konev, I.S.; Zakharov, M.V.; Zheltov, A.S.; Grechko, A.A.; Sharokin, M.N.; and Telegin, K.F. *The Great March of Liberation.* Translated by David Fidlon. Moscow, U.S.S.R., 1972.

Kubovy, Aryeh L. "The Silence of Pope Pius XII and the Beginnings of the 'Jewish Document.' " *Yad Vashem Studies* 6 (1967).

Lambert, Gilles. *Operation Hazalah.* Translated by Robert Bullen and Rosette Letellier. Indianapolis, 1974.

Laqueur, Walter. *Russia and Germany: A Century of Conflict.* Boston, 1967.

————. *The Terrible Secret: The Suppression of Information About Hitler's Final Solution.* Boston, 1980.

Leschnitzer, Adolf. *The Magic Background of Modern Anti-Semitism: An Analysis of the German-Jewish Relationship.* New York, 1955.

Lester, Elenore and Werbell, Frederick E. "The Lost Hero of the Holocaust: The Search for Sweden's Raoul Wallenberg." *New York Times Magazine,* 30 March 1980, pp. 20ff.

Lévai, Jenö. *Eichmann in Hungary.* Budapest, 1961.

————. *Gömbös Gyula és a magyar fajvédok a hitlerizmus bölcsojénél..* Budapest, 1938.

————. *Hungarian Jewry and the Papacy.* London, 1968.

Levin, Nora. *The Destruction of European Jewry, 1933-1945.* New York, 1968.

Lewy, Günter. *The Catholic Church and Nazi Germany.* London, 1964.

Lichten, Joseph L. "The Mystery of a War Hero." *The American Scandinavian Review* 44 (1956): 241-244.

Lindahl, Mac. "Budapest Will Remember." *American-Swedish Monthly* 39 (1945): 9.

Lindström, Ulla. *Och Regerengen Salt Kvar.* Stockholm, 1968.

Littell, Franklin. *The Crucifixion of the Jews.* New York, 1974.

Luryi, Yuri. "On the 35-Year-Old Trail of a Missing Hero." *Maclean's,* 2 March 1981, pp. 16-18.

Macartney, C.A. *A History of Hungary, 1929-1945.* 2 vols. New York, 1957.

————. "Hungarian Foreign Policy During the Inter-War Period, With Special Reference to the Jewish Question." In *Jews and Non-Jews in Eastern Europe, 1918-1945,* edited by Béla Vago and George Mosse. New York, 1974.

McCormick, Anne O'Hare. "A Russian Pot Shot at the Policy of Neutrality." *New York Times,* 18 June 1952, p. 26.

Mandelstam, Nadezhta. *Hope Against Hope.* Translated by Max Hayward. 1971. Reprint. New York, 1971.

Manvell, Roger and Fraenkel, Heinrich. *Himmler.* New York, 1965.

————. *The Incomparable Crime: Mass Extermination in the Twentieth Century: The Legacy of Guilt.* New York, 1967.

Marschalko, Lajos. *The World Conquerors: The Real War Criminals.* Translated by A. Suranyi. London, 1958.

Masur, Norbert. *En Jude Talar med Himmler.* Stockholm, 1945.

Massing, Paul W. *Rehearsal for Destruction: A Study of Political Anti-Semitism in Imperial Germany.* New York, 1949.

Medalie, George Z. "Overseas Activities in 1944." *The American Jewish Committee's Annual Report* (1944): 97-99.

Mindszenty, Jozsef Cardinal. *Memoirs.* Translated by Richard and Clara Winston. New York, 1974.

Montgomery, John Flourney. *Hungary, the Unwilling Satellite.* New York, 1947.

Mora, Sylvester and Zwierniak, Peter. *La Justice Soviétique.* Rome, 1945.

Morse, Arthur D. *While Six Million Died: Chronicle of American Apathy.* 1967. Reprint. New York, 1975.

Nagy-Talavera, Nicholas. *The Green Shirts and the Others.* Stanford, 1970.

Naumann, Berend. *Auschwitz.* New York, 1966.

Nazi Massacre of the Jews and Others: Some Practical Proposals Made by the Archbishop of Canterbury and Lord Rochester in Speeches on March 23rd 1943 in the House of Lords. London, 1943.

Neususs-Hunkel, Ermenhild. *Die SS.* Hanover, 1956.

Nils, André. *Power Balance of Non-Alignment.* Stockholm, 1967.

Nork, Karl. *Hell in Siberia.* Translated by E. Brockett. London, 1957.

Oakley, Stewart. *A Short History of Sweden.* New York, 1966.

Palóczy, Horvath G. *In Darkest Hungary.* London, 1945.

Paneth, Philip. *Eichmann: Technician of Death.* New York, 1960.

Pilch, Judah, ed. *The Jewish Catastrophe in Europe.* New York, 1968.

Pinson, Koppel S. *Essays on Antisemitism.* 2d rev. ed. New York, 1946.

Poliakov, Leon. *Harvest of Hate: The Nazi Program for the Destruction of the Jews in Europe.* 1954. Reprint. Westport, Conn., 1971.

Powers, Francis G., and Gentry, Curt. *Operation Overflight: The Story of U-2 Spy Pilot, Francis Gary Powers.* New York, 1970.

Pulzer, Peter G.J. *The Rise of Political Anti-Semitism in Germany and Austria.* New York, 1964.

Reddaway, Peter. *The Forced Labor Camps in the USSR Today: An Unrecognized Example of Modern Inhumanity.* London, 1973.

————. *Uncensored Russia: Protest and Dissent in the Soviet Union.* New York, 1972.

———— and Bloch, Sidney, *Psychiatric Terror: How Soviet Psychiatry Is Used to Suppress Dissent.* New York, 1977.

Reichmann, Eva G. *Hostages of Civilisation: The Social Sources of National Socialist Anti-Semitism.* Reprint. Westport, Conn., 1951.

Reitlinger, Gerald. *The Final Solution: The Attempt to Exterminate the Jews of Europe.* 2d rev. ed. Cranbury, N.J., 1961.

Reston, James. "Swedes Believe Neutrality Has Strategic Advantages." *New York Times,* 27 July 1949, p. 3.

————. "Swedish Neutrality Is Firm Despite Debates in the West." *New York Times,* 25 July 1949, p. 3.

Reynolds, Quentin; Katz, Ephraim; and Aldouby, Zwy. *Minister of Death: The Adolf Eichmann Story.* New York, 1960.

Rhodes, Anthony. *The Vatican in the Age of the Dictators, 1922-1945.* 1973. Reprint. New York, 1974.

Riedl, Franz. "Die Juden in Ungarn." *Volk und Reich* 15 (1939): 107-135.

Rittenberg, Louis. "The Crisis in Hungary." *Contemporary Jewish Record,* no. 3 (1939), pp. 20-31.

Ritter, Gerhard. *The German Resistance: Carl Goerdeler's Struggle Against Tyranny.* Translated by R.T. Clark. facs. ed. Plainview, N.Y., 1958.

Robinson, Jacob. *And the Crooked Shall Be Made Straight: The Eichmann Trial, the Jewish Catastrophe, and Hannah Arendt's Narrative.* New York, 1965.

———— and Friedman, Philip. *Guide to Jewish History Under Nazi Impact.* 1960. Reprint. New York, 1974.

Roeder, Bernahard. *Katorga: An Aspect of Modern Slavery.* Translated by L. Kochan. London, 1958.

Ruland, Fritz. "Ungarns Kampf gegen das Judentum." *Volkstum im Sudösten* 18 (1942): 123-127.

Russell, Lord of Liverpool. *The Record, the Trial of Eichmann.* New York, 1963.

Sabille, Jacques. "Das tragische Epos Raoul Wallenberg." In *Das dritte Reich und die Juden.* Edited by Leon Poliakov and Josef Wulf. Berlin-Grunewald, 1955, pp. 416-420.

Sandberg, Moshe. *My Longest Year: In the Hungarian Labour Service and in the Nazi Camps.* Edited by Livia Rothkirchen. Jerusalem, 1968.

Schellenberg, Walter. *The Labyrinth: Memoirs of Walter Schellenberg.* New York, 1956.

Schoenberner, Gerhard. *The Yellow Star: The Persecution of the Jews in Europe, 1933-1945.* New York, 1973.

Scott, Franklin D. "Sweden Steering Between the Rocks." In *The United States and Scandinavia.* Cambridge, Mass., 1950, pp. 260-273.

The Secret Speech. London, 1976.

Shalamov, Varlam. *Graphite.* Translated by John Glad. New York, 1981.

Shilkrot, Boris. "Bericht aus Vladimir." *Allgemeine Judusche Wochenzeitung,* 30 August 1974.

Shirer, William. *The Rise and Fall of the Third Reich: A History of Nazi Germany.* New York, 1960.

Shtemenko, General S.M. *The Last Six Months.* Translated by Guy Daniels. New York, 1978.

Sjöquist, Eric. *Affären Raoul Wallenberg.* Stockholm, 1974.

Solomon, Michael. *Magadan.* New York, 1971.

Solzhenitsyn, Aleksandr L. *The Gulag Archipelago: An Experiment in Literary Investigation.* Translated by Thomas P. Whitney and Harry Willetts. 4 vols. New York, 1975.

Spiro, Edward. *Spy Trade.* New York, 1972.

Stern, Fritz R. *The Politics of Cultural Despair: A Study in the Rise of the Germanic Ideology.* California Library Reprint Series. Berkeley, 1974.

Svartz, Nanna. *Steg för Steg.* Stockholm, 1968.

Swedish Foreign Ministry. *White Papers—Raoul Wallenberg, 1944-1949.* Stockholm, 1980.

Syrkin, Marie. *Blessed Is the Match.* New York, 1947.

Tal, Uriel. *Religious and Anti-religious Roots of Modern Anti-Semitism.* New York, 1971.

Tenenbaum, Joseph. *Race and Reich: The Story of an Epoch.* 1956. Reprint. Westport, Conn., 1957.

Tingsten, Herbert. *The Debate on the Foreign Policy of Sweden 1918-1939.* Translated by Joan Bulman. London, 1949.

Toynbee, Arnold J. *Hitler's Europe.* Reprint. New York, 1954.

Tregubov, J.A. *Vosem Let vo Vlasti Lubjanki.* Frankfurt/M, 1957.

Tucker, Robert C. *The Soviet Critical Mind: Studies in Stalinism and Post-Stalin Change.* New York, 1963.

United Nations War Crimes Commission. *Law Reports of Trials of War Criminals.* 15 vols. London, 1947-49.

U.S. Congress. Senate. Committee on the Judiciary. *Hearings to Investigate the Administration of the Internal Security Act and Other Internal Security Laws.* 93rd Cong., 1st sess., 1973.

Utriksdepartementet. *Raoul Wallenberg: Dokumentsamling rorände efterorskningarna efter år 1957.* Stockholm, 1965.

Vago, Béla. "Budapest Jewry in the Summer of 1944: Otto Komoly's Diaries." *Yad Vashem Studies* 8 (1970): 81-105.

Vámbéry, Rustem. *Hungary—To Be or Not to Be.* New York, 1946.

Villius, Hans and Villius, Elsa. *Fallet Raoul Wallenberg.* Stockholm, 1965.

Vörös, Marton. *Även för din skull.* Stockholm, 1978.

Warburg, Gustav. "Rescuing Hungarian Jewry." *The Jewish Monthly,* October 1947, pp. 26-31.

War Refugee Board. *History of the War Refugee Board With Selected Documents.* January 22, 1944-September 15, 1945.

Weinberg, Gerhard L. *The Foreign Policy of Hitler's Germany: 1933-1936.* Chicago, 1971.

Weissburg, Alex. *Advocate for the Dead: The Story of Joel Brand.* London, 1958.

Weissmandel, Michael Dov. *Min hametzar.* New York, 1960.

Werbell, Fredrick E., and Clarke, Thurston. *Lost Hero: The Mystery of Raoul Wallenberg.* New York, 1981.

Werth, Alexander. *Russia at War 1941-1945.* New York, 1964.

Wheaton, Eliot Barculo. *The Nazi Revolution: Prelude to Calamity.* New York, 1969.

Wighton, Charles. *Eichmann: His Career and Crimes.* London, 1961.

Wigmans, Johan H. *Ten Years in Russia and Siberia.* Translated by Arnout de Waal. London, 1964.

Wolin, Simon and Slusser, Robert M., eds. *The Soviet Secret Police.* New York, n.d.

World Committee for the Victims of German Fascism. *The Brown Book of the Hitler Terror and the Burning of the Reichstag.* 1933. Reprint. New York, n.d.

Wulf, Joseph. *Raoul Wallenberg: Il Fut Leur Esperance.* Tournai, Belgium, 1968.

Yad Vashem. *Blackbook of Localities Whose Jewish Population Was Exterminated by the Nazis.* Jerusalem, 1965.

Zorin, Libushe. *Soviet Prisons and Concentration Camps: An Annotated Bibliography 1917-1980.* Newtonville, Mass., 1980.

Zywulska, Krystyna. *I Came Back.* Translated by Krystyna Cenkalska. London, 1951.

INDEX

Raoul Wallenberg
Angel of Rescue

This is the dramatic story of Raoul Wallenberg, a young Swedish diplomat who went into the "lair of the hyenas" to save the Jews of Budapest from the death camps of Adolf Eichmann. It examines the roots of Hungarian anti-Semitism, why Hungary became involved with Nazi Germany in World War II, and how changing relations between Hungary and Germany doomed many Hungarian Jews, yet saved others.

Abundant personal testimonies from survivors lend immediacy to the superhuman efforts of Wallenberg and his colleagues. His wily diplomacy, clever ruses, and heroic interventions saved thousands of Budapest Jews from the SS and the Arrow Cross, the Hungarian fascists. His volunteer organization provided sustenance, protection, and hope for many Jews.

Newly released documents from Vatican archives tell the unknown story of the role the Roman Catholic Church played as his ally in Hungary. The rescue efforts of Wallenberg, the papal nuncio, and other neutral diplomats provide an inspirational chapter in the grim story of the Holocaust.

For the Jews, Budapest's capture by the Red Army meant salvation; for Wallenberg, it meant the chance to rebuild Hungary. When he approached the Soviets with his plans, they rewarded his efforts with arrest. While the world hailed him as a hero, the Soviets imprisoned him as a spy.

(conti...

Testimony from returning prisoners presents evidence of his continued survival in camps throughout the Gulag. While sharply critical of the weak efforts of neutral Sweden to gain his release, the author expresses hope that renewed interest in Wallenberg, generated by granting him American citizenship, will finally end his unjust confinement. Some startling new evidence offers a possible explanation of Soviet motives for continuing his imprisonment after officially declaring him dead.

This definitive biography of Raoul Wallenberg is based on exhaustive research by Harvey Rosenfeld, editor of *Martyrdom and Resistance,* the longest-running periodical devoted to the Holocaust.

ISBN 0-87975-177-0

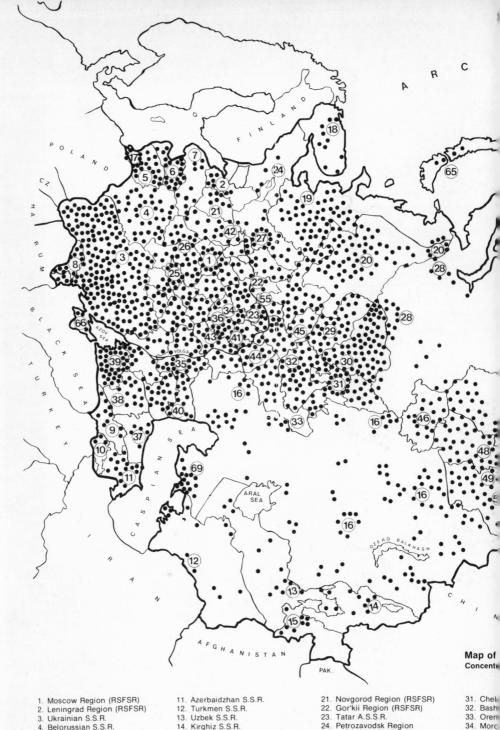

Map of
Concent...

1. Moscow Region (RSFSR)
2. Leningrad Region (RSFSR)
3. Ukrainian S.S.R.
4. Belorussian S.S.R.
5. Lithuanian S.S.R.
6. Latvian S.S.R.
7. Estonian S.S.R.
8. Moldavian S.S.R.
9. Georgian S.S.R.
10. Armenian S.S.R.

11. Azerbaidzhan S.S.R.
12. Turkmen S.S.R.
13. Uzbek S.S.R.
14. Kirghiz S.S.R.
15. Tadzhik S.S.R.
16. Kazakh S.S.R.
17. Kaliningrad Region (RSFSR)
18. Murmansk Region (RSFSR)
19. Arkhangel'sk Region (RSFSR)
20. Komi A.S.S.R.

21. Novgorod Region (RSFSR)
22. Gor'kii Region (RSFSR)
23. Tatar A.S.S.R.
24. Petrozavodsk Region
25. Orel, Kursk, Tula, Kaluga, Lipetsk Regions (RSFSR)
26. Pskov, Vladimir, Bryansk, Kalinin, Smolensk Regions (RSFSR)
27. Vologda, Kostroma, Kirov, Izhevsk Regions (RSFSR)
28. Tyumen' Region (RSFSR)
29. Perm' Region (RSFSR)
30. Sverdlovsk Region (RSFSR)

31. Chel...
32. Bash...
33. Oren...
34. Mord...
35. Volg...
36. Penz...
37. Kalm... A.S....
38. Stavr...
39. Kras... and ...
40. Astra...